For the Love of ACT Math

by

Michael Cerro
Max McMahon
Abbey J. Neer, Ph.D.
Chris Reddick

Published by Private Prep
Printed by Kindle Direct Publishing, An Amazon.com Company
Original cover art by Ryan Lause
Version 2021-2022

Acknowledgments

From Chris:

To my partner, best friend, and roommate, Gianna, for putting up with my obsessions. Your patience reminds me every day how to love properly.

To my older sister, Yvonne, and younger brother, Kaiya, for a life time of reminding me that I can in fact do better.

To my father. Through example you constantly remind me that learning is a life long habit.

To my mother. You are my role model.

From Michael:

A lot of Private Preppers helped make this journey easy and possible. For me personally, I would like to thank Lindsay Bressman, Erin Muskat, and Abbey Neer.

From Max:

Thanks to Nana, Auntie Ei, and Auntie Ann for your continued guidance. I miss you all each and every day.

Thanks to Annie & Rich (my parents), Meg & Keara (my sisters), and all my family and friends for your unwavering love and support. I wouldn't be who I am without you

Thanks to my old teachers Mr. Santaloci, Mrs. Blume, Mr. Piede, Ms. Chua, Mr. Scibilia, and Mrs. Hoell. You did, and continue to inspire in me a passion for education. I cannot tell you how valuable your teachings have been throughout my career.

And thank you to my girlfriend for putting up with me throughout this whole book writing process.

From Abbey:

To Jean, my grandmother: Thank you for all your words of wisdom and advice. Your constant example of empathy inspires my path into creating equitable content for all students.

To Kathryn, my mother and best friend: Thank you for all the laughter throughout my life, and for nurturing me into the resilient and strong woman I am today, I owe it all to your example!

Contents

ACT MATH GENERAL STRATEGIES

Welcome to *for the Love of ACT Math*. This text is designed to guide you through the content of the ACT Math section, with explanations and strategies optimized for test performance.

That means we aren't fully teaching the concepts the test uses, but rather are trying to give you enough of a system to get questions right and right fast.

The ACT Math section is a 60 minute 60 question barrage of topics. The test draws from middle school and high school Mathematics up to but not including Calculus. Questions are multiple choice, with 5 answer possibilities. The test is scored out of 36 points, which is scaled and curved based on the difficulty of the specific section and how test-takers perform on it.

The test can roughly be divided into 1-25, 25-48, and 48-60 in terms of zones of difficulty. Early problems use simple math and single-step approaches, but like to confuse with words, words, and more words!

The ACT is (currently) an integral part of the college application process, and has been since 1959! Throughout its lifetime, the ACT has undergone numerous transformations and these changes have led to confusion among students. So let's begin by debunking these outdated and incorrect statements about the ACT:

1. ALL QUESTIONS ARE UNIQUE...

The ACT Test Question writers are not creative; they reuse the same types of wording and questions test after test. In Part 4 we will familiarize you with the five general types of questions, and how to approach each kind.

2. TOO MANY QUESTIONS, TOO LITTLE TIME...

The ACT is designed for a student to complete 60 questions in 60 minutes (or your total time if you have an accommodation), so each question should take about 1 minute to solve. Therefore, keep the strategies simple, do not try any complex methods unless specifically asked. We will go into more detail about pacing in a later section on timing strategies.

3. QUESTION DIFFICULTY IS RANDOMLY ASSORTED...

Do not overlook that the test begins with the easiest questions and ends with the more difficult questions. This means questions #1-30 are generally easier than questions #31-60.

4. SKIPPING IS BETTER THAN GUESSING...

You do not receive any penalty for guessing! Therefore it is in your favor to answer every question, even if you are unsure of the answer. If you leave a question blank by skipping, it will be counted as an incorrect answer, and your score will be penalized. Keep in mind that if you can eliminate at least one answer, your odds of getting to the correct answer have increased from a 1 in 5 to a 1 in 4 chance. The more you can eliminate, the better your odds of choosing the correct answer.

5. ALWAYS SOLVE FOR X ...

Sometimes, the question is not necessarily ONLY testing if you are able to find x (or whatever variable), but really, if at 8AM, you are paying attention! Once you think you found the answer, go back and re-read the question to make sure it is not asking for the sum of your values for x, $x + 4$, or anything other than **JUST** x.

These general strategies will help you with any question you approach, whether it's super simple or more complicated.

1. READ THE QUESTION STATEMENT, FIRST

Often the ACT hides the actual question in a body of text. Find the "?" and then read that statement first. It is often the last sentence of the question.

2. LOOK AT THE ANSWER CHOICES

Unlike exams and tests given in school, the ACT is multiple choice. The answers can tell you A LOT about the answer you are seeking! Remember the answer must be within these 5 choices.

3. SET-UP THE PROBLEM

Sometimes, this is all that is asked to answer the question–think expression based This will be discussed in more depth in Part 3 where we discuss pathways.

4. CHECK BACK IN WITH ANSWER CHOICES FREQUENTLY

Now that you have set up the problem, does your answer resemble any of the answer choices yet? Check back in to the answer choices throughout the solving process, your answer should start looking like the answer choices.

5. SIMPLIFY LAST

The ACT can and will include special values and expressions in their answer choices. It is in your best interest to check-in with the answer choices BEFORE simplifying your answer.

6. RE-READ THE QUESTION

Once you've found your answer, re-read the question. Oftentimes the ACT will bait you to solve for x, however to answer the question correctly you may need to go one step further.

7. CHOOSE AN ANSWER

Now you're ready to choose your answer!

Problem solving in math can look very different from one person to another, and the ACT does not penalize you for using one solution method over another. Most math problems, including on the ACT, can be solved in various ways. Familiarizing yourself with all solving methods will help you work through those tricky problems.

Your method of solving may heavily depend on the question and the answer types. Be sure to check out the answers and read only the question statement prior to determining the best method for solving.

WORK FORWARD

Some questions will feel most natural to work forwards to solve, just like in your coursework. When working forwards be sure to set-up the problem and continue to solve, if necessary.

WORK BACKWARDS

Other questions, you may find that using the answers and working backwards helps you get to the answer quicker. Particularly with expression based questions, it can be time consuming to solve the problem forward when you can plug in the answers to the question or plug in a value for the variable.

BE FLEXIBLE

Sometimes you will find that you will begin to work one direction with a solution, and then become stuck. When this happens, be flexible and try to work in the other direction, this may help you find clarity and get closer to the question's solution.

let's PRACTICE

1. What is the value of $\log_2 16$?

    A. $\dfrac{1}{2}$

    B. 2

    C. 3

    D. 4

    E. 6

FORWARDS
① USE LOG DEFINITION

$\log_a b = c$ $a^c = b$
TO THE

SO THEN $\log_2 16 \rightarrow 2^x = 16$

For an expression based question like the one above, it may be the best fit to **start forwards**. This question involves logs, which often appear in the second half of the test making this question more challenging. It may be that you are able to recall the definition of a log to translate it to an exponential expression, but then become stuck on how to solve for a variable as an exponent.

Looking at the answer choices, you should notice that they are numerical. *Numerical answer choices with expression based questions are ideal* for **working backwards** at some point in solving the problem. Once you have the exponential function, you can begin plugging in the answer choices for x.

The question now is what answer choice is the best to start with, if you do not have any intuition towards an answer choice, or like in this example the answer choices are relatively close to one another, it's advised to start with the middle value. That way if the middle value yields you an answer that is too large, you know to try a smaller value next, or if it yields a number that is too small, you know to try a larger value. **Here the middle answer choice is 3, it's the approximate middle value between $\dfrac{1}{2}$ and 6**.

BACKWARDS
② PLUG IN ANSWER CHOICES FOR X

$2^3 = 8$ TOO SMALL, TRY A LARGER VALUE

$2^4 = 16$ ✓

It's very important to keep in mind that it's entirely OKAY, reasonable and sometimes the best option to shift direction to solve ACT Math problems. There are no instructions for telling us how to solve the problem.

Unrelated to math, but necessary to solve the problem is the assumption that you are familiar with the monetary values of American coins. However, being a current high school student means you may not use coins frequently enough to recall their values. A quarter is $0.25, a dime is $0.10, a nickel $0.05 and a penny is $0.01. Remember, there are no instructions for telling us how to solve the problem.

Now, let's try another example.

2. Joe found $13.22 in pennies, nickels, dimes, and quarters while walking home from school one week. When he deposited this money in the bank he noticed that he had twice as many dimes as pennies, 1 more dime than nickels, and 1 fewer quarters than nickels. How many quarters did he find that week?

    F. 18
    G. 19
    H. 28
    J. 29
    K. 32

BACKWARDS
① START WITH THE MIDDLE
   ANSWER CHOICE OF 28
Q=28 SO THEN WE HAVE:
29=N 30=D 15=P
WHICH COMES OUT TO
$(28 \times 0.25) + (30 \times 0.1) + (29 \times 0.05) + (15 \times 0.01)$
   7   +   3   +   1.45   +   0.15
      = $11.60 ← TOO SMALL
              TRY LARGER

Lengthy word problems like above are time intensive. One way to save time is to work backwards. Working backwards allows you to start checking what answers would work instead of using time finding the answer choice through algebra.

After trying $Q = 28$ and noticing the calculations for the monetary amount is less than needed, you can feel secure that the answer must be more than 28 Quarters.

Try a larger answer choice. The next would be 29 Quarters, however this leads to a non-integer (whole number) for the number of pennies. Because this is physically impossible, the answer to the question must be $Q = 32$, Answer choice E. It is not necessary to check $Q = 32$, because you know the answer has to be more than 28 Quarters (remember you JUST checked this answer rigorously) and there is no other option.

② TRY A LARGER ANSWER CHOICE
$Q=29$, SO THEN
$N=30$ $D=31$ $P=15.5$ NOT POSSIBLE MUST BE Q=32
* THERE IS NO NEED TO CHECK Q=32

This differs from what we are used to with coursework, where we often need to check our work. **You do not need to check your work on the ACT, therefore eliminating answer choices through reason is a valid way to solve a problem**. This may feel uncomfortable at first, however this will diminish over time. You will notice that it **saves** a significant amount of **time**, and **yields higher accuracy**.

But what if you decide that you understand this question well enough to work forward to determine the answer? Below is the bulk of the solution: we did not include the arithmetic here, as it's lengthy and prone to error. Hopefully this helps elucidate that this type of problem is not only time saving to work backwards, but simpler as well.

Eventually, you will find that $Q = 32$, but it is a lengthy and arguably painful algebraic experience when compared to the process of working backwards. Again, it does not matter the path you take to solve ACT questions. While you may solve this type of question forwards at school, it's not necessarily the most time efficient route.

FORWARDS
① SETUP EQUATIONS
$13.22 = 0.01P + 0.1D + 0.05 + 0.25Q$
$D = 2P$
$N + 1 = D$
$N - 1 = Q$
② EXPRESS EACH EQUATION ABOVE IN TERMS OF Q

$N - 1 = Q \rightarrow Q + 1 = N$
PLUG IN FOR "N"
$D = N + 1 \rightarrow (Q + 1) + 1 = Q + 2 = D$
PLUG IN FOR "D"
$2P = D \rightarrow 2P = Q + 2 \rightarrow \frac{Q+2}{2} = P$

③ PLUG INTO THE FIRST EQUATION AND SOLVE FOR "Q"
$13.22 = 0.01(\frac{Q+2}{2}) + 0.05(Q+1) + 0.1(Q+2) + 0.25Q$

3. In the circle with center Z shown, the length of radius $\overline{ZW}$ is 7 cm, the length of $\overline{WX}$ is 2 cm and $\overline{WX}$ is perpendicular to radius $\overline{YZ}$ at X. When angle $\angle WZY$ is measured in degrees, which of the following expressions represents the length, in centimeters of the minor arc $\overset{\frown}{WY}$?

Image

A. $\dfrac{7\pi}{180}\sin^{-1}\left(\dfrac{2}{7}\right)$

B. $\dfrac{14\pi}{180}\cos^{-1}\left(\dfrac{2}{7}\right)$

C. $\dfrac{14\pi}{180}\sin^{-1}\left(\dfrac{2}{7}\right)$

D. $\dfrac{14\pi}{180}\tan^{-1}\left(\dfrac{2}{7}\right)$

E. $\dfrac{7\pi}{180}\cos^{-1}\left(\dfrac{2}{7}\right)$

Step #3 in the General Strategies highlights the idea that sometimes the answer on the ACT can be found alone by setting up the problem. There are no rules that you can not set up the problem in two separate parts, especially when tricky trigonometry is involved.

Before we can start the solution process, we have to determine the goal of the question. Again, avoid reading block text, and instead focus on the question statement. Here, calls for the length of arc $\overset{\frown}{WY}$, however the answer choices are in terms of a trigonometric function. It is recommended that you mark-up visual based questions to identify the value, or length you are solving for.

Part of setting the problem up is deciding which trigonometric ratio is appropriate given the sides of the right triangle. Specifically here we are given the opposite and hypotenuse, therefore it is sine! Just that allows you to eliminate the 3 out of the 5 options for answers. *This can be the step where you shift directions and begin to work backward.*

FORWARDS
① ALL ANSWER CHOICES INVOLVE
SOHCAHTOA, SET IT UP
└ GIVEN OPP. AND HYP.
$\sin\theta = \frac{2}{7}$
ELIMINATE B, D AND E

Part of setting the problem up is deciding which trigonometric ratio is appropriate given the sides of the right triangle. Specifically, here, we are given the opposite and hypotenuse, there it is **sine**! Just *that* allows you to eliminate 3 out of the 5 answer choices. *This can be the step where you shift directions and begin to work backwards and use the answer choices (see backwards solution).* However, continuing to work forwards, we can use the arc length formula. If you plug in the radius value of 7 for r and simplify in terms of θ, you will find that you will get $\dfrac{7\pi}{180}$ which resembles answer choice **A** over **C**.

Without relying on setting up the problem, initially you can work backwards just as easily here. A key feature when working with any visuals based question is that the figures are drawn to scale. We will go into more detail regarding specific techniques for visuals later.

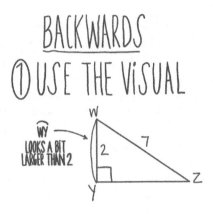

BACKWARDS
① USE THE VISUAL

Here we can use the visual to find arc $\overparen{WY}$, on the curved side that has a height of 2, meaning that the answer must be a number a little bit larger than 2.

A. $\dfrac{7\pi}{180} \sin^{-1}\left(\dfrac{2}{7}\right) \approx \mathbf{2.028}$

② PLUG THE ANSWER CHOICES
INTO CALCULATOR
SHOULD BE IN ↑
DEGREE MODE

B. $\dfrac{14\pi}{180} \cos^{-1}\left(\dfrac{2}{7}\right)$

C. $\dfrac{14\pi}{180} \sin^{-1}\left(\dfrac{2}{7}\right)$

D. $\dfrac{14\pi}{180} \tan^{-1}\left(\dfrac{2}{7}\right)$

E. $\dfrac{7\pi}{180} \cos^{-1}\left(\dfrac{2}{7}\right)$

Only one option shows a value around, but slightly larger than 2, which is **A**. As stated in the working forwards direction, if you set up the problem first and recognized the trigonometric function here was sine, then you could reduce the amount of answers you plug into your calculator and check.

Timing is the most important skill to master on the ACT. The better you are with pacing, the more questions you will be able to answer without guessing! Keep in mind that the perfect timing strategy for one student may not be the best strategy for another. It may take trying more than one or a combination of the three strategies below to find the best timing strategy for you. If you have timing accommodations, you can adjust the 60 minutes mentioned below to your total time.

REDUCE THE TEST

When the 60 questions of the ACT Math section are just too daunting, you can reduce the test down to a smaller number of questions in an hour instead of 60. **This strategy provides a method to train yourself to gradually complete more of the test**.

First you choose your benchmark, or end point, then for the remaining questions you choose an answer choice to bubble in the rest. Do not stress that you are not finishing the test—looking at the general scaling of the test, you do not need to necessarily finish to yield a desirable score. Accuracy is more important, and this is highly affected by timing pressure. When you are rushing to finish all 60 questions, you are not going to perform your best.

Below is a very general starting point, based on your diagnostic score and personal goals the benchmark may need to be adjusted.

FOCUS ON QUESTIONS #1-45

A starting benchmark place would be to focus on the first 30-45 questions. The reasoning behind this is that generally a raw score within the range of 30-45 will yield you a Math score upwards of 21. If you choose to complete 30-45 questions in 60 minutes this equates to 80 -120 seconds per question vs. 60 seconds per question.

GRADUALLY ADD ON

Once you are comfortable completing 30-45 questions in an hour, it's time to gradually add on more questions to complete within time. A suggested amount would be about 5 questions added for a new benchmark, which means 8 seconds less per question. It's important to choose reasonable additions when applying this method, otherwise your benchmark number will also feel daunting.

PAGE BY PAGE

Another method for breaking-up the test into smaller, more manageable chunks is to take the test **page-by-page**. This strategy works best once you have experimented with other strategies and have established your pacing goal. The idea here is that you will allot a certain amount of time per page depending on the number of questions on the page.

DETERMINE TIME PER PAGE

Your pacing per question is dependent on your specific goals. You can combine this strategy with the reducing the test strategy to gain a sense of how much time you should give to each question: for example if you are reducing the test to 30 questions, then each question should be paced for about 120 seconds per question, and then you can use the number of questions per page to determine the time per page. For example, if the page contains four questions this equates to 8 minutes. Alternatively, if your goal is to complete the test in its entirety each question should be adjusted to 60 seconds per question, and therefore you should aim to complete the page in 4 minutes.

GRADUALLY SPEED UP

Remember that your goal pace is a place to work towards. Be sure to set realistic goals. For example, if your goal is to complete a 4-question page in 8 minutes you can start with 8.5 minutes and gradually shave down 5-10 seconds per question until you reach your goal. Shaving off increments of 5-10 seconds per question may seem like a very short amount of time, but it does add up!

CONSIDER THE DIFFICULTY LEVEL

Remember the test gradually becomes more difficult as you work towards #60. Be mindful of this when determining a pace: you may want to give yourself less time for earlier questions and more time for the later more challenging questions.

WATCH THE CLOCK

It sounds simple, but when we are working a timed section, taking a practice test or a real test the time seems to escape us much much quicker than normal! So if we watch the clock we will have a better idea of where our pacing stands and how to improve it.

HAVE TIME & QUESTION BENCHMARKS

Everyone's benchmarks will be a little different depending on their specific goals, so it's important to not compare yourself to anyone. It's all about personal growth! It's also important to recognize that throughout your ACT preparation journey your goals will evolve with you.

With watching the clock it's imperative that you create benchmarks with time, questions, or both! Some ideas of benchmarks are below.

REACH # 30 BY...

#30 is the middle of the test making it a natural place for a benchmark. A beginning goal would be to reach this point with exactly half the time left, as you have 30 more questions to complete. Overtime, this goal can evolve with you, as you begin to consistently hit this benchmark you can shave off 30 second intervals ($\tilde{1}$ second a question) until you hit a new benchmark of 25-28 minutes elapsed or 32-35 minutes remaining.

WITH 25-30 MINUTES LEFT...

Another method of a benchmark is to focus on the time remaining or elapsed. If you are working without a watch, and you are solely relying on the proctor and a clock, then remaining time may be easier. That said, you will want to make a goal for about half the time left, a quarter of the time left and so on. Again, keep in mind that these goals are subject to change with you! With half the time left a beginning goal could be to have half the questions complete, or more than half (ideal). With a quarter of the time remaining ($\tilde{1}$5 minutes), maybe you would like to be past question 45 ($3/4$ or more of the questions complete).

WORK BACKWARDS THROUGH THE SECTION

The idea behind this strategy is to begin with more difficult questions first, and work toward the easier questions. Recall in the misconceptions section, we elucidated that the ACT math section starts with the easiest questions and ends with the most challenging questions.

When beginning a test, we want to get the first question we answer correct! As a result, we spend the most time on that question. By working backwards we shift that time to a more complex question, instead of #1.

Another benefit of working backwards is that we are no longer working uphill in difficulty! Instead we are working downhill, starting with the hardest and ending with the easiest. By starting with the most difficult, the earlier numbered questions will begin to appear easier than the previous later numbered questions; this will increase your pace allowing you to complete the earlier questions in less time than previously possible.

Below are two starting points for this strategy. You can begin with starting at #30 and gradually build up to starting at #60 by pushing back 5-10 questions once accuracy of 70-80% or more is achieved below that start point. It's all about comfort levels and what works best!

START AT #30

Question #30 is the elusive tipping point into the medium level difficulty questions. Starting in the dead middle of the test and working backwards will support you in working towards finishing this portion in less than half the time of the section. The first 30 questions are easy to medium difficulty, so ideally these should take less time than the last 30 more complex questions. When starting at #30 and moving backwards, you will still have 30 more challenging questions to complete, so it is important to pace yourself with this strategy. If your aim is to finish the full section, you should aim to have about 35-40 minutes remaining once you have completed the first 30.

START AT #60

Suggested start point for those who feel comfortable with the last 15 questions when working untimed, but under a time crunch feel overwhelmed by these problems. Others may work their way up to starting at #60, by adding 5-10 more questions gradually in timed sections for homework. When starting at #60, you will want to watch the clock and have a time goal to get to #30, or so. It is suggested that the first 30 questions take less than a minute to compete, therefore about 22-25 minutes remaining is a reasonable goal if you are finding that those questions need about 45 seconds for a solution.

TRUST THE PROCESS

Starting to work backwards can feel intimidating at first, you are generally moving a bit slower than you would taking the test forwards. This is normal! It is suggested to first try this strategy untimed, for a full section or two.

Try to notice if you feel the difference in your confidence in the questions. Did the questions in the beginning feel easier, or more straight forward? Take less time? Did your accuracy improve anywhere, like in the last 15 questions? Or the first 30 questions? You may want to try an untimed section two times to really decide if this method could work for you, before moving on to seeing its benefits in a timed section and finally a practice test!

On the ACT you will encounter 5 answer formats–numbers, special values, expressions, phrases and visuals. There are some general strategies surrounding answer choices that can lead you to the correct answer **faster**.

<u>Before</u> and <u>after</u> reading the question, you likely turn your attention to the answer choices. Here it is key to **make note of some differences**. Recognizing the differences can help you eliminate answer choices, once you begin to solve.

5 answer FORMATS:

1. NUMBERS:

Number answer format describes when the answer choices are just numbers. (Note: π is a number, not a variable). Often the answer choices differences will focus on whether or not the value is **negative** or **positive**. Do not overlook this!!! When you return to start solving, and set up the problem, there at some point in solving you will be able to recognize if the answer is **negative** or **positive**, this is where you can **ELIMINATE** answer choices.

EXAMPLE:

A. -9
B. -1
C. 3
D. 6
E. 9

2. SPECIAL VALUES:

Special Values format refers to the answer choices that contain values that do not appear to be student friendly. Often they contain roots, complex numbers, rationalized numbers, etc. While it is easy to get overwhelmed by the convoluted wording of the answer, keep in mind that it means you likely **do not** have to **simplify your answer**! A general rule of thumb when deciding if an answer choice is a special value or not, is if the answer could be simplified further–to a numerical value.

Aside from the true value of the answer, the differences here will focus on:

- Positive or negative values

- Operations between roots and constants–addition, subtraction, multiplication, division

- Very large/small values

- Same types of values in each answer

EXAMPLE:

A. $4\sqrt{7}$

B. $4\sqrt{7} + 8$

C. 8

D. 14

E. 16

3. EXPRESSIONS:

Expression answers choices which are not values, but expressions with a mixture of variables, often x, and numbers.

Here some key differences to spot between expression answer choices:

- Adding or subtracting specific terms

- Negative or positive variables

- Differing powers of leading terms

- Differing number of terms

- Missing terms

- Differences in denominators and numerators

EXAMPLE:

A. $x^2 - y^2 = 16$

B. $(x - 8)^2 + (y - 4)^2 = 16$

C. $\dfrac{(x + 8)^2}{4} - \dfrac{(y + 4)^2}{2} = 1$

D. $\dfrac{(x + 8)^2}{16} + \dfrac{(y + 4)^2}{4} = 1$

E. $\dfrac{(x - 8)^2}{16} + \dfrac{(y - 4)^2}{4} = 1$

4. PHRASES:

Instead of numbers or expressions, phrase answer choices provide answers in word phrases in plain English. Sometimes answer choices resemble the ACT science section and similar strategies can be used here–focus on the **differences**. Other times, the phrases of each choice are completely disconnected from one another, here still focus on finding the differences. The differences with this answer type are most dependent on the question.

EXAMPLE:

A. 2 imaginary numbers
B. 2 positive real numbers
C. 1 negative and 1 positive real number
D. 1 negative real number only
E. 1 real number, which is 0

5. VISUALS:

Another answer choice method is visual answer choices, like graphs or shapes. The idea remains the same: find the differences, focus on those and try to eliminate answer choices from there.

Some Key Differences in Visual Answer choices:

- Negative/Positive Graphs

- X-intercepts, including roots/zeros, and y-intercepts

- Multiplicity of roots/zeros if a polynomial

- Order of the polynomial

- Center/focus of a conic

EXAMPLE:

4.

F.

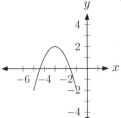

J.

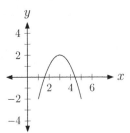

G.

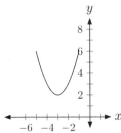

K.

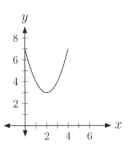

H.

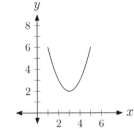

let's PRACTICE

Given the following answer choices determine the key differences between them, and classify them as a numerical, special value, expression, phrases or visuals answer choice.

1. Classify as: Numerical, Special Value, Expression, Phrases, or Visual. Then identify their key differences.
   A. $24 - 6\pi$
   B. $24 - 9\pi$
   C. $36 - \frac{9}{2}\pi$
   D. $36 - 3\pi$
   E. $36 - 9\pi$

2. Classify as: Numerical, Special Value, Expression, Phrases, or Visual. Then identify their key differences.
   F. $(6, 0)$
   G. $\left(4\frac{1}{2}, 1\frac{1}{2}\right)$
   H. $(1, 2)$
   J. $(0, -2)$
   K. $(-3, 0)$

3. Classify as: Numerical, Special Value, Expression, Phrases, or Visual. Then identify their key differences.
   A. -54
   B. -9
   C. -3
   D. 0
   E. 6

4. Classify as: Numerical, Special Value, Expression, Phrases, or Visual. Then identify their key differences.
   F. add up to $180°$
   G. add up to $90°$
   H. are each greater than $90°$
   J. are each $90°$
   K. are each less than $90°$

5. Classify as: Numerical, Special Value, Expression, Phrases, or Visual. Then identify their key differences.
   A. $\sqrt{2}$
   B. 2
   C. 4
   D. $\sqrt{34}$
   E. 8

6. Classify as: Numerical, Special Value, Expression, Phrases, or Visual. Then identify their key differences.

   F. 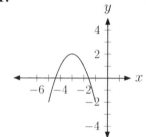   G.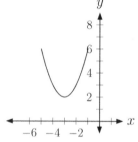

   H. 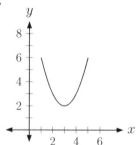   J.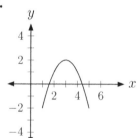

   K.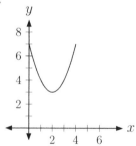

let's CHECK

Remember key differences are subjective, and the list given in this section is not exhaustive for any of the questions above. It's important to understand that key differences should help you differentiate between the answer choices to guide you to the answer quicker, so someone may see other differences.

1 Special Value/ Expression

This answer choice is a special value, recall the general rule of thumb to ask yourself if the answer could be easily simplified to a numerical value. However, if you decided that it was an expression instead, that is also a valid answer. Regardless of the answer choice type, the key differences remain the crucial component here.

Some key differences:

- first term of 24 or 36
- Subtracting a whole number or fraction of π
- If a whole number of π, subtracting 3π, 6π or 9π

2 Numerical

Coordinate points are student friendly, and therefore are numerical answer choices.

Some key differences:

- positive versus negative coordinate values
- x-intercept or y-intercept values
- x - coordinate values
- y-coordinate values

3 Numerical

Some key differences:

- Zero value
- Negative versus positive value
- Large absolute value (-54) versus, smaller values

4 Phrases

The answer choices here are describing the relationship between two angles. We may not have the question in front of us, but the phrase of "add up to 180°" alludes that we are talking about the sum of two or more angles.

Some key differences:

- Complementary versus supplementary angles
- Angles independently are obtuse, acute, or right

5 Special Value/ Numerical

Square roots, or any roots for that matter are not super student friendly, and can be classified as a special value, they also can be simplified further into an exact numerical value. However, some of the other answer choices are numerical, making that work as a classification here as well.

Some key differences:

- Whole number or a root
- Big root or small root

6 Visual

Not all visuals will be linear, in this cause the answer choices are lines. When the answer choices are not lines,but other polynomials, watch for x and y-intercept differences, and roots.

Some key differences:

- Negative versus positive slope
- y-intercept value of -4, 2 or 4
- x-intercept value of -2, 2 or 4
- Slope value

On the ACT you will find 4 main question types–**word problems, expression based questions, visuals based questions and cluster questions**. Building on the previous section (Part 5), recall that previewing the answer choices is essential! This will get you thinking about the problem before you've read it. For each question type, there are a few general strategies that if followed can facilitate choosing the correct answer.

1. WORD PROBLEMS:

On the ACT the word problems can be broken down further into two distinct types–Paragraph and 2-Sentences. The first tends to be a block of text, while the second is much more concise–usually about 2 sentences. The general strategies here are as follows:

- **Read the last sentence, FIRST.**

  Generally speaking, the last sentence is where the actual question is hidden. To save time, particularly with rather lengthy questions, it's best to read the question statement first and then go back and gather any information you may need from previous sentences. Avoid reading full sentences!!!

- **Then, look at the answers, yes, before setting the problem up!**

  Referring back to the previous section regarding the answer choices, these provide very useful information as to what to expect for your answer. Is the question answered, once x is found, or does something like $x + 5$, ACTUALLY answer the question? What about if the answer is positive?, negative?

- **Now, set-up the problem. Afterwards refer back to the answers, especially if the answer choice is given as an expression!**

  Oftentimes we will rush to simplify the answer or solve for the variable, however it's important to remember that the ACT will ask for you to just set-up the problem instead of fully solving. This is why familiarizing yourself with the answer choices is so important!!

- **If numerical answer choices, keep solving. But check back frequently!**

  Remember to keep checking back to the answer choices, you may not need to finish solving the question to see the answer! This step requires a bit of practice on your end, it does not come natural to intermittently stop and check the answers. However, if you were able to differentiate between the answer choices then this step will save you a significant amount of time!

- **Choose your answer.**

let's PRACTICE

1. The area of a new rectangular playground will be 210 ft^2. The playground will have a log border that has a total length of 74 ft. What are the dimensions of the playground, in feet?

   A. 7 by 30
   B. 8 by 29
   C. 10 by 21
   D. 14 by 15
   E. 16 by 21

2. A pool holds 880,000 liters of water (1 L = 1,000 m^3) and is 10 meters long. Which of the following could be the width and height of the pool, respectively?

   F. 22 m, 4 m
   G. 20 m, 5 m
   H. 18 m, 6 m
   J. 17 m, 5 m
   K. 16 m, 6 m

3. The next week, Joe found $120.96 while walking home from school. When he deposited the money in the bank, he noticed that he had three times as many quarters as pennies, 1 more quarters than nickels, and 1 fewer nickels than dimes. How many nickels did Joe find that week?

   A. 50
   B. 100
   C. 299
   D. 300
   E. 301

4. Tickets for a high school's theater production cost $5 each when bought in advance and $10 each when bought at the door. The theater group's goal is at least $2,000 in ticket sales for opening night. The theater sold 140 opening-night tickets in advance. What is the minimum number of tickets they need to sell at the door on opening night to make their goal?

   F. 50
   G. 130
   H. 140
   J. 150
   K. 200

let's CHECK

1. A 2. F 3. C 4. G

2. EXPRESSION BASED QUESTIONS:

Expression based questions are the most straightforward of the questions on the ACT, and yet somehow they are still able to be overcomplicated. Sometimes, the question is **JUST** the expression, and other times it's more wordy–and within that there are times where the words matter or not at all! For simplicity purposes we can classify the expression based questions as expression only, expression + words, and expression (words), respectively. The same basic strategy can be used to solve for all three types, but there are some specifics we will get into as well.

- **Go straight to the answers.**

  The words for the most part here are a distraction, the answers tell you more about what the question is asking. After you understand what the answer will look like, go back to the expression.

- **Focus on the expression, only.**

  Wherever you can minimize reading on the ACT Math, do so! Often the ACT gives too much information, and it can completely cause you to lose focus on solving the question.

- **Identify the route to go from the expression to the answer choices.**

  The solution to these types of questions revolves around transforming the expression to the answer choices, whether it is simplifying or solving for the solution. Remember that even if the solution involves solving for x or any variable, the ACT is known to make you go one step further, so be sure to read the question to make sure you are solving the problem and not on math autopilot.

- **Using the answer choices, begin the transformation from expression to answer choices.**

  Yes, the answer is the transformation, so begin! Can you simplify the constants or coefficients first, and does that help you identify the answer immediately!? This step really showcases the power of the previous section, understanding the differences can help you decide which step to do first or which step is the answer realizing step.

- **Read the question!**

  It may seem strange that the second to last step is to read the question, but this step allows you to make sure you answered correctly. If you are solving for a variable, this step may be moved up to ensure you do not go down the wrong path. If the question is an expression only, or an expression question where the words do not matter, then this step may be skipped entirely.

- **Choose your answer.**

let's PRACTICE

1. Which of the following is the sum of the solutions to
    the equation $x^2 - 24x = 0$.

    A. -48

    B. -24

    C. 12

    D. 24

    E. 48

2. If $12x = -8(5 - x)$, then $x = ?$

    F. -10

    G. -2

    H. 0

    J. 2

    K. 10

3. If $i^2 = -1$, which of the following is equivalent to

    $$\frac{1}{1-i} \cdot \frac{1+i}{1+i} \, ?$$

    A. $1 - i$

    B. $1 + i$

    C. i

    D. $\dfrac{-(1+i)}{2}$

    E. $\dfrac{1+i}{2}$

4. If x and y are integers, x is negative and $x^3 y^5 > 0$,
    which of the following must be true?

    F. $y > 0$

    G. $x - y > 0$

    H. $xy > 0$

    J. $y - x > 0$

    K. $xy^2 > 0$

3. VISUALS BASED QUESTIONS:

These questions involve a clearly labeled and accurately scaled visual that the problem revolves around. Above the visual will either be a block of text or a few sentences. Often the text only describes the figure, and is not necessary to read. It is best advised to not read any text, and if you have to then do your best to only read the question statement.

It's important to point out that the visual is drawn to scale—that means if the angle looks less than 90°, then it is an acute angle. Or if a length looks smaller, then it is indeed a smaller length.

- **Focus on the visual.**

  The words of the question likely solely describe the visual. Based on the type of visual, it can be clearly labeled or obvious what you need to find to solve the problem from the visual alone. Sometimes it will be labeled x, other times you will need to use the last sentence of the question to determine what the question is asking.

- **Re-read the answer choices.**

  You should get into the habit of reading the answer choices first, then taking a look at the visual and then back to the answer choices. After studying the visual, the answer will provide you with insight to solve the problem.

- **Avoid reading the question if you can./Read the question statement only.**

  At first, not reading the question initially or in its entirety will feel awkward, but trust the process. Often the wording of the question can distract from solving the answer by giving extraneous information, or it describes the figure in a convoluted way. Keep in mind that visuals are labeled correctly and to scale, and the labeling alone can tell you what to solve for.

  If you must read the question, minimize the amount of words you read! Try to keep it to the final sentence or the sentence asking the question. This way you avoid reading any redundant descriptions of figures.

- **Set-up the problem, sometimes this is enough.**

  As you may recall from the last part, the ACT sometimes is just asking you to set up the problem, often leaving the answer in an expression. After you set up the problem, check back in to the answer choices. You may have just completed the problem, or you may be able to eliminate many answer choices.

- **Continue to solve the problem and check in with the answer choices.**

  If the answer choices are not given in expressions, but in numerical or special values, then you will need to continue to solve the problem. Throughout your process of solving, keep checking back into the answer choices–you may be able to eliminate more answer choices intermittently and get to the answer choice faster!

- **Choose your answer.**

  Now you're ready to choose your answer.

let's PRACTICE

1. After all of the shows, a high school recorded their final ticket sales. Tickets purchased in advanced cost $8 and tickets purchased at the door cost $12. The table below shows the tickets sold per night both in advance and at the door.

	Friday	Saturday
Advanced	85	123
At the door	152	101

For which night did the school earn more in ticket sales, and by how much?

A. Friday, by $308
B. Friday, by $300
C. Saturday, by $120
D. Saturday, by $300
E. Saturday by $308

2. Rectangle $ABCD$ has a side length of 20 and a width of 15. What is the distance of $\overline{AC}$?

F. $10\sqrt{5}$
G. $15\sqrt{2}$
H. $45\sqrt{2}$
J. 25
K. 35

3. In the right triangle $\triangle ABC$, $\sin(B) = \dfrac{3}{5}$. Which of the following expressions is equal to $\cos(B)$?

A. $\dfrac{2}{5}$

B. $\dfrac{1}{2}$

C. 1

D. $\dfrac{5}{3}$

E. $\dfrac{4}{5}$

4. Which expression gives the area of the trapezoid shown below?

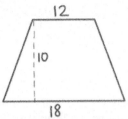

F. $\dfrac{(10)(15)}{2}$

G. $\dfrac{(10)(30)}{2}$

H. $\dfrac{(10)(18)}{2}$

J. $\dfrac{(10)(12)}{2}$

K. $\dfrac{(10)(12)(18)}{2}$

let's CHECK

1. A 2. J 3. E 4. G

4. CLUSTER QUESTIONS:

Cluster questions are the type of questions that are all related to block text alongside a figure or table. Think of these types of questions as similar to the ACT Science section, with the block text and figure/table as the passage. With this similarity in mind, here is how to approach these questions:

- **Re-look at the answer choices.**

  After reading the question, you may find that the question, while related to the passage, has a big enough disconnect that you can answer the question without the passage. You also could begin to eliminate answer choices, or determine differences, as we have highlighted in the previous section. The next two steps may be taken out of their order. If you do not need to necessarily use the passage, skip the next step, whereas if you do need to use the passage, proceed to the next step.

- **Ask yourself "What?" , "Where?"**

  You may find that you need to use **some of the passage**, but before you spend the time to read the entire passage, ask yourself "What you are looking for?" and "Where might that be in the passage?". This will help you avoid reading more than necessary, again remember the ACT writers are professional confusers! The information you may need to solve the problem could be in clearly labeled figures or tables where it is redundant to read their descriptions.

- **Set-up the problem.**

  After you have all the information necessary to solve the problem, set it up! Remember that the answer choices should communicate the form they want your answer–so be sure to simplify your answer just enough to look like the answer choices.

  If you must read the question, minimize the amount of words you read! Try to keep it to the final sentence or the sentence asking the question. This way you avoid reading any redundant descriptions of figures.

- **Set-up the problem, sometimes this is enough.**

  As you may recall from the last part, the ACT sometimes is just asking you to set up the problem, often leaving the answer in an expression. After you set up the problem, check back in to the answer choices. You may have just completed the problem, or you may be able to eliminate many answer choices.

- **Choose your answer.**

  Now you're ready to choose your answer.

let's PRACTICE

Use the following information to answer questions 1-2.

A new data storage provider by the name of DigiStore advertises the following plans:

Digistore Data Plans
500 GB for $89.99 per month
1,000 GB for $119.99 per month
2,000 GB for $159.99 per month
The charge for each additional GB is $0.50
Taxes are NOT included

1. Jessica buys the $89.99 plan, and Saphira buys the $119.99 plan. To the nearest cent, how much more is the before-tax charge per GB for the 500 GB on Jessica's plan than for 1,000 GB on Saphira's plan?
    A. 0.06 $/GB
    B. 0.12 $/GB
    C. 0.18 $/GB
    D. 0.30 $/GB
    E. 0.36 $/GB

2. Emily chose the $159.99 plan. There are certain months when she uses more than 1,750 GB of storage. For a month in which she uses x GB of storage space, where x is an integer greater than 1,750, which of the following expressions gives the amount, in dollars, of her bill before any taxes are added?
    F. $0.50x$
    G. $159.99 + 0.50x$
    H. $159.99 + 0.50(1,750 - x)$
    J. $159.99 + 0.50(1,750 + x)$
    K. $159.99 + 0.50(x - 1,750)$

Use the following information to answer questions 3-4.

The Private Prep Preschool held its annual book fair for 3 days. The total profit for the 3 days was $2,510. The profit, in dollars, is shown for each of the 3 days in the bar graph below.

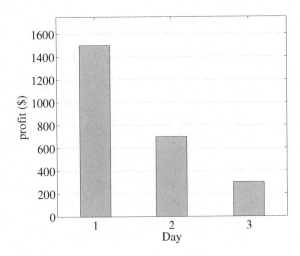

3. The mean profit per day that the preschool made during the 3-day period is closest to which of the following?
    A. $ 310
    B. $ 700
    C. $ 840
    D. $ 1,250
    E. $ 1,500

4. Approximately what percent of the book fair's profit over the 3 days did the preschool make on Day 2?
    F. 15%
    G. 20%
    H. 30%
    J. 40%
    K. 60%

let's CHECK

1. A 2. K 3. C 4. H

Now, let's explore how to use this book properly to help you perform at your best on the ACT.

Read it, crush it, get better?

There are six Chapters in this book. Each Chapter is divided into Sections, which focus on a specific topic, concept, or approach.

1.6 PERIMETER AND AREA

① Draw a picture (for ALL geometry)

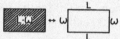

② Write BOTH formulas

③ Fill in for all quantities you have, and solve for what you need.

The TOP of each Section teaches the concept and shows how to properly approach your work.

1. The top of a rectangular table has an area of 24 square feet and a length of 6 feet. What is the perimeter, in feet, of the table?
   A. 10
   B. 16
   C. 20
   D. 24
   E. 26

① 24   ?(L)
   6(w)

② L·W = Area   what we need
   L·W·L·W = Perimeter

③ → $\frac{6L}{6} = \frac{24}{6}$ → L=4

→ 4·6·4·6 = P → P = $\boxed{20}$

Below that, we show how to properly FORMAT your work by solving a few example problems.

Ok. So when I'm solving the problems in each Section, I should make my work look as much like the examples as possible?

Yes. The purpose of showing the work laid out is for you to imitate layout as closely as possible.

At the end of each Chapter is a quiz. In addition, there is a Mid Book Test after Chapter 3, and two full Practice Tests at the end of the book.

I think you're ready to go! Before we get into Chapter One's concepts, however, let's do a quick skills check and practice some math foundations.

There won't really be explicit questions on these ideas, but the terminology and grammar skills will be used throughout all the problems.

0.1 COMBINING LIKE TERMS

1. Which of the following is a simplified form of the expression $3(2 + 5x) + 10 - 4x$?

   A. $-11x + 16$
   B. $-11x - 4$
   C. $-x + 4$
   D. $11x - 4$
   E. $11x + 16$

   handwritten: $6 + 15x + 10 - 4x$
   $16 + 11x$

2. Which of the following is a simplified form of the expression $3(2 - 5x) - 10 + 4x$?

   F. $-11x + 16$
   G. $-11x - 4$
   H. $-x + 4$
   J. $11x - 4$
   K. $11x + 16$

   handwritten: $6 - 15x - 10 + 4x$
   $-4 - 11x$

3. If $3 + 2x = 19$, then $x = ?$

   A. 8
   B. 11
   C. 24
   D. 33
   E. 38

   handwritten: $x = 8$

4. If $3 + 2x = 19$, then $3x = ?$

   F. 8
   G. 11
   H. 24
   J. 33
   K. 38

5. If $13 - 5x = 14$, then $x = ?$

   A. $-\dfrac{27}{5}$
   B. $-\dfrac{1}{5}$
   C. $\dfrac{1}{14}$
   D. $\dfrac{1}{5}$
   E. $\dfrac{27}{5}$

   handwritten: $x = -\dfrac{1}{5}$

6. If $13 - 5x = 14$, then $5x = ?$

   F. $-\dfrac{27}{5}$
   G. $-\dfrac{1}{5}$
   H. -1
   J. 1
   K. $\dfrac{27}{5}$

7. Which of the following is a simplified form of the expression $5(2 - 3x) - 5x - 2$?

   A. $-20x + 8$
   B. $-20x + 12$
   C. $-8x + 8$
   D. $8x + 12$
   E. $20x - 8$

   handwritten: $10 - 15x - 5x - 2$
   $8 - 20x$

8. Which of the following is a simplified form of the expression $5(2 - 3x) - (5x - 2)$?

   F. $-20x + 8$
   G. $-20x + 12$
   H. $-8x + 8$
   J. $8x + 12$
   K. $20x - 8$

   handwritten: $10 - 15x - 5x + 2$
   $12 - 20x$

0.2 ABSOLUTE VALUE

1. $|1 + 2| = ?$ 3
   - A. -3
   - B. -1
   - C. 1
   - D. 2
   - **E.** 3

2. $|1 - 2| = ?$
   - F. -3
   - G. -1
   - **H.** 1
   - J. 2
   - K. 3

3. $-3|-4 + 5| = ?$
   - A. -27
   - **B.** -3
   - C. -2
   - D. 3
   - E. 27

4. $-3|-4 - 5| = ?$
   - **F.** -27
   - G. -3
   - H. -2
   - J. 3
   - K. 27

5. What is the value of $2|4 - 9| - (5 + 6)$? $10 - 11$
   - **A.** -1
   - B. 1
   - C. 15
   - D. 21
   - E. 37

6. What is the value of $2|4 - 9| - 4(5 + 6)$? $10 - 44$
   - **F.** -34
   - G. -15
   - H. -1
   - J. 15
   - K. 54

7. What is the value of $-2(1 + 2) - 4|5 - 5|$? -6
   - A. -46
   - B. -40
   - **C.** -6
   - D. 6
   - E. 40

8. What is the value of $-2(1 + 2) - 4|5 + 5|$? $-6 - 40$ -46
   - **E.** -46
   - G. -40
   - H. -6
   - J. 6
   - K. 40

0.3 SCIENTIFIC NOTATION

1. The number 123, when written in correct scientific notation, is written as which of the following?
   - **A.** 12.3×10^{-2}
   - **B.** 1.23×10^{-1}
   - **C.** 1.23×10^1
   - **D.** 1.23×10^2
   - **E.** 12.3×10^1

2. The number 0.123, when written in correct scientific notation, is written as which of the following?
   - **F.** 12.3×10^{-2}
   - **G.** 1.23×10^{-1}
   - **H.** 1.23×10^{-2}
   - **J.** 1.23×10^1
   - **K.** 12.3×10^2

3. The number 945 000 000 000 is equivalent to which of the following expressions?
   - **A.** 9.45×10^{-13}
   - **B.** 9.45×10^{-11}
   - **C.** 9.45×10^{-10}
   - **D.** 9.45×10^{11}
   - **E.** 9.45×10^{13}

4. The number 0.000 000 000 094 5 is equivalent to which of the following expressions?
   - **F.** 9.45×10^{-13}
   - **G.** 9.45×10^{-11}
   - **H.** 9.45×10^{-10}
   - **J.** 9.45×10^{11}
   - **K.** 9.45×10^{13}

5. The number 400, 000, when written in correct scientific notation, is written as which of the following?
   - **A.** -40×10^{-5}
   - **B.** -4×10^{-4}
   - **C.** -4×10^4
   - **D.** 4×10^4
   - **E.** 4×10^5

6. The number 420, 200, when written in correct scientific notation, is written as which of the following?
   - **F.** -4202×10^{-5}
   - **G.** -4.202×10^{-4}
   - **H.** 4.202×10^4
   - **J.** 4.202×10^5
   - **K.** 42.02×10^5

7. The number 0.000 000 000 001 is equivalent to which of the following expressions?
   - **A.** 1×10^{-12}
   - **B.** 1×10^{-11}
   - **C.** 1×10^{-10}
   - **D.** -1×10^{11}
   - **E.** -1×10^{12}

8. The number 0.000 203 000 is equivalent to which of the following expressions?
   - **F.** -20.3×10^{-4}
   - **G.** -2.03×10^{-4}
   - **H.** 2.03×10^{-4}
   - **J.** 20.3×10^{-4}
   - **K.** 2.03×10^4

0.4 SIMPLIFYING RADICALS

1. Which of the following is the most simplified form of the expression $\sqrt{27}$?
   A. $3\sqrt{3}$
   B. $3\sqrt{9}$
   C. $9\sqrt{3}$
   D. $3i\sqrt{3}$
   E. $9i\sqrt{3}$

2. Which of the following is the most simplified form of the expression $\sqrt{-27}$?
   F. $3\sqrt{3}$
   G. $3\sqrt{9}$
   H. $9\sqrt{3}$
   J. $3i\sqrt{3}$
   K. $9i\sqrt{3}$

3. If $\sqrt{a} = b$ and $a = 36$, $b = ?$
   A. 6
   B. 72
   C. $1,296$
   D. $\dfrac{36}{2}$
   E. $\dfrac{1,296}{4}$

4. If $\sqrt{a} = b$ and $b = 36$, $a = ?$
   F. 6
   G. 72
   H. $1,296$
   J. $\dfrac{36}{2}$
   K. $\dfrac{1,296}{4}$

5. Consider the equation: $5\sqrt{45} = a\sqrt{5}$. Which of the following is the value of a ?
   A. 3
   B. 5
   C. 9
   D. 15
   E. 45

6. Consider the equation: $-4\sqrt{-24} = a\sqrt{6}$. Which of the following is the value of a ?
   F. $-8i$
   G. $-6i$
   H. $-4i$
   J. $6i$
   K. $8i$

7. What is the value of the expression $\sqrt{\dfrac{z}{m-4}}$ when $m = 2$ and $z = -24$?
   A. -3
   B. 3
   C. $2\sqrt{3}$
   D. $2i$
   E. $-2i\sqrt{3}$

$$\sqrt{\frac{-24}{-2}} = \sqrt{12} = 2\sqrt{3}$$

8. What is the value of the expression $\sqrt{\dfrac{a-10}{b-4}}$ when $a = 46$ and $b = 6$?
   F. -3
   G. 3
   H. $3\sqrt{2}$
   J. $2i$
   K. $-3i\sqrt{2}$

$$\sqrt{\frac{36}{2}} = \sqrt{18} = 3\sqrt{2}$$

1. The improper fraction $\frac{13}{12}$ is equivalent to which of the following?

   A. $1\frac{13}{12}$

   B. $1\frac{5}{12}$

   C. $1\frac{1}{12}$

   D. $1\frac{1}{6}$

   E. $1\frac{1}{3}$

2. The improper fraction $\frac{23}{5}$ is equivalent to which of the following?

   F. $2\frac{3}{5}$

   G. $2\frac{6}{5}$

   H. $4\frac{6}{5}$

   J. $4\frac{4}{5}$

   K. $4\frac{3}{5}$

3. What is the sum of $2\frac{4}{7}$ and $3\frac{1}{3}$?

   A. $5\frac{5}{10}$

   B. $5\frac{19}{21}$

   C. $5\frac{5}{21}$

   D. $-1\frac{5}{21}$

   E. $-1\frac{5}{10}$

   $2\frac{12}{21} + 3\frac{7}{21}$

   $5\frac{19}{21}$

4. What is the sum of $3\frac{1}{4}$ and $2\frac{5}{6}$?

   F. $6\frac{1}{12}$

   G. $6\frac{6}{10}$

   H. $6\frac{5}{24}$

   J. $5\frac{1}{12}$

   K. $5\frac{5}{24}$

   $3\frac{6}{24} + 2\frac{20}{24}$

   $6\frac{1}{12}$

5. What is the difference of $4\frac{1}{4}$ and $2\frac{5}{6}$?

   A. $1\frac{1}{12}$

   B. $1\frac{5}{12}$

   C. $2\frac{1}{12}$

   D. $2\frac{5}{12}$

   E. $5\frac{5}{12}$

   $4\frac{6}{24} - 2\frac{20}{24}$

   $1\frac{10}{24} = 1\frac{5}{12}$

6. Michele is building a fence around her rectangular garden. The length of her garden is $2\frac{2}{5}$ inches and the width of her garden is $3\frac{3}{4}$ inches. How many linear feet of fence does Michele need to have to fully enclose her garden?

   F. $5\frac{5}{8}$

   G. $5\frac{5}{9}$

   H. 9

   J. $10\frac{5}{9}$

   K. $12\frac{3}{10}$

   $2\frac{8}{20} \qquad 3\frac{15}{20}$

   $6\frac{3}{20}$

   $12\frac{6}{20} = 12\frac{3}{10}$

0.6 FACTORS AND MULTIPLES

1. Which of the following is a multiple of 7?
   - **A.** 7
   - **B.** 17
   - **C.** 27
   - **D.** 37
   - **E.** 71

2. Which of the following is a multiple of 8?
   - **F.** 12
   - **G.** 20
   - **H.** 28
   - **J.** 32
   - **K.** 38

3. What is the least common multiple of 15 and 20?
   - **A.** 20
   - **B.** 60
   - **C.** 100
   - **D.** 300
   - **E.** 7,500

4. What is the greatest common factor of 15 and 20?
   - **F.** 1
   - **G.** 4
   - **H.** 5
   - **J.** 15
   - **K.** 20

5. Which of the following is a factor of 3?
   - **A.** 1
   - **B.** 6
   - **C.** 12
   - **D.** 13
   - **E.** 30

6. Which of the following is a factor of 12?
   - **F.** 5
   - **G.** 6
   - **H.** 20
   - **J.** 24
   - **K.** 120

7. Which of the following is NOT a factor of $12x$?
   - **A.** $3x$
   - **B.** 6
   - **C.** $6x$
   - **D.** $12x$
   - **E.** $24x$

8. Two cities, City X and City Y, have regular weather patterns. City X rains every third day and City Y rains every sixth day. If the current day is a day where both City X and City Y have rain, how many days will pass until it rains in both cities?
   - **F.** 3
   - **G.** 6
   - **H.** 9
   - **J.** 12
   - **K.** 18

1. Which of the following numbers is an *integer*?
   A. 1.7
   B. $\sqrt{5}$
   C. π
   D. 5
   E. $\dfrac{11}{2}$

2. Which of the following numbers is *rational*?
   F. $\sqrt{7}$

   G. $\sqrt{\dfrac{25}{3}}$

   H. $\sqrt{\dfrac{25}{9}}$

   J. $\sqrt{\dfrac{50}{5}}$

   K. $\sqrt{\dfrac{1}{10}}$

3. Which of the following numbers represents a *real number*?
   A. $3 + 4i$
   B. $4i$
   C. $i^2\sqrt{7}$
   D. $3 - 4i$
   E. $25i^3$

4. Which of the following numbers represents a *complex number*?
   F. $3i$
   G. $4i^3$
   H. $\sqrt{-49}$
   J. $3 - 4i$
   K. $25i^3$

5. Which of the following choices represents an *expression*?
   A. $a + b = 2$

   B. $3a - 4b = 5$

   C. $\dfrac{a}{b} = 10$

   D. $a^2 b^3 c^{10}$

   E. $a^2 = 36$

6. Which of the following choices represents an *equation*?
   F. $a + b$

   G. $3a - \dfrac{4}{5}b$

   H. $\dfrac{a}{b} = 10$

   J. $a^2 b^3 c^{10}$

   K. $a^2 - 36$

7. Consider equilateral triangle ABC with side lengths of 5. Which of the following represents the *sum of the interior angles* of triangle ABC?
   A. $60°$
   B. $90°$
   C. $120°$
   D. $180°$
   E. $360°$

8. Consider all quadrilaterals with four different side lengths and a perimeter of 24. Which of the following represents the *sum of the interior angles* of those quadrilaterals?
   F. $90°$
   G. $180°$
   H. $270°$
   J. $360°$
   K. $540°$

1. The distance-versus-time graph below represents Sally Mae's walk to work on Thursday.

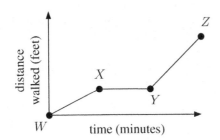

Which of the following statements could describe what Sally Mae did during the time interval covered by the horizontal line segment $\overline{XY}$?

A. She walked due east.

B. She walked up a hill.

C. She walked on level ground.

D. She walked at a faster speed than the line segment $\overline{WX}$

E. She stopped to find her phone.

2. Teller conducted a survey of a group of 10th-grade students to determine which of the 4 classes, Math, Chemistry, History, and English, were the most popular. Each student who responded to the survey selected his or her favorite class. The circle graph below shows the number of students who selected each of the 4 classes. How many students chose History?

F. 5
G. 7
H. 12
J. 29
K. 60

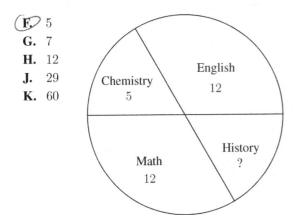

3. An engineer conducted an experiment consisting of a rolling 6-sided cube with the digits 1 through 6 on its faces, 1 digit per face. The cube was rolled 30 times, and after each roll, the number appearing on the top face was recorded. The data of the experiment is presented in the graph below. Which digit appeared least often, and which digit appeared most often, respectively?

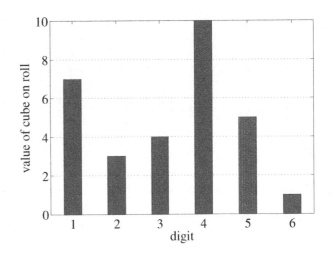

A. 1 and 4
B. 2 and 6
C. 3 and 5
D. 6 and 1
E. 6 and 4

4. Jefferson High School has 680 juniors and seniors currently enrolled. Students were asked whether or not they were attending the homecoming football game.

Grade	Yes	No	Total
Juniors	160	150	310
Seniors	210	160	370
Total	370	310	680

How many seniors are NOT attending the game?

F. 50
G. 160
H. 210
J. 310
K. 370

0.9 VENN DIAGRAMS

Questions 1-3 pertain to the following information.

Anton is the director of basketball and softball at Hollow's East High School. He recorded how many student athletes currently participate in each sport. His results are shown in the Venn diagram below:

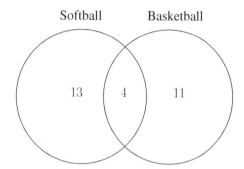

1. How many students at Hollow's East High School participate in both softball and basketball?
   A. 4
   B. 11
   C. 13
   D. 17
   E. 28

2. How many students at Hollow's East High School participate in softball *only*?
   F. 4
   G. 11
   H. 13
   J. 17
   K. 28

3. How many students at Hollow's East High School participate in softball?
   A. 4
   B. 11
   C. 13
   D. 17
   E. 28

Questions 4-6 pertain to the following information.

The Venn diagram below displays how many students at Hollow's East High School attend the advanced Physics, Math, and English courses.

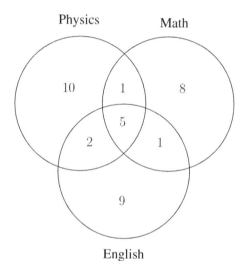

4. How many students at Hollow's East High School attend advanced English *only*?
   F. 5
   G. 9
   H. 10
   J. 17
   K. 36

5. How many students at Hollow's East High School attend advanced English?
   A. 5
   B. 9
   C. 10
   D. 17
   E. 36

6. How many students at Hollow's East High School attend both Physics and Math?
   F. 1
   G. 6
   H. 8
   J. 10
   K. 18

0.10 STEM AND LEAF PLOT

1. Consider the following stem and leaf plot:

stem	leaf
1	0, 5, 8
2	0, 0, 1

Which of the following is the set of numbers organized in the stem and leaf plot?
A. 0, 5, 8, 0, 0, 2
B. 1, 0, 5, 8, 2, 0, 0, 1
C. 1, 6, 9, 2, 2, 3
D. 10, 15, 18, 20, 20, 21
E. 1,058 & 2,001

2. Consider the following stem and leaf plot:

stem	leaf
3	0, 5, 8
4	7
5	1,7,7,7

Which of the following is the set of numbers organized in the stem and leaf plot?
F. 0, 15, 24, 28, 5, 35, 35, 35
G. 3, 0, 5, 8, 4, 7, 5, 1, 7, 7, 7
H. 3, 8, 11, 11, 6, 12, 12, 12
J. 30, 35, 38, 47, 51, 57, 57, 57
K. 30, 35, 38, 47, 50, 51, 52, 53, 54

3. Consider the following stem and leaf plot:

stem	leaf
3	0, 5, 8
4	7
5	1,7,7,7

Which of the following is the average of the set of numbers organized in the stem and leaf plot?
A. 4
B. 46.5
C. 47
D. 51
E. 57

Questions 4-6 pertain to the following information.

Kyla surveyed her fifteen grammar classmates to find out what grade each classmate received on the end of the year final project. She tabulated the survey in the stem and leaf plot below:

stem	leaf
7	8, 8, 9, 9
8	1, 1, 1, 3, 3, 4, 5, 8, 9
9	3, 7

4. Which grade appeared most often in Kyla's survey?
F. 1
G. 78
H. 79
J. 80
K. 81

5. Kyla received the highest grade in the grammar class. Which grade did she receive for the end of the year final project?
A. 9
B. 70
C. 80
D. 90
E. 97

6. To the nearest whole number, what was the average grade of the end of the year final project for all fifteen students in Kyla's grammar class?
F. 8
G. 81
H. 84
J. 90
K. 97

Chapter 1 covers questions found early on in the Math section, typically in the 1-25 region. These types may continue to show up throughout the test, so keep an eye out.

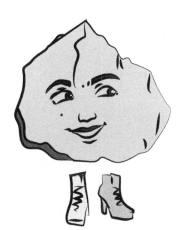

Instructions are laid out with the hopes of guiding your written work. Try to imitate steps and layout when solving the first few probelms - obviously everyone has their own way of working, but try to give ours a shot first :)

① Group x terms together ② Get x alone.

→ $x + 15 = 3x - 7$

Remove terms by following } | Addition +/−
Multiplication ×/÷
Exponents ✓/−
Parentheses ( )

---

1. Consider the equation $3x - 2 = 10$. What is the value of x?

A. 2

B. $\dfrac{8}{3}$

C. 3

D. 4

E. 10

① $3x - 2 = 10$ ✓ x is in one place

② $3x - 2 = 10$

$+2 \quad +2$ ᴬ

$3x = 12$

$\div 3 \quad \div 3$ ᴹ

$x = 4$

---

2. Consider the equation $3x + 1 = -2x + 11$. What is the value of x?

$5x = 10$

F. -11

G. -2

H. 2

J. 2.4

K. 11

① Group x terms together.

$3x + 1 = -2x + 11$

$+2x \quad +2x$

② $5x + 1 = 11$

$-1 \quad -1$ ᴬ

$5x = 10$

$\div 5 \quad \div 5$ ᴹ

$x = 2$

---

3. If $\dfrac{10}{3}\sqrt{x} + \dfrac{7}{6}\sqrt{x} = 9$, which of the following values of x satisfies the given equation?

A. 4

B. 6

C. 9

D. 27

E. 54

① Group x terms together.

$\left(\dfrac{10}{3} + \dfrac{7}{6}\right)\sqrt{x} = 9$

② $\dfrac{9}{2}\sqrt{x} = 9$

$\div \dfrac{9}{2} \quad \div \dfrac{9}{2}$ ᴹ

$\sqrt{x} = 2$

$\sqrt{x}^2 = 2^2$ ᴱ

$x = 4$

Notice that "undo"ing operations means using the inverse operation on them. Subtraction gets rid of addition, and vice versa. Squares get rid of square roots!

4. If $x + 7 = -2$, what is the value of x?
   - F. -9
   - G. -5
   - H. 3
   - J. 5
   - K. 9

5. If $x - 2 = -7$, what is the value of x?
   - A. -9
   - B. -5
   - C. 3
   - D. 5
   - E. 9

6. If $2x + 12 = 10$, what is the value of $2x$?
   - F. -11
   - G. -2
   - H. -1
   - J. 1
   - K. 11

7. If $2x + 5 = 11$, then $2x = ?$
   - A. 2
   - B. 3
   - C. 4
   - D. 5
   - E. 6

8. If $5x + 23 = 17$, what is the value of x?
   - F. $-\dfrac{6}{5}$
   - G. -2
   - H. 0
   - J. $\dfrac{6}{5}$
   - K. 8

9. Consider the equation $5x + 4 = -x - 8$. What is the value of x?

   $6x = -12$

   $x = -2$

   - A. -2
   - B. 0
   - C. 2
   - D. 4
   - E. 6

10. Consider the equation $-2x - 3 = -6x + 9$. What is the value of x?

    $4x = 12$

    $x = 3$

    - F. -4
    - G. -3
    - H. 3
    - J. 4
    - K. 12

11. Which value of x satisfies the equation:

    $$\frac{2x - 8}{6} = -2$$

    - A. -30
    - B. -10
    - C. -2
    - D. 8
    - E. 10

12. Which value of x satisfies the equation:

    $$\frac{5}{2x + 7} = -\frac{10}{4x + 2}$$

    - F. -10
    - G. -2
    - H. 2
    - J. 10
    - K. 40

13. What value of x makes this equation $4(3x - 7) = 13$ true?

   A. $-\dfrac{5}{4}$

   B. $\dfrac{41}{12}$

   C. $\dfrac{5}{3}$

   D. $\dfrac{20}{3}$

   E. $\dfrac{41}{3}$

14. What value of x makes this equation $-3(4x - 5) = 27$ true?

   F. $-\dfrac{8}{3}$

   G. $-\dfrac{11}{6}$

   H. -1

   J. 1

   K. $\dfrac{11}{6}$

15. What value of x makes this equation $-2(5 - x) = -3x - 5$ true?

   A. $-\dfrac{5}{4}$

   B. $-\dfrac{4}{5}$

   C. -1

   D. 1

   E. $\dfrac{5}{4}$

16. A researcher used the formula $F = \dfrac{1}{2}dcv^2$ to model the force of air resistance on a falling object, where F is the force, d is the density of air, c is a constant, and v is the velocity of the object. Which of the following gives the density of air in terms of F, c, and v?

   F. $d = \dfrac{F}{2cv^2}$

   G. $d = \dfrac{2F}{cv^2}$

   H. $d = \dfrac{F}{cv^2}$

   J. $d = \dfrac{2F}{\sqrt{cv}}$

   K. $d = \dfrac{F}{2cv}$

17. The kinetic energy of an object is defined by $KE = \dfrac{1}{2}mv^2$, where KE is the kinetic energy of the object, m is the mass of the object, and v is the velocity of the object. Which of the following gives the mass of the object in terms of the velocity and kinetic energy?

   A. $m = \dfrac{2KE}{v^2}$

   B. $m = \dfrac{2KE}{\sqrt{v}}$

   C. $m = \dfrac{\frac{1}{2}KE}{v^2}$

   D. $m = \dfrac{\frac{1}{2}KE}{\sqrt{v^2}}$

   E. $m = \dfrac{\sqrt{2KE}}{v^2}$

18. The cost of a rental car can be modeled as $C = 0.42m + 20d$, where C is the cost of the car in dollars, m is the distance the car was driven in miles, and d is the length of the rental period in days. Which of the following expressions gives m in terms of d and C?

F. $m = C - 47.6d$

G. $m = \dfrac{C}{0.42} - 20d$

H. $m = (0.42)(C - 20d)$

J. $m = \dfrac{C - 20d}{0.42}$

K. $m = \dfrac{C - 20d}{42}$

19. Consider the following equation:

$$\frac{1}{4}x - \frac{1}{5}x = 1$$

Which of the following values of x satisfies the equation?

A. 1
B. 4
C. 5
D. 20
E. 400

20. Consider the following equation:

$$\frac{1}{4}x - \frac{1}{5}x = 20$$

Which of the following values of x satisfies the equation?

F. 1
G. 4
H. 5
J. 20
K. 400

21. Consider the following equation:

$$\frac{1}{2}x + \frac{2}{3}x = 42$$

Which of the following values of x satisfies the equation?

A. 49
B. 42
C. 36
D. 7
E. 6

22. Consider the following equation:

$$-\frac{2}{3}x + 3 = \frac{1}{3}x - \frac{1}{4}x$$

Which of the following values of x satisfies the equation?

F. -12
G. -4
H. -3
J. 3
K. 4

23. If $\dfrac{2x + 3y}{x - y} = \dfrac{1}{2}$, what is the value of $\dfrac{x}{y}$?

A. $-\dfrac{7}{3}$

B. $-\dfrac{3}{7}$

C. $\dfrac{3}{7}$

D. $\dfrac{7}{3}$

E. $\dfrac{14}{3}$

24. If $\dfrac{3x - y}{2x + 5y} = \dfrac{2}{3}$, what is the value of $\dfrac{x}{y}$?

F. $\dfrac{13}{5}$

G. $\dfrac{17}{8}$

H. $\dfrac{3}{2}$

J. $\dfrac{8}{17}$

K. $\dfrac{5}{13}$

When setting up ratios, check that both of the TOPS are the same type of thing. Then check that the LEFT side only contains one set of data. Units can help a lot here!

Item A with attribute A. Item B with attribute B.

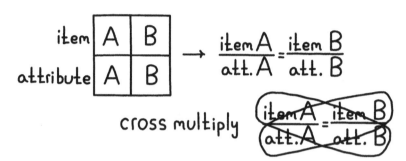

1. On a certain map of Colorado, one inch represents 15 miles. How many miles do $3\frac{4}{5}$ inches represent?

   A. 19
   B. 49
   C. 57
   D. 60
   E. 77

$$\frac{\text{inches}}{\text{miles}} = \frac{\text{inches}}{\text{miles}}$$

$$\frac{1 \text{ in}}{15 \text{ mi}} = \frac{3.8 \text{ in}}{X \text{ mi}}$$

$$1 \cdot X = 15 \cdot 3.8$$

$$X = \boxed{57}$$

2. The ratio of boys to girls in Mr. Owen's math class is 3 to 5. If there are 10 girls in the class on a given day, how many boys are there in the class on that day?

   F. 16
   G. 6
   H. 15
   J. 3
   K. 17

$$\frac{\text{boys}}{\text{girls}} = \frac{\text{boys}}{\text{girls}}$$

(ratio)   (in class)
  ↓   ↓

$$\frac{3}{5} = \frac{X}{10}$$

$$3 \cdot 10 = 5 \cdot X$$

$$\boxed{X = 6}$$

3. Samantha goes to the grocery store to purchase cheese. The store sells cheese for $5 per pound. Samantha wants to purchase 12 pounds of cheese. How much will Samantha have to pay?
(Note: Ignore sales tax for Samantha's purchase.)
A. $2.40
B. $5.00
C. $12.50
D. $30.00
E. $60.00

4. Mr. Caraco gives each student two stickers when they show up on time. If 18 people show up on time, how many stickers will Mr. Caraco give to his students?
F. 45
G. 36
H. 20
J. 18
K. 6

5. A baking recipe that yields 30 brownies requires $1\frac{1}{4}$ scoops of sugar. When the ingredients in this recipe are increased proportionally, how many scoops of sugar are required for the recipe to yield 120 brownies?
A. $4\frac{3}{4}$
B. 5
C. 30
D. $37\frac{1}{2}$
E. 120

6. Deena asked a random sample of 20 sophomore students which of four colors they liked best. 9 answered red, 4 answered blue, 4 answered yellow, and 3 answered green. Deena plans to order 200 colored pencils in the proportions, by color, of the students' preferences. How many blue pencils will she order?
F. 4
G. 8
H. 32
J. 40
K. 90

7. Steven has a jar containing 28 blue jelly beans and 72 red jelly beans. What is the ratio of blue jelly beans to red jelly beans in the jar?
A. 1:7
B. 1:18
C. 7:18
D. 7:25
E. 18:7

8. The ratio of the sides of a triangle are 3:4:5. If the length of the longest side is 15 inches, what is the perimeter, in inches, of the triangle?
F. 54
G. 36
H. 12
J. 9
K. 6

9. If a 12 foot tree casts a shadow 30 feet long, how long of a shadow would a 30 foot tree cast at the same time and place?
A. 12 feet
B. 30 feet
C. 42 feet
D. 72 feet
E. 75 feet

10. If $x = 12$ and $y = 6$ when $\frac{8}{x} = \frac{k}{y}$, what is the value of x when $y = 15$?
F. 1
G. 4
H. 6
J. 8
K. 30

11. A certain farm raises only chickens and pigs. The ratio of chickens to pigs on that farm is 5:3. If there are currently 160 animals in total, how many pigs would they need to add to the farm so that the ratio of chickens to pigs would be 2:3?
A. 60
B. 80
C. 90
D. 150
E. 250

1.3 PROBABILITY

There are 15 marbles. 6 are red and 9 are blue. What is the probability of picking a blue marble?

$$\frac{\text{target}}{\text{total}} \rightarrow \frac{\#\text{ of blue marbles}}{\#\text{ of total marbles}} \rightarrow \boxed{\frac{9}{15}}$$

1. Darius has 200 marbles in a bag. Two marbles are purple, two are brown, and the rest are pink. What is the chance that Darius will pick a purple marble at random?

$$\frac{\text{target}}{\text{total}} \rightarrow \frac{\text{purple}}{\text{all}} \rightarrow \frac{2}{200} = \boxed{\frac{1}{100}}$$

   A. $\frac{1}{100}$

   B. $\frac{2}{100}$

   C. $\frac{2}{50}$

   D. $\frac{2}{25}$

   E. $\frac{1}{10}$

To find the probability of two events occuring back to back, multiply their individual probabilities!

2. There are 22 students in the drama club. There are 5 freshman, 5 sophomores, 6 juniors, and 6 seniors in the club. The club president cannot be a freshman. John Carlo, a senior, runs against 3 juniors for club president. What is the probability that he gets elected?

$$\frac{\text{target}}{\text{total}} \rightarrow \frac{\text{chosen}}{\text{running}} \rightarrow \boxed{\frac{1}{4}}$$

watch out for problems that dont ask for the $\frac{\text{target}}{\text{total}}$ setup you were expecting.

   F. $\frac{17}{22}$

   G. $\frac{5}{22}$

   H. $\frac{4}{22}$

   J. $\frac{6}{22}$

   K. $\frac{1}{4}$

Playing cards show up a lot in Probability problems, so it's good to know there are 52 cards in a deck. There are 4 suits, which means 13 of each suit.

So the probability of drawing a king is 4/52, since there is one king per suit?

Yes exactly! And the probability of picking a Heart is 1/4, since there are 4 suits.

3. The key club after school meets every Wednesday. There are 20 members in the club, 3 of which are officers: President, Vice President, and Treasurer. Vanessa, who is in the key club, is NOT an officer. A random member of the club is selected. What are the odds of choosing Vanessa?

A. $\dfrac{1}{20}$

B. $\dfrac{1}{17}$

C. $\dfrac{3}{20}$

D. $\dfrac{3}{17}$

E. $\dfrac{17}{20}$

4. Tami has 7 white marbles, 4 blue marbles, and 5 red marbles. What are the odds that that she picks either a white or a blue marble at random?

F. $\dfrac{4}{7}$

G. $\dfrac{5}{16}$

H. $\dfrac{7}{16}$

J. $\dfrac{8}{16}$

K. $\dfrac{11}{16}$

5. A normal deck of cards, with 52 in total, is spread out face down on a tabletop. A card is randomly selected. What are the odds of selecting a heart, placing it back on the tabletop, then selecting a second heart?

(Note: A normal deck of cards contains four suits — clubs, diamonds, hearts, and spades — each with the same quantity of cards.)

A. $\dfrac{1}{52} \cdot \dfrac{1}{51}$

B. $\dfrac{1}{52} \cdot \dfrac{1}{52}$

C. $\dfrac{13}{52} \cdot \dfrac{12}{51}$

D. $\dfrac{13}{52} \cdot \dfrac{13}{51}$

E. $\dfrac{13}{52} \cdot \dfrac{13}{52}$

6. Madison is playing a game that requires her to throw a dart at a target while blindfolded. The target is in the shape of a circle and has a radius of 6 inches. The wall behind the target is in the shape of a rectangle and has dimensions of 84 inches by 100 inches. If Madison throws the dart randomly, assuming the dart hits the space within the dimensions of the wall, which is closest to the percent chance that that she hits the target and not the wall?

F. 1.3%

G. 2.2%

H. 2.8%

J. 3.6%

K. 5.7%

7. Adam has a library of books with either a blue, gray, or black cover. If Adam has 11 blue books, 10 gray books, and 25 books in total, what are the odds that Adam randomly picks a black book from his library?

A. $\dfrac{11}{25}$

B. $\dfrac{4}{25}$

C. $\dfrac{2}{5}$

D. $\dfrac{1}{5}$

E. $\dfrac{1}{25}$

8. Madison is taking a 6-question multiple choice quiz in math class with 4 choices for each question. If she guesses randomly on all 6 questions, what is the probability that she will get every question correct?

F. $\dfrac{1}{4096}$

G. $\dfrac{1}{1296}$

H. $\dfrac{1}{512}$

J. $\dfrac{1}{64}$

K. $\dfrac{1}{24}$

1.4 MEAN, MEDIAN, MODE, MIDPOINT

$$\frac{\text{sum of things}}{\text{\# of things}} = \text{Average/Mean}$$

$$\left(\begin{array}{cc}\text{average} & \text{average} \\ \text{of x values,} & \text{of y values}\end{array}\right) = \text{Midpoint}$$

$$\text{Middle Number} = \text{Median}$$

Mean = Average = Midpoint.

They all *mean* the same thing!

sigh Good one.

---

1. Dan got an 88, 86, 91, and 82 on the first four of five total tests that he would need to take in his history class. What would Dan need to get on his final exam to get an overall average of 89 for all five test grades?

   A. 98
   B. 97
   C. 96
   D. 95
   E. 94

   Sum of things = 88+86+91+82+x = 347+x
   \# of things = 5
   Average = 89

   $$\frac{347+x}{5} = 89 \;\rightarrow\; 5\left(\frac{347+x}{5}\right) = 5(89)$$

   $$347+x = 445$$
   $$\underline{-347 \qquad -347}$$
   $$\boxed{x = 98}$$

---

2. What is the midpoint of the line segment whose endpoints are located at $(3, 11)$ and $(7, 7)$?

   F. $(5, 9)$
   G. $(10, 18)$
   H. $(11, 3)$
   J. $(4, 4)$
   K. $(-1, 3)$

   $$\left(\begin{array}{cc}\text{average} & \text{average} \\ \text{of x values,} & \text{of y values}\end{array}\right)$$
   $$\downarrow$$
   $$\left(\frac{3+7}{2}, \frac{11+7}{2}\right)$$
   $$\downarrow$$
   $$\boxed{(5, 9)}$$

Median problems almost always require you to re-write the data from low to high. Tedious, but not too hard :)

If you have an even number of data points, then two numbers will be in the "middle". The Median is the Average of these two numbers!

3. The average temperature, in degrees Fahrenheit, per month of Brooklyn, New York in 2016 were: 31, 43, 50, 50, 65, 70, 81, 89, 72, 60, 42, and 28. What is the median average temperature, in degrees Fahrenheit?

A. 50
B. 55
C. 60
D. 63
E. 88

4. The Hicksville Comets scored 52, 71, 58, 60, and 65 points in their first five games of the season, respectively. What is the average points scored per game?

F. 65
G. 61.2
H. 57.4
J. 50
K. 42

5. Martha plays a game of darts and hits the board with the following values: 3, 3, 3, 5, 6, 17, 17, 17, 17, 19, and 19. What is the mode of Martha's game of darts?

A. 3
B. 5
C. 6
D. 17
E. 19

6. What is the median of the following data set:

$$3, -4, 7, 5, -2, 5, 0$$

F. 0
G. 2
H. 3
J. 5
K. 14

7. Jill has completed 5 tests this semester and has achieved scores of 74, 92, 83, 89, and 77. What score must she average over the next two tests to average at least an 85 on all 7 tests?

A. 59
B. 83
C. 85
D. 90
E. 95

8. Stephen has a test average of an 88 after taking 3 exams. He has one exam left and wants to finish the year with exactly a 90 test average. What does Stephen need to score on his last exam?

F. 88
G. 90
H. 92
J. 96
K. 100

9. The height, in inches, of the eleven students in Ms. Morena's kindergarten class are as follows: 34, 36, 41, 32, 40, 45, 30, 40, 26, 33, and 36. A new student enters Ms. Morena's class and the median height of the twelve students is 35 inches. Which of the following could be the height, in inches, of the new student?

A. 32
B. 36
C. 37
D. 39
E. 41

10. On Monday, 10 students took an exam in Mr. Herbert's Algebra class, and their results averaged to a score of 86. When Stephen, who was out sick on Monday, took the exam, the class average for all 11 students improved to a score of 87. What score did Stephen receive on the exam?

F. 87
G. 88
H. 90
J. 93
K. 97

11. Evan completed a survey at his local mall. He recorded the number of siblings for 35 random people and tabulated his data in the data shown below.

Siblings	Frequency
0	5
1	12
2	9
3	5
4	2
5	2

To the nearest tenth, what is the average number of siblings per person surveyed?

A. 1
B. 1.8
C. 2
D. 2.5
E. 5.8

12. The average of 5 numbers is 91. What is the fifth number if the first 4 numbers are 78, 92, 96, and 94?

    F. 90
    G. 91
    H. 92
    J. 93
    K. 95

13. In Ms. Marino's Biology class, students are growing a certain type of cactus under different environmental conditions. The height of each student's cactus, in centimeters, at the end of 10 weeks is recorded in the stem and leaf plot below.

stem	leaf
1	0, 1, 4
2	0, 0, 2, 6, 8
3	1, 2, 4, 4, 4, 9
4	0, 2, 5, 6, 6, 9

What is the median height of the students' data at the end of the 10 week period?

    A. 31
    B. 32
    C. 33
    D. 34
    E. 36

14. The average of 5 numbers is 83. If one of those numbers is 15, what is the average of the other four numbers?

    F. 16.6
    G. 68
    H. 80
    J. 83
    K. 100

15. To determine the overall test score for each student in a semester, Mr. Gomez deletes the lowest test score and calculates the average of the remaining test scores. Cheryl took all 5 tests and earned the following test scores in Mr. Gomez's class this semester: 81, 83, 88, 92 and 99. What overall test score did Cheryl earn in Mr. Gomez's class this semester?

    A. 88.0
    B. 88.9
    C. 90.0
    D. 90.5
    E. 91.0

16. A data set has 20 elements. The 20 elements in a second data set are obtained by multiplying each element in the first data set by 10. The 20 elements in a third data set are obtained by decreasing each element of the second data set by 8. The median of the third data set is 40. What is the median of the first data set?

    F. −12
    G. 4.8
    H. 12
    J. 48
    K. 480

17. In his grading policy, Mr. McMahon drops the highest and lowest of scores of the 10 tests he gives each semester. Keara has calculated the mean and median of her 10 tests scores. Which of the following statements *must* be true when Mr. McMahon applies his grading policy to Keara's test scores?

    A. The mean of her scores will be higher
    B. The mean of her scores will be lower
    C. The median of her scores will be higher
    D. The median of her scores will be lower
    E. The median of her scores will remain the same

18. The height of each player, in inches, on the Chester High School basketball team is as follows:

$$65, 66, 66, 68, 68, 68, 70, 71, 72$$

The league has ruled this year that the average of height of players on each team cannot exceed 68 inches. Chester High School has room for one additional player on its roster. What is the maximum height, in inches, that the additional player can be that still allows Chester High School to comply with the rules of the league?

F. 61
G. 62
H. 64
J. 66
K. 67

19. Line segment AB has endpoints $A\,(1,0)$ and $B\,(7,4)$. What is the midpoint of line segment AB?

A. $(4,2)$
B. $(4,4)$
C. $(7,0)$
D. $(8,2)$
E. $(8,4)$

20. Line segment YZ has endpoints $Y\,(-11,2)$ and $Z\,(-5,5)$. What is the midpoint of line segment YZ?

F. $\left(-8,\frac{7}{2}\right)$
G. $(-8,7)$
H. $(-6,3)$
J. $\left(-6,\frac{7}{2}\right)$
K. $(-6,7)$

21. Line segment MN has midpoint $(0,0)$ and endpoint $N\,(6,2)$. What are the coordinates of M?

A. $(-6,-2)$
B. $(-6,0)$
C. $(3,0)$
D. $(3,1)$
E. $(7,2)$

Questions 22-23 pertain to the following information.

Consider the stem and leaf plot shown below.

stem	leaf
3	2, 2, 4, 5
4	3, 5, 5, 5, 7, 8
5	0, 2, 2, 3, 5, 6, 9
6	1, 5, 7

22. What is the median of this data set?

F. 46
G. 47
H. 48
J. 49
K. 50

23. What is the mode of this data set?

A. 2
B. 5
C. 32
D. 45
E. 52

24. Line segment AB has midpoint $(-2,1)$ and endpoint $A\,(3,-4)$. What are the coordinates of B?

F. $(-7,6)$
G. $(-1,-3)$
H. $\left(-1,-\frac{3}{2}\right)$
J. $\left(1,-\frac{3}{2}\right)$
K. $\left(\frac{1}{2},-\frac{3}{2}\right)$

Least Common Multiple

→ start with the first answer choice

→ $\dfrac{\text{answer choice}}{\text{each given } \#}$ = integer ✓

Greatest Common Factor

→ start with the last answer choice.

→ $\dfrac{\text{each given } \#}{\text{answer choice}}$ = integer ✓

---

1. What is the least common multiple of 5, 15, 30, and 40?
   A. 1
   B. 5
   C. 120
   D. 9,000
   E. 90,000

For LCM, don't worry about testing ALL the numbers - you want to find the smallest one that works. Start small and move on only if it breaks.

LCM

→ Divide ANSWERS by GIVEN

① Start dividing.

$\dfrac{1}{40}$	$\dfrac{5}{40}$	$\dfrac{120}{40}$	$\dfrac{9000}{40}$	$\dfrac{90,000}{40}$
✗	✗	3	225	2,250

② Next: ÷30

$\dfrac{120}{30}$	$\dfrac{9000}{30}$	$\dfrac{90,000}{30}$
4 ↑	300	3,000

120 is looking good!

$\dfrac{120}{15} = 8$ $\dfrac{120}{5} = 24$ ✓

LCM = $\boxed{120}$

---

2. What is the greatest common factor of $10x^2y^3 + 15x^3y$?
   F. $5x^2y$
   G. 5
   H. $15x^3y^3$
   J. $5x^3y^3$
   K. $150x^5y^5$

GCF

→ Divide GIVEN by ANSWERS
   NOTE: variables make it easier, as the LOWEST power of x and y given is the GCF

$10\underset{\uparrow}{\underline{x^2}}y^3 + 15x^3\underset{\uparrow}{\underline{y}}$

limit for x   limit for y

$\boxed{F}$ G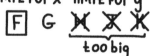

too big

3. What is the least common multiple of 5, 20, and 40?
   A. 5
   B. 10
   C. 20
   D. 30
   E. 40

4. What is the greatest common factor of 30, 50, and 80
   F. 5
   G. 10
   H. 30
   J. 80
   K. 1,200

5. What is the least common multiple of 12, 18 and 27?
   A. 3
   B. 4
   C. 27
   D. 108
   E. 5,832

6. Which of the following is NOT a factor of 108?
   F. 1
   G. 3
   H. 8
   J. 54
   K. 108

7. What is the least common denominator of the fractions $\dfrac{3}{13^2 \cdot 15}$ and $\dfrac{4}{13^4 \cdot 11^2}$?
   A. $11 \cdot 13 \cdot 15$
   B. $11^2 \cdot 13^2 \cdot 15^2$
   C. $11^2 \cdot 13^4 \cdot 15$
   D. $11^2 \cdot 13^7 \cdot 15$
   E. $11^4 \cdot 13^8 \cdot 15^2$

8. The prime factors of a number n are 2, 5, 7, and 17. Which of the following CANNOT be a factor of n?
   F. 1
   G. 10
   H. 14
   J. 24
   K. 34

9. If e will be the value of the numerator, which of these could be the denominator x for all integer values of a, b, c, d, e and x such that $\dfrac{a}{3} + \dfrac{b}{4} + \dfrac{c}{8} + \dfrac{d}{12} = \dfrac{e}{x}$?
   A. 12
   B. 24
   C. 96
   D. 384
   E. 1152

10. Two light beacons flash at different frequencies: one every 10 seconds and the other every 12 seconds. Beginning at a time when both lights flashed simultaneously, how many seconds will pass by until the lights flash simultaneously again?
    F. 10
    G. 12
    H. 30
    J. 60
    K. 120

11. In a math competition, teams are made up of either 6, 7, or 8 members. What is the minimum amount of prize money that can be offered to guarantee that each member of the winning team takes home the same, whole dollar amount, regardless of how many members are on the team?
    A. $21
    B. $56
    C. $168
    D. $210
    E. $336

① Draw a picture (for ALL geometry)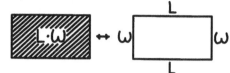

② Write BOTH formulas

③ Fill in for all quantities you have, and solve for what you need.

1. The top of a rectangular table has an area of 24 square feet and a length of 6 feet. What is the perimeter, in feet, of the table?

   A. 10
   B. 16
   C. 20
   D. 24
   E. 26

   ①

   24   ?(L)

   6(ω)

   ② L·W = Area

   what we need

   L+W·L+W = Perimeter

   ③ → $\frac{6L}{6} = \frac{24}{6}$ → L=4

   → 4·6·4·6 = P → P = $\boxed{20}$

2. A rectangle has a length one more than its width. If its area is 56, what is its perimeter?

   F. 7
   G. 30
   H. 56
   J. 60
   K. 112

   ①

   56   ω

   ω+1

   ② ω(ω+1)=56

   2ω·2(ω+1)=P

   ③ → ω(ω+1)=7·8 → ω = 7

   → 2(7)·2(8)=P → P = $\boxed{30}$

Did you know that diagrams on the ACT are almost always drawn to scale? That can help narrow down answers if you find yourself stuck.

3. Consider a rectangle with a perimeter of 34 and an area of 70. If the width and length of the rectangle are represented by w and l, respectively, which of the following systems of equations is valid?

A. $w + l = 34$
$wl = 70$

B. $2w + 2l = 34$
$wl = 70$

C. $w + l = 70$
$wl = 34$

D. $2w + 2l = 70$
$wl = 34$

E. $2w + l = 34$
$2wl = 70$

4. What is the perimeter of a square with an area of 49 square feet?

F. 2
G. 7
H. 11
J. 14
K. 28

5. Consider rectangular $ABCD$ where side $AB = 13$ and side $BC = 6$. What is the area, in square feet, of rectangle $ABCD$?

A. 36
B. 38
C. 78
D. 96
E. 169

6. Max is planting a rectangular garden with dimensions 20 feet by 15 feet. If he wants to enclose the garden with a fence, how many feet of fencing does he need to purchase?

F. 30 ft
G. 40 ft
H. 70 ft
J. 150 ft
K. 300 ft

7. In a rectangle, the width is 1 less than three times the length. If the length of the rectangle is 7, what is the area of the rectangle?

A. 13
B. 20
C. 27
D. 54
E. 140

8. Sheena is building a frame around the border of a rectangular window. The length of the window is 2.5 feet and the width of the window is 1 foot. How many linear feet of border does Sheena need?

F. 2.5
G. 3.5
H. 6
J. 6.5
K. 7

9. Owen is constructing a rectangular playpen for his puppies. The outside borders of the playpen will be made of a soft fabric, as well as one inside border running parallel to the long side of the playpen that separates the playpen into two halves. If w and l represent the width and length of the playpen, respectively, and $l > w$, which expression would yield the total amount of linear feet of fabric Owen would need to construct the playpen?

A. $w + l$
B. $2w + l$
C. $2w + 2l$
D. $3w + 2l$
E. $2w + 3l$

10. Consider all possible rectangles with an area of 36 and perimeter P. Which of the following inequalities constrains all possible perimeters?

F. $P \geq 24$
G. $P \geq 36$
H. $P \geq 48$
J. $P \geq 72$
K. $P \geq 144$

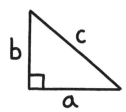

$$a^2 + b^2 = c^2 \qquad \text{Distance} \rightarrow \Delta x^2 + \Delta y^2 = d^2$$

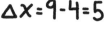

$$\Delta x \text{ means "change in } x\text{"}$$
$$\Delta y \text{ means "change in } y\text{"}$$

$$(4,3) \rightarrow (9,1)$$
$$\Delta x = 9 - 4 = 5$$
$$\Delta y = 1 - 3 = -2$$

The Pythagorean Theorem works only on RIGHT Triangles. It describes how the two legs relate to the Hypotenuse.

1. A 50 foot ladder is resting against a wall. If the base of the ladder is 15 feet from the wall, to the nearest tenth, how high up on the wall does the ladder reach?

   A. 15.9
   B. 25.0
   C. 37.6
   D. 43.3
   E. 47.7

$$a^2 + b^2 = c^2$$
$$15^2 + b^2 = 50^2$$
$$-15^2 \qquad -15^2$$

$$a = 15$$
$$c = 50$$
$$b = ?$$

$$\sqrt{b^2} = \sqrt{50^2 - 15^2}$$
$$b = \sqrt{2275} = \boxed{47.7}$$

2. What is the distance between the points $(-5, 13)$ and $(12, 13)$ in the (x, y) coordinate plane?

   F. 7
   G. 12
   H. 13
   J. 17
   K. 18

$$\Delta x^2 + \Delta y^2 = d^2$$
$$17^2 + 0^2 = d^2$$
$$\sqrt{17^2} = \sqrt{d^2}$$
$$\boxed{17} = d$$

$$\Delta x = 12 - (-5) = 17$$
$$\Delta y = 13 - 13 = 0$$

3. Consider a right triangle with legs of length 3 and 4. How long is the hypotenuse?

   A. 2
   B. 3
   C. 4
   D. 5
   E. 6

4. What is the length of the diagonal of a rectangle whose length is 7 cm and width is 24 cm?

   F. 8 cm
   G. 25 cm
   H. 31 cm
   J. 62 cm
   K. 696 cm

5. Consider a right triangle with a leg 5 units long and a hypotenuse 13 units long. How long, in units, is the length of the other leg?

   A. 5
   B. 7
   C. 9
   D. 11
   E. 12

6. Right triangle ABC has legs of length $x+2$ and $x+4$. Which of the following correctly gives the length of the hypotenuse of triangle ABC?

   F. $2x+6$
   G. $2x^2+20$
   H. $\sqrt{2x^2+6}$
   J. $\sqrt{2x^2+20}$
   K. $\sqrt{2x^2+12x+20}$

7. A rectangle with side lengths 5 cm and 12 cm is inscribed inside a circle. What is the length, in cm, of the diameter of the circle?

   A. 13
   B. 17
   C. 34
   D. 60
   E. 72

8. A certain right triangle has legs of length 7 cm and 10 cm. The length of the hypotenuse, in centimeters, is between

   F. 7 and 8.
   G. 10 and 11.
   H. 12 and 13.
   J. 14 and 16.
   K. 16 and 18.

9. If Ben lives 20 miles due south of his parents and 20 miles due east of his sister, to the nearest mile, what is the straight-line distance between Ben's parents and sister?

   A. 10 miles
   B. 14 miles
   C. 20 miles
   D. 28 miles
   E. 40 miles

10. What is the distance, in coordinate units, between $(2,2)$ and $(5,-2)$?

   F. 3
   G. 4
   H. 5
   J. 6
   K. 7

Simple translations:

is → =

more than, sum, and → +

difference, less than → −

percent → $\frac{}{100}$

of, product → ×

quotient, ratio, per → ÷

consecutive → $x, x+1, x+2...$

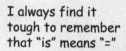

The essence of Word Problems is translating them into math equations.

I always find it tough to remember that "is" means "="

① ② ③ ④ ⑤

1. What is 40% of 15?

   A. 6
   B. 25
   C. 37.5
   D. 40
   E. 55

① ② ③ ④ ⑤

what is 40% of 15
↓   ↓   ↓   ↓   ↓
x   = $\frac{40}{100}$ · 15

$x = 0.40 \cdot 15$

$\boxed{x = 6}$

Almost all translation goes Left to Right, just like the sentence is written.

One tricky exception is "A less than B", which swaps the order to B − A.

① ② ③ ④ ⑤ ⑥

2. Three times the difference of a number and 5 is equal to 12. Which of the following is the number?

   F. 3 ↖ ⑦
   G. 4
   H. 6
   J. 9
   K. 12

① ② ④ ③ ⑤ ⑥ ⑦
↓ ↓ ↓ ↓ ↓ ↓ ↓
3 · (x − 5) = 12

$\dfrac{3(x-5)}{3} = \dfrac{12}{3}$

$x - 5 = 4$

$+5 \quad +5$

$\boxed{x = 9}$

3. Marissa earns $38 per hour for the first 40 hours she works in a week. For every hour after the first 40 hours that she works in a week, she earns one and a half times her regular hourly rate. If Marissa worked 46 hours in a week, how much does she make?

    A. $1,748

    B. $1,824

    C. $1,862

    D. $1,919

    E. $2,622

4. What percent of 150 is 30% of 300?

    F. 15%

    G. 30%

    H. 45%

    J. 60%

    K. 75%

5. Maxine's car travels 33 miles for every gallon of gas. On a road trip with a total distance of 512 miles, to the nearest gallon of gas, about how many gallons will Maxine's car use?

    A. 7

    B. 8

    C. 15

    D. 16

    E. 33

6. During their summer break from school, Hortencia and Alex decide to paint houses to earn money. Hortencia charges a flat rate of $350 per house that she paints, while Alex charges an hourly fee of $18 per hour. If both Hortencia and Alex paint one house this week, what is the least number of hours that Alex must paint in order to make more money than Hortencia?

    F. 17

    G. 18

    H. 19

    J. 20

    K. 21

7. At Jake's Theatre, the entrance fee for a movie is $3.50 for children and $7.00 for adults. Which of the following correctly shows the total entrance fee to a movie for a group of 10 children and x adults?

    A. $7(x + 3.50)$

    B. $3.50(10) + 7x$

    C. $(3.50 + 7)x$

    D. $3.50(x + 7)$

    E. $7(10) + 3.50x$

8. A number subtracted from 22 is negative. Which of the following could be the number?

    F. -23

    G. -22

    H. -21

    J. 22

    K. 23

9. Renting space at Shervin's Self Storage costs $12 per square-foot. If Julio wants to rent a space at Shervin's Self Storage that has dimensions a feet by b feet, what will be the total cost, in dollars, that he can expect to pay?

    A. $12(a \cdot b)$

    B. $\dfrac{a \cdot b}{12}$

    C. $\dfrac{a + b}{12}$

    D. $12\left(\dfrac{a}{b}\right)$

    E. $\dfrac{12}{a \cdot b}$

10. A package of 12 pens is $9.75 at Ben's Discount. A package of 18 pens is $12.25 at Bob's Savings. Which store is cheaper per pen and by how much?

    F. Ben's Discount at $0.81 cheaper

    G. Ben's Discount at $0.68 cheaper

    H. Bob's Savings at $0.13 cheaper

    J. Bob's Savings at $0.68 cheaper

    K. Both stores charge the same amount per pen

1. The number 80 is decreased by 15%. What is the result?
   A. 15
   B. 55
   C. 65
   D. 68
   E. 80

$$80 - (15\% \text{ of } 80) = X$$
$$80 - (.15 \cdot 80) = X$$
$$80 - (\quad 12 \quad) = X$$
$$\boxed{68 = X}$$

2. Carl bought tape at the hardware store for 15 dollars. After an 8.5 percent tax was added, how much did Carl pay in total?
   F. $12.75
   G. $15.09
   H. $15.85
   J. $16.28
   K. $29.60

$$15 + (8.5\% \text{ of } 15) = X$$
$$15 + (.085 \cdot 15) = X$$
$$15 + (\quad 1.275 \quad) = X$$
$$16.278 = \boxed{X \sim 16.28}$$

3. The original purchase price of a dress is $84. Elizabeth has a coupon for 25% off and the sales tax is 7%. What is the final purchase price of the dress for Elizabeth?
   A. $5.88
   B. $22.47
   C. $63.00
   D. $67.41
   E. $89.88

Discounted price:
$$84 - (25\% \text{ of } 84)$$
$$84 - (.25 \cdot 84)$$
$$84 - (21)$$
$$63$$

Price with tax:
$$63 + (7\% \text{ of } 63) = X$$
$$63 + (.07 \cdot 63) = X$$
$$63 + (4.41) = X$$
$$\boxed{67.41 = X}$$

These are simply a special type of "Words to Equations". Since they are a bit tricky, let's do some extra practice!

Keep in mind "Percent" literally means "Of 100", so 35% is 35/100.

4. 23% of 200 is what number?

    F. 23
    G. 30
    H. 40
    J. 46
    K. 123

5. If 80% of a number is 60, what is 60% of that number?

    A. 60
    B. 45
    C. 75
    D. 80
    E. 100

6. The city of Dupont received 32.60 inches of rainfall last year. This year, the amount of rainfall Dupont received was 10% greater than last year. How much rainfall did Dupont receive this year?

    F. 3.26 inches
    G. 32.70 inches
    H. 32.93 inches
    J. 33.60 inches
    K. 35.86 inches

7. A basketball team of a high school is holding try-outs. Fifteen players attend the try-out. The coach of the basketball team will cut 20% of the players attending the try-out and the remaining players are placed on the roster of the basketball team. How many players make the roster of the basketball team?

    A. 3
    B. 5
    C. 12
    D. 15
    E. 20

8. From 2014 to 2015, Kyleema's long jump record improved by 10%. From 2015 to 2016, Kyleema's long jump record improved by 20%. How much greater is Kyleema's long jump record in 2016 than in 2014?

    F. 30%
    G. 32%
    H. 35%
    J. 40%
    K. 42%

9. Johan wants to buy a toy for his nephew. The original sales price of the toy is $25. The store selling the toy is having a sale and Johan can buy the toy at the discounted price of $20. What is the percent savings of the toy that Johan purchased?

    A. 5%
    B. 15%
    C. 20%
    D. 25%
    E. 30%

10. Bobby earns $62,000 a year before taxes. After taxes he receives 68% of his income. How much money does Bobby earn after taxes?

    F. $19,840
    G. $42,160
    H. $62,000
    J. $81,840
    K. $104,160

11. Jenny owns $200 worth of shares of a certain stock at the start of the day on Monday. The price of a stock increased by 5% on Monday, 10% on Tuesday, and 3% on Wednesday. What is the value of Jenny's shares, to the nearest cent, at the end of the day on Wednesday?

    A. $18.18
    B. $218.42
    C. $236.51
    D. $237.93
    E. $328.60

12. What is $\frac{1}{5}$% of 3?

    F. $\dfrac{3}{5}$
    G. $\dfrac{1}{15}$
    H. $\dfrac{3}{100}$
    J. $\dfrac{1}{500}$
    K. $\dfrac{3}{500}$

1.10 SohCahToa

→ If two sides are given and you need the third side, use **pythagorean theorem**.

→ But if two sides are given and you need a trig function use **SOHCAHTOA**

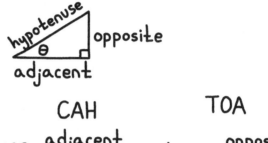

SOH

$\sin\theta = \dfrac{\text{opposite}}{\text{hypotenuse}}$

CAH

$\cos\theta = \dfrac{\text{adjacent}}{\text{hypotenuse}}$

TOA

$\tan\theta = \dfrac{\text{opposite}}{\text{adjacent}}$

1. Consider a right triangle ABC, with right angle at B, where $\overline{AB} = 10$ and $\overline{BC} = 24$. What is the value of $\tan A =$?

   A. $5/12$
   B. $5/13$
   C. $12/13$
   D. $12/5$
   E. $13/5$

   SOHCAH(TOA)

   $\tan A = \dfrac{\text{opposite}}{\text{adjacent}} = \dfrac{24}{10} = \boxed{\dfrac{12}{5}}$

2. Consider a right triangle XYZ, with angles X, Y, and Z opposite sides x, y, and z, respectively. If X is a right angle, what is the value of $\cos Z$?

   F. x/y
   G. x/z
   H. y/x
   J. y/z
   K. z/x

   SOH(CAH)TOA

   $\cos Z = \dfrac{\text{adjacent}}{\text{hypotenuse}} = \boxed{\dfrac{y}{x}}$

> Trigonometry might look scary to some, but these problems are some of the easiest and most consistent problems in the Math section. They are very plug-and-play and predictable!

3. In right triangle ABC, side $AB = 6$ inches, side $BC = 8$ inches, and the angle between sides AB and BC is $90°$. Which of the following is NOT true of triangle ABC?

    A. $\tan A = \dfrac{8}{6}$

    B. $\sin A = \dfrac{8}{10}$

    C. $\cos A = \dfrac{6}{8}$

    D. $\cos C = \dfrac{8}{10}$

    E. $\tan C = \dfrac{6}{8}$

4. For right $\triangle ABC$, $\angle CBA$ is $90°$, $\angle BAC$ is $50°$ and $\overline{AB}$ is 7. What is the length of $\overline{AC}$?

    F. $\dfrac{7}{\cos 50°}$

    G. $\dfrac{7}{\sin 50°}$

    H. $\dfrac{7}{\tan 50°}$

    J. $7\cos 50°$

    K. $7\sin 50°$

5. In right $\triangle DEF$, hypotenuse $\overline{DF}$ is 300 feet and the measure of $\angle D$ is $35°$. What is the length, in feet, of $\overline{DE}$?

    A. $\dfrac{300}{\cos 35°}$

    B. $\dfrac{300}{\sin 35°}$

    C. $\dfrac{300}{\tan 35°}$

    D. $300\cos 35°$

    E. $300\sin 35°$

6. In right $\triangle XYZ$, leg $\overline{XZ}$ is 30 feet and leg $\overline{XY}$ is 40 feet. What is the cosine of $\angle Z$?

    F. $\dfrac{3}{4}$

    G. $\dfrac{3}{5}$

    H. $\dfrac{4}{5}$

    J. $\dfrac{5}{4}$

    K. $\dfrac{5}{3}$

7. Consider right triangle ABC, where C is the right angle and sides a, b, and c are opposite angles A, B, and C, respectively. What is the sine of $\angle A$?

    A. $\dfrac{a}{c}$

    B. $\dfrac{c}{a}$

    C. $\dfrac{c}{b}$

    D. $\dfrac{b}{c}$

    E. $\dfrac{a}{b}$

8. Consider a right triangle where one acute angle measures $70°$ and the length of the hypotenuse is 40 inches. What is the length, in inches, of the leg adjacent to the $70°$ angle?

    F. $\dfrac{40}{\cos 70°}$

    G. $\dfrac{40}{\sin 70°}$

    H. $\dfrac{40}{\tan 70°}$

    J. $40\cos 70°$

    K. $40\sin 70°$

9. If the angle of depression from the top of a 300 foot lighthouse to a boat is $72°$, how far is the boat from the bottom of the lighthouse?

    A. $\dfrac{300}{\cos 72°}$

    B. $\dfrac{300}{\sin 72°}$

    C. $\dfrac{300}{\tan 72°}$

    D. $300\cos 72°$

    E. $300\sin 72°$

10. Gianna can see a cat stuck in a tree that is 32 feet away on level ground from where she stands. The angle of elevation from Gianna's feet to the cat is $15°$. To the nearest foot, how high up is the cat from the ground?

    F. 8

    G. 9

    H. 15

    J. 30

    K. 31

That's all for Chapter 1. The problem concepts we covered may show up once or a half dozen times on any given test.

Sadly, they won't show up in order or labeled, so we ought to practice them in a mixed, timed review quiz!

Don't take a quiz absent-mindedly. Do set up a time and space to take it with total focus and all your energy.

Find a place where you can concentrate, but know a few ambient distractions can be good for you. Learn how to focus through some noise - but don't answer your phone every 5 minutes.

If 20 minutes seems comfortable, take on another challenge and attempt to label every question with its parent chapter. Practicing ID'ing problem types is super useful!

More than anything, it's a quiz, not a test. This is an opportunity to make mistakes and find out where you need to improve. Don't sweat the results too hard and let it affect your confidence.

CHAPTER ONE QUIZ
15 Minutes — 20 Questions

DIRECTIONS: Solve each problem, choose the correct answer, and then fill in the corresponding oval on your answer document.

Do not linger over problems that take too much time. Solve as many as you can; then return to the others in the time you have left for this test.

You are permitted to use a calculator on this test. You may use your calculator for any problems you choose,

but some of the problems may be best done without using a calculator.

Note: Unless otherwise stated, all of the following should be assumed.

1.   Illustrative figures are NOT necessarily drawn to scale.
2. Geometric figures lie in a plane.
3. The word *line* indicates a straight line.
4. The word *average* indicates arithmetic mean.

---

1. What is the least common multiple of 15, 25 and 35?
    A. 35
    B. 50
    C. 525
    D. 1,025
    E. 13,125

2. A bag of McNutter's Supreme Nut Mix contains 48 cashews and 112 raisins. What is the ratio of cashews to raisins in this bag?
    F. 2:5
    G. 3:7
    H. 4:9
    J. 5:11
    K. 6:13

3. At the grocery store, Dana bought a bag of apples for $4.60, a jar of peanut butter for $3.20, and a bottle of soda for $1.75. The clerk at the register added a sales tax of 7% on the price of Dana's purchase. To the nearest cent, how much did Dana pay in total?
    A. $8.64
    B. $9.20
    C. $9.80
    D. $10.22
    E. $11.14

Use the following information for questions 4-6.

Max tracked the number of regular season games his favorite football team won over the last 10 seasons.

Years since 2007	0	1	2	3	4	5	6	7	8	9
Wins	10	12	8	10	9	9	7	6	6	11

4. Which of the following statements is true?
    F. The mean and the median are equal
    G. The range of the data is 7
    H. The mean is greater than the median
    J. The mode of the data set is 6
    K. The median is greater than the mean

5. Based on the data, what is the probability that the number of wins was a prime number?
    A. $1/10$
    B. $1/5$
    C. $2/5$
    D. $3/5$
    E. $4/5$

6. What was the percent increase in their number of wins from 2015 to 2016?
    F. $45.\overline{4}\%$
    G. $54.\overline{5}\%$
    H. $83.\overline{3}\%$
    J. $154.\overline{5}\%$
    K. $183.\overline{3}\%$

7. A formula for the pressure in a cylinder is $P = \frac{kT}{V}$, where T is the temperature of the gas, V is the volume of the cylinder, and k is a constant. Which of the following expressions gives V in terms of P, k, and T?

A. $V = \dfrac{kP}{T}$

B. $V = \dfrac{kT}{P}$

C. $V = kTP$

D. $V = \dfrac{P}{kT}$

E. $V = \dfrac{TP}{k}$

8. The average number of points scored per game by each of the 12 players on the Jefferson High School basketball team is 11.2. A new player joins the team and causes the average number of points scored per game by each player to rise to 13.4. How many points does this new player score on average in each game?

F. 15.2
G. 26.4
H. 28.6
J. 32.1
K. 39.8

9. Martin has a bag of five different colored candies. He has 8 red candies, 14 blue candies, 6 yellow candies, 12 orange candies, and 9 green candies. If he draws one candy at random from the bag, what is the probability that it is NOT blue?

A. 14:49
B. 20:35
C. 26:41
D. 30:49
E. 35:49

10. In art class, Lin cuts a right triangle out of a sheet of paper with dimensions 9 inches by 13 inches. Which of the following is closest to the length, in inches, of the hypotenuse of the right triangle?

F. 13
G. 14
H. 16
J. 17
K. 18

Use the following information to answer questions 11-14.

Consider triangle ABC below, where $\angle C$ is a right angle, $\overline{AC} = 5$, and $\overline{AB} = 13$.

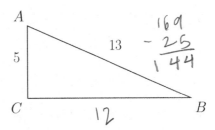

11. What is $\cos B$?

A. $5/13$
B. $5/12$
C. $12/13$
D. $12/5$
E. $13/12$

12. What is the area of triangle ABC?

F. 30
G. 32.5
H. 60
J. 65
K. 78

13. Which of the following expressions does NOT represent the length of $\overline{BC}$?

A. $5\tan A$

B. $\sqrt{169 - 25}$

C. $13\sin A$

D. $\sqrt{(13 - 5)^2}$

E. $\dfrac{5}{\tan(90 - A)^\circ}$

14. Another triangle, $\triangle DEF$, has sides in proportion to $\triangle ABC$ such that $\dfrac{\overline{AB}}{\overline{DE}} = \dfrac{\overline{BC}}{\overline{EF}} = \dfrac{\overline{AC}}{\overline{DF}}$. If $\overline{DF} = 15$, what is the length of $\overline{DE}$?

F. 15
G. 24
H. 31
J. 36
K. 39

15. When solved for q, what is $p = \dfrac{q+1}{2}$?

    A. $q = \frac{1}{2}p - 1$

    B. $q = p - \frac{1}{2}$

    C. $q = 2p - 1$

    D. $q = 2p$

    E. $q = 2p + 2$

16. Argilia plans to lay a fence around her garden, which is in the shape of a square. If her garden has an area of 324 square feet, how many feet of fencing will she need to buy in order to completely enclose the garden?

    F. 36

    G. 72

    H. 112

    J. 168

    K. 212

17. In right triangle ABC, $\overline{AB} = 5$ inches, $\overline{BC} = 12$ inches, and the angle between $\overline{AB}$ and $\overline{BC}$ is 90°. Which of the following could NOT be true of triangle ABC?

    A. $\tan A = \dfrac{12}{5}$

    B. $\sin A = \dfrac{5}{13}$

    C. $\cos A = \dfrac{5}{13}$

    D. $\cos C = \dfrac{12}{13}$

    E. $\tan C = \dfrac{5}{12}$

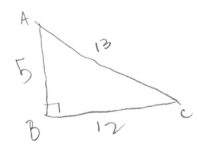

Use the following information to answer questions 18-20.

Wyatt is planning a bowling birthday party at one of three alleys. All have different pricing structures for group events depending on the number of people, p, and the total number of games, g, bowled. Al's Alleys charges a flat fee to rent the lanes for an unlimited number of games and a per-person price for shoe rentals. Bill's charges a lower lane rental fee and a fee per game bowled, but has free shoe rental. Cane's Lanes does not have a lane rental fee but they charge each person for shoe rentals and a fee for each game bowled. Their pricing structures are summarized in the table below:

Company	Lane Rental	Shoe Rental	Per Game Fee
Al's Alleys	$300	$2	—
Bill's Bowls	$100	—	$7
Cane's Lanes	—	$10	$10

18. Which of the following equations represents the total cost, B, of a bowling party at Bill's?

    F. $B = 100 + 7g$

    G. $B = 7p + 100pg$

    H. $B = 100 + 7pg$

    J. $B = 100p + 7g$

    K. $B = 700pg$

19. If a total of 18 games were to be bowled, at least how many people would need to attended Wyatt's birthday party for Al's Alley's to be cheaper than Cane's Lanes?

    A. 12 bowlers

    B. 13 bowlers   324

    C. 14 bowlers

    D. 15 bowlers

    E. 16 bowlers   332

20. If Wyatt limits his guest list to 10 people they would have time to bowl a total of 4 games. For this scenario, which of the following correctly lists the 3 venues from the cheapest to the most expensive?

    F. Bill's < Al's Alleys < Cane's Lanes

    G. Cane's Lanes < Al's Alleys < Bill's

    H. Cane's Lanes < Bill's < Al's Alleys

    J. Bill's < Cane's Lanes < Al's Alleys

    K. Al's Alleys < Cane's Lanes < Bill's

Welcome to Chapter 2!

We'll be covering the second part of problems 1 through 25 on the ACT.

Chapter 2 focuses on basic concepts that students of mine continually find frustrating.

These topics are often new concepts, not emphasized enough, or take a lot of practice to understand well. However, they are largely single-step ideas and appear early on in the ACT.

Marjorie has 4 shirts, 2 pairs of pants, and 2 pairs of shoes. How many different outfits are possible?

→ multiply the numbers. $\underbrace{4}_{\text{shirts}} \times \underbrace{2}_{\text{pants}} \times \underbrace{2}_{\text{shoes}} = \boxed{16}$

1. Darius needs to design a jacket for his class in fashion design. He can choose one of 10 colors, one of 4 stitching patterns, and one of 6 different materials for his jacket. How many different jackets can Darius design?

   A. 20
   B. 80
   C. 120
   D. 160
   E. 240

$\underbrace{10}_{\text{colors}} \times \underbrace{4}_{\text{stitching}} \times \underbrace{6}_{\text{materials}} = \boxed{240}$

2. A school has 65 freshmen, 55 sophomores, 80 juniors, and 70 seniors. If one member from each class is elected to the student council, how many different councils are possible?

   F. 4
   G. 67.5
   H. $65 + 55 + 80 + 70$
   J. $(65 + 55)(80 + 70)$
   K. $(65)(55)(80)(70)$

$\underbrace{65}_{\text{9th}} \times \underbrace{55}_{\text{10th}} \times \underbrace{80}_{\text{11th}} \times \underbrace{70}_{\text{12th}}$

$\boxed{65 \cdot 55 \cdot 80 \cdot 70}$

Combinations are a breeze!
Simply multiply the numbers :)

A lot of Probability and Trigonometry topics on the ACT are straightforwards, since the subject matter is less heavily emphasized in the classroom.

3. How many ways can five different books be arranged on a shelf?

   A. 5
   B. 15
   C. 25
   D. 120
   E. 3125

4. This year's Snowball Dance is attended by 35 students from East Lake High School and 51 students from Bowman North High School. For a certain dance, chaperones must pair one student from East Lake High School with one student from Bowman North High School. How many different pairs of two students are possible for the dance?

   F. 86
   G. 240
   H. 890
   J. 1,785
   K. 2,010

5. Jerome's teacher in statistics class has instructed each student in the class to create a three digit number. In this assignment, digits 0-9 will be used and both the first digit and the last digit of the three digit number cannot have the values 0, 1 or 2. How many different three numbers can Jerome create?

   A. 256
   B. 490
   C. 512
   D. 1024
   E. 1600

6. In a standard deck of 52 cards, how many two-card hands are possible?

   F. 52
   G. 52^2
   H. $\frac{1}{2}(52)(51)$
   J. $(52)(51)$
   K. $52^2 - 51^2$

7. Jenn has 3 different styles of shoes, 4 different styles of pants, and 5 different styles of t-shirts. If she wants to wear an outfit to the movies consisting of 1 pair of shoes, 1 pair of pants, and 1 t-shirt, how many different outfits can she choose from?

   A. 12
   B. 30
   C. 48
   D. 60
   E. 72

8. If you roll two standard six sided die, how many different sums are possible?

   F. 6
   G. 7
   H. 11
   J. 12
   K. 36

9. Andre is arranging his plants in a line in his windowsill. He has four different plants: one fikus tree, one sage bush, one fern, and one cactus. How many different ways can he arrange the plants in a line in his windowsill?

   A. 24
   B. 64
   C. 72
   D. 108
   E. 256

10. Nina has 3 pairs of pants, 8 shirts, and 2 pairs of shoes. If Nina picks 1 pair of pants, 1 shirt, and 1 pair of shoes to wear, how many different outfits are possible?

   F. 48
   G. 24
   H. 12
   J. 8
   K. 3

Laws:

Multiplying with the same base (add exponents) → $a^2 \cdot a^3 = a^{2+3} = a^5$

Distribute into parentheses → $(a^2 b^5)^2 = a^{2 \cdot 2} b^{5 \cdot 2} = a^4 b^{10}$

Dividing with the same base (subtract exponents) → $\dfrac{a^5}{a^3} = a^{5-3} = a^2$

Negative exponents → $a^{-3} = \dfrac{1}{a^3}$ $\dfrac{1}{c^{-2}} = c^2$

Method:

① Group like terms

② Follow the rules above

Note:
$x^1 = x$
$x^0 = 1$

---

1. Which of the following is equivalent to the expression $(n^3)^3 \cdot \dfrac{2}{n}$?

   $(n^3)^3 \cdot \dfrac{2}{n} \rightarrow \left[\dfrac{(n^3)^3}{n^1}\right] 2 \rightarrow \left[\dfrac{n^9}{n^1}\right] 2 \rightarrow \boxed{2n^8}$

   A. 2
   B. $2n^5$
   C. $2n^8$
   D. $2n^9$
   E. $2n^{10}$

2. For all nonzero values of a, b, and c, which of the following expressions is equivalent to $\dfrac{30a^6b^{12}c}{5a^3b^3}$?

   F. $-25a^2b^9$
   G. $6a^3b^9c$
   H. $6a^2b^4c$
   J. $25a^2b^9$
   K. $35a^9b^{15}$

   each variable should be simplified separately

   $\dfrac{30a^6b^{12}c}{5a^3b^3} \rightarrow \left(\dfrac{30}{5}\right)\left(\dfrac{a^6}{a^3}\right)\left(\dfrac{b^{12}}{b^3}\right)\left(\dfrac{c}{1}\right)$

   $6 \cdot a^3 \cdot b^9 \cdot c = \boxed{6a^3b^9c}$

This is exactly what my work looks like when I solve exponent problems. Detailed work makes it clear and quick!

3. $3ab^3c^5 \cdot 2a^2b^4c^4 =$
A. $5a^3b^7c^9$
B. $5a^2b^{12}c^{20}$
C. $6abc$
D. $6a^3b^7c^9$
E. $6a^2b^{12}c^{20}$

4. Which of the following represents an integer?
F. $(\sqrt{2})(\sqrt{8} + 16)$
G. $2(\sqrt{3} + \sqrt{10})$
H. $(\sqrt{5})(\sqrt{9})$
J. $(\sqrt{4} + 5)(\sqrt{4} - 5)$
K. $(\sqrt{7} + \sqrt{18})$

5. For all real integer values of n where $n \neq 0$, what is the value of $\dfrac{3n^4}{3n^3}$?

A. 3
B. $3n$
C. n
D. $n^{4/3}$
E. n^7

6. For what real number value of w is the equation $(x^5)^6(x^3)^4 = x^w$ true?
F. 12
G. 20
H. 23
J. 42
K. 90

7. Which of the following correctly gives the relationship between a, b, c, and d given that $(x^a)^b \cdot x^c = x^d$?
A. $a^b \cdot c = d$

B. $ab + c = d$

C. $a \cdot b \cdot c = d$

D. $\dfrac{a}{b} - c = d$

E. $\dfrac{a}{b} + c = d$

8. Whenever a, b, x, and y are positive integers, which of the following expressions is equivalent to $x^{ab}y^a$?
F. $(xy)^{ab}$
G. $(x^b + y)^a$
H. $(x^by)^a$
J. $(x + y)^{ab}$
K. x^by^a

9. Let a and b be nonzero real numbers such that $3^{a+2} = 3b$. Which of the following is an expression for 3^{a+4} in terms of b?

A. $\dfrac{1}{27b}$

B. $\dfrac{1}{9b}$

C. $27b$

D. $81b$

E. $243b$

10. Which of the following expressions is equivalent to $(4x^{-2}y^5z)(-9x^7y^{-4}z)$?
F. $-36x^2y^2z^2$
G. $-36x^5yz^2$
H. $27x^3y^2z^2$
J. $36x^3y^2z^2$
K. $36x^2y^3z^3$

11. Which expression is equivalent to $\dfrac{(3a^2b^4c)(4a^3b^2c)}{6abc^2}$?
A. $2a^4b^5$
B. $2a^4b^5c^{-2}$
C. $2a^6b^8$
D. $72a^4b^5c^{-2}$
E. $72a^5b^6$

$$f(x) = 3x^2 - 2 \qquad \text{Then} \quad f(A) = 3A^2 - 2$$
$$f(B+1) = 3(B+1)^2 - 2$$
$$f(\sim\!\sim) = 3(\sim\!\sim)^2 - 2$$

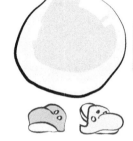

Think "FILL IN THE BLANK"

Whatever is in the parentheses replaces every "x" in the equation. After that, it's on to careful number crunching!

1. The functions f and g are defined such that $f(x) = 4x - 1$ and $g(x) = 2x^2$. Which of the following correctly gives the value of $f(g(-2))$?

    A. -33
    B. -31
    C. 24
    D. 31
    E. 162

$$f(g(-2)) = ?$$

Always evaluate the inner most function and work your way out.

$$g(-2) = 2(-2)^2 = 8$$
$$g(-2) = 8$$
$$f(g(-2)) = 4(g(-2)) - 1$$
$$f(8) = 4(8) - 1 = \boxed{31}$$

2. If $f(x) = \dfrac{3x^2 - 15x + 2}{-5x - 8}$, what is $f(-2)$?

    F. $8/9$
    G. 10
    H. 22
    J. 52
    K. 88

$$f(\_) = \frac{3(\_)^2 - 15(\_) + 2}{-5(\_) - 8}$$
$$f(-2) = \frac{3(-2)^2 - 15(-2) + 2}{-5(-2) - 8}$$
$$= \frac{12 + 30 + 2}{10 - 8}$$
$$= \boxed{22}$$

3. If $f(x) = 5x^2 - 3x + 7$, what is $f(-3)$?

   A. -47
   B. -29
   C. 1
   D. 43
   E. 61

4. If $f(x) = x^2 - 7$ and $g(x) = 4x + 3$, what is $g(f(4))$?

   F. $19/9$
   G. 28
   H. 39
   J. 171
   K. 354

5. The function p is defined by $p(x) = x^2 + 11x + 28$. Which of the following could be the value of b if $p(b) = 0$?

   A. -7
   B. -1
   C. 0
   D. 4
   E. 7

6. What is the value of $g(4)$ when $g(x) = \dfrac{x^2 - 9}{x + 3}$?

   F. -1
   G. $-\dfrac{5}{7}$
   H. 1
   J. $\dfrac{25}{7}$
   K. 20

7. The functions f and g are defined such that $f(x) = 6x^2 - 5$ and $g(x) = 15x + 10$. For the value of a such that $g(a) = 55$, what is the value of $f(a)$?

   A. 26
   B. 32
   C. 49
   D. 225
   E. 660

8. The function ∇ is defined by the relation $\nabla(a, b, c) = a^b - c$. Which answer below correctly gives the value of $\nabla(3, 2, 1)$?

   F. -2
   G. -1
   H. 7
   J. 8
   K. 9

9. A pentagon has a maximum of 5 diagonals and an octagon has a maximum of 20 diagonals. Which of the following functions represents the maximum number of diagonals, d, in a polygon with number of sides, n?

   A. $d(n) = \dfrac{n(n-3)}{2}$
   B. $d(n) = n$
   C. $d(n) = 2(n + 2)$
   D. $d(n) = \dfrac{5n}{2}$
   E. $d(n) = \dfrac{2n}{5}$

10. If $f(x) = 3x - 5$, For which of the following functions $g(x)$ would $f(g(x)) = x$?

    F. $g(x) = \dfrac{x + 5}{3}$
    G. $g(x) = \dfrac{x}{3} + 5$
    H. $g(x) = 5x - 3$
    J. $g(x) = 3x + 5$
    K. $g(x) = \dfrac{x - 3}{5}$

11. If $f(x) = x^2 - 7$ and $g(x) = 3x + 4$, which of the following represents $f(g(x))$?

    A. $3x^2 - 9$
    B. $9x^2 - 9$
    C. $3x^2 + 17x + 9$
    D. $9x^2 + 24x + 9$
    E. $9x^2 + 24x + 23$

Roots = Solutions = x-intercepts.
Each phrase wants values of x that make the equation = 0

$$y = ax^2 + bx \cdot c$$

① If an answer choice says "x-4" or similar, try plugging in "4" and see if it equals 0.

③ Sum of roots = $\frac{-b}{a}$
Product of roots = $\frac{c}{a}$

② Difference of squares
$$x^2 - A^2 = (x + A)(x - A)$$

④ Perfect squares
$$(x + B)^2 = x^2 + 2xB \cdot B^2$$

1. Which of the following expressions is a factor of the polynomial $x^2 - 9x + 20$?

A. $x - 3$
B. $x - 11$
C. $x - 5$
D. $x + 4$
E. $x + 5$

Method 1:

A) $3^2 - 9(3) \cdot 20 = 2$ ✗
B) $11^2 - 9(11) \cdot 20 = 42$ ✗
C) $5^2 - 9(5) \cdot 20 = 0$ ✔

2. For $x^2 \neq 36$, $\dfrac{(x+6)^2}{x^2 - 36} = ?$

F. $x + 6$

G. $x - 6$

H. $(x + 6)(x - 6)$

J. $\dfrac{x+6}{x-6}$

K. $\dfrac{x-6}{x+6}$

Method 2:

$$\frac{(x+6)^2}{(x^2-36)} \rightarrow \frac{(x+6)(x+6)}{(x+6)(x-6)}$$

$$\rightarrow \frac{\cancel{(x+6)}(x+6)}{\cancel{(x+6)}(x-6)} \rightarrow \boxed{\frac{(x+6)}{(x-6)}}$$

Factoring is a big subject that takes a lot of time to master.

But this is the ACT...

... which is why I'm showing you shortcuts and tricks! They won't solve everything, but they are effective and quick.

3. Which of the following expressions is equivalent to $(2x + 8)(2x - 8)$?

   A. $4x$

   B. $16x + 64$

   C. $4x^2 - 64$

   D. $x^2 - 64$

   E. $4x^2 - 16x - 64$

4. Which of the following is the factored form of $x^2 - 3x - 10$?

   F. $(x - 2)(x - 5)$

   G. $(x + 2)(x - 5)$

   H. $(x - 2)(x + 5)$

   J. $(x + 2)(x + 5)$

   K. $(x - 3)(x - 10)$

5. Which of the following is the factored form of $x^2 + 15x - 34$?

   A. $(x - 17)(x - 2)$

   B. $(x + 17)(x - 2)$

   C. $(x - 1)(x + 34)$

   D. $(x + 1)(x + 34)$

   E. $(x - 6)(x - 6)$

6. The quadratic equation $14x^2 = 30x$ can be solved by factoring. Which of the following states the solutions?

   F. $x = 0$ or $x = 1$

   G. $x = 0$ or $x = \dfrac{15}{7}$

   H. $x = 1$ or $x = -1$

   J. $x = 1$ or $x = \dfrac{15}{7}$

   K. $x = -\dfrac{15}{7}$ or $x = \dfrac{15}{7}$

7. What is the product of the two solutions to the equation $4x^2 + 6x - 10 = 0$?

   A. -10

   B. $-\dfrac{5}{2}$

   C. 1

   D. $\dfrac{3}{5}$

   E. 5

8. Which of the following expressions is a factor of the polynomial $5x^2 + 9x - 2$?

   F. $(x - 1)$

   G. $(x + 1)$

   H. $(x - 2)$

   J. $(5x + 1)$

   K. $(5x - 1)$

9. For what values of x is the expression $\dfrac{1}{x^2 - 16}$ undefined?

   A. -1 and 1

   B. -2 and 2

   C. -4 and 4

   D. $-\dfrac{1}{4}$ and $\dfrac{1}{4}$

   E. $-\dfrac{1}{2}$ and $\dfrac{1}{2}$

10. What is the solution set of x for the quadratic equation $x^2 - 15x = -50$?

    F. $x = -10, x = 5$

    G. $x = -5, x = -10$

    H. $x = 0, x = 25$

    J. $x = 5, x = -10$

    K. $x = 10, x = 5$

11. For $x^2 \neq 4$, $\dfrac{(x - 2)^2}{x^2 - 4} =$?

    A. $x + 2$

    B. $x - 2$

    C. $(x + 2)(x - 2)$

    D. $\dfrac{x - 2}{x + 2}$

    E. $\dfrac{x - 4}{x + 4}$

12. If $a \neq -b$ and $a + b = a^2 - b^2$, then $a - b =$

    F. 0

    G. 1

    H. $a + b$

    J. $2a$

    K. Cannot be determined from the given information

Finding slope → From an equation: From points:

→ solve for y

→ $y = mx + b$
↑
slope!

→ $m = \dfrac{y_2 - y_1}{x_2 - x_1}$

✳ Given two lines $y = mx + b$ & $y = nx + c$

→ parallel if
    same slope $m = n$, $b \neq c$

→ same line if $m = n$ AND $b = c$
  (infinite solutions)

→ perpendicular if $m = -\dfrac{1}{n}$
  negative reciprocal

A "reciprocal" is a flipped number. 5 turns to 1/5, and 3/7 becomes 7/3.

1. What is the slope of the line given by the equation $3x + 7y = -21$?

    A. -3

    B. $-\dfrac{3}{7}$

    C. $-\dfrac{7}{3}$

    D. 3

    E. 7

solve for y

$3x + 7y = -21$
$-3x \qquad\quad -3x$

$\dfrac{7y = -3x - 21}{7} \qquad \dfrac{}{7}$

$y = \boxed{\dfrac{-3}{7}} x - 3$

2. Which of the following equations represent a line perpendicular to the line $y = 4x - 7$?

    F. $y = -4x$

    G. $y = -4x + 7$

    H. $y = -\dfrac{1}{4}x$

    J. $y = \dfrac{1}{4}x$

    K. $y = \dfrac{1}{4}x + 7$

$y = 4x - 7$
↓
$m = 4$

→ For a perpendicular line the slope must be $-\dfrac{1}{m} = -\dfrac{1}{4}$. The answer must be $\boxed{H}$.

3. When graphed in the standard (x, y) coordinate plane, the line $x + 6y - 5 = 0$ and has a slope of:

A. 5

B. $-\dfrac{6}{5}$

C. $-\dfrac{1}{6}$

D. $-\dfrac{5}{6}$

E. -6

4. What is the y-intercept of the line $2x = 3y - 6$ when graphed in the standard (x, y) coordinate plane?

F. 1

G. 2

H. 3

J. 4

K. 6

5. In the standard (x, y) coordinate plane, what is the x-intercept of the line represented by $y = 8x + 10$?

A. $-\dfrac{5}{4}$

B. -1

C. 1

D. 8

E. 10

6. A line that is parallel to the line $y = -\dfrac{1}{2}x + 6$ and has a y-intercept of 3 has an x-intercept at which point?

F. $(-6, 0)$

G. $(-3, 0)$

H. $(-1.5, 0)$

J. $(3, 0)$

K. $(6, 0)$

7. What is the slope of the line containing the points $(-6, 4)$ and $(-8, -3)$ in the standard (x, y) coordinate plane?

A. $-\dfrac{7}{2}$

B. -2

C. $-\dfrac{1}{14}$

D. $\dfrac{7}{2}$

E. 14

8. Which of the following is always true about any line with an undefined slope?

F. The line is parallel to the y-axis

G. The line is a horizontal line

H. The line passes through the origin

J. The equation of the line begins with $y =$

K. The line has zero x-intercepts

A slope of 0 creates a flat, horizontal line, like y = 2

Perpendicular to a horizontal line would be a vertical line.

Perpendicular to m = 0 is m = -1/0, or "undefined". So vertical lines have "undefined" slope!

9. What is true about the relationship in the coordinate plane between the lines $y = \frac{2}{3}x + 7$ and $y = \frac{2}{3}x - 5$?

A. The lines are parallel
B. The lines are perpendicular
C. The lines are neither parallel nor perpendicular
D. The lines are the same line
E. Cannot be determined from the given information

10. Which of the following equations represents a line parallel to the line $y = \frac{5}{2}x$?

F. $5x + 2y = 10$
G. $5x - 2y = 10$
H. $2x + 5y = 10$
J. $2x - 5y = 10$

K. $x = \frac{5}{2}y$

11. What values of g and h would make the system of equations below perpendicular?

$$4x + 7y = 17$$
$$gx + hy = 37$$

A. $g = -7, h = -4$
B. $g = -4, h = 7$
C. $g = 4, h = 7$
D. $g = 7, h = -4$
E. $g = 17, h = 37$

12. For what value of n will the following system of equations have no solution?

$$2x - 3ny = 4$$
$$6x - y = 5$$

F. $1/9$
G. $1/6$
H. $1/3$
J. 1
K. 3

13. Which of the following is the equation of a line that is perpendicular to the line $5y - 4x = 9$?

A. $y = -\dfrac{5}{4}x + 10$

B. $y = \dfrac{4}{5}x + 6$

C. $y = \dfrac{9}{5}x + 4$

D. $y = 4x - 6$

E. $y = x + 1$

14. In the system of equations shown below, what value of d will create a system of equations that has no solutions?

$$10x + 7y = 12$$
$$15x + dy = 14$$

F. 5

G. $4\dfrac{2}{3}$

H. 10.5

J. 12

K. 21

15. The system of equations below has multiple solutions, all of which satisfy the equation $y = 4 - \dfrac{4}{3}x$. If it can be determined, what is the value of k?

$$4x + 3y = 12$$
$$12x + ky = 36$$

A. 6

B. 9

C. 12

D. 15

E. Cannot be determined from the given information

2.6 CIRCLES, SECTORS, AND ARCS

Perimeter a.k.a Circumference

$2\pi r$

Arc length

$\dfrac{\theta}{360} \cdot 2\pi r$

Area

πr^2

Sector Area

$\dfrac{\theta}{360} \cdot \pi r^2$

---

1. The area of a circle is 81π square centimeters. What is the circle's circumference, in centimeters?

  A. 9π

  B. 12π

  C. 18π

  D. 36π

  E. 81π

$$A = \pi r^2 = \frac{81\pi}{\pi} \quad \frac{81\pi}{\pi}$$

$$\sqrt{r^2} = \sqrt{81}$$

$$r = 9$$

$$C = 2\pi r = 2\pi 9 = \boxed{18\pi}$$

---

2. Tony recorded the number of items he has in his kitchen in the table below. If he converted his table into a pie chart, what would be the central angle of the sector labeled "potatoes"?

Item	Number
Eggs	5
Tomatoes	15
Potatoes	16

  F. $16°$

  G. $160°$

  H. $180°$

  J. $240°$

  K. $360°$

Pie charts are circles

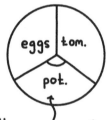

The size of "potatoes" represents its piece of the total.

$$\frac{16}{5 \cdot 15 \cdot 16} = \frac{16}{36}$$

$$\text{angle} = 360° \left(\frac{16}{36}\right) = \boxed{160°}$$

3. Amy orders a 16" diameter pizza and cuts the pizza into 8 slices of equal area. If Amy eats 3 slices, in square inches, how much pizza did Amy eat?

   A. 16π

   B. 24π

   C. 32π

   D. 48π

   E. 256π

$$A = \pi r^2 = 64\pi$$

$$\text{Sector} = \left(\frac{3}{8}\right) \cdot A$$

$$= \frac{3}{8} \cdot 64\pi$$

$$= \boxed{24\pi}$$

Sectors and Arcs are simply pieces of Area and Circumference.

What about "central angles"?

That same "piece" of 360 degrees. 1/3 of a circle is (1/3)*(360)

4. Sarah is installing a fence around her garden, which is in the shape of a semicircle with radius 7 yards. The garden is fully enclosed due to the fence continuing from one end of the semicircle to the other, in a straight-line. Which of the following is closest to the perimeter, in yards, of the garden?

   F. 28 yards

   G. 29 yards

   H. 36 yards

   J. 51 yards

   K. 58 yards

$= \frac{1}{2} \text{Circumference} \cdot \text{Diameter}$

$$\frac{1}{2}(2 \cdot 7\pi) \cdot (2 \cdot 7) \sim \boxed{36}$$

5. The diameter of a circle is 9 centimeters. What is the circle's circumference, in centimeters?

  A. 9π
  B. 13.5π
  C. 20.25π
  D. 45π
  E. 81π

6. The area of a circle is 36π square centimeters. What is the circle's diameter, in centimeters?

  F. 6
  G. 12
  H. 18
  J. 36
  K. 72

7. A circle in the standard (x, y) coordinate plane has its center at $(0,0)$ and passes through the point $(5, 12)$. What is the area, in square coordinate units, of this circle?

  A. 13π
  B. 17π
  C. 39π
  D. 169π
  E. 676π

8. A circle has an area of 16π. If the diameter of a second circle is three times larger than the diameter of original circle, what is the area of the second circle?

  F. 4π
  G. 12π
  H. 48π
  J. 144π
  K. 256π

9. What is the length, in inches, of a $30°$ arc of a circle whose circumference is 60 inches?

  A. $\frac{2}{\pi}$
  B. 2
  C. 4
  D. 5
  E. 5π

10. Mr. Samihr wants to build a fence around his garden in the shape of a half circle, as shown in the diagram below. If the garden has a diameter of 20 feet, what will be the total length of fencing, in feet, that Mr. Samihr should buy?

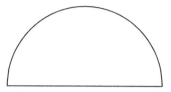

  F. 20
  G. $20 + 10\pi$
  H. $20 + 20\pi$
  J. 30π
  K. 40π

11. Points D and E lie on a circle with center O. The circle has radius 10 meters. The measure of $\angle DOE$ is $27°$.

  What is the length, in meters, of minor arc $\overset{\frown}{DE}$?

  A. 0.75π
  B. 1.5π
  C. 3π
  D. 4.5π
  E. Cannot be determined from the given information

12. Points A and B lie on a circle with center C. The circle has radius 12 meters. The measure of $\angle ACB$ is $60°$.

  What is the length, in meters, of minor arc $\overset{\frown}{AB}$?

  F. 2π
  G. 4π
  H. 8π
  J. 12π
  K. 16π

13. In the circle shown below, central angle $\angle AOB$ measures $40°$, and arc $\overset{\frown}{AB}$ is 2π centimeters long. How many centimeters long is the circle's radius?

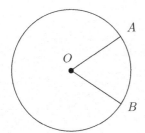

A. 4.5
B. 9
C. 18
D. 20
E. 24

14. A sector of a circle has an area equal to $\frac{13}{20}$ of the area of the circle. What is the measure of the sector's central angle?

F. 117°
G. 126°
H. 183°
J. 202°
K. 234°

15. A circular pizza with an 18-inch diameter is cut into 12 equal slices. If the pizza is one-inch thick, what is the *volume*, in cubic inches, of a single slice of the pizza?

A. $\dfrac{27}{4}\pi$

B. 27π

C. $\dfrac{243}{4}\pi$

D. 81π

E. 324π

16. In the circle shown below, central angle $\angle AOB$ measures $30°$, and arc $\overarc{AB}$ is 1.5π centimeters long. How many centimeters long is the circle's radius?

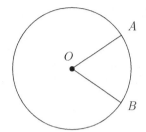

F. 3

G. 4.5

H. 9

J. 12

K. 18

17. In the figure below, ABC is a right triangle, where $\overline{AB} = 3$ and $\overline{BC} = 6$, and $\overline{DC}$ is perpendicular to $\overline{AB}$. $\overline{DC}$ is a radius of circle C. What is the length of arc $\overarc{BD}$?

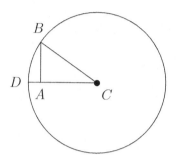

A. $\dfrac{\pi}{6}$

B. π

C. 3π

D. 8π

E. 12π

18. In circle O shown below, the space between consecutive points is equal, each line segment contains the center of the circle, and the area of the sector bound by points A, D, and O and minor arc $\overset{\frown}{AD}$ is 54π. What is the diameter of the circle?

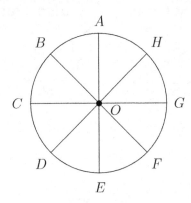

F. 12
G. 18
H. 24
J. 36
K. 144

19. In the circle with center C shown below, the length of radius $\overline{BC}$ is 9, the length of $\overline{AB}$ is 3, and $\overline{AB}$ is perpendicular to radius $\overline{CD}$ at A. When $\angle BCD$ is measured in degrees, which of the following represents the length of arc $\overset{\frown}{BD}$?

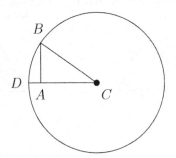

A. $\dfrac{\pi}{20}\left(\sin^{-1}\dfrac{1}{3}\right)$

B. $\dfrac{\pi}{20}\left(\cos^{-1}\dfrac{1}{3}\right)$

C. $\dfrac{\pi}{20}\left(\tan^{-1}\dfrac{1}{3}\right)$

D. $\dfrac{\pi}{10}\left(\sin^{-1}\dfrac{1}{3}\right)$

E. $\dfrac{\pi}{10}\left(\cos^{-1}\dfrac{1}{3}\right)$

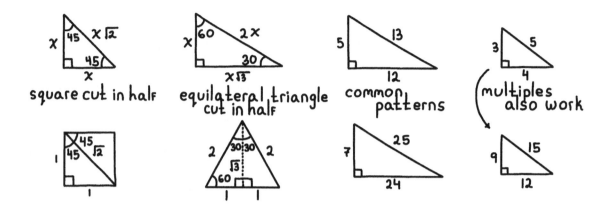

square cut in half   equilateral triangle   common   (multiples
                      cut in half   patterns   also work)

1. What is the length, in feet, of the diagonal of a square with sides of length 8 feet?

   A. 8
   B. $8\sqrt{2}$
   C. $8\sqrt{3}$
   D. 16
   E. $16\sqrt{2}$

   Special Triangles are patterns for shortcuts, nothing more!

   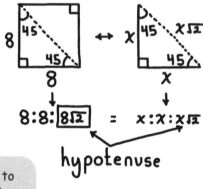

   $8:8:\boxed{8\sqrt{2}} = x:x:x\sqrt{2}$

   hypotenuse

   They are Integer Solutions to the Pythagorean Theorem :)

2. A rectangle has a diagonal of 10 cm. Which of these are possible values of the length and width of the rectangle?

   F. 1 and 9
   G. 2 and 8
   H. 5 and 9
   J. 6 and 8
   K. 7 and 7

   special triangles
   3 4 5   5 12 13
   6 8 ⑩   10 24 25
   9 12 15

   → The diagonal of a rectangle creates a right triangle.
   → Always check special right triangle multiples as a shortcut.
   * Hypotenuse = 10 fits $\frac{6}{\ell}$ $\frac{8}{w}$ $\frac{10}{d}$

   $\boxed{6 \text{ and } 8}$

   This makes them very clean to use in problems, so they show up constantly ... especially multiples of 3/4/5!

3. Which of the following sets of three numbers could be the lengths, in feet, of the sides of a $45°$ - $45°$ - $90°$ triangle?

A. $2, 2\sqrt{3}, 4$

B. $3, 3, 3$

C. $3, 4, 5$

D. $4, 4, 4\sqrt{2}$

E. $5, 5\sqrt{2}, 10$

4. Which of the following sets of three numbers could be the lengths, in feet, of the sides of a $30°$ - $60°$ - $90°$ triangle?

F. $2, 2\sqrt{3}, 4$

G. $3, 3, 3$

H. $3, 4, 5$

J. $4, 4, 4\sqrt{2}$

K. $5, 5\sqrt{2}, 10$

5. Consider isosceles right triangle KLM, where the hypotenuse KL has a length of $2\sqrt{6}$. What is the length, in feet, of side KM?

A. 2

B. $2\sqrt{2}$

C. $2\sqrt{3}$

D. $2\sqrt{5}$

E. 6

6. What is the length, in feet, of the diagonal of a square with sides of length 12 feet?

F. 12

G. $12\sqrt{2}$

H. $12\sqrt{3}$

J. 16

K. $16\sqrt{2}$

7. What is the length of the hypotenuse of a right triangle whose short leg is 4 inches and is across from a $30°$ angle?

A. 4

B. $4\sqrt{2}$

C. $4\sqrt{3}$

D. 8

E. $8\sqrt{3}$

8. What is the length, in feet, of the side lengths of a square with a diagonal of length 12 feet?

F. 6

G. $6\sqrt{2}$

H. 12

J. $12\sqrt{2}$

K. $12\sqrt{3}$

9. Consider equilateral triangle ABC with side lengths of 8 inches each. What is the area of triangle, in square inches, of triangle ABC?

A. $8\sqrt{3}$

B. $16\sqrt{3}$

C. 64

D. 256

E. 512

10. Consider isosceles right triangle MNO with hypotenuse $\overline{MN} = 20$ inches. What is the perimeter, in inches, of triangle MNO?

F. $20\sqrt{2} + 10$

G. $20\sqrt{2} + 20$

H. $10\sqrt{2} + 10$

J. $10\sqrt{2} + 20$

K. $30\sqrt{2}$

2.8 SOHCAHTOA WORD PROBLEMS

Given: ANGLE and SIDE
Goal: Another side

① Draw triangle and label

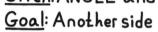
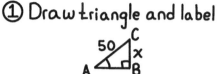

② Use given sides to pick trig function.

$\sin A = \frac{O}{H}$

③ Setup equation and solve for x.

$\sin A = \frac{x}{50}$

---

1. In right triangle $\triangle DEF$ shown below, $\overline{DF}$ is 300 feet and the measure of $\angle D$ is $35°$. What is the length, in feet, of $\overline{DE}$?

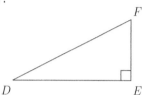

①

② SOH (CAH) TOA

$\cos(D) = \frac{adjacent}{hypotense}$

③ $\cos(35) = \frac{x}{300}$

$x = \boxed{300\cos(35)}$

A. $\dfrac{300}{\cos(35°)}$

B. $\dfrac{300}{\sin(35°)}$

C. $\dfrac{300}{\tan(35°)}$

D. $300\cos(35°)$

E. $300\sin(35°)$

Trigonometry problems always seem so straightforward! I love it.

2. Natalie, atop a cliff 0.25 miles tall, observes a ship approaching at $15.4°$ North of West. Which expression gives the distance between the ship and the shore?

cliff

$15.4°$

?

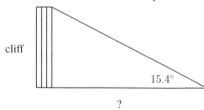

② SOHCAH (TOA)

$\tan = \frac{opposite}{adjacent}$

③ $\tan(15.4) = \frac{0.25}{x}$

$x = \boxed{\dfrac{0.25}{\tan(15.4)}}$

F. $\dfrac{0.25}{\sin(15.4°)}$

G. $\dfrac{0.25}{\tan(15.4°)}$

H. $0.25\sin(15.4°)$

J. $0.25\tan(15.4°)$

K. $0.25\cos(15.4°)$

3. Which of the following gives the length of side x in the right triangle shown below in terms of angle θ and hypotenuse z?

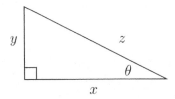

A. $z\cos(\theta°)$

B. $z\sin(\theta°)$

C. $z\tan(\theta°)$

D. $\dfrac{z}{\cos(\theta°)}$

E. $\dfrac{z}{\sin(\theta°)}$

4. As shown in the diagram below, a ship is approaching the shore of an island with a steep cliff face. Atop the cliff sits a lighthouse that is approximately 0.3 kilometers above sea level. The captain of the ship measures the angle of elevation between his ship and the lighthouse to be approximately 2.5°. Which of the following, if solved, would correctly give the distance between the ship and the shore of the island, in kilometers?

(Note: Figure not drawn to scale.)

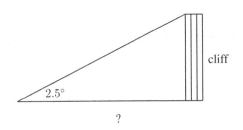

F. $\dfrac{0.3}{\tan(2.5°)}$

G. $\dfrac{0.3}{\sin(2.5°)}$

H. $\dfrac{0.3}{\cos(2.5°)}$

J. $0.3\tan(2.5°)$

K. $0.3\sin(2.5°)$

5. To clean the gutters on the roof of his house, Tom leans a 30 foot ladder against the base of his house at a 56° angle of elevation from the ground, as shown in the diagram below. Which of the following, when correctly solved, gives the height of Tom's house in feet?

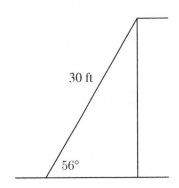

A. $\dfrac{30}{\sin(56°)}$

B. $\dfrac{30}{\cos(56°)}$

C. $30\sin(56°)$

D. $30\cos(56°)$

E. $30\tan(56°)$

6. Point M lies on side $\overline{JK}$ of rectangle $NJKL$ as shown below. The measure of $\angle KLM$ is 51° and the length of $\overline{KL}$ is 12 feet. Which of the following expressions is the length, in feet, of $\overline{MK}$?

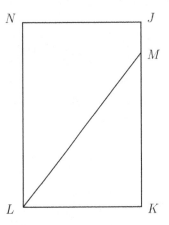

F. $12\sqrt{3}$

G. $12\sqrt{2}$

H. $12\tan(51°)$

J. $12\cos(51°)$

K. $\dfrac{12}{\tan(51°)}$

If any of these topics feel fuzzy or new, take on some extra practice. The topics are not complex, so an extra hour of practice can really cement progress.

For Word Problems, read the last sentence first. It orients your mind to what you're trying to do! Then return to the problem, knowing the goal.

If a Geometry problem has a visual already, many times the word problem describing it is redundant. Try using the last sentence of the word problem and the image to solve. This isn't always true, but shows up enough to use it.

CHAPTER TWO QUIZ
20 Minutes — 20 Questions

DIRECTIONS: Solve each problem, choose the correct answer, and then fill in the corresponding oval on your answer document.

Do not linger over problems that take too much time. Solve as many as you can; then return to the others in the time you have left for this test.

You are permitted to use a calculator on this test. You may use your calculator for any problems you choose, but some of the problems may be best done without using a calculator.

Note: Unless otherwise stated, all of the following should be assumed.
1. Illustrative figures are NOT necessarily drawn to scale.
2. Geometric figures lie in a plane.
3. The word *line* indicates a straight line.
4. The word *average* indicates arithmetic mean.

---

1. What is the slope of the line given by the equation $12x - 6y = 5$?
   A. $1/2$
   B. $5/12$
   C. $6/5$
   D. 2
   E. $12/5$

2. Which of the following expressions is equal to $(2x^2y)^3 \cdot xy^2$?
   F. $6x^6y^5$
   G. $6x^6y^6$
   H. $8x^6y^5$
   J. $8x^7y^5$
   K. $8x^7y^6$

3. What is the circumference, in inches, of a circle that has an area of 144π square inches?
   A. 12π
   B. 24π
   C. 36π
   D. 144π
   E. 288π

4. What is the length of a side of an equilateral triangle whose height is $5\sqrt{3}$?
   F. 5
   G. $5\sqrt{3}$
   H. 10
   J. $10\sqrt{3}$
   K. 15

5. The function $g(x)$ is defined for all x such that $g(x) = 4x^2 - 11x + 6$. What is the value of $g(-3)$?
   A. 9
   B. 16
   C. 25
   D. 36
   E. 75

6. In shop class, Raquel is designing a piece of stained glass in the shape of a square. Raquel would like the square piece of glass to have an area of 81 square inches. How many inches long is the diagonal of the piece of glass?
   F. 9
   G. 11.2
   H. 12
   J. $9\sqrt{2}$
   K. $9\sqrt{3}$

7. Emilio is in charge of choosing party decorations for the senior prom dinner at West Bishop Memorial High School. In a catalogue, he finds 12 different styles of banners, 6 different kinds of balloons, 4 different types of streamers, and 3 different styles of confetti. How many different possible combinations of party decorations can Emilio choose?

A. 25

B. 45

C. 112

D. 864

E. 1,728

8. What is the equation of the line in the standard (x, y) coordinate plane passing through the points $(1, 4)$ and $(-2, 6)$?

F. $y = -\dfrac{2}{3}x + \dfrac{14}{3}$

G. $y = -\dfrac{2}{3}x + 6$

H. $y = \dfrac{3}{2}x + \dfrac{5}{3}$

J. $y = \dfrac{3}{2}x + 4$

K. $y = -\dfrac{1}{4}x + \dfrac{9}{7}$

9. A pizza with a diameter of 12 inches is cut into 8 equal slices. What is area of one slice of pizza?

A. 4.5π

B. 9π

C. 12π

D. 18π

E. 36π

10. Equilateral triangle $\triangle ABC$ has sides of length 10 inches. How many inches long is the altitude connecting vertex A to side $\overline{BC}$?

F. 5

G. $5\sqrt{2}$

H. $5\sqrt{3}$

J. 10

K. $10\sqrt{3}$

Use the following information to answer questions 11-13.

In Erica's garden there are 5 trees with straight line pathways between some, as shown in the figure below. The birch, elm, and maple trees are equidistant from each other, while the pine tree is equidistant from the birch tree and maple tree. The measure of the angle from the birch tree to the maple tree to the pine tree is 45° and the distance between the birch tree and the maple tree is 100 meters.

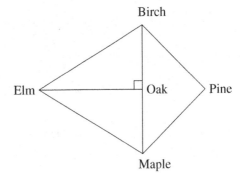

11. What is the measure of the angle from the elm tree to the birch tree to the pine tree?

A. 45°

B. 60°

C. 90°

D. 105°

E. 120°

12. The distance from the elm tree to the oak tree is how much less than the distance from the elm tree to the maple tree, to the nearest tenth of a meter?

F. 13.4 meters

G. 27.9 meters

H. 29.2 meters

J. 36.6 meters

K. 86.6 meters

13. Starting at the pine tree, Erica walked around the entire perimeter of the garden, passing every tree except the oak tree, and ended up back where she started. To the nearest meter, how far did Erica walk?

A. 241 meters

B. 300 meters

C. 341 meters

D. 400 meters

E. 500 meters

Use the following information to answer questions 14-17.

In the figure below, rhombus $ABCD$ has diagonals that intersect at E:

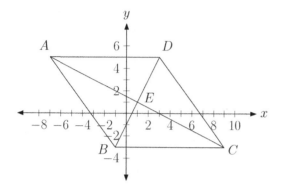

14. What is the midpoint of line segment $\overline{AB}$?

F. $(-4, 5)$

G. $(-4, 1)$

H. $(-3, 5)$

J. $(1, -4)$

K. $(1, 1)$

15. Which of the following is NOT the slope of one of the line segments on the graph?

A. $-4/3$

B. $-1/2$

C. 0

D. $1/2$

E. 2

16. Which of the following are true about the relationship between diagonals $\overline{AC}$ and $\overline{BD}$ in coordinate units?

    I. They are congruent
    II. They bisect each other
    III. The are parallel
    IV. They are perpendicular

F. I and III only

G. II only

H. IV only

J. II and IV only

K. I, II, and IV only

17. How much longer is diagonal $\overline{AC}$ than diagonal $\overline{BD}$?

A. $4\sqrt{5}$

B. 12

C. $8\sqrt{5}$

D. 24

E. $12\sqrt{5}$

Use the following information to answer questions 18-20.

The figure below depicts a Go Kart tire whose inner diameter is 6" and whose outer diameter is 10". The tire has 12 spokes connecting with one another at the center.

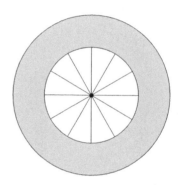

18. What is the inner circumference of the tire, in inches?

F. 3π

G. 4π

H. 6π

J. 10π

K. 12π

19. What is the angle formed between each of the tire's spokes?

A. $15°$

B. $20°$

C. $30°$

D. $36°$

E. $45°$

20. If the area of the tire is found by subtracting the area of the inner circle from the area of the outer circle, what is the area of the tire?

F. 9π

G. 16π

H. 25π

J. 36π

K. 64π

Welcome to Chapter 3.

This marks our progression into the middle section of the ACT. This realm begins somewhere around 25 and lasts into the mid 40s.

This middle section gets more difficult in one of two ways. Either the problem still uses straightforward calculation but now requires many steps to complete, or the test writers ask you to intepret and relate systems and graphs.

Probability and Trigonometry get a little more in depth coverage, but still remain some of the easier problems in the section.

With multiple layers of work comes the need to structure your work more clearly. It will be important to write each step clearly. All this writing translates to more time, so you may find speed becoming a tough factor.

① Write out every variable, what they represent, and their given values.

② Plug all given values into the given equation, and solve.

1. The number of kittens, N, born per week at Kal's Animal Sanctuary can be modeled by the equation $N(t) = \frac{2t^2+7}{t+1}$, where t is the number of weeks since Kal opened his sanctuary. According to this model, how many kittens will be born in week 8?

   A. 15
   B. 18
   C. 26
   D. 34
   E. 51

① N = # of kittens
   t = # of weeks

   $N(t) = \frac{2t^2 + 7}{t+1}$ $t = 8$ $N = ?$

② $N(8) = \frac{2(8)^2 + 7}{8+1} = \frac{2(64) + 7}{9} = \frac{128 + 7}{9} = \frac{135}{9} = \boxed{15}$

This is a great topic to start on for Chapter 3. These problems look TERRIFYING, full of insane equations and references to math you barely remember or may never have heard at all!

2. The formula for continuously compounding interest is $A = Pe^{rt}$, where A is the amount of money presently in an account, P is the starting principle P, r is the interest rate, and t is the time in years since the principle was deposited. Euler's number, e, is a constant whose value is approximately equal to 2.718. If Kyle puts $5,000 into an account that earns 8% interest when he starts college, how much money will he have in his account when he graduates exactly 4 years later?

   F. $5,416.44
   G. $6,802.44
   H. $6,885.64
   J. $11,127.70
   K. $122,662.65

① A = money in account, t = time in years
   P = initial amount of money in account
   r = interest rate,

   $A = Pe^{rt}$, $P = 5,000$, $r = 0.08$, $t = 4$, $e = 2.718$

② $A = 5,000 \cdot 2.718^{(0.08)(4)}$
   $A = 5,000 \cdot 1.38$
   $A = \boxed{6,885.64}$

In reality, they are some of the easiest on the entire test. These problems give you an equation, and then tell you exactly what to plug into it! All that's left is a little algebra to find "x".

3. The approximate distance in meters, d, traveled by a rock as it falls from a cliff can be modeled by the equation $d(t) = 4.9t^2$, where t is the time the rock has been falling in seconds. According to this model, for how many seconds has a rock been falling if it has covered a distance of 176.4 meters?

A. 6
B. 18
C. 36
D. 7,200
E. 36,024

4. A certain investment firm models the total revenue, R, in millions of dollars of one of its mutual funds using the equation $R(t) = 0.04t^3 - 0.5t^2 - 0.8t + 6$, where t is the number of years since the mutual fund was created. Based on this model, how much total revenue will the mutual fund have made, in millions of dollars, 15 years after it was created?

F. 12.2
G. 16.5
H. 18.1
J. 24.6
K. 31.7

5. The number of diagonals of a polygon with n sides can be calculated using the formula $\dfrac{n(n-3)}{2}$. How many more diagonals exist in a dodecagon (12 sides) than in a decagon (10 sides)?

A. 12
B. 19
C. 27
D. 35
E. 54

6. For a certain species of flower, the recommended daytime temperate range in degrees Fahrenheit is $59° < F < 68°$. Given the formulas $C = \dfrac{5}{9}(F - 32)$, where C is the temperature in degrees Celsius and F is the temperature in degrees Fahrenheit, what is the corresponding daytime temperature range in degrees Celsius for the plant?

F. $0° < C < 5°$
G. $5° < C < 10°$
H. $10° < C < 15°$
J. $15° < C < 20°$
K. $20° < C < 25°$

7. For his birthday last year, Jeremy's parents bought him an ant colony. Since his birthday, Jeremy has kept track of the population of ants in the colony and has come up with the expression $160(1.6)^{.25t}$ to model the colony's population t weeks after his birthday. According to his model, approximately how many ants will be in the ant colony 12 weeks after his birthday?

A. 256
B. 655
C. 2,844
D. 10,108
E. 45,035

8. David's Biology class is studying the growth of bacterial cells in petri dishes. In David's petri dish, the number of bacterial cells, N, that are alive t hours after the start of the experiment can be modeled by the equation $N(t) = N_0(2)^{0.12t}$, where N_0 is the initial number of cells in the petri dish. Approximately how many hours has the experiment been running if there are 1.2×10^9 cells alive in David's petri dish and the colony initially started with 3.2×10^6 cells?

F. 3
G. 17
H. 71
J. 83
K. 164

9. Annual interest can be calculated using the formula $A = A_o(1 + r)^t$, where A is the current amount, A_o is the starting amount, r is the interest rate, and t is the time in years. If $\$20,000$ is put into an account that earns 4.5% annual interest, how much interest would the account earn over the next 84 months if no money is withdrawn and no additional funds are deposited?

A. $\$26,300.00$
B. $\$27,117,96$
C. $\$27,217.24$
D. $\$29,800$
E. $\$269529.32$

10. The formula for continuously compounding interest is $A = Pe^{rt}$, where A is the amount of money in the account, P is the principal initial investment, r is the interest rate and t is the time in years. Euler's number, e, is a constant whose value is approximately equal to 2.718. If Mindy puts $\$1,000$ into an account that earns 11% interest, how much money will she have in her account 36 months later?

F. $\$1,390.92$
G. $\$4,293.56$
H. $\$4,819.28$
J. $\$10,927.87$
K. $\$12,623.33$

3.2 GEOMETRIC & ARITHMETIC SEQUENCES

① Write your term numbers

② Make buckets or blanks

③ Fill in given values

④ Determine the difference or ratio

⑤ Fill in the blanks

1st 2nd 3rd 4th 5th 6th

_____ _____ _____ _____ _____ _____

2   4   6   ___   ___   ___

arithmetic
difference = +2

the 6th term is 12

1st 2nd 3rd 4th 5th 6th

_____ _____ _____ _____ _____ _____

2   4   8   ___   ___   ___

geometric
ratio = x2

the 6th term is 64

---

1. What is the sixth term in the geometric sequence 1, −2, 4, ...?

   A. −128
   B. −32
   C. −8
   D. 16
   E. 64

   This chart might look long, but even I make it every time I hit a sequence problem.

   ① 1st 2nd 3rd 4th 5th 6th

   ② _____ _____ _____ _____ _____ _____

   ③ 1   -2   4   ___   ___   ___

   ④ geometric, ratio = -2

   ⑤ 1   -2   4   -8   16   -32

   the 6th term is -32

---

2. What is the difference between the 5th and 8th terms of the arithmetic sequence 4, 7, 10, ...?

   F. 3
   G. 6
   H. 8
   J. 9
   K. 14

   Yeah, I find it super useful to visualize the sequences. Then I just have to find the target!

   ① 1st 2nd 3rd 4th 5th 6th 7th 8th

   ② _____ _____ _____ _____ _____ _____ _____ _____

   ③ 4   7   10   ___   ___   ___   ___   ___

   ④ arithmetic, difference = +3

   ⑤ 4   7   10   13   16   19   22   25

   8th − 5th = 25 − 16 = 9

3. In an arithmetic sequence that has an odd number of terms, the first term is -3 and the last term is 27. What is the middle term?

A. 6
B. 9
C. 12
D. 15
E. 18

4. What is the common ratio of a sequence containing the consecutive terms 32, 8, 2, and $1/2$?

F. $1/4$
G. $1/2$
H. 2
J. 4
K. 24

5. What is the seventh term in the geometric sequence $-\dfrac{1}{2}, 1, -2, \ldots$?

A. -32
B. -16
C. 16
D. 32
E. 64

6. Ignacio is writing a computer program that he plans to finish in 12 days. He writes 15 additional lines of code every day and wrote 0 lines of code on his first day. How many lines of code will Ignacio write on the 12th day?

F. 165
G. 180
H. 210
J. 240
K. 270

7. The sum of the five terms in an arithmetic sequence is 150 and the common difference is 8. What is the value of the second term?

A. 14
B. 22
C. 30
D. 38
E. 46

8. In the arithmetic sequence 8, 9.5, 11, ..., 21.5, how many terms are there between the numbers 11 and 21.5, exclusive?

F. 5
G. 6
H. 7
J. 9
K. 12

9. In an infinite geometric sequence, the first four terms are 12, 6, 3, and 1.5. Which of the following is NOT true?

A. The fifth term is 0.75
B. There are no negative terms
C. The sum of all terms is 24
D. The common difference is $1/2$
E. The common ratio is $1/2$

10. During a period of rapid growth, a certain species of inchworm grows 10% per day. If an inchworm of this species begins this period of growth with a length of 2.50 centimeters, approximately how long, in centimeters, will it be four days later?

F. 3.21
G. 3.54
H. 3.60
J. 3.66
K. 3.72

① Stack your two equations such that all variables of the same type sit on top of one another.

$$y + 2x = 7 \qquad \to \qquad 2x + y = 7$$
$$3x + 2y = 12 \qquad \qquad 3x + 2y = 12$$

② Decide which variable you want to solve for, and eliminate the other one.

    — Multiply the top and/or bottom equation(s) by coefficients that will cause the variable destined for elimination to have the same coefficients in both equations.

    — Subtract the two equations.

$$2(2x + y) = 2(7) \qquad \to \qquad 4x + 2y = 14$$
$$3x + 2y = 12 \qquad \qquad \underline{3x + 2y = 12}$$
$$\boxed{x = 2}$$

> If you get hit with a crazy pair, another method is to solve for y and plug both equations into your graphing calculator to find the intersection of the lines.

1. What is the value of y in the system of equations below?

$$4w + y = 16$$
$$w + y = 11$$

    A. -2

    B. 1

    C. $\dfrac{5}{3}$

    D. $\dfrac{28}{3}$

    E. $\dfrac{38}{3}$

$$4w + y = 16$$
$$w + y = 11$$
↓
we are trying to solve for y.
so we should eliminate w.
↓

$$4w + y = 16 \qquad \to \qquad 4w + y = 16$$
$$4(w + y) = 4(11) \qquad \qquad 4w + 4y = 44$$
$$\underline{}$$
$$\frac{-3y}{-3} = \frac{-28}{-3}$$
$$\boxed{y = \frac{28}{3}}$$

2. If the system of equations shown below has an infinite number of solutions, what is the value of c?

$$8x + 14y = 36$$
$$12x + 21y = 9c$$

    F. 2

    G. 3

    H. 6

    J. 9

    K. 54

$$8x + 14y = 36$$
$$12x + 21y = 9c$$
↓
Infinite solutions means that they are the same line, so we want to eliminate both x and y.
↓

$$3(8x + 14y) = 3(36) \qquad \to \qquad 24x + 42y = 108$$
$$2(12x + 21y) = 2(9c) \qquad \qquad 24x + 42y = 18c$$
$$0 = 108 - 18c$$
$$+18c \qquad +18c$$
$$\frac{18c}{18} = \frac{108}{18}$$
$$\boxed{c = 6}$$

3. In the (x, y) solution to the system of equations below, the value of y is which of the following?

$$5x = 3$$
$$2x + 3y = 5$$

A. $\dfrac{3}{5}$

B. $\dfrac{19}{15}$

C. $\dfrac{25}{21}$

D. $\dfrac{25}{18}$

E. 3

4. When the system of equations below is solved for a and b, what is the value of b?

$$5a + 12b = 36$$
$$5a + b = 14$$

F. 2
G. 4
H. 11
J. 14
K. 22

5. What is the value of b in the following system of equations?

$$3a = 21$$
$$20 - 2a = 2b$$

A. 3
B. 6
C. 7
D. 12
E. 24

6. If the system of equations shown below has an infinite number of solutions, what is the value of c?

$$2x + 3y = 7$$
$$4x + 6cy = 14$$

F. -7
G. -1
H. 1
J. 2
K. 7

7. What is the value of $3n$ in the following system of equations?

$$m = 5$$
$$4m - 3n = 11$$

A. 3
B. 6
C. 9
D. 12
E. 15

8. What (r, t) value will satisfy the system of equations shown below?

$$-2t + r = -10$$
$$4t + 2r = 8$$

F. $(-4, 0)$
G. $(-3, \frac{7}{2})$
H. $(-3, 3)$
J. $(-1, \frac{1}{2})$
K. $(-1, 1)$

9. If the system of equations shown below has an infinite number of solutions, what is the value of k?

$$3x + 12y = 16$$
$$4x - 8ky = 21\tfrac{1}{3}$$

A. -2
B. -1
C. 1
D. 2
E. 8

10. If $3x + 5y = 7$ and $6x + 8y = 10$, what is the value of $9x + 11y$?

F. 3
G. 9
H. 13
J. 14
K. 20

Many word problems involve systems of equations. A common type that does is cost vs. total amount.

→ Apples & Oranges

Bought 10   Apples = $1

Spent $16   Oranges = $3

① Apples + Oranges = 10   → $x + y = 10$

② $1(Apples) + $3(Oranges) = $16 → $1x + 3y = 16$

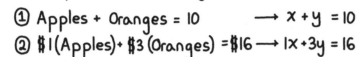

The "Cost vs. Things" problem shows up extremely often.

1. The senior class at Birch North High School is sponsoring a costume party. Each student wearing a costume will pay an admission price of $4, and each student NOT wearing a costume will pay an admission price of $6. A total of $436 was collected from the 91 students who paid admission. How much of the amount was collected from students NOT wearing a costume?

A. $110
B. $125
C. $165
D. $180
E. $216

Costume: "C" $4
No costume: "n" $6

things → $n + C = 91$

cost → $6n + 4c = 436$

goal: $6n = ?$

$$\begin{array}{r} 6n + 4c = 436 \\ -4n + 4c = 91 \cdot 4 \\ \hline 2n = 72 \\ n = 36 \\ 6n = \boxed{216} \end{array}$$

2. The Evanston High School music room has 108 seats, which are arranged in rows. The number of seats in each row is 3 less than the number of rows. How many rows of seats are there in the music room?

F. 6
G. 9
H. 12
J. 18
K. 36

① $s = $ # of seats per row
   $r = $ # of rows

$s = r - 3$ $sr = 108$

② $s = (r-3)$ $sr = 108$

$(r-3)r = 108$

$r^2 - 3r = 108$

$ -108 -108$

$r^2 - 3r - 108 = 0$

$(r+9)(r-12) = 0$

$\cancel{r-9} \quad \boxed{r = 12}$

3. The sum of the real numbers a and b is 21. Their difference is 9. What is the value of ab?

A. 15
B. 21
C. 28
D. 45
E. 90

4. Sun will order boxes of yellow highlighters and boxes of blue highlighters for her classroom. The table below gives the number of highlighters in each box and the price per box.

Color	Number in each box	Price per box
Yellow	20	$6
Blue	30	$8

Sun will order a total of 60 boxes of highlighters for a total price of $400. Which of the following systems of equations gives a true relationship between the y boxes of yellow highlighters and b boxes of blue highlighters that Sun will order?

F. $y + b = 60 \qquad 6y + 8b = 400$
G. $y + b = 60 \qquad 20y + 30b = 400$
H. $y + b = 400 \qquad 20y + 30b = 60$
J. $6y + 8b = 60 \qquad 20y + 30b = 400$
K. $6y + 8b = 400 \qquad 20y + 30b = 60$

5. John and Kevin are encyclopedia salesmen. Last month, not only did they each sell the same number of encyclopedias, they both made the exact same amount of money. John works for himself and makes $40 for each set of encyclopedias he sells. Kevin works for a company that pays him $300 per month, but Kevin only makes $25 for each set of encyclopedias he sells. How many encyclopedias did they each sell?

A. 5
B. 12
C. 20
D. 75
E. 800

6. At TMC movie theaters, adult tickets cost $14 and kids tickets cost $6. On Friday night, TMC made a total of $11,348 from selling a total of 1,006 tickets. How many adult tickets were sold?

F. 212
G. 342
H. 448
J. 664
K. 712

7. A pool containing 200 gallons of water is filling at a rate of 15 gallons per hour. A second pool contains 500 gallons of water and is draining at a rate of 25 gallons per hour. In how many hours will the two pools contain the same amount of water?

A. 7.5
B. 10
C. 17.5
D. 30
E. 70

8. For a school pep rally, the basketball team sold pom-poms and foam fingers. The pom-poms sold for $7 and the foam fingers sold for $5. The team made a total of $600 by selling 106 items. How many foam fingers did the basketball team sell?

F. 7
G. 35
H. 53
J. 71
K. 99

9. Stephen and Diana are the star performers and organizers for their high school musical. The musical costs current high school students $5 and non-students $8 to attend opening night. If 800 people attend opening night and Stephen and Diana collect $5,500 in revenue, how much money did Stephen and Diana collect from non-students?

A. $300
B. $500
C. $1,500
D. $4,000
E. $5,500

1. Which of the following augmented matrices represents the system of linear equations below?

$$x + 3y = 12$$
$$7x - y = 1$$

A. $\begin{bmatrix} 1 & 3 & | & 12 \\ 7 & 1 & | & 1 \end{bmatrix}$

B. $\begin{bmatrix} 1 & 3 & | & 12 \\ 7 & -1 & | & 1 \end{bmatrix}$

C. $\begin{bmatrix} 1 & 3 & | & 12 \\ 7 & -1 & | & -1 \end{bmatrix}$

D. $\begin{bmatrix} 1 & 3 & | & 12 \\ -7 & -1 & | & 1 \end{bmatrix}$

E. $\begin{bmatrix} 1 & 3 & | & 12 \\ -7 & -1 & | & 1 \end{bmatrix}$

A Matrix, or matrices if there are many, is just another way to organize information. It is not a message from the future or a new mode of thought.

Remember : anything that looks "above your paygrade" difficult or foreign is probably a simple problem. Wild or outside topics do not get complex, but instead are more of a general knowledge test.

Two matrices of the same size can be added

$$\begin{bmatrix} a & b \\ c & d \end{bmatrix} + \begin{bmatrix} r & s \\ t & v \end{bmatrix} = \begin{bmatrix} a+r & b+s \\ c+t & d+v \end{bmatrix}$$

→ multiply any constants first

→ add corresponding pieces

$$3\begin{bmatrix} a & b \\ c & d \end{bmatrix} - 2\begin{bmatrix} m & n \\ o & p \end{bmatrix} = \begin{bmatrix} 3a-2m & 3b-2n \\ 3c-2o & 3d-2p \end{bmatrix}$$

2. $3 \begin{bmatrix} 2 & 3 \\ 4 & 5 \end{bmatrix} + 2 \begin{bmatrix} 1 & 2 \\ -2 & 0 \end{bmatrix} = ?$

F. $\begin{bmatrix} 7 & 8 \\ -1 & 0 \end{bmatrix}$

G. $\begin{bmatrix} 8 & 13 \\ 8 & 15 \end{bmatrix}$

H. $\begin{bmatrix} 6 & 4 \\ -8 & 0 \end{bmatrix}$

J. $\begin{bmatrix} 8 & 4 \\ -4 & 0 \end{bmatrix}$

K. $\begin{bmatrix} 6 & 13 \\ 12 & -6 \end{bmatrix}$

$$3 \begin{bmatrix} 2 & 3 \\ 4 & 5 \end{bmatrix} + 2 \begin{bmatrix} 1 & 2 \\ -2 & 0 \end{bmatrix}$$

$$\downarrow \qquad \qquad \downarrow$$

$$\begin{bmatrix} 6 & 9 \\ 12 & 15 \end{bmatrix} + \begin{bmatrix} 2 & 4 \\ -4 & 0 \end{bmatrix}$$

$$\downarrow$$

$$\begin{bmatrix} 8 & 13 \\ 8 & 15 \end{bmatrix}$$

For speed, try checking the math for just the upper left hand corner of each matrix first. It should eliminate a few answer choices!

3. What is the value of a in the matrix equation shown below?

$$a \begin{bmatrix} -2 & 6 \\ -1 & 0 \end{bmatrix} = \begin{bmatrix} 4 & -12 \\ 2 & 0 \end{bmatrix}$$

A. -6
B. -4
C. -2
D. 5
E. 8

① $a \begin{bmatrix} -2 & 6 \\ -1 & 0 \end{bmatrix} = \begin{bmatrix} 4 & -12 \\ 2 & 0 \end{bmatrix}$

$\begin{bmatrix} -2a & 6a \\ -a & 0 \end{bmatrix} = \begin{bmatrix} 4 & -12 \\ 2 & 0 \end{bmatrix}$

② $-2a = 4 \qquad 6a = -12$

$a = \boxed{-2} \qquad a = \boxed{-2}$

$-a = 2$
$a = \boxed{-2}$

Fact : Corresponding spots in equal matrices are equal.

4. What is the value of x in the matrix equation shown below?

$$b \begin{bmatrix} 3 & 5 \\ 2 & -4 \end{bmatrix} = \begin{bmatrix} 9 & x \\ 6 & -12 \end{bmatrix}$$

F. -1
G. 0
H. 3
J. 12
K. 15

6. $3\begin{bmatrix} 2 & -7 \\ 5 & 1 \end{bmatrix} - \begin{bmatrix} 1 & -6 \\ 15 & -8 \end{bmatrix} = ?$

F. $\begin{bmatrix} 5 & -15 \\ 0 & 11 \end{bmatrix}$

G. $\begin{bmatrix} 3 & -13 \\ 20 & -7 \end{bmatrix}$

H. $\begin{bmatrix} 5 & 15 \\ 0 & 10 \end{bmatrix}$

J. $\begin{bmatrix} 3 & -6 \\ 30 & 27 \end{bmatrix}$

K. $\begin{bmatrix} -5 & -15 \\ 0 & -10 \end{bmatrix}$

5. $\begin{bmatrix} 4 & 7 \\ 3 & 2 \end{bmatrix} + \begin{bmatrix} 5 & 1 \\ 8 & -3 \end{bmatrix} = ?$

A. $\begin{bmatrix} 5 & 12 \\ 0 & 10 \end{bmatrix}$

B. $\begin{bmatrix} 9 & 7 \\ 11 & 2 \end{bmatrix}$

C. $\begin{bmatrix} 1 & 15 \\ 4 & 7 \end{bmatrix}$

D. $\begin{bmatrix} 20 & 7 \\ 24 & -6 \end{bmatrix}$

E. $\begin{bmatrix} 9 & 8 \\ 11 & -1 \end{bmatrix}$

7. What is the value of k in the matrix equation shown below?

$$\begin{bmatrix} 1 & -1 \\ -1 & 1 \end{bmatrix} - \begin{bmatrix} 2k & 3 \\ -3 & 2 \end{bmatrix} = \begin{bmatrix} 5 & -4 \\ 2 & -1 \end{bmatrix}$$

A. -4
B. -2
C. 0
D. 2
E. 4

8. What is the value of y in the matrix equation shown below?

$$-2 \begin{bmatrix} -3 & 4 \\ -1 & 1 \end{bmatrix} + \begin{bmatrix} 4 & -2 \\ 0 & 6 \end{bmatrix} = \begin{bmatrix} 10 & x \\ 2 & y \end{bmatrix}$$

F. -10
G. 0
H. 2
J. 4
K. 8

9. Which of the following augmented matrices represents the system of linear equations below?

$$-5x + 7y = 10$$
$$x - 2y = -4$$

A. $\begin{bmatrix} -5 & 7 & | & 10 \\ 1 & 2 & | & -4 \end{bmatrix}$

B. $\begin{bmatrix} -5 & 7 & | & -10 \\ 1 & -2 & | & -4 \end{bmatrix}$

C. $\begin{bmatrix} -5 & 7 & | & 10 \\ 1 & -2 & | & -4 \end{bmatrix}$

D. $\begin{bmatrix} -5 & 7 & | & -10 \\ -1 & -2 & | & -4 \end{bmatrix}$

E. $\begin{bmatrix} -5 & 7 & | & 10 \\ -1 & -2 & | & -4 \end{bmatrix}$

10. $5 \begin{bmatrix} 3 & 8 \\ -4 & 0 \end{bmatrix} = ?$

F. $\begin{bmatrix} 15 & 40 \\ -20 & 0 \end{bmatrix}$

G. $\begin{bmatrix} 8 & 13 \\ 1 & -4 \end{bmatrix}$

H. $\begin{bmatrix} 15 & 8 \\ -4 & 0 \end{bmatrix}$

J. $\begin{bmatrix} -15 & -40 \\ 20 & 0 \end{bmatrix}$

K. $\begin{bmatrix} 15 & 20 \\ -10 & 0 \end{bmatrix}$

11. $\begin{bmatrix} 1 & -1 \\ -1 & 1 \end{bmatrix} + 5 \begin{bmatrix} 1 & 0 \\ 0 & -1 \end{bmatrix} = ?$

A. $\begin{bmatrix} 5 & -1 \\ -1 & -6 \end{bmatrix}$

B. $\begin{bmatrix} 5 & -1 \\ 1 & -4 \end{bmatrix}$

C. $\begin{bmatrix} 6 & -1 \\ 1 & -4 \end{bmatrix}$

D. $\begin{bmatrix} 6 & -1 \\ -1 & -6 \end{bmatrix}$

E. $\begin{bmatrix} 6 & -1 \\ -1 & -4 \end{bmatrix}$

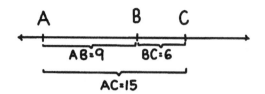

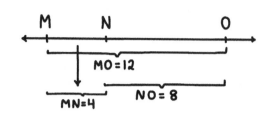

→ Adjacent: add (AB·BC = AC)   → Overlap: subtract (MO-NO=MN)

1. Points A, B, C, and D lie in that order on a number line. If $AD = 28$, $AC = 17$, and $BD = 14$, what is the length of BC?

A. 3
B. 5
C. 21
D. 31
E. 59

Remember the Venn Diagram method: (sum of pieces) - (total) = Overlap.

In this case, (AC + BD) - AD = BC

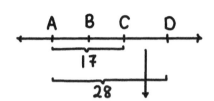

$$CD = 28 - 17 = 11$$

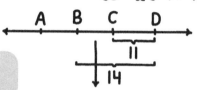

$$BC = 14 - 11 = \boxed{3}$$

2. Circle O with diameter $\overline{DG}$ is drawn below. If $\angle EOG = 95°$ and $\angle DOF = 140°$, what is the measure of $\angle EOF$?

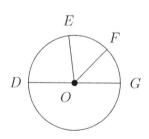

F. 55°
G. 70°
H. 95°
J. 140°
K. 180°

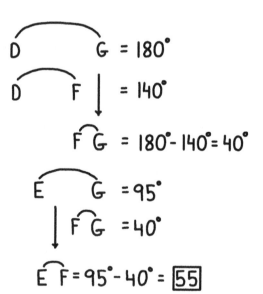

$$\overparen{DG} = 180°$$

$$\overparen{DF} = 140°$$

$$\overparen{FG} = 180° - 140° = 40°$$

$$\overparen{EG} = 95°$$

$$\overparen{FG} = 40°$$

$$\overparen{EF} = 95° - 40° = \boxed{55}$$

3. In the line segment shown below, the length of $\overline{AB}$ is 10 cm and the length of $\overline{BC}$ is 30 cm. What is the distance, in centimeters, between C and the midpoint of $\overline{AB}$?

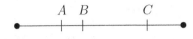

A. 20
B. 30
C. 35
D. 38
E. 40

4. Points A, B, C, D, and E lie on a number line such that point E is between points A and B, point C is between points A and E, and Point D is between points B and E. Which of the following *must* be true?

F. $AC > BD$
G. $CD > BD$
H. $CD > EB$
J. $AD > CE$
K. $AE > CB$

5. For the line segment below, the ratio of the length of $\overline{LM}$ to the length of $\overline{MN}$ is 1:3. If it can be determined, what is the ratio of the length of $\overline{LM}$ to the length of $\overline{LN}$?

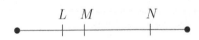

A. 1:2
B. 1:4
C. 3:1
D. 4:1
E. Cannot be determined from the given information

6. Samantha is organizing the boys basketball and football teams and has 60 student athletes attend a tryout. Samantha recruits 15 boys for basketball and 52 boys for football from the tryout. What is the minimum amount of boys that will need to be recruited for both?

F. 0
G. 7
H. 8
J. 15
K. 37

7. On a number line, point A is placed at -8, B placed at -3, C placed at 1, and placed D at 7. A point travels from A to D, then from D to B, then from B to C, and finally back to A. What was the total distance that the point traveled?

A. 0
B. 15
C. 22
D. 30
E. 38

8. On a circle, Point B is located 8 inches clockwise from Point A, Point D is located 8 inches counter clockwise from Point A, and Point C is both 1 unit counterclockwise from Point B and 12 units counter clockwise from point A. How far apart are points C and D along the circle?

F. 3
G. 4
H. 5
J. 20
K. 29

9. Two radio stations are 150 miles apart along a straight highway. The first, $WACK$, has a signal that broadcasts for 87 miles. The second, $WIZE$, has a signal that broadcasts for 92 miles. For how many miles can both radio stations be heard along the highway?

A. 5
B. 29
C. 58
D. 63
E. 121

10. Circle O is drawn below. If $\angle DOA = 140°$, $\angle DOC = 90°$, and $\angle AOB = 95°$, what is the measure of $\angle BOC$?

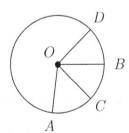

F. 25°
G. 35°
H. 45°
J. 55°
K. 65°

<u>Patterns from linear inequalities:</u>

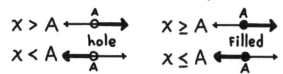

$x > A$ hole $x \geq A$ filled

$x < A$ $x \leq A$

More trick patterns for speed! But if this leaves you with two answer choices, set the inside equal to A to find the proper points.

<u>Patterns from absolute values:</u>

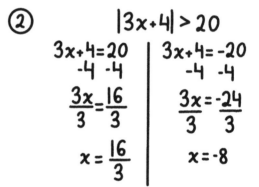

$|\sim\sim| < A$ } to find the endpoints, plug in for x so that $\sim\sim = A$

$|\sim\sim| > A$

tricks { $|\sim| > -A$ $\mathbb{R}$

$|\sim| < -A$ $\emptyset$

1. Which of the following is the graph of the inequality $|3x + 4| > 20$?

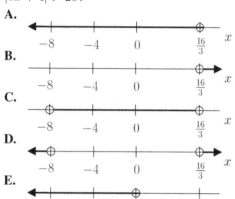

A.
   -8 -4 0 $\frac{16}{3}$ x

B.
   -8 -4 0 $\frac{16}{3}$ x

C.
   -8 -4 0 $\frac{16}{3}$ x

D.
   -8 -4 0 $\frac{16}{3}$ x

E.
   -8 -4 0 $\frac{16}{3}$ x

Here, the patterns immediately identify D as correct. I went ahead and did step 2 to practice my point above.

① $|3x+4| > 20$

② $|3x+4| > 20$

$3x+4 = 20$ $3x+4 = -20$
$\quad -4 \quad -4$ $\quad -4 \quad -4$

$\dfrac{3x}{3} = \dfrac{16}{3}$ $\dfrac{3x}{3} = \dfrac{-24}{3}$

$x = \dfrac{16}{3}$ $x = -8$

$-8 \quad \dfrac{16}{3}$

2. Which of the following is the graph of the inequality $|x| \leq 3$?

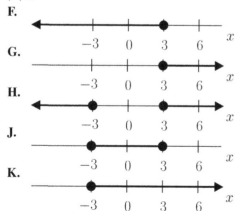

F.
   -3 0 3 6 x

G.
   -3 0 3 6 x

H.
   -3 0 3 6 x

J.
   -3 0 3 6 x

K.
   -3 0 3 6 x

① $|x| \leq 3$

② $|x| \leq 3$

$x = 3 \quad | \quad x = -3$

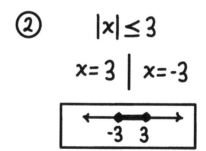

$-3 \quad 3$

3. Which of the following graphs shows the solution set for the inequality $2x + 5 \geq 7$?

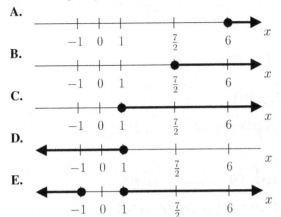

4. Which of the following is that of the solution set to the graph below?

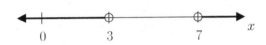

F. $x < 3$ or $x > 7$
G. $x < 3$ and $x > 7$
H. $x > 3$ or $x < 7$
J. $x > 3$ and $x < 7$
K. $x \neq 3$ and $x \neq 7$

5. Which of the following is the graph of the inequality $|2x - 5| < 11$?

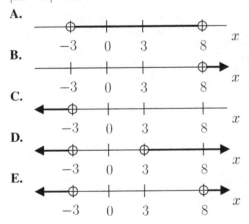

6. Which of the following number line graphs represents the solution set of the equation $x^2 + 4 = 5$?

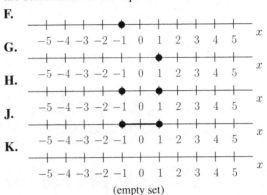

(empty set)

7. Which of the following graphs illustrates the solution set for the system of inequalities $2x + 6 < 10$ and $9x > -6$?

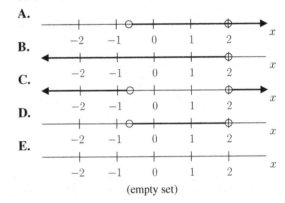

(empty set)

8. Which of the following number line graphs represents the solution set of the equation $x^2 + 5 = 4$?

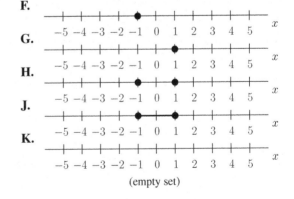

(empty set)

① Given a clear shape comparison,

$$\frac{\text{small shape}}{\text{big shape}} = \frac{\text{small shape}}{\text{big shape}}$$

② If shapes are unclear, find related sides by writing equal angles above each other.

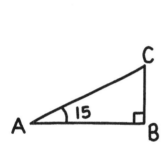
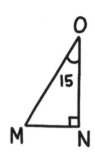
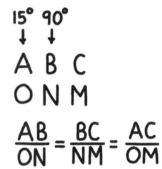

15° 90°
↓ ↓
A B C
O N M

$$\frac{AB}{ON} = \frac{BC}{NM} = \frac{AC}{OM}$$

1. Shown below are similar triangles $\triangle ABC$ and $\triangle DEF$ with $\angle A \cong \angle D$ and $\angle B \cong \angle E$. The length of $\overline{AB}$ is 4 inches, $\overline{BC}$ is 7 inches, and $\overline{DE}$ is 3 inches. What is the length, in inches, of $\overline{EF}$?

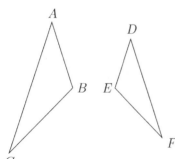

A. $3\frac{5}{7}$
B. 5
C. $5\frac{1}{4}$
D. 6
E. $9\frac{1}{3}$

A B C
↓ ↓
D E F

$$\frac{AB}{DE} = \frac{BC}{EF}$$

$$\frac{4}{3} = \frac{7}{x} \quad \text{cross multiply!}$$

$$4x = 21$$

$$x = \boxed{\frac{21}{4}}$$

This is a useful method to go from equal angles to corresponding sides in similar triangles. Notice how AB ends up over DE, and BC over EF, which is how we translate them into the fractions below.

2. The sides of one triangle are 7, 13, and 15 inches long, respectively. In a second triangle similar to the first, the shortest side is 8 inches long. To the nearest tenth of an inch, what is the length of the longest side of the second triangle?

F. 6.4

G. 9.2

H. 11.6

J. 14.4

K. 17.1

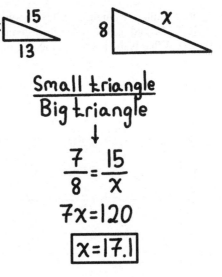

$$\frac{\text{Small triangle}}{\text{Big triangle}}$$
↓
$$\frac{7}{8} = \frac{15}{x}$$
$$7x = 120$$
$$\boxed{x = 17.1}$$

3. In the figure below, $\overline{BE}$ is parallel to $\overline{CD}$. If $\overline{AB} = 3$, $\overline{BC} = 5$, and $\overline{CD} = 12$, what is the length of $\overline{BE}$?

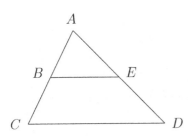

A. 4

B. 4.5

C. 6

D. 7

E. 7.5

$$\frac{\text{Small triangle}}{\text{Big triangle}}$$
↓
$$\frac{AB}{AC} = \frac{BE}{CD}$$
$$\frac{3}{8} = \frac{x}{12}$$
$$36 = 8x$$
$$\boxed{4.5} = x$$

Look out that the BIG triangle here, ACD, uses all of side AC and not just BC or AB. The overlapping similar triangles are tricky - it can be easier to redraw ACD and ABE separately.

4. Shown below are similar triangles $\triangle ABC$ and $\triangle ZYX$ with $\angle A \cong \angle Z$ and $\angle B \cong \angle Y$. The given lengths are in meters. What is the length, in meters, of $\overline{YZ}$?

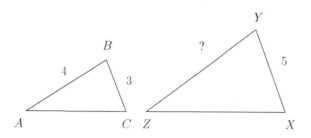

   F. 6
   G. $6\frac{2}{3}$
   H. $7\frac{1}{3}$
   J. 8
   K. $8\frac{1}{2}$

5. In the figure below, triangle ABC is similar to triangle DEF. Angles A, B, and C measure $45°$, $60°$, and $75°$, respectively. What is the measure of $\angle F$?

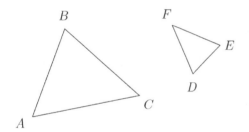

   A. $15°$
   B. $45°$
   C. $60°$
   D. $75°$
   E. $135°$

6. Given the 2 similar right triangles shown below, with side lengths given in inches, what is the area of the smaller triangle, in square inches?

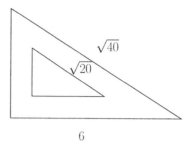

   F. $\sqrt{2}$
   G. 2
   H. $2\sqrt{2}$
   J. $2\sqrt{3}$
   K. 3

7. In the figure shown below, $\overline{AB}$ is parallel to $\overline{DE}$. The given lengths are in meters. What is the length, in meters, of $\overline{AB}$?

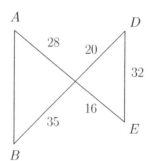

   A. $44\frac{4}{5}$
   B. 48
   C. $54\frac{1}{2}$
   D. 56
   E. 70

8. A triangle has side lengths 3, 4, and 6 inches. The shortest side of a similar, second, triangle is 9 inches. What is the length of the longest side, in inches, of the second triangle?

 F. 9
 G. 15
 H. 18
 J. 39
 K. 44

9. Veronica is standing next to a 22 foot tree on a sunny day. Veronica measures the shadow of the tree on the ground to be 40 feet long. If Veronica's shadow is 10 feet long at the same moment she measures the tree's shadow, how tall is Veronica?

 A. 5 feet 5 inches
 B. 5 feet 6 inches
 C. 7 feet 5 inches
 D. 6 feet 5 inches
 E. 18 feet 2 inches

10. Consider right triangles ABC and EDC in the figure below. If $\overline{AE} = 10$, $\overline{EC} = 5$, and $\overline{AB} = 9$, what is the length of $\overline{DC}$?

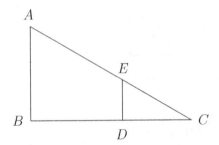

 F. 4
 G. 5
 H. 7
 J. 9
 K. 10

11. A triangle has side lengths 7, 8, and 12 inches. The shortest side of a similar, second, triangle is 10 inches. Approximately what is the perimeter, to the nearest inch, of the second triangle?

 A. 10
 B. 19
 C. 27
 D. 39
 E. 45

12. In the figure below, points D, E, and F are the midpoints of their respective sides of triangle ABC. A circle is inscribed in ABC and another is circumscribed about triangle ABC. Which of the following statements is NOT true about the figure?

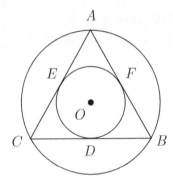

 F. $\overline{AB} = \overline{BC}$
 G. The radius of the inner circle is half the radius of the outer circle
 H. Triangle ABC is equilateral
 J. The ratio of the perimeter of triangle ABC to the length of $\overline{AB}$ is 3:1
 K. The area of the inner circle is half the area of the outer circle

	Points	Functions	
	(a b)	$y = F(x)$	$y = ax^2$
Translate by (5,9)	(a+5, b+9)	$y-9 = F(x-5)$	$y-9 = a(x-5)^2$
Reflect over x-axis	(a, -b)	$y = -F(x)$	$y = -ax^2$
Reflect over y-axis	(-a, b)	$y = F(-x)$	$y = a(-x)^2$
Dilate around the origin by a factor of 3	(3a, 3b)	$y = 3F(x)$	$y = 3a(x)^2$

1. In the standard (x, y) coordinate plane, the graph of $y = x^2$ is shifted 6 units up and 3 units right. Which of the following is an equation of the translated graph?

   A. $y = (x + 6)^2 + 3$
   B. $y = (x - 6)^2 + 3$
   C. $y = (x - 3)^2 - 6$
   D. $y = (x + 3)^2 - 6$
   E. $y = (x - 3)^2 + 6$

$y = x^2$ translate by (3,6)

↓

$$\boxed{y = (x-3)^2 + 6}$$

2. In the standard (x, y) coordinate plane, the point $P(1, -4)$ is reflected across the y axis to point P'. Which of the following gives the coordinates of point P'?

   F. $(-4, -1)$
   G. $(-1, -4)$
   H. $(-1, 4)$
   J. $(1, 4)$
   K. $(4, 1)$

P(1,-4)

↓

reflect across y-axis

↓

$$\boxed{P'(-1,-4)}$$

Translation is the most common problem type. The key is to remember that the sign is Inversely related.

That means a negative moves values Right or Up, and a Positive moves them Left or Down.

3. Point D lies on the coordinate plane at $(7, -3)$. What would the new coordinates be after a reflection over the x-axis?

A. $(7, 3)$

B. $(7, -3)$

C. $(-3, 7)$

D. $(-7, 3)$

E. $(-7, -3)$

4. Which of these represents the equation of the function $f(x) = x^2$, shifted 3 units down and 5 units to the left?

F. $f(x) = (x + 5)^2 - 3$

G. $f(x) = (x - 5)^2 - 3$

H. $f(x) = (x + 5)^2 + 3$

J. $f(x) = (x - 3)^2 + 5$

K. $f(x) = (x + 3)^2 - 5$

5. The line $y = \dfrac{2}{3}x + 5$ is reflected over the y-axis. What is the new equation of this line?

A. $y = \dfrac{2}{3}x - 5$

B. $y = -\dfrac{2}{3}x + 5$

C. $y = -\dfrac{2}{3}x - 5$

D. $y = \dfrac{3}{2}x + 5$

E. $y = -\dfrac{3}{2}x + 5$

6. The line $y = -\dfrac{5}{2}x + 7$ is reflected over the x-axis. What is the new equation of the line?

F. $y = \dfrac{2}{5}x + 7$

G. $y = \dfrac{5}{2}x + 7$

H. $y = \dfrac{5}{2}x - 7$

J. $y = -\dfrac{2}{5}x + 7$

K. $y = -\dfrac{2}{5}x - 7$

7. In the standard (x, y) coordinate plane, the point $Q(-6, -1)$ is reflected across the x axis to point Q'. Which of the following gives the coordinates of point Q'?

A. $(-6, 1)$

B. $(-1, -6)$

C. $(1, 6)$

D. $(6, -1)$

E. $(6, 1)$

8. In the standard (x, y) coordinate plane, the point $M(3, 4)$ undergoes the translation $T_{(x-3, y-4)}$ to point M'. Which of the following gives the coordinates of point M'?

F. $(0, 0)$

G. $(0, 8)$

H. $(6, 0)$

J. $(6, 8)$

K. $(9, -16)$

9. Grid lines are shown at 1-unit intervals in the standard (x, y) coordinate plane below. Some of the 1-by-1 squares are shaded in the grid. What is the least number of additional 1-by-1 squares that must be shaded so the total shaded region will be symmetric about the y-axis?

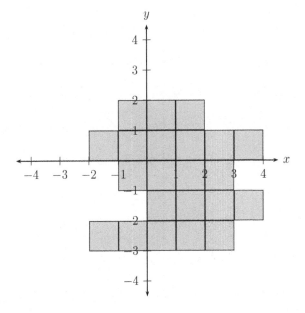

A. 6

B. 8

C. 9

D. 10

E. 12

10. The graphs of $f(x)$ and $g(x)$ are shown in the standard (x, y) coordinate plane below. Which of the following expressions represents $g(x)$ in terms of $f(x)$?

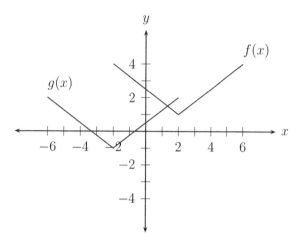

    F. $g(x) = f(x - 2) + 4$
    G. $g(x) = f(x - 4) + 2$
    H. $g(x) = f(x + 2) + 4$
    J. $g(x) = f(x + 4) + 2$
    K. $g(x) = f(x + 4) - 2$

11. The function shown below represents a transformation of the graph $y = |x|$ in the standard (x, y) coordinate plane. Which of the following equations represents this graph?

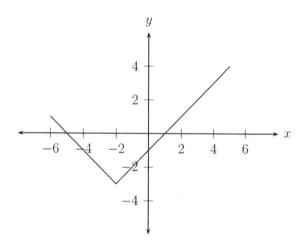

    A. $y = |x - 3| - 2$
    B. $y = |x - 2| - 3$
    C. $y = |x + 2| - 3$
    D. $y = |x + 2| + 3$
    E. $y = |x + 3| + 2$

12. Two parabolas are graphed in the standard (x, y) coordinate plane below. Which of the following is the line of symmetry for these two parabolas?

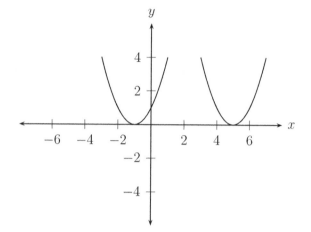

    F. $y = 2$
    G. $y = -2$
    H. $x = -2$
    J. $x = 2$
    K. $y = x$

3.10 CHAPTER THREE QUIZ

It's about time to get CUMULATIVE! Multi step problems can only happen with plenty of materials, so be sure to review Chapters 1 & 2 as well.

Feeling good? Try doing 1 - 10 in 10 minutes, and then 11 - 20 in another 10 minutes. This will stop momentum and train you to focus on command.

For Geometry problems, ALWAYS draw a diagram!

For the Chapter quiz and really every problem all the time, continue to take a moment to identify the problem type and topic. Simply writing down a major related formula can often solve a problem immediately :)

CHAPTER THREE QUIZ
20 Minutes — 20 Questions

DIRECTIONS: Solve each problem, choose the correct answer, and then fill in the corresponding oval on your answer document.

Do not linger over problems that take too much time. Solve as many as you can; then return to the others in the time you have left for this test.

You are permitted to use a calculator on this test. You may use your calculator for any problems you choose, but some of the problems may be best done without using a calculator.

Note: Unless otherwise stated, all of the following should be assumed.
1. Illustrative figures are NOT necessarily drawn to scale.
2. Geometric figures lie in a plane.
3. The word *line* indicates a straight line.
4. The word *average* indicates arithmetic mean.

---

1. What is the value of x in the matrix equation shown below?

$$k \begin{bmatrix} 1 & 0 \\ 0 & -1 \end{bmatrix} = \begin{bmatrix} 3 & x \\ 0 & -3 \end{bmatrix}$$

   A. -1
   B. 0
   C. 3
   D. 12
   E. 15

2. Daniella's cat Stella, who is now 4 years old, has been increasing in weight since she was born. Stella's weight in pounds can be approximately modeled by the equation $W(t) = 0.04t^2 - 0.5t + 0.9$, where t is Stella's age in months. Based on this model, to the nearest pound, how heavy was Stella when she was 2 years and 6 months old?

   F. 7 pounds
   G. 9 pounds
   H. 16 pounds
   J. 20 pounds
   K. 22 pounds

3. What is the value of b in the system of equations below?

$$6a + b = 20$$
$$a + b = 12.5$$

   A. -4
   B. 1.5
   C. $7/4$
   D. $20/3$
   E. 11

Use the following information to answer questions 4-6

Bobby used to earn \$20 per week for his allowance until he made the following deal with his parents: For the next 20 weeks, his allowance will start at \$0.01 per week and then double each week.

4. Which of the following functions represents the amount Bobby will receive in a given week (w)?

   F. $f(w) = 0.01(2)^w$
   G. $f(w) = 0.01(2)^{w-1}$
   H. $f(w) = 2(0.01)^w$
   J. $f(w) = 2(0.01)^{w-1}$
   K. $f(w) = \dfrac{2}{0.01^{w-1}}$

5. How much will Bobby earn, to the nearest cent, in his new deal during week 18?

   A. \$655.35
   B. \$1,310.72
   C. \$2,621.44
   D. \$5,242.88
   E. \$7,023.23

6. For which week will Bobby's earnings for his new deal surpass those from his old deal?

   F. Week 10
   G. Week 11
   H. Week 12
   J. Week 16
   K. His new deal will not surpass his old deal

7. At the Fright Nights Haunted House, tickets for children cost \$7 each and tickets for adults cost \$11 each. On Saturday night, a total of 488 tickets were sold, earning a total of \$4,496. How many adult tickets were sold?

   A. 218

   B. 240

   C. 270

   D. 288

   E. 310

8. In the standard (x, y) coordinate plane, the point $A(-2, 3)$ is reflected across the x axis to point A'. Which of the following gives the coordinates of point A'?

   F. $(2, 3)$

   G. $(2, -3)$

   H. $(-2, 3)$

   J. $(-2, -3)$

   K. $(-3, -2)$

9. Triangle ABC has sides of length 6, 12 and 17 and is similar to triangle WXY. If the shortest side of triangle WXY is 18, what is the perimeter of triangle WXY?

   A. 44

   B. 46

   C. 64

   D. 88

   E. 105

10. At a local office supplies store, Doreen submits the following order for new packs of sticky notes:

Color	Number of sticky notes per pack	Price per pack
Green	100	\$3
Yellow	120	\$4

   Doreen will order a total of 30 packs of sticky notes for a total price of \$105. If g represents the number of packs of green sticky notes and y represents the number of packs of yellow sticky notes, which of the following systems of equations can be solved to correctly yield the total number of sticky notes in Doreen's order?

   F. $g + y = 30 \qquad 3g + 4y = 105$

   G. $g + y = 30 \qquad 100g + 120y = 105$

   H. $g + y = 105 \qquad 3g + 4y = 30$

   J. $3g + 4y = 30 \qquad 100g + 120y = 105$

   K. $3g + 4y = 105 \qquad 100g + 120y = 30$

Use the following information to answer questions 11-13

Three students, Arthur, George, and Frank, are all saving for a school trip. During the first week, each of them saved \$8. Arther chose to increase the amount he saved by the same amount each week. George increased the amount he saved by the same factor each week. Frank decided, after an arbitrary increase the first week, to make the amount he saved a function of the previous two weeks. The first four weeks of savings (starting with their initial amounts) are listed in the table below.

	Week 1	Week 2	Week 3	Week 4
Arthur	8	16	24	32
George	8	12	18	27
Frank	8	13	21	34

11. Which of the following statements regarding the table is NOT true?

   A. Arthur's progression is an arithmetic sequence

   B. George's progression is a geometric sequence

   C. Frank's progression is neither arithmetic nor geometric

   D. The common difference of Arthur's sequence is 8

   E. The common difference of George's sequence is 1.5

12. Which of the following functions can be used to determine the amount Arthur saved, a, for any week, n, after week 1?

   F. $a_n = \frac{13}{8}(a_{n-1})$

   G. $a_n = a_{n-1} + \frac{5}{8}(a_{n-1})$

   H. $a_n = 8 + a_{n-1}$

   J. $a_n = 1.5(a_{n-1})$

   K. $a_n = a_{n-1} + a_{n-2}$

13. If their goal was to each save \$200, who accomplished that goal first and how long did it take them?

   A. Arthur - 26 weeks

   B. George - 9 weeks

   C. George - 10 weeks

   D. Frank - 8 weeks

   E. Frank - 9 weeks

14. Which of the following augmented matrices represents the system of linear equations below?

$$2x - 3y = 7$$
$$x - 5y = -2$$

F. $\begin{bmatrix} 2 & -3 & | & 7 \\ 1 & -5 & | & -2 \end{bmatrix}$

G. $\begin{bmatrix} 2 & -3 & | & -7 \\ 1 & -5 & | & 2 \end{bmatrix}$

H. $\begin{bmatrix} 2 & -3 & | & 7 \\ -1 & 5 & | & -2 \end{bmatrix}$

J. $\begin{bmatrix} 2 & 3 & | & -7 \\ -1 & -5 & | & 2 \end{bmatrix}$

K. $\begin{bmatrix} 2 & -3 & | & 7 \\ -1 & -5 & | & -2 \end{bmatrix}$

15. In the line segment shown below, the length of $\overline{AB}$ is 22 cm and the length of $\overline{BC}$ is 18 cm. What is the distance, in centimeters, between the midpoint of $\overline{AB}$ and the midpoint of $\overline{AC}$?

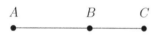

A. 9
B. 11
C. 18
D. 20
E. 40

16. Which of the following graphs shows the solution set for the inequality $3x + 7 \geq -8$?

F.
G.
H.
J.
K.

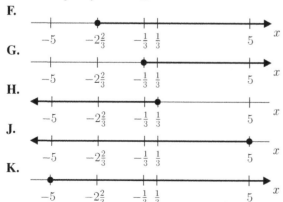

Use the following information to answer questions 17-20.

A vertical flagpole with a length of 21 feet casts a shadow on the ground based on the position of the sun. At 12:00 P.M., the angle, θ, that the suns rays make with the flagpole is $0°$. In time, θ increases at a rate of $15°$ per hour until it reaches a value of $90°$ at 6:00 P.M.

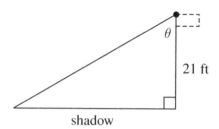

shadow

17. When the length of the shadow is 35 feet long, how long of a shadow will a 6' tall person standing next to the flagpole cast?

A. 3.6'
B. 8'
C. 10'
D. 20'
E. 25'

18. Which of the following expressions represents the length of shadow as a function of θ?

F. $21 \sin \theta$
G. $21 \tan \theta$
H. $21 \cos \theta$
J. $\dfrac{21}{\sin \theta}$
K. $\dfrac{21}{\tan \theta}$

19. To the nearest degree, what would be the value of θ when the distance from the top of the flagpole to the end of the shadow was twice the distance from the top of the flagpole to the ground?

A. 27°
B. 30°
C. 45°
D. 60°
E. 64°

20. At 3:00 P.M., the length of the shadow will be equal to the length of the flagpole. At what time will the length of the shadow be twice as large as the length of the flagpole?

   F. 4:14 P.M.
   G. 4:46 P.M.
   H. 5:14 P.M.
   J. 5:46 P.M.
   K. 6:00 P.M.

———————————

MID-BOOK REVIEW

The math that appears in Chapters 1-3 shows up all over the ACT. Sometimes the problems are true to the types we have given you so far, while others can be more deceiving or complex.

This cumulative review is intended to completely solidify your foundation before moving into the concepts of the second half. As such, take this mid-test as an accuracy test more than a timed speed situation.

In fact, I would recommend treating it as an open-book exam! You're welcome to flip through to find the proper solution concept for a problem, but be sure to take notes in the process. It's better to use proper technique when solving tough problems and build the proper connections in your memory :)

MID-BOOK REVIEW
60 Minutes — 60 Questions

DIRECTIONS: Solve each problem, choose the correct answer, and then fill in the corresponding oval on your answer document.

Do not linger over problems that take too much time. Solve as many as you can; then return to the others in the time you have left for this test.

You are permitted to use a calculator on this test. You may use your calculator for any problems you choose,

but some of the problems may be best done without using a calculator.

Note: Unless otherwise stated, all of the following should be assumed.
1. Illustrative figures are NOT necessarily drawn to scale.
2. Geometric figures lie in a plane.
3. The word *line* indicates a straight line.
4. The word *average* indicates arithmetic mean.

---

1. What is $|(6)(-7) - (5)(-3)|$?
   A. -57
   B. -27
   C. 9
   D. 27
   E. 57

2. If $\sqrt{x + 1} = 9$, what is the value of x?
   F. -4
   G. 2
   H. 4
   J. 80
   K. 82

3. A six player game involves a bag that contains 6 red, 5 green, 11 yellow, and 8 blue marbles. Players will take turns selecting a marble from the bag without replacement. If a player selects a green marble they lose the game. What is the probability that the first person who selects a marble will NOT lose the game?
   A. $^5/_6$
   B. $^1/_6$
   C. $^1/_5$
   D. $^3/_4$
   E. $^1/_4$

4. Michael opens up a new box of crayons. There are 80 total crayons in the box, of which Michael likes to use 20. What percent of the crayons does Michael like to use?
   F. 20%
   G. 25%
   H. 50%
   J. 60%
   K. 80%

5. If $x = 9$ and $y = 12$ when $\dfrac{x}{4} = \dfrac{k}{y}$, what is the value of y when $x = 6$?

   (Note: k is a constant)
   A. 8
   B. 9
   C. 18
   D. 24
   E. 27

6. If the midpoint of $\overline{AB}$ is $(1, 5)$ and Point B is at $(9, 10)$, then what are the coordinates of point A?
   F. $(5, 7.5)$
   G. $(4, 2.5)$
   H. $(7, 0)$
   J. $(0, 7)$
   K. $(-7, 0)$

Questions 7-9 pertain to the following information.

Sophia had an average test grade of 88 and a median score of 85 on five tests in a marking period. She received a different score on each of her five tests. All test scores were whole numbers out of a possible 100 points and Sophia did not earn a perfect score on any test.

7. Her teacher allowed her to do test corrections for each test, which added 5 points to each of her tests. How would adding 5 points to each test score affect her mean and median?

    A. The mean will increase by 5, but the median will stay the same
    B. The median will increase by 5, but the mean will stay the same
    C. Both the median and mean will increase by 5
    D. Both the mean and median will stay the same
    E. The median will increase by 5 and the mean will increase by 25

8. Which of the following *must* be true in order to explain the difference between her median and mean?

    F. The two test scores above 85 were farther from the median than the two tests below 85
    G. The two test scores above 85 were closer to the median than the two tests below 85
    H. Her highest score was farther from the median than her lowest score
    J. Her highest score was closer the median than her lowest score
    K. She only had one test below the median and two tests above the median

9. Suppose l, m, and h, represent Sophia's lowest, median, and highest test scores, respectively. If Sophia scored an 83 and a 93 on two of the five exams, and $l < 83 < m < 93 < h$, what is the maximum range of Sophia's scores?

    A. 3
    B. 10
    C. 16
    D. 19
    E. 20

10. Awesome Automotive Company has an option for customers to buy the car that they are leasing at its current market value. The market value of a car depreciates at a rate of 20% per year. If a customer has a three-year lease on a new car that is worth $35,000$, how much will it cost to buy the car once the lease ends?

    F. $280
    G. $14,000
    H. $17,080
    J. $17,920
    K. $60,480

11. What is the distance between the points $(1, 2)$ and $(3, 4)$ in the standard (x, y) coordinate plane?

    A. 1
    B. $\sqrt{2}$
    C. 2
    D. $2\sqrt{2}$
    E. 8

12. In the figure below, $m\angle A = m\angle C = 80°$ and $m\angle D = m\angle E = 130°$. What is the measure of $\angle B$?

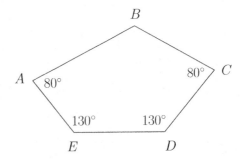

    F. 50°
    G. 60°
    H. 120°
    J. 130°
    K. 150°

13. Which of the following augmented matrices represents the system of equations shown below?

$$6x + 11y = 43$$
$$4x - 7y = -43$$

A. $\begin{bmatrix} 6 & 11 & | & 43 \\ 4 & -7 & | & -43 \end{bmatrix}$

B. $\begin{bmatrix} 6 & 11 & | & -43 \\ 4 & -7 & | & 43 \end{bmatrix}$

C. $\begin{bmatrix} 6 & 11 & | & 43 \\ 4 & 7 & | & -43 \end{bmatrix}$

D. $\begin{bmatrix} 6 & -7 & | & 43 \\ 4 & 11 & | & -43 \end{bmatrix}$

E. $\begin{bmatrix} 6 & 11 & | & -43 \\ 4 & 7 & | & 43 \end{bmatrix}$

14. Mrs. Sanders likes to assign group projects to her students. On Monday, she divided her entire class evenly into groups of 3. On Tuesday, she divided her entire class evenly into groups of 5. On Wednesday, two students were absent so she divided the class evenly into groups of 4. What is the minimum number of students that Mrs. Sanders could have in her class?

F. 15
G. 20
H. 28
J. 30
K. 60

15. To the nearest inch, what is the perimeter of a square that has a diagonal 17 inches long?

A. 12 inches
B. 24 inches
C. 48 inches
D. 68 inches
E. 96 inches

16. Which of the following expressions is equivalent to $(-7x^2 + 8x - 12) - (-3x^2 + 8x + 5)$?

F. $-4x^2 - 17$
G. $-4x^2 + 16x + 7$
H. $-10x^2 - 16x - 7$
J. $10x^2 + 17$
K. $21x^2 + 64x - 60$

17. On his first day at the gym, Tripp completes 50 reps on the bench press. His goal is to complete 5 more reps each day than the previous day. If Tripp meets but does not exceed his goal, how many reps will he complete on the 20th day?

A. 95
B. 100
C. 145
D. 150
E. 200

18. If the probability of picking a red marble from a bag is $5/18$ and there are 54 total marbles in the bag, how many marbles in the bag are NOT red?

F. 13
G. 15
H. 36
J. 39
K. 49

19. The force, F, in Newtons, of an object is modeled by the equation:

$$F = \frac{md}{t^2}$$

where m is the mass of the object in kilograms, d is the distance the object is from collision in meters, and t is the amount of time the object travels in seconds. What is the mass of an object that hits a wall with a force of 1000 Newtons after traveling 200 meters in 5 seconds?

A. 8 kg
B. 25 kg
C. 125 kg
D. 625 kg
E. 8,000 kg

20. If $\dfrac{(x^a)^b}{x^c x^d} = x^y$, which of the following represents the value of y in terms of a, b, c & d?

F. $ab - c - d$
G. $ab - cd$
H. $a + b - c - d$
J. $ab - c + d$
K. $\dfrac{ab}{c + d}$

21. Winnie has a circular patch of land 100 ft in diameter. She wants to fence off a garden that divides the path of land into two identical regions, as shown in the figure below. If she will fence off the entire perimeter of the garden, how many feet of fencing will she need?

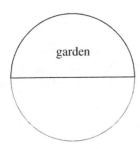

garden

A. $25\pi + 100$
B. $25\pi + 200$
C. $50\pi + 100$
D. $50\pi + 200$
E. $100\pi + 200$

22. Which of the following is NOT true about the infinite geometric sequence $-16, 8, -4, 2 \dots$?

F. The common ratio is $-1/2$
G. The 8th term is $1/8$
H. If n is odd, then the term a_n is negative
J. Each term is smaller than the previous term
K. The sum of the series is $-10\ 2/3$

23. A school play usually charges $8 admission for a performance, but last night offered $5 tickets for anybody who brought a donation for the school clothing drive. For the performance, the 450 seat auditorium was filled to capacity. If the proceeds from the tickets totaled $2,637, how many people did NOT make a donation to the clothing drive?

A. 56
B. 90
C. 129
D. 165
E. 321

24. In isosceles right triangle WXY, $\sin \angle WXY = \dfrac{\sqrt{2}}{2}$. Which of the following is equal to $\tan \angle WXY$?

F. 1
G. $\sqrt{2}$
H. 2
J. $2\sqrt{2}$
K. $3\sqrt{2}$

25. Which value of x would make the equation $3^x(3^7) = 27$ true?

A. -5
B. -4
C. -3
D. 2
E. 4

26. If $g(x) = \dfrac{-2x^2 + 7x + 4}{2x + 1}$, what is $g(-4)$?

F. -113
G. -8
H. 0
J. 8
K. 113

27. If a rectangular garden has a perimeter of 140 feet and an area of 1,000 square feet, what are the dimensions of the garden?

A. 20 ft by 50 ft
B. 25 ft by 40 ft
C. 25 ft by 45 ft
D. 30 ft by 40 ft
E. 35 ft by 35 ft

28. If $\sin A$ in the figure below is $\frac{8}{17}$, what is $\tan A$?

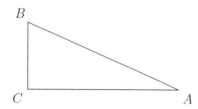

F. $\frac{8}{15}$

G. $\frac{8}{17}$

H. $\frac{15}{17}$

J. $\frac{15}{8}$

K. $\frac{17}{8}$

29. What values of g and h, respectively, would result in the system of equations below having perpendicular lines?

$$4x + 7y = 17$$
$$gx + hy = 37$$

A. $(-7, 4)$

B. $(-4, 7)$

C. $(\ 7, 4)$

D. $(\ 8, 14)$

E. $(\ 14, -4)$

30. In a certain marketing class, the final grades for each student is determined by deleting the lowest and highest test scores, then averaging the remaining test scores. Deyanira took every test and achieved the following scores: 71, 82, 86, 91, 98, 73, and 94. Which of the following is closest to Deyanira's final grade in the marketing class?

F. 81

G. 85

H. 87

J. 89

K. 91

31. If both x and y are integers such that the greatest common factor of x^2y^5 and x^4y is 175, which of the following could be the value of y?

A. 5

B. 7

C. 25

D. 35

E. 49

32. The figure below shows the graph of the function $f(x) = x^2$. Which of the following graphs shows the graph of $-f(x+3) + 2$?

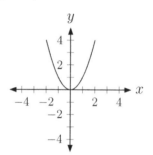

F.   **J.**

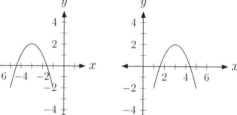

G.   **K.**

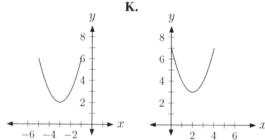

H.

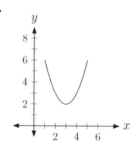

Questions 33-35 pertain to the following information.

At a grocery store the cost of several items can be found on the table below.

Item	Cost
Bananas	$0.75 each
Cheese	$3 per pound
Lemons	5 for $2
Bacon	$5 per pound
Chips	$1.50 per bag*

(*Note: This item has a 7% sales tax.)

33. If Dale purchased 8 bananas, 2.5 pounds of cheese, 3 lemons, and 4 pounds of bacon, what was the total cost of Dale's purchase?

  A. $32.43

  B. $34.70

  C. $37.13

  D. $39.50

  E. $42.27

34. If Jack has $15 to spend, how many bags of chips could he buy?

  F. 8

  G. 9

  H. 10

  J. 11

  K. 12

35. Which of the following scenarios could be represented by the matrix equation below?

$$4 \begin{bmatrix} \$0.75 & \$0.40 \\ \$3 & \$5 \end{bmatrix} = \begin{bmatrix} \$3 & \$1.60 \\ \$12 & \$20 \end{bmatrix}$$

  A. The cost of buying 4 of each of the first 4 items

  B. The average cost of the 4 items that do not require sales tax

  C. The amount of refund that would be issues after returning one of each of 4 items

  D. The amount that 5 items would cost if tax were not included

  E. The unit price of 4 items

36. Which expression is equivalent to $\dfrac{2}{\sqrt{3}+7}$?

  F. $\dfrac{14 - 2\sqrt{3}}{-46}$

  G. $\dfrac{14 - 2\sqrt{3}}{-4}$

  H. $\dfrac{-14 + \sqrt{3}}{-46}$

  J. $\dfrac{-14 + 2\sqrt{3}}{-46}$

  K. $\dfrac{-14 + 2\sqrt{3}}{-4}$

37. When Bonnie did her inventory at the three locations of her clothing store, she found that she had 110 shirts, 70 pairs of pants, and 40 hats in stock at her main street location, 65 shirts, 40 pairs of pants, and 25 hats in stock at her uptown location, and 125 shirts, 90 pairs of pants, and 85 hats in stock at her downtown location. If Bonnie sells shirts for $30, pants for $50 and hats for $10, what is the total value of her inventory?

  A. $6,500

  B. $16,100

  C. $19,500

  D. $20,500

  E. $32,500

38. A ladder is placed against a building so that the top of the ladder rests 30 feet from the base of the building. If the angle formed by the ladder and the ground has a cosine of $\dfrac{5}{13}$, to the nearest foot, how long is the ladder?

  F. 13 feet

  G. 25 feet

  H. 28 feet

  J. 33 feet

  K. 38 feet

39. If Terry deposits $500 into an account that earns 7% annual interest, approximately how many years will it take until the amount of money in his account is double his initial deposit?

  A. 1.3

  B. 7.1

  C. 9.9

  D. 10.2

  E. 35

40. A barn contains pigs and chickens. Farmer Jim Bob asked his smart aleck farm-hand Charlie to count the number of pigs, p, and the number of chickens, c, in the barn. Charlie reported that he counted a total of 237 animals who have a total of 652 legs. Which of the following system of equations could farmer Jim Bob use to determine how many pigs and chickens are in his barn?

F. $p - c = 237$
$4p - 2c = 652$

G. $p + c = 237$
$2p + 4c = 652$

H. $p + c = 652$
$4p + 2c = 237$

J. $p + c = 237$
$4p + 2c = 652$

K. $p + c = 652$
$2p + 4c = 237$

41. The ratio of the circumference of Circle A to the circumference of Circle B is 3:1. If Circle B has a radius of 8, what is the diameter of Circle A?

A. $^{11}/_3$
B. 24
C. 48
D. 144
E. 512

42. Katie constructed a garden in the shape of a right triangle where the shortest side is half the length of the longest side. If the sum of the shortest and longest sides is 33 feet, what is the length, in feet, of the remaining side?

F. 11
G. $11\sqrt{3}$
H. 22
J. $22\sqrt{2}$
K. $22\sqrt{3}$

43. When going on vacation, Joey packed 3 pairs of pants, 5 shirts, 2 pairs of shoes and 4 hats, one of which is his lucky Seattle Pilots hat. How many different combinations of outfits (consisting of 1 of each item) could Joey wear that would include wearing his Seattle Pilots hat?

A. 4
B. 14
C. 30
D. 60
E. 120

44. Which of the following equations gives a function $f(x)$ such that $f(3) = 21$?

F. $f(x) = 3x + 18$
G. $f(x) = x + 21$
H. $f(x) = 2x^2 + 3$
J. $f(x) = 3x + 21$
K. $f(x) = 3x^2 + 21$

45. Josephine turns on the weather report and hears, "And there is a $^3/_{10}$ chance it will rain on Sunday. For all you aspiring mathematicians out there, that means that there is a $^1/_5$ chance that we will get rain on *both* days this weekend." Even though Josephine missed Saturday's forecast, what could she deduce are the chances of rain on Saturday?

A. $^3/_{50}$
B. $^1/_{10}$
C. $^1/_2$
D. $^2/_3$
E. $^7/_{10}$

46. What values of x are not in the domain of

$$f(x) = \frac{1}{x^3 - 25x}?$$

F. 0 only
G. 5 only
H. 0 and 5
J. -5 and 5
K. $-5, 0,$ and 5

47. At the end of the week, Hector emptied his pockets and found out that he had \$7.50 in change. If he has twice as many dimes as pennies, three more nickels than dimes, and three more dimes than quarters, how many quarters does Hector have?

A. 8
B. 11
C. 12
D. 17
E. 22

48. Which of the following expressions is a factor of the quadratic expression $2x^2 - 7x - 15$?

F. $2x - 3$
G. $x - 5$
H. $x - 3$
J. $2x + 5$
K. $x + 5$

49. If the system of equations shown below has no solution, which of the following numbers can NOT be the value of c?

$$8x + 14y = 36$$
$$12x + 21y = 9c$$

A. 2
B. 3
C. 6
D. 9
E. 54

50. A medical helicopter is located 18 kilometers west and 23 kilometers north of St. Mary's Hospital. There is an emergency 7 kilometers south and 3 kilometers west of St. Mary's Hospital. How far, in kilometers, is the straight-line distance the helicopter is from the emergency?

F. $12\sqrt{5}$
G. $12\sqrt{6}$
H. $16\sqrt{2}$
J. $15\sqrt{5}$
K. $17\sqrt{5}$

51. Al, Bob, and Carl are all standing 75 feet apart from one another. To the nearest foot, if Bob runs in a straight line towards Carl, what is the closest he will get to Al?

A. 75 feet
B. 65 feet
C. 53 feet
D. 43 feet
E. 38 feet

52. In rectangle $EDCB$ below, $m\angle ABC = 32°$, $\overline{BC} = \overline{AB}$, and $\overline{BC} = 13$. To the nearest whole number, what is the length of line segment $\overline{AD}$?

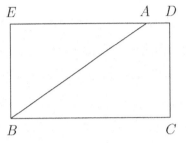

F. 2 cm
G. 3 cm
H. 7 cm
J. 11 cm
K. 13 cm

53. In the figure below, $\overline{AB}$ is parallel to $\overline{GH}$ and points C, D, E, and F are the midpoints of $\overline{AG}, \overline{BH}, \overline{CG}$ & $\overline{DH}$ respectively. If $\overline{AB}$ is 15 cm long and $\overline{GH}$ is 9 cm long, how long is $\overline{EF}$?

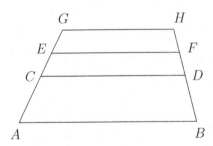

A. 6 cm
B. 10.5 cm
C. 11 cm
D. 12 cm
E. 13.5 cm

54. If $\dfrac{2x - y}{x + 2y} = \dfrac{2}{3}$, what is the value of $\dfrac{x}{y}$?

   F. $\dfrac{1}{7}$

   G. $\dfrac{1}{4}$

   H. $\dfrac{4}{7}$

   J. $\dfrac{5}{2}$

   K. $\dfrac{7}{4}$

55. Heron's formula for the area of a triangle, A, is:

$$A = \sqrt{S(S - a)(S - b)(S - c)}$$

where $S = \dfrac{a + b + c}{2}$, and a, b, c represent the three side lengths of the triangle. To the nearest square unit, what is the area of the triangle below?

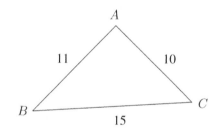

   A. 18
   B. 21
   C. 36
   D. 55
   E. 82

56. A group of students placed 5 rabbits in a closed population and monitored the number of rabbits, R, over a period of several months, m. They discovered that the number of rabbits after any given month can be modeled using the equation $R_m = R_{m-1} + R_{m-2}$. The data for the first 3 months appear in the table below:

Months	Rabbits
0	5
1	8
2	13
3	21

How many rabbits will be in the population at the end of the 6th month?

   F. 45
   G. 55
   H. 73
   J. 89
   K. 144

57. In Circle B shown below, $\overline{AB}$ is 6 units long, $\overline{AD}$, which is perpendicular to $\overline{BC}$, is 4 units long, and central angle ABC is measured in degrees. What is the length of $\overset{\frown}{AC}$ in terms of π?

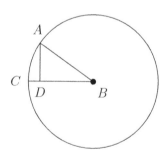

   A. $\dfrac{\pi \sin^{-1}(2/3)}{30}$

   B. $\dfrac{\pi \cos^{-1}(2/3)}{30}$

   C. $\dfrac{\pi \tan^{-1}(2/3)}{30}$

   D. $\dfrac{\pi \sin^{-1}(2/3)}{60}$

   E. $\dfrac{\pi \tan^{-1}(2/3)}{60}$

58. What is the point of intersection of the medians of the triangle whose vertices are $(1, 2)$, $(4, 8)$ and $(7, -4)$?

F. $(4, 2)$

G. $(2.5, 5)$

H. $(4, -1)$

J. $(5.5, -2)$

K. $(12, 6)$

59. Consider the equation for standard deviation, σ, below:

$$\sqrt{\frac{(v_1)^2 + (v_2)^2 + ... + (v_n)^2}{n}}$$

where v_1 represents the difference of the first element and the mean of the set, v_2 represents the difference of the second element and the mean of the set, and so forth, and n is the total amount of elements in the set. What is the standard deviation, to the nearest tenth, of the following 5 numbers: 88, 75, 83, 77, and 82?

A. 1.4

B. 4.6

C. 5.2

D. 9.0

E. 10.3

60. Col. Jessep is the captain of a submarine. He has two torpedoes remaining, each with a $1/3$ chance of hitting the battle ship that is his target. If either torpedo hits, the battle ship will sink. If Col. Jessep fires both torpedoes, what are the chances that he sinks the battleship?

F. $2/6$

G. $2/3$

H. $1/9$

J. $4/9$

K. $5/9$

Welcome to Chapter 4.
We're about to get VISUAL.

This chapter focuses on challenging Geometry concepts. The idea is after this chapter, they Won't be challenging anymore :)

With shapes, there is a lot of overlap between concepts. Sometimes this is useful, as you can use a tool you learned earlier. Sometimes it can be distracting, launching you in the incorrect direction at first.

Identification of problem type will be more important than ever.

Memorization of various formulae is always frustrating to students, but time and accuracy are in limited supply when taking the ACT. Having all those Area and Volume formulae on call will speed testing up mightily.

So far I have in my notes :

- Always draw a diagram
- Write a formula immediately
- Look for special triangles
- Label the goal and/or type

I love it! Keep up the good work :)

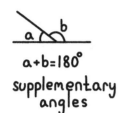

a+b=180°
supplementary
angles

c = d
vertical
angles

e=f
alternate
interior

h+g+i=180°
triangle angles
add to 180°

1. Consider the figure below where points D, A, and C are collinear. What is the measure of $\angle BAC$?

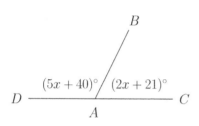

$(5x+40)+(2x+21)=180$
$7x+61=180$
$-61 \quad -61$
$\dfrac{7x}{7}=\dfrac{119}{7}$
$x=17$
$2(17)+21=\boxed{55}$

A. $17°$
B. $34°$
C. $55°$
D. $72°$
E. $125°$

These problems often have a ton of simple steps. Start filling out whatever you can see and keep it moving - the pieces always connect eventually!

2. In the figure below $\overline{AB} = \overline{BC}$, $\angle B = 40°$, $\angle D = 50°$, and $\angle F = 55°$. What is the measure of $\angle G$?

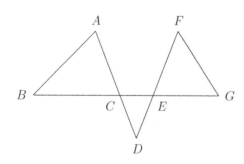

① triangle angles add to 180°

$40+x+x=180$
isosceles
$2x=140$
$x=70$

② vertical angles, then another △ → 180°
$70+50+x=180$
$x=60$

③ vertical angles, △ → 180°
$60+55+x=180$
$x=\boxed{65}$

F. $55°$
G. $60°$
H. $65°$
J. $70°$
K. $75°$

3. Consider the figure below where points P, M, and O are collinear, $\angle PMN = 6x + 10$ and $\angle NMO = 4x$. What is the degree measure of the larger angle?

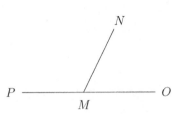

   A. $28°$
   B. $54°$
   C. $68°$
   D. $98°$
   E. $112°$

4. In the figure below lines l and m are $\parallel$ and $\overline{AB} = \overline{BC} = \overline{AC}$. What is the measure of the exterior angle at $\angle C$?

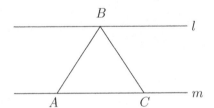

   F. $55°$
   G. $70°$
   H. $110°$
   J. $120°$
   K. $140°$

5. In the figure below $\overline{AB} = \overline{BC} = \overline{CD} = \overline{DE}$ and $\angle BAC = 20°$. What is the measure of $\angle CDE$?

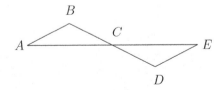

   A. $20°$
   B. $40°$
   C. $110°$
   D. $140°$
   E. $160°$

6. In the figure below $l \parallel m$, $\angle EDC = 51°$, and $\overline{AB} = \overline{BC}$. What is the measure of $\angle B$?

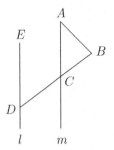

   F. $78°$
   G. $68°$
   H. $51°$
   J. $48°$
   K. $40°$

7. In the figure below $FG \parallel BE$, $\overline{HA} = \overline{AC}$, and $\overline{DC}$ bisects $\angle ACE$. If the measure of $\angle AHC = 60°$, What is the measure of $\angle CDG$?

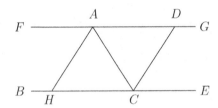

   A. $120°$
   B. $110°$
   C. $70°$
   D. $55°$
   E. $40°$

8. In the figure below $l \parallel m$, the exterior angle at B is $a°$, and line $\overline{AC}$ bisects $\angle DCB$. In terms of a, what *must* be the measure of $\angle CAB$?

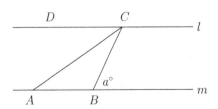

   F. $\frac{1}{2}a°$
   G. $(180 - a)°$
   H. $a°$
   J. $(180 - \frac{1}{2}a)°$
   K. $(90 - \frac{1}{2}a)°$

9. In the figure below lines a and b are $\parallel$, L lies on both $\overline{JN}$ and $\overline{KM}$, and two angle measures are given. What is the measure of $\angle JKL$?

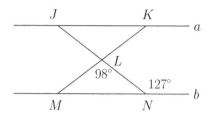

A. $47.5°$

B. $29°$

C. $45°$

D. $53°$

E. $98°$

10. In the figure below lines a, b, and c are parellel, and lines l and m are parallel. One angle is given. What is the sum of angles x and y?

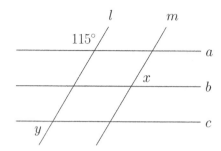

F. $230°$

G. $180°$

H. $140°$

J. $130°$

K. $65°$

11. Consider the figure below where $\angle ABC = 129°$, the slope of $\overline{AB} = 0$ and $\overline{DC}$ is a vertical line. What is the measure of $\angle DCB$?

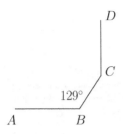

A. 61°
B. 90°
C. 129°
D. 141°
E. 151°

12. In the figure below, a laser beam emanating from Point Q bounces off three mirrors and hits a sensor. The angle the laser hits the mirror is equivalent to the angle the laser reflects off. If the laser bounces off the first mirror at a $40°$ angle, the first mirror intersects the second mirror at a $80°$ angle and the second mirror intersects the third at a $75°$ angle, what is the measure of $\angle x$?

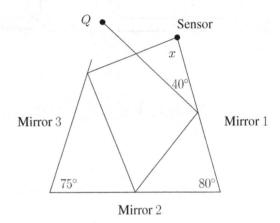

F. 45°
G. 60°
H. 70°
J. 80°
K. 110°

A triangle has 180 degrees. A rectangle has 360 degrees. A pentagon has 540 degrees. Notice the pattern?

The general formula for degrees in a polygon is (sides - 2) times 180 degrees

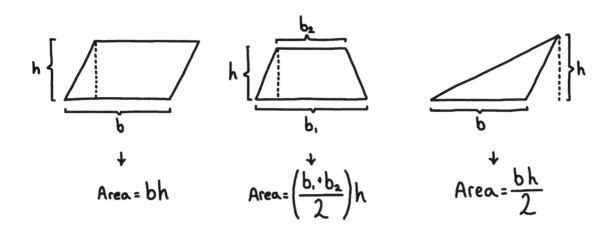

$$\text{Area} = bh \qquad \text{Area} = \left(\frac{b_1 + b_2}{2}\right)h \qquad \text{Area} = \frac{bh}{2}$$

1. What is the area of the triangle with vertices $A(-3, 5)$, $B(-3, -3)$, and $C(3, 2)$?

$$\text{Area} = \frac{bh}{2}$$

$$\text{Area} = \frac{6 \cdot 8}{2} = \boxed{24}$$

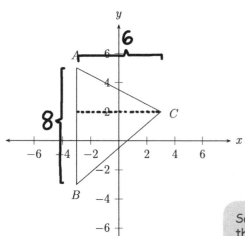

Sometimes shapes are given as coordinates. In these cases, "height" will be the difference of the y-coordinates if the base is horizontal, or x-coordinates if the base is vertical.

A. 18

B. 20

C. 24

D. 40

E. 48

2. In quadrilateral $ABCD$ shown below, angles B and C are right angles, side AB is 5 inches, side BC is 4 inches, and side DC is 8 inches. In square inches, what is the area of quadrilateral $ABCD$?

$$\text{Area} = \frac{(b_1 + b_2)}{2} h$$

$$\text{Area} = \left(\frac{5+8}{2}\right) 4 = \boxed{26}$$

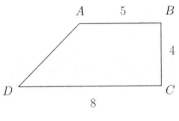

F. 12
G. 25
H. 26
J. 32
K. 36

Remember that the "midline" of a trapezoid is the average of the bases! So if that's given, you're halfway to area already.

Uh, midline?

A midline is a point that connects the midpoints of the two slanted sides.

3. What is area of parallelogram $ACED$, if $AD = 7$, $AB = 4$, and $AC = 5$?

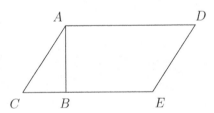

A. 6
B. 12
C. 27
D. 28
E. 35

4. Consider rectangle $ABCD$, where $\overline{CD} = 5$ and $\overline{AC} = 13$. What is the area of rectangle $ABCD$?

F. 12
G. 34
H. 47
J. 60
K. 65

5. Consider parallelogram $ABCD$ shown below. The length of $\overline{AB}$, $\overline{ED}$, and $\overline{AD}$, is 10, 12, and 13, respectively. $\overline{ED}$ is perpendicular to $\overline{AB}$. What is the area of parallelogram $ABCD$?

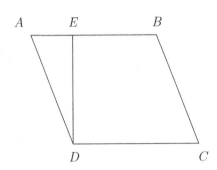

A. 60 ft^2
B. 65 ft^2
C. 120 ft^2
D. 130 ft^2
E. 156 ft^2

6. What is the area of the trapezoid $ACED$ below if $AD = 15, AC = 6, CE = 13$, and altitude $CB = 12$?

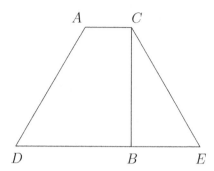

   F. 54
   G. 156
   H. 168
   J. 180
   K. 195

7. A square and a rectangle have the same area. The width of the rectangle is 14 inches and the length of the rectangle is 56 inches. What is the length, in inches, of a side of the square?

   A. $2\sqrt{14}$
   B. 14
   C. 21
   D. 28
   E. 112

8. The perimeter of trapezoid $ABCD$ is 39, If $AD = 10$ and $BC = 7$, what is the area of the trapezoid?

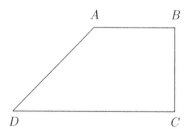

   F. 17
   G. 47.5
   H. 70
   J. 77
   K. 154

9. Emmy is tiling the floor of her kitchen, which is in the shape of a rectangle, as shown in the figure below. The sides of the kitchen are $x + 1$ and $x - 2$. Which of the following expressions gives the perimeter of Emmy's kitchen in terms of x?

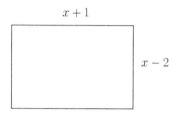

   A. $2x - 1$
   B. $4x - 2$
   C. $4x + 4$
   D. $5x + 1$
   E. $x^2 - x - 2$

10. In the figure below, all sides are in feet and all interior non-reflexive angles are 90°. What is the area, in square feet, of the figure?

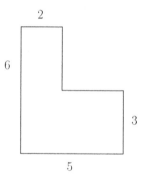

   F. 15
   G. 18
   H. 21
   J. 27
   K. 30

11. The swimming pool at Thompson High School is in the shape of a rectangle. It has a width of 50 feet and an area of 4000 square feet. The school wants to lay a strip of tile along the two shorter sides of the pool and one of the longer sides, leaving one longer side not tiled. What is the length of tile, in feet, the school should buy?

    A. 80
    B. 100
    C. 180
    D. 260
    E. 800

12. Square $ABEF$ and parallelogram $ACDG$ are shown in the figure below, with side lengths given in centimeters. What is the ratio of the area of $ABEF$ to the area of $ACDG$?

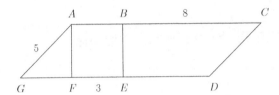

    F. 9:64
    G. 9:121
    H. 3:8
    J. 3:11
    K. 3:5

13. A hexagon has 1 side of length y cm, 3 sides of length $(y - 4)$ cm each, 1 side of length 8 cm, and 1 side of length $2y$ cm. What is the perimeter, in centimeters, of the hexagon?

    A. $6y - 4$
    B. $6y + 4$
    C. $5y + 4$
    D. $5y - 6$
    E. $4y + 4$

14. In the parallelogram below, Points A, B, C, and D are located at $(6, 7), (-1, 7), (-3, 2)$ and $(4, 2)$ respectively. What is the area of the parallelogram?

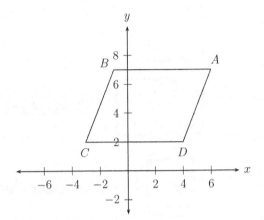

    F. 25
    G. 29
    H. 35
    J. 49
    K. 51

15. Stevens High School plans to lay a foundation of concrete for a new outdoor patio, which is in the shape of the figure shown below. 1 bag of concrete will pave an area of 500 square meters. How many bags of concrete should the school buy to fully pave the patio?

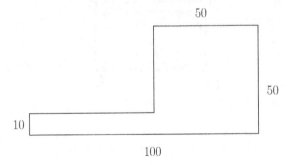

    A. 1
    B. 3
    C. 4
    D. 6
    E. 10

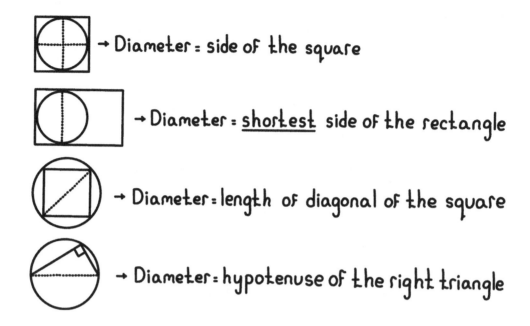

→ Diameter = side of the square

→ Diameter = __shortest__ side of the rectangle

→ Diameter = length of diagonal of the square

→ Diameter = hypotenuse of the right triangle

1. A circle with center K is inscribed inside rectangle $ABCD$, as shown in the figure below. If $\overline{AB} = 12$ inches and $\overline{BC} = 4$ inches, what is the area, in square inches, of the circle with center K?

   A. 4π
   B. 8π
   C. 12π
   D. 16π
   E. 48π

Diameter = 4
↓
radius = 2
↓
$A = \pi r^2 = \pi(2)^2 = \boxed{4\pi}$

2. Four congruent circles are set inside square $ABCD$ such that each circle is tangent to exactly two sides of the square and exactly two adjacent circles. If each circle has an area of 16π square feet, what is the area, in square feet, of square $ABCD$?

   F. 16
   G. 32
   H. 64
   J. 128
   K. 256

$2D$ = side of square (s)

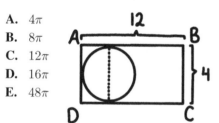

① Find diameter.

$\dfrac{\pi r^2}{\pi} = \dfrac{16\pi}{\pi}$

$\sqrt{r^2} = \sqrt{16}$

$r = 4 \rightarrow D = 8$

② Find square area.

$S = 2D = 2(8) = 16$

$S = 16$

$S^2 = 16^2 = \boxed{256}$

3. Square $WXYZ$ is inscribed inside circle with center O. If the square has an area of 100 square inches, what is the area, in square inches, of circle O?

   A. 10π

   B. 20π

   C. 25π

   D. 50π

   E. 100π

4. A circle is tangent to 3 sides of a rectangle whose dimensions are 8×15. What is the area of the circle?

   F. 16π

   G. 56.25π

   H. 64π

   J. 120π

   K. 225π

5. Rectangle $BCDE$ is inscribed in circle A, where $\overline{ED} = 5$ and diameter $\overline{BD} = 13$. To the nearest tenth, what is the area of circle A?

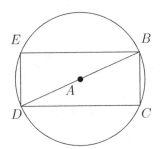

   A. 42.3

   B. 60

   C. 132.7

   D. 169

   E. 530.9

6. Four congruent circles are set inside square $WXYZ$ such that each circle is tangent to exactly two sides of the square and exactly two adjacent circles. If each circle has an area of 36π square feet, what is the area, in square feet, of square $ABCD$?

   F. 64

   G. 128

   H. 256

   J. 512

   K. 576

7. Square $ABCD$ is inscribed inside a circle with center O. If square $ABCD$ has an area of 36 square inches, what is the area, in square inches, of circle O?

   A. 6π

   B. 9π

   C. 18π

   D. 36π

   E. 72π

8. In the figure below, circle A with radius 5 is inscribed in a square. What is the area of the square?

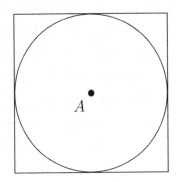

   F. 25

   G. 31

   H. 40

   J. 25π

   K. 100

9. A cube is inscribed in a sphere with side lengths of 10 centimeters. What is the radius, in centimeters, of the sphere?

   A. $5\sqrt{2}$

   B. $5\sqrt{3}$

   C. $10\sqrt{2}$

   D. $10\sqrt{3}$

   E. 10π

Three dimensions? Uh oh ...

Hint : the SPACE DIAGONAL of a cube is equal to (side)*(the square root of 3). Combine that with the two dimensional method :)

① Draw the largest possible rectangle around the given shape.

② Subtract the area of all of the smaller shapes that are outside of the shaded region and inside of the largest shape.

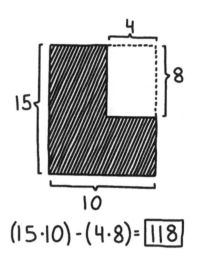

$(15 \cdot 10) - (4 \cdot 8) = \boxed{118}$

Big shape - Small shape = Shaded Area

1. To make a project in art class, Marcus needs to cut four holes through a piece of wood. Each hole is in the shape of a circle with a radius of 1 inch, and the piece of wood has dimensions 6 inches by 11 inches, as shown in the figure below. What will be the remaining area of wood after Marcus bores out the four holes?

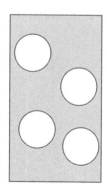

Big shape - Small shape

Rectangle - Circle x 4

$LW - 4(\pi r^2)$

$(6)(11) - 4(\pi (1)^2)$

$\boxed{66 - 4\pi}$

A. $34 - 8\pi$
B. $34 - 4\pi$
C. $34 + 8\pi$
D. $66 - 4\pi$
E. $34 - 2\pi$

I often find "Big Shape - Small Shape" is all you really need.

2. Rectangle $ABCD$ has a width of 5 feet and a length of 12 feet and is inscribed in circle O, as shown in the figure below. What is the area, in square feet, of the shaded region?

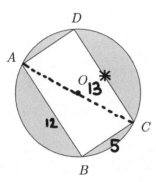

F. $60 - 42.25\pi$
G. $60 - 26\pi$
H. $26\pi - 60$
J. $42.25\pi - 60$
K. 110

Big shape - Small shape

Circle - Rectangle

* $\pi r^2 - LW$

$\pi(6.5)^2 - (5)(12)$

$$\boxed{42.25\pi - 60}$$

* Diameter = Diagonal of ABCD

$r = \dfrac{d}{2} = \dfrac{13}{2} = 6.5$

3. What is the area of the shaded region bound by, the lines $-7x + 2y = -21$, $-3x + 5y = 20$, the x-axis, and the y-axis?

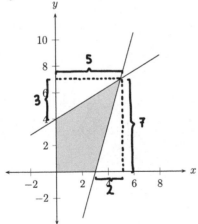

A. 15
B. 20.5
C. 25
D. 30.5
E. 35

Big shape - Small shape

Rectangle - 2 Triangles

$(5 \cdot 7) - \left[\left(\dfrac{5 \cdot 3}{2} \right) + \left(\dfrac{2 \cdot 7}{2} \right) \right] = \boxed{20.5}$

4. Circle O is inscribed inside square $ABCD$, as shown below. If square $ABCD$ has an area of 25 cm^2 what is the area of the shaded region?

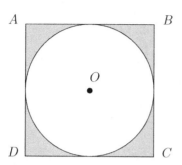

F. $25 - 6.25\pi$

G. $25 - 10\pi$

H. $25 - 25\pi$

J. $6.25 - 25\pi$

K. $6.25 - 5\pi$

6. Square $KLMN$ is inscribed in circle O and has an area of 64 meters^2, as shown in the figure below. What is the area of the shaded region?

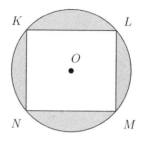

F. $64 - 32\pi$

G. $64 - 16\pi$

H. $16\pi - 64$

J. $32\pi - 64$

K. $128\pi - 64$

5. In the figure below, circle O has diameter $\overline{AC}$ with length 16. B is the midpoint of $\overline{OC}$. What is the area of the shaded region?

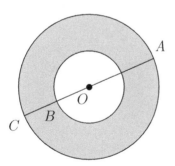

A. 16π

B. 48π

C. 64π

D. 80π

E. 192π

7. In the figure below, equilateral triangle ABC has sides of length 16, and each of the three congruent circles has an area of approximately 25. To the nearest tenth, what is the area of the *non*-shaded region?

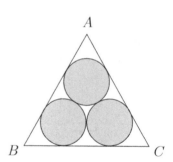

A. 20.4

B. 35.9

C. 53.0

D. 107.6

E. 110.9

8. In the rectangle $ABCD$ below, $AE = 3$, $AD = 7$, and $CD = 10$. What is the area of the shaded region?

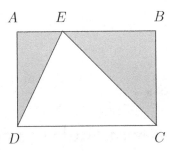

F. 10.5
G. 24.5
H. 35
J. 42
K. 70

9. In triangle ABC below, X, Y, and Z are the midpoints of $\overline{AB}$, $\overline{BC}$, and $\overline{AC}$ respectively. If the area of triangle XYZ is 17, what is the area of the shaded region?

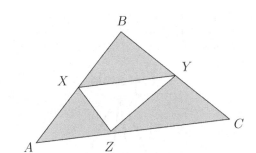

A. 17
B. 34
C. 51
D. 68
E. 85

10. What is the area of the shaded region bound by $-x + 2y = 6$, $5x + 3y = 35$, the x-axis, and the y-axis?

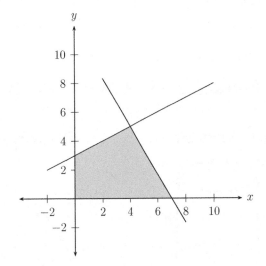

F. 20.3
G. 22.5
H. 23
J. 23.5
K. 30

A lot of these problems use special triangles and inscribed shapes to give a deceivingly small amount of information up front. Use the relationships you know to build out sides, values, and relationships before you dive into finding area.

Volume = Area of the base × Height

Surface area = sum of the area of all of the sides

Cylinder

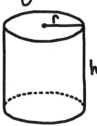

Base = circle

$$V = (\pi r^2) h$$

$$SA = 2(\pi r^2) + \pi dh$$

Triangular prism

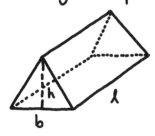

Base = triangle

$$V = \left(\frac{bh}{2}\right) \ell$$

Rectangular prism

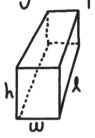

Base = rectangle

$$V = (\ell w) h$$

If the shape goes to a point, $\frac{1}{3}$ volume.

Cone

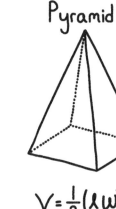

$$V = \frac{1}{3}(\pi r^2) h$$

Pyramid

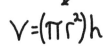

$$V = \frac{1}{3}(\ell w) h$$

1. A swimming pool in the shape of a right rectangular prism has a length of 13 feet and a width of 15 feet. The volume of water in the pool is 2,650 cubic feet. To the nearest foot, what is the depth of water in the pool?

   A. 14
   B. 16
   C. 17
   D. 19
   E. 22

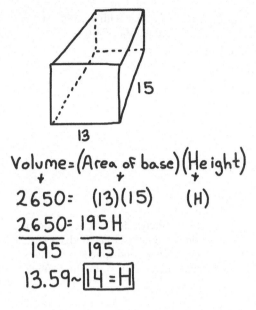

Volume = (Area of base)(Height)

$2650 = (13)(15) \quad (H)$

$2650 = 195H$

$\dfrac{2650}{195} = \dfrac{195H}{195}$

$13.59 \sim \boxed{14 = H}$

2. In Nandini's engineering class, students are designing a wooden ramp, as shown in the figure below. She is assigned to paint every side of the ramp green. What is the total surface area Nandini will have to paint?

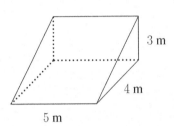

3 m

4 m

5 m

   F. 30m^2
   G. 39m^2
   H. 47m^2
   J. 51m^2
   K. 72m^2

Surface Area = Sum of the area of all the sides

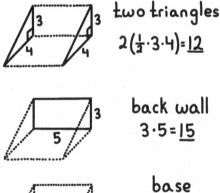

two triangles

$2(\frac{1}{2} \cdot 3 \cdot 4) = \underline{12}$

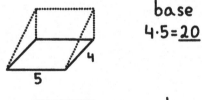

back wall

$3 \cdot 5 = \underline{15}$

base

$4 \cdot 5 = \underline{20}$

top

$5 \cdot 5 = \underline{25}$

$\underline{SA} = 12 \cdot 15 \cdot 20 \cdot 25 = \boxed{72}$

Make sure you don't miss any sides ...

... or count ones they aren't asking for! Some problems ignore a base or sides, so check in with that before you choose an answer.

3. What is the surface area of a box with a width of 1.5 feet, a length of 4 feet, and a height of 3 feet?
   A. 8.5 square feet
   B. 18 square feet
   C. 32 square feet
   D. 40 square feet
   E. 45 square feet

4. Each edge of a cube is 3 inches long. Each edge of a second cube is triple the length of each edge of the first cube. The volume of the second cube is how many cubic inches bigger than the volume of the first cube?
   F. 27
   G. 81
   H. 512
   J. 702
   K. 729

5. The volume of a right circular cylinder is 35 cm³. If the cylinder is 5 cm tall, what is the approximate radius of the base of the cylinder, to the nearest tenth of a centimeter?
   A. 1.1 cm
   B. 1.5 cm
   C. 2.2 cm
   D. 2.7 cm
   E. 7.0 cm

6. Darryl is filling a rectangular pool with water. The pump Darryl uses can pour water at a rate of 2 cubic feet per minute. If the pool is 20 feet long, 15 feet wide, and 6 feet deep, how long will it take Darryl to fill the pool, in hours?
   F. 10 hours
   G. 15 hours
   H. 18 hours
   J. 600 hours
   K. 900 hours

7. If a 2 liter bottle of lemonade is poured into a cylindrical pitcher whose diameter is 5 inches, approximately how many inches high, at minimum, must the pitcher be in order to for the entire bottle to fit in the pitcher? (Note: 1 liter = 61 cubic inches)
   A. 6 inches
   B. 7 inches
   C. 8 inches
   D. 9 inches
   E. 10 inches

8. A pyramid has a square base with lengths of 8 inches. If the slant height of the pyramid is $4\sqrt{3}$ inches long, what is the sum of all eight edges of the pyramid?
   F. 8
   G. 12
   H. $32\sqrt{3}$
   J. 64
   K. $64\sqrt{3}$

9. A rectangular pool is filled with $10,000$ ft^3 of water and has a maximum depth of 10 feet. If the dimensions of the floor of the pool are 50 feet by 30 feet, what is the depth of the water in the pool?

A. $6^2/_3$ feet
B. 10 feet
C. 20 feet
D. $33^1/_3$ feet
E. 125 feet

10. What is the lateral area of a cone whose height is 24 inches and whose circumference is 14π inches?

(Note: the slant height, s, of a cone is given by the formula $s = \sqrt{r^2 + h^2}$ and the lateral surface area of a cone, L, is given by the formula $L = \pi rs$)

F. 168π
G. 175π
H. 336π
J. 350π
K. $4{,}375\pi$

11. An ant walks along the edge of a spherical basketball, following the line shown below. When the ant returns to its starting point, it has a walked a distance of 9π feet. What is the surface area of the sphere?

(Note: the surface area, SA, of a sphere is given by $SA = 4\pi r^2$, where r is the sphere's radius.)

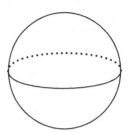

A. 9π square feet
B. 20.5π square feet
C. 36π square feet
D. 81π square feet
E. 121.5π square feet

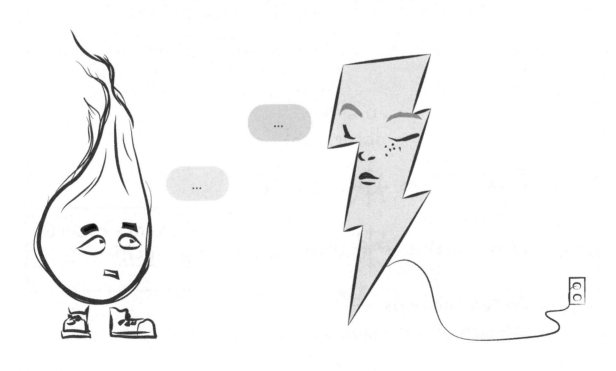

$$y = ax^2 + bx + c$$

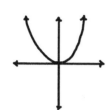

big a squishes

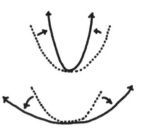

fraction a widens

negative a flips

y-intercept $= c$

The letters a, b, c are essential to most Quadratic calculations. To find them, first solve for y. The coefficients of each power of x are what we are looking for. Note that "x" does not come with the a, b, or c!

Above, the values for a & c give us clues to the shape of the graph. Below, all 3 values allow us to find solutions.

In addition, the Vertex of a parabola sits at x = -b/2a. Plug that point back into the equation to find the y-value of the Vertex.

$$D = b^2 - 4ac$$

˙discriminant˙

$D > 0 \rightarrow 2$ real solutions $\quad (x-r)(x-s) = 0$

$D = 0 \rightarrow 1$ real solution $\quad (x-r)^2 = 0$

$D < 0 \rightarrow$ no real solutions
(solutions are imaginary)

Quadratic formula
$$x = \frac{-b \pm \sqrt{D}}{2a}$$

1. The equation of the two parabolas graphed on the standard (x, y) coordinate plane below are $f(x) = mx^2 + nx + p$ and $g(x) = ax^2 + bx + c$. Which of the following *must* be true?

→ Given that g(x) is wider than F(x) a must be smaller than m.

$\boxed{a < m}$

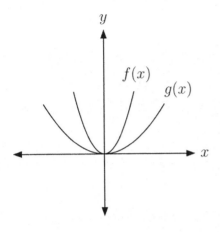

A. $b < n$

B. $m = a$

C. $m < a$

D. $a < m$

E. $b = n$

2. How many zeros, real and/or imaginary, does $f(x)$, function below, contain?

$$f(x) = 3x^2 + 6x + 3$$

a = 3

b = 6

c = 3

$D = b^2 - 4ac$

$D = 6^2 - 4 \cdot 3 \cdot 3$

$D = 0 \rightarrow$ $\boxed{\text{one real root}}$

F. 1 real zero

G. 2 real zeros

H. 2 imaginary zeros

J. 1 real and 1 imaginary zero

K. $f(x)$ contains no zeros

3. The graph of the function $f(x)$ is shown in the figure below. Which of the following is true about the roots of $f(x)$?

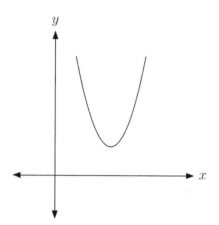

    A. $f(x)$ has two real, non-zero roots
    B. $f(x)$ has one real root and one imaginary root
    C. $f(x)$ has one positive real root and one negative real root
    D. $f(x)$ has two imaginary roots
    E. $f(x)$ has one negative imaginary root

4. The function $w(x)$ is defined for all values of x such that $w(x) = 4x^2 - 5x - 2$. Which of the following is true about the zeros of $w(x)$?
    F. $w(x)$ has 2 imaginary zeros
    G. $w(x)$ has 1 real zero
    H. $w(x)$ has 2 real zeros
    J. $w(x)$ has 1 real zero and 1 imaginary zero
    K. $w(x)$ has no zeros

5. The graphs of two functions, $f(x) = px^2 + m$ and $g(x) = rx^2 + t$ are shown in the figure below. Which of the following statements is true about the values of p, m, r and t?

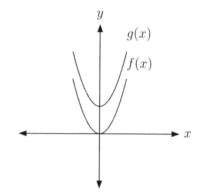

    A. $m > t$
    B. $m < t$
    C. $p > r$
    D. $p < r$
    E. $\dfrac{p}{m} > \dfrac{r}{t}$

6. Two functions, $p(x)$ and $r(x)$ are defined such that $p(x) = 2x^2 + 5x - 2$ and $r(x) = -6$. For what real values of x does $p(x) = r(x)$?
    F. $x = -4$ only
    G. $x = -4$ and $x = -2$
    H. $x = -3$ and $x = 0$
    J. $x = -2$ and $x = 2$
    K. There are no real values of x such that $p(x) = r(x)$

7. What is the x-coordinate of the vertex of the parabola $g(x) = 2x^2 - 9x + 10$?

A. $x = -\dfrac{9}{4}$

B. $x = -\dfrac{10}{9}$

C. $x = \dfrac{9}{4}$

D. $x = \dfrac{9}{2}$

E. $x = 5$

8. The graph of the function $g(x)$ is shown in the standard (x, y) coordinate plane below. Which of the following functions could be equal to $g(x)$?

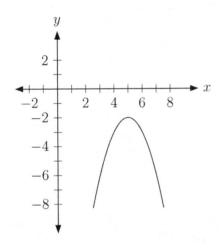

F. $-2x^2 - 10x - 14$
G. $-x^2 - 10x + 12$
H. $-x^2 + 10x - 27$
J. $x^2 - 10x + 27$
K. $2x^2 + 6x + 2$

9. The functions $f(x) = x^2$ and $g(x) = ax^2 + bx + c$ are shown in the standard (x, y) coordinate plane below. Which of the following statements *must* be true about the values of a, b and c?

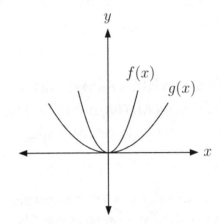

A. $c > 1$
B. $a < 1$
C. $a > 1$
D. $b > c$
E. $-\dfrac{b}{2a} > 1$

10. If the function $h(x) = ax^2 - 6x + 3$ has 1 real solution, what must be true about the value of a?

F. $a = -3$
G. $a = 1$
H. $a = 3$
J. $a = 6$
K. $a = 12$

<u>Given:</u> Trig Function

<u>Goal</u>: Another trig function

example:
$\tan(x) = \dfrac{a}{b}$. What is $\sin(x)$?

① Draw a right triangle. Write out SOHCAHTOA, and fill in the right triangle accordingly.

SOHCAH⟨TOA⟩

$\tan(x) = \dfrac{\text{opposite}}{\text{adjacent}} = \dfrac{a}{b}$

② Use the Pythagorean theorem to solve for the missing side.

$a^2 + b^2 = c^2$

$\sqrt{a^2 + b^2} = c$

③ Use SOHCAHTOA to solve for the trig function needed.

⟨SOH⟩CAHTOA

$\sin(x) = \dfrac{\text{opposite}}{\text{hypotenuse}} = \boxed{\dfrac{a}{\sqrt{a^2 + b^2}}}$

---

1. In right triangle XYZ, $\sin X = \dfrac{x}{z}$. What is the value of $\cos X$??

   A. $\dfrac{x}{y}$

   B. $\dfrac{y}{x}$

   C. $\dfrac{y}{z}$

   D. $\dfrac{z}{x}$

   E. $\dfrac{z}{y}$

① ⟨SOH⟩CAHTOA

$\sin(x) = \dfrac{O}{H} = \dfrac{x}{z}$

② We don't need to use the Pythagorean theorem.

③ SOH⟨CAH⟩TOA

$\cos(x) = \dfrac{A}{H} = \boxed{\dfrac{y}{z}}$

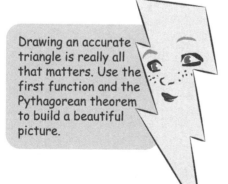
Drawing an accurate triangle is really all that matters. Use the first function and the Pythagorean theorem to build a beautiful picture.

2. If $\tan \theta = \dfrac{a}{b}$, what is the value of $\cos \theta$ in terms of a and b?

F. $\dfrac{a}{\sqrt{a^2 + b^2}}$

G. $\dfrac{b}{\sqrt{a^2 + b^2}}$

H. $\dfrac{\sqrt{a^2 + b^2}}{a}$

J. $\dfrac{\sqrt{a^2 + b^2}}{b}$

K. $\dfrac{b}{a}$

① SOHCAH(TOA)

a ◺ b $\tan(\theta) = \dfrac{O}{A} = \dfrac{a}{b}$

② $a^2 \cdot b^2 = c^2$

$\sqrt{a^2 \cdot b^2} = c$

③ SOH(CAH)TOA

a ◺ b

$\cos(\theta) = \dfrac{A}{H} = \boxed{\dfrac{b}{\sqrt{a^2 \cdot b^2}}}$

---

3. If $\sin A = \dfrac{8}{17}$, what is $\tan A$?

A. $\dfrac{8}{17}$

B. $\dfrac{15}{17}$

C. $\dfrac{8}{15}$

D. $\dfrac{15}{8}$

E. $\dfrac{17}{8}$

4. If $\cos A = \dfrac{5}{13}$, what is $\sin A$?

F. $\dfrac{5}{13}$

G. $\dfrac{12}{13}$

H. $\dfrac{5}{12}$

J. $\dfrac{13}{5}$

K. $\dfrac{12}{5}$

5. Consider right triangle ABC with hypotenuse $\overline{AB}$. If $\tan B = \dfrac{4}{3}$, what is $\sin A$?

A. $\dfrac{3}{4}$

B. $\dfrac{3}{5}$

C. $\dfrac{4}{3}$

D. $\dfrac{4}{5}$

E. $\dfrac{5}{3}$

6. Consider right triangle ABC with hypotenuse $\overline{AB}$. If $\cos A = \dfrac{4}{5}$, what is $\sin B \tan B$?

F. $\dfrac{3}{4}$

G. $\dfrac{3}{5}$

H. $\dfrac{4}{3}$

J. $\dfrac{5}{4}$

K. $\dfrac{16}{15}$

7. If $0 \leq \theta \leq \dfrac{\pi}{2}$ and $\sin \theta = \dfrac{\sqrt{2}}{2}$, then $\tan \theta = ?$

    A. $\dfrac{1}{2}$

    B. $\dfrac{\sqrt{2}}{2}$

    C. 1

    D. $\sqrt{2}$

    E. 2

8. Consider right triangle MNO with hypotenuse $\overline{MN}$. If $\cos M = \dfrac{24}{25}$, what is $\sin M \tan N$?

    F. $\dfrac{24}{25}$

    G. $\dfrac{7}{25}$

    H. $\dfrac{7}{24}$

    J. $\dfrac{24}{7}$

    K. $\dfrac{25}{7}$

9. Consider right triangle ABC with right angle C. If $\sin A = \dfrac{a}{c}$, what is the length of $\overline{AC}$ in terms of a and c?

    A. $\sqrt{a^2 - c^2}$

    B. $\sqrt{a^2 + c^2}$

    C. $\sqrt{c^2 - a^2}$

    D. $\sqrt{c^2 + a^2}$

    E. $\sqrt{(c - a)^2}$

10. Consider right triangle XYZ with hypotenuse $\overline{XY}$. If $\overline{XY} = 26$, and $\cos Y = \dfrac{5}{13}$, what is the length of $\overline{XZ}$?

    F. 5

    G. 10

    H. 12

    J. 13

    K. 24

11. Right triangle ABC with side lengths 8 cm, 15 cm and 17 cm are opposite angles A, B, and C, respectively. Which of the following is NOT a possible relationship for this triangle?

A. $\sin A = \dfrac{8}{17}$

B. $\cos A = \dfrac{15}{17}$

C. $\cos B = \dfrac{8}{17}$

D. $\tan A = \dfrac{8}{15}$

E. $\tan B = \dfrac{17}{15}$

12. Consider right triangle XYZ with hypotenuse $\overline{XY}$. If $\overline{XZ} = 12$, and $\sin X = \dfrac{3}{5}$, what is the length of $\overline{XY}$?

F. 12

G. 15

H. 18

J. 21

K. 24

13. Right triangle ABC with sides of length 3 cm, 4 cm and 5 cm opposite angles A, B, and C, respectively. Which of the following is NOT a possible relationship for this triangle?

A. $\tan B = \dfrac{4}{3}$

B. $\cos A = \dfrac{4}{5}$

C. $\cos B = \dfrac{3}{5}$

D. $\sin A = \dfrac{4}{5}$

E. $\tan A = \dfrac{3}{4}$

14. A ladder is placed against a building so that the top of the ladder rests 30 feet from the base of the building. If the angle formed by the ladder and the ground has a cosine of $\dfrac{5}{13}$, to the nearest foot, how long is the ladder?

F. 13 feet

G. 25 feet

H. 28 feet

J. 33 feet

K. 38 feet

$$MPH \rightarrow Ft/min$$

$$\underbrace{\frac{miles}{hour}}_{starting} \cdot \underbrace{\frac{feet}{}}_{top} \cdot \underbrace{\frac{}{minutes}}_{bottom} \rightarrow \frac{60\ \cancel{miles}}{1\ \cancel{hour}} \cdot \frac{5280\ Ft}{1\ \cancel{mile}} \cdot \frac{1\ \cancel{hour}}{60\ minutes}$$

1. Anette is running a race at her local high school. She ran 5 miles in 42 minutes. What was Anette's average speed, in *feet per second*?

   (Note: 1 mile = 5,280 feet)

   $$\frac{5\ \cancel{mi}}{42\ \cancel{min}} \cdot \frac{5280\ Ft}{1\ \cancel{mi}} \cdot \frac{1\ \cancel{min}}{60\ sec} = \boxed{\frac{(5)(5280)\ Ft}{(42)(60)\ sec}}$$

   A. $\dfrac{(5)(5,280)}{(42)(60)}$

   B. $\dfrac{(5)}{(5,280)(42)(60)}$

   C. $\dfrac{(5)(5,280)(42)}{(60)}$

   D. $\dfrac{(5,280)}{(5)(42)(60)}$

   E. $\dfrac{1}{(5)(5,280)(42)(60)}$

Dimensional analysis problems are not their own problem type per se, but frequently show up as part of multi-step problems.

Take a moment to practice targeting goal units and properly lining up starting units so that everything cancels properly.

2. Carl is going to cover his bathroom floor with tile. The dimensions of the bathroom are 5 feet by 10 feet. The length of a side of each square tile is 6 inches. What is the minimum number of tiles Carl will need to purchase cover his bathroom floor?

   F. $50/36$

   G. 36

   H. 50

   J. 200

   K. 300

   ① Convert all units, so they are the same.

   $$\frac{10\ \cancel{Ft}}{1} \cdot \frac{12\ in}{1\ \cancel{Ft}} \rightarrow 120\ in$$

   $$\frac{5\ \cancel{Ft}}{1} \cdot \frac{12\ in}{1\ \cancel{Ft}} \rightarrow 60\ in$$

   ② Convert to area.

   Floor area   Tile area

   $120\ in \cdot 60\ in$ $6\ in \cdot 6\ in$

   $7,200\ in^2$ $36\ in^2$

   ③ Now compare! $\rightarrow \dfrac{7,200\ in^2}{36\ in^2} = \boxed{200}$

3. Shima will mix 1 fluid ounce of fertilizer in water for every 40 square feet of soil. At this rate, which of the following expressions gives the number of gallons of fertilizer that Shima will mix in water for 0.5 acres of soil?

(Note: 1 acre = 43,560 square feet; 1 gallon = 128 fluid ounces)

A. $\dfrac{(0.5)(40)(128)}{43,560}$

B. $\dfrac{(0.5)(40)}{(128)(43,560)}$

C. $\dfrac{(0.5)}{(40)(128)(43,560)}$

D. $\dfrac{(0.5)(43,560)}{(40)(128)}$

E. $\dfrac{(0.5)(43,560)(128)}{(40)}$

4. Uyi is planning to build a wire fence around his back lot, which is in the shape of a rectangle with dimensions 48 feet by 56 feet. Uyi would like the fence to cover all four sides of his lot. Uyi's local hardware store only sells wire fencing in units of yards. How many total yards of fence should Uyi purchase to fully enclose his lot?
(Note: 1 yard. = 3 feet.)

F. 24
G. $69\frac{1}{3}$
H. 104
J. 624
K. 2,688

5. Grandpa Joseph likes to speak in riddles. When his granddaughter asks how old he is, Grandpa Joseph says that he is 551,880 hours older than she is. If Grandpa Joseph's granddaughter is 9 years old, approximately how old is Grandpa Joseph?

A. 63 years old
B. 67 years old
C. 70 years old
D. 71 years old
E. 72 years old

6. Shantrea's new art gallery is in the shape of a square with a side length of 9 yards. What is the area of Shantrea's art gallery in units of square feet?

F. 9
G. 27
H. 81
J. 243
K. 729

7. Horatio takes his new kitten to the veterinarian for a check up. The veterinarian tells Horatio that his kitten weighs approximately 98 grams. Which of the following is closest to the weight of Horatio's kitten in pounds?
(Note: 1,000 grams = 1 kilogram. 1 kilogram = 2.20 pounds)

A. 0.098
B. 0.216
C. 2.156
D. 6.514
E. 21.560

8. The African Cheetah holds the record for the fastest running speed of any land animal. The top speed recorded for an African Cheetah is approximately 74.6 miles per hour. Approximately how fast is this in units of feet per second?

F. 35
G. 82
H. 109
J. 135
K. 4,476

9. Marcia buys a new jewelry box in the shape of a rectangular prism while on a trip to Spain. The prism has dimensions of 12 cm by 16 cm by 22 cm. What is the approximate volume of the jewelry box in cubic inches?
(Note: 1 inch = 2.54 cm.)

A. 84
B. 258
C. 4,224
D. 10,728
E. 69,219

1. Voter identification cards in a certain state consist of 2 letters taken from the 26 letters, A through Z, following by 4 digits taken from the 10 digits, 0 through 9. Which of the following expressions gives the number of distinct voter identification cards that are possible given that repetition of both letters and digits is NOT allowed?

A. $10^4 \cdot 26^2$

B. $(10 + 26)^3$

C. $2(26)^2(10)^4$

D. $(4 + 2)^{26+10}$

E. $26 \cdot 25 \cdot 10 \cdot 9 \cdot 8 \cdot 7$

odds of letters   odds of numbers

$26 \cdot 25 \cdot 10 \cdot 9 \cdot 8 \cdot 7$

drops by one each step
as we use a value

$(26)(25)(10)(9)(8)(7)$

2. In how many different ways can the letters in the word MISSISSIPPI be rearranged?

F. $\dfrac{11!}{(4!)(4!)(2!)}$

G. $\dfrac{4!}{(11!)(4!)(2!)}$

H. $\dfrac{(11!)(4!)}{(4!)(2!)}$

J. $\dfrac{(11!)(2!)}{(4!)(4!)(2!)}$

K. $\dfrac{(11!)(4!)(2!)}{(4!)}$

Reordering/Rearranging

$\dfrac{(\text{\# of letters})!}{(\text{\# of repeats of 1st repeating letter})! \ (\text{\# of repeats of 2nd repeating letter})!}$

$\dfrac{(\text{MISSISSIPPI})!}{(\text{SSSS})!(\text{IIII})!(\text{PP})!} \rightarrow \boxed{\dfrac{(11)!}{(4)!(4)!(2)!}}$

3. If a student council will elect a president, vice president, and treasurer from among its 12 members, which of the following expressions represents the number of possible councils?

A. $_{12}P_3$

B. $_{12}C_3$

C. $12!$

D. 12^3

E. $(12!)(11!)(10!)$

$_{\#}P_x \rightarrow$ Pick x from $\#$, order matters.

$\underline{ex:}$ phone numbers, license plates

$_{\#}C_x \rightarrow$ Choose x items from $\#$ items, order doesn't matter.

$\underline{ex:}$ buying items, friends at a party

$\underline{\text{Elections}} \rightarrow$ order MATTERS as a different order swaps positions.

4. The first question on a 2-question quiz offers 5 answers, and exactly 1 answer must be chosen. The second question offers 6 answers, and exactly 1 answer must be chosen. The quiz has how many possible combinations of answers?

F. 2
G. 5
H. 11
J. 30
K. 60

5. The table below shows the price of 4 different kinds of fruit on sale at Dale's Fruit Market. Dale's Fruit Market has 30 of each type of fruit in stock. Horatio's mother allows him to choose any two pieces of fruit to take home. Assuming Horatio chooses 2 pieces of fruit, how many different total costs are possible?

Fruit	Cost per piece
Apple	$0.60
Plum	$0.52
Peach	$0.75
Apricot	$0.36

A. 10
B. 12
C. 16
D. 20
E. 24

6. A baseball manager will select 15 of the 27 players at the baseball tryout to join the baseball team. Which of the following expressions represents the number of possible teams the manager can select?

F. $_{27}P_{15}$
G. $_{27}C_{15}$
H. $(_{27}C_{15})(_{27}P_{15})$
J. $12!$
K. $(27!)(26!)(25!)$

7. The AV club won a contest that will allow it to send 4 of its 13 members to comic-con. If they are going to choose 4 names out of a hat, how many different combinations of members could they send?

A. 46
B. 52
C. 715
D. 17,160
E. 28,561

8. Let X and Y be independent events. Denote $P(X)$ as the probability that Event X will occur, and denote $P(X \cap Y)$ as the probability that Events X and Y both occur. Which of the following equations *must* be true?

F. $P(X \cup Y) = P(X) + P(Y) - (P(X) \cdot P(Y))$
G. $P(X) = 1 - P(Y)$
H. $P(X \cap Y) = P(X) \cdot P(Y)$
J. $P(X \cap Y) = P(X) + P(Y)$
K. $P(X) = P(Y)$

9. Which of the following expressions gives the number of distinct permutations of all of the letters in the word SYSTEM?

A. $6!$
B. $4(4!)$
C. $\dfrac{6!}{4!}$
D. $\dfrac{6!}{2!}$
E. $\dfrac{6!}{2!2!}$

10. A student council consists of three seniors, three juniors, three sophomores, and three freshmen. The president must be a senior, but the vice president and the treasurer could be any student council member. Assuming the selection of officers is random, which of the following statements about this student council must NOT be true?

F. Jimmy, a senior on the council, has a 1 in 3 chance of being president
G. There are 330 different councils possible
H. Timmy, a junior on the council, has a 1 in 12 chance of being treasurer
J. There is an approximately 1.81% random chance that all 3 officers will be seniors
K. Kimmy, a freshmen, has a 1 in 12 chance of being president

11. In the state of Petoria, license plate consists of two letters followed by four digits (0-9). If repetition of any character is NOT allowed, how many unique license plates are possible?

A. 3,276,000
B. 6,760,000
C. 32,292,000
D. 35,880,000
E. 41,127,840

12. In how many different ways can the letters in the word STRAPS be rearranged?

    F. 21
    G. 30
    H. 36
    J. 360
    K. 720

13. A skiing race involves 10 racers. Gold, silver, and bronze medals are awarded for placing 1st, 2nd, and 3rd, respectively. Which of the following expressions represents the possible number of different medalists receiving gold, silver, and bronze?

    A. $_{10}P_3$
    B. $_{10}C_3$
    C. $(_{10}C_3)(_{10}P_3)$
    D. $10!$
    E. $(10)(10)(10)$

14. Stanley is creating a new password for his e-mail account. His password consists of 7 characters. The first and last character are digits (0-9), and the remaining characters are letters from the English alphabet. There are no repeating characters in Stanley's password. Which of the following expressions represents the number of different passwords Stanley can create?

    F. $10^2 \cdot 26^5$
    G. $10 \cdot 2 + 26 \cdot 5$
    H. $9^2 \cdot 26^5$
    J. $(9)(26)(25)(24)(23)(22)(8)$
    K. $(10)(26)(25)(24)(23)(22)(9)$

15. A committee will be formed from a group of 15 men and 18 women. The committee will consist of 7 men and 7 women. Which of the following expressions represents the possible number of different committees that can be formed?

    A. $_{33}C_{14}$
    B. $_{18}P_7$
    C. $(_{15}C_7)(_{18}P_7)$
    D. $(_{15}P_7)(_{18}P_7)$
    E. $(_{15}C_7)(_{18}C_7)$

16. Marissa is looking to form a key club at school. 13 boys and 14 girls apply for the key club. Marissa has enough spots to accept 10 students. What is the probability Marissa randomly selects 4 boys and 6 girls to join the key club?

    F. $\dfrac{(_{13}C_4)(_{14}C_6)}{_{27}C_{10}}$
    G. $\dfrac{(_{13}P_4)(_{14}P_6)}{_{27}P_{10}}$
    H. $\dfrac{(_{14}C_4)(_{13}C_6)}{_{27}C_{10}}$
    J. $\dfrac{(_{14}P_4)(_{13}P_6)}{_{27}P_{10}}$
    K. $\dfrac{(_4C_{13})(_6C_{14})}{_{10}C_{27}}$

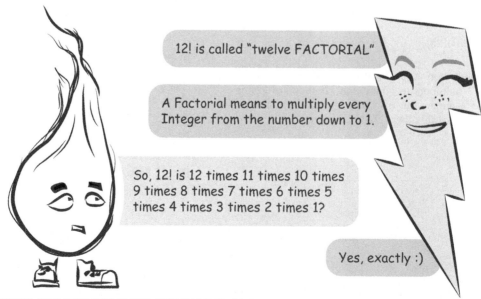

12! is called "twelve FACTORIAL"

A Factorial means to multiply every Integer from the number down to 1.

So, 12! is 12 times 11 times 10 times 9 times 8 times 7 times 6 times 5 times 4 times 3 times 2 times 1?

Yes, exactly :)

Hey, notice that the time allowed is getting longer. Because the Math section increases in difficulty, it is hard to train an even pace. Later problems can simply take longer, so adjust your expectations accordingly.

This quiz is exploring later parts of the test, and later parts of the test often include multi step problems. The concept identification from earlier quizzes is still essential, but many concepts may be needed to solve a single problem.

The multiple-step nature of problems means it is more important than ever to write your work clearly.

Keep an eye out for tricky last steps, such as problems wanting "2x - y" or "2a" instead of "x" or "a" alone.

CHAPTER FOUR QUIZ
25 Minutes — 20 Questions

DIRECTIONS: Solve each problem, choose the correct answer, and then fill in the corresponding oval on your answer document.

Do not linger over problems that take too much time. Solve as many as you can; then return to the others in the time you have left for this test.

You are permitted to use a calculator on this test. You may use your calculator for any problems you choose, but some of the problems may be best done without using a calculator.

Note: Unless otherwise stated, all of the following should be assumed.
1. Illustrative figures are NOT necessarily drawn to scale.
2. Geometric figures lie in a plane.
3. The word *line* indicates a straight line.
4. The word *average* indicates arithmetic mean.

---

1. Andrea plans to build a fence around the four sides of her rectangular garden to keep out rabbits. Her garden has an area of 750 square feet and has a width of 25 feet. What is the total length of fencing Andrea must buy in order to completely fence her entire garden?

   A. 55 feet
   B. 110 feet
   C. 130 feet
   D. 160 feet
   E. 200 feet

2. In the figure below all line segments intersect at right angles, the base has a length of 20 units, and the height of the figure is 12 units. What is the perimeter, in units, of the entire figure?

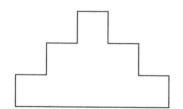

   F.   9
   G.   24
   H.   36
   J.   64
   K.   240

3. The Stevens Point swimming pool is in the shape of a right rectangular prism with a length of 60 feet and a width of 45 feet. When the pool is completely filled, the volume of water in the pool is 32,400 cubic feet. How deep is the pool to the nearest foot?

   A.   8
   B.   10
   C.   12
   D.   14
   E.   16

4. Circle O is inscribed inside square $ABCD$, as shown in the figure below. Square $ABCD$ has an area of 100 square feet. What is the area, in square feet, of the shaded region?

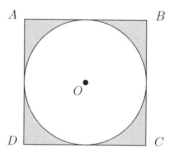

   F. $100 - 25\pi$
   G. $100 - 50\pi$
   H. $100 - 100\pi$
   J. $100\pi - 100$
   K. $25\pi - 50$

5. The length of the sides of a certain cube is n inches long. The length of each side of a second cube is $3n$ inches long. How many times larger is the surface area of the second cube than the first?

    A. 3

    B. 6

    C. 9

    D. 27

    E. 81

6. In right triangle ABC with hypotenuse $\overline{AB}$, $\cos B = \dfrac{5}{13}$. What is the value of $\tan A$?

    F. $\dfrac{5}{12}$

    G. $\dfrac{5}{13}$

    H. $\dfrac{12}{5}$

    J. $\dfrac{12}{13}$

    K. 1

7. At SmartWare Technologies, identification codes each consist of the following sequence: 1 digit, 4 letters, 1 digit. For any code, the digits (0-9) may be the same, but the letters, each from the 26 letters of the English alphabet, must all be different. Which of the following expressions below gives the probability that a randomly selected identification code contains the word CHIP, spelled correctly?

    A. $\dfrac{10^2}{10^2(26^4)}$

    B. $\dfrac{10^2}{10^2(26)(25)(24)(23)}$

    C. $\dfrac{10^2}{10(9)(26)(25)(24)(23)}$

    D. $\dfrac{10^2(4)(3)(2)(1)}{10^2(26^4)}$

    E. $\dfrac{10^2(4)(3)(2)(1)}{10^2(26)(25)(24)(23)}$

Use the following information to answer questions 8-10.

The table below shows the results of a survey from the 75 people who participated in a track team's short distance (sprints and hurdles) tryouts.

Question	Yes	No
Did you run sprints?	57	18
Did you run hurdles?	46	29

In total, 20 students made the team. Of them, 5 were exclusively sprinters, 3 were exclusively hurdlers, and the rest ran in both events.

8. During the tryout, given that a student ran hurdles, what is the probability that that student also ran sprints?

    F. $28/75$

    G. $46/75$

    H. $28/57$

    J. $9/23$

    K. $14/23$

9. If both the captain and the assistant captain will be chosen from among those who ran both events, how many different pairs of captain and assistant captain are possible from those who made the team?

    A. 15

    B. 66

    C. 132

    D. 380

    E. 522

10. While the people who ran both events were trying out, those who just ran sprints and those who just ran hurdles played each other in a game of dodgeball. If the teams were 5 against 5, which of the following represents the number of unique games that were possible?

    F. $(_{18}C_5)(_{29}C_5)$

    G. $(_{18}P_5)(_{29}P_5)$

    H. $(_{57}C_5)(_{46}C_5)$

    J. $_{47}C_{10}$

    K. $_{47}P_{10}$

11. The figure below shows lines $\overline{WX} \parallel \overline{YZ}$, line segments $\overline{WY}$ and $\overline{XY}$, and two angle measures. What is the measure of $\angle WYX$?

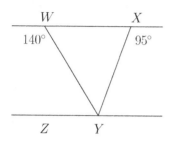

- **A.** 35°
- **B.** 38°
- **C.** 42°
- **D.** 55°
- **E.** 64°

12. A committee will be selected from a group of 15 women and 20 men. The committee will consist of 7 women and 4 men. Which of the following expressions gives the number of different committees that could be selected from these 35 people?

- **F.** $_{35}P_{11}$
- **G.** $(_{15}P_7)(_{20}P_4)$
- **H.** $_{35}C_{11}$
- **J.** $(_{35}C_{11})(_{35}C_{11})$
- **K.** $(_{15}C_7)(_{20}C_4)$

13. A circle with diameter 20 inches is inscribed inside a square. What is the perimeter, in inches, of the square?

- **A.** 40
- **B.** 80
- **C.** 160
- **D.** 320
- **E.** 400

Use the following information to answer questions 14-16.

In the figure below, a circle has been inscribed in a rhombus.

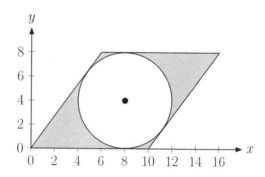

14. Which of the following represents the equation of this circle?

- **F.** $(x - 8)^2 + (y - 4)^2 = 4$
- **G.** $(x + 4)^2 + (y + 8)^2 = 4$
- **H.** $(x - 8)^2 + (y - 4)^2 = 16$
- **J.** $(x + 8)^2 + (y + 4)^2 = 16$
- **K.** $(x - 4)^2 + (y - 8)^2 = 16$

15. What is the circumference of the inscribed circle shown above?

- **A.** 2π
- **B.** 4π
- **C.** 8π
- **D.** 16π
- **E.** 32π

16. What is the area, in square coordinate units, of the shaded region?

- **F.** $80 - 16\pi$
- **G.** $80 - 8\pi$
- **H.** $80 - 4\pi$
- **J.** $40 - 16\pi$
- **K.** $40 - 8\pi$

Use the following information to answer questions 17-20.

A pyramid. shown below, has a square base with an area of $10,000$ m^2 and a height that is 80% of the length of one of the edges of the base. A surveyor is standing 150 meters from the center of the base of the pyramid and is a straight-line distance of 170 meters from the top of the pyramid with an angle of elevation of θ.

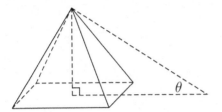

17. To the nearest meter, how far is the surveyor from the closest point at the base of the pyramid?

    A.   50 meters

    B.   86 meters

    C.   100 meters

    D.   125 meters

    E.   137 meters

18. According to the information given, what is the volume of the pyramid?

(Note: The equation for the volume, V, of a pyramid is $V = 1/3Bh$, where B is the area of the base and h is the length of the height.)

    F. $80,000$ m^3

    G. $266,666.\overline{6}$ m^3

    H. $500,000$ m^3

    J. $800,000$ m^3

    K. $1,100,000$ m^3

19. To the nearest degree, which of the following is the angle of elevation from the surveyor to the top of the pyramid?

    A. $25°$

    B. $28°$

    C. $30°$

    D. $41°$

    E. $49°$

20. Which of the following is closest to the total surface area of the pyramid?

    F. $14,700$ m^2

    G. $18,600$ m^2

    H. $27,200$ m^2

    J. $28,900$ m^2

    K. $31,400$ m^2

This Chapter begins to explore the more one-off and strange topics of the last portion of the Math section. While important, and potentially a bit confusing, there's no guarantee any of these concepts will actually show on the test.

Late test problems are tough, so if you don't know the content well or have a strong strategy for working quickly, you can get in deep water with limited time. It's the nature of the test that not all of the tough topics will show up every time, and thus you must over prepare.

But before diving into this late work, build a strong foundation. Work on Chapters 1 through 4 until problems 1 through 40 are very strong and consistent. The more the fundamentals are at a muscle-memory level of mastery, the more room you'll have to store all the new information.

Vertical asymptote (VA):

$h(x) = \dfrac{f(x)}{g(x)} \rightarrow$ x=va for whatever x value makes the BOTTOM zero.

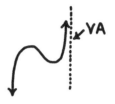

Horizontal asymptote (HA):

→ If the degree of the numerator is larger, then there is no HA.

ex: $\dfrac{x^2+4}{x+1}$, $\dfrac{x^4+x^2-9}{x^3}$

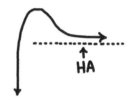

→ If the degree of the denominator is larger, the HA is $y=0$.

ex: $\dfrac{x+1}{x^2+4}$, $\dfrac{x^2-5}{x^3-7}$

→ If the degrees are the SAME, the HA is y=(ratio of coefficients).

ex: $\dfrac{x^2+1}{x^2+4}$ $\dfrac{8x^3-2}{2x^3}$

HA → $y=1$, HA → $y=\dfrac{8}{2}=4$

You might not need to know this, but if the degree of the numerator is only ONE larger than the denominator, we have what's called a SLANT ASYMPTOTE.

In that case, the coefficients work out to the slope, which is usually the question.

1. In the standard (x, y) coordinate plane, when $m \neq 0$ and $n \neq 0$, the graph of $f(x) = \dfrac{6x - m}{x + n}$ has a vertical asymptote at:

x + n = 0
- n - n
$\boxed{x = -n}$

A. $x = y$

B. $x = -m$

C. $x = -n$

D. $x = 6$

E. $x = -\dfrac{m}{n}$

Set the bottom equal to zero!

2. In the standard (x, y) coordinate plane, when $a \neq 0$ and $b \neq 0$, the graph of $f(x) = \dfrac{4x + b}{x - a}$ has a horizontal asymptote at:

→ The degrees are the same, so the HA is the ratio of the coefficients.

$y = \boxed{4}$

F. $y = a$

G. $y = -a$

H. $y = \dfrac{4}{a}$

J. $y = 4$

K. $y = -\dfrac{b}{a}$

Quick trick : plug in a HUGE number for x and round to get the Horizontal Asymptote

3. The graph of $y = \dfrac{3x - 5}{x + 4}$ in the standard (x, y) coordinate plane has a vertical asymptote with equation $x = ?$

A. -4
B. $-5/4$
C. 3
D. $5/3$
E. 9

5. Which equation represents a horizontal asymptote for the function $f(x) = \dfrac{6x + a}{2x + b}$ for values of a and b where $a \neq b$?

A. $x = 3$
B. $y = 3$
C. $y = 3x$
D. $y = \dfrac{3a}{b}$
E. $y = \dfrac{-a}{b}$

4. Which of the following values of x would make the expression, $\dfrac{4}{x^2 - 25}$, undefined?

F. 5 only
G. -5 only
H. 0 only
J. -5 and 5
K. $-5, 0$, and 5

6. Which of the following is the vertical asymptote of the function $f(x) = \dfrac{x^2 + 4x}{x^2 - 3x - 28}$?

F. $y = 1$
G. $y = 0$
H. $x = 7$
J. $x = -4$
K. $x = 0$

Vertical asymptotes occur when the bottom is zero, true. However, if this also makes the top equal zero, we might have what is called a HOLE.

To check for holes, factor the top and bottom of quadratic fractions and cancel repeat factors BEFORE looking for Vertical Asymptotes.

7. What is the horizontal asymptote of the equation $y = \dfrac{x - 6}{2x + 2}$ when graphed in the standard (x, y) coordinate plane?

    A. $y = 1$
    B. $y = 1/2$
    C. $y = 2$
    D. $y = 6$
    E. $y = 3$

8. Which of the following functions does NOT contain an asymptote?

    F. $f(x) = x^3 + 3$

    G. $f(x) = \dfrac{x^2}{x - 5}$

    H. $f(x) = \dfrac{x}{x^2 - 25}$

    J. $f(x) = \dfrac{x^3 + 5}{x - 5}$

    K. $f(x) = \dfrac{5 - x}{x}$

9. Which of the following correctly lists all asymptotes of the equation $f(x) = \dfrac{3}{x + 1}$?

    A. $x = -1$
    B. $y = 0$
    C. $x = 0, y = -1$
    D. $x = -1, y = 0$
    E. $x = 1, y = 3$

10. Which of the following is the horizontal asymptote of the function $f(x) = \dfrac{x^2 + 4x}{x^2 - 3x - 28}$?

    F. $y = 0$
    G. $y = 1$
    H. $y = 7$
    J. $y = -4$
    K. $x = 1$

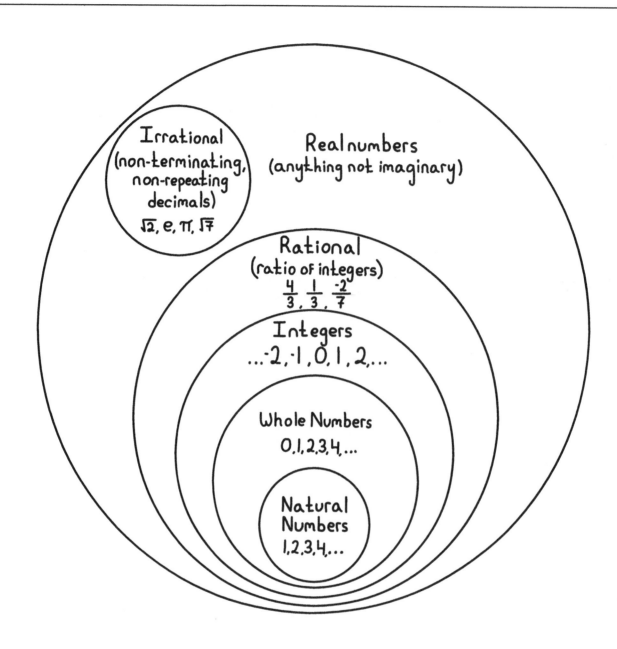

Real numbers
(anything not imaginary)

Irrational
(non-terminating,
non-repeating
decimals)
$\sqrt{2}, e, \pi, \sqrt{7}$

Rational
(ratio of integers)
$\frac{4}{3}, \frac{1}{3}, \frac{-2}{7}$

Integers
...-2,-1, 0, 1, 2,...

Whole Numbers
0,1,2,3,4,...

Natural
Numbers
1,2,3,4,...

I recommend using 2, 3, and 5 as numbers to guess. Try doing "2 & 3" and then "3 & 2" as reversing order can show a change sometimes.

Method:
Number properties questions can be solved by choosing and plugging in numbers.

→ BUT your objective is to ELIMINATE 4 not just confirm 1.

1. When $8 \leq x \leq 12$ and $5 \leq y \leq 8$, the smallest possible value for $\dfrac{4}{x-y}$ is:

   A. $\dfrac{4}{9}$

   B. $\dfrac{4}{7}$

   C. $\dfrac{1}{2}$

   D. $\dfrac{1}{4}$

   E. $\dfrac{4}{5}$

→ To make $\frac{4}{x-y}$ as small as possible, we will need to make the denominator as large as possible.

→ To make x-y as large as possible, we need the largest possible x and the smallest possible y.

→ Let x=12 and y=5 $\dfrac{4}{12-5} = \boxed{\dfrac{4}{7}}$

2. Which of the following statements is ALWAYS true for integers a and b?
   F. If a and b are both negative, $a - b$ is negative
   G. If a is negative and b is positive, $a + b$ is negative
   H. If a is positive and b is negative, $a + b$ is positive
   J. If a is negative and b is positive, $a - b$ is negative
   K. If a and b are both positive $a - b$ is positive

F) Let a=-2 and b=-5
   -2-(-5)=3   3 is not negative.

G) Let a=-2 and b=5
   -2+5=3   3 is not negative.

H) Let a=2 and b=-5
   2+(-5)=-3   -3 is not positive.

K) Let a=2 and b=5
   2-5=-3   -3 is not positive.

   $\boxed{J}$ must correct.

3. If $|x| + x = 0$, which of the following is true about x?
   A. x is a negative real number
   B. x must be equal to zero
   C. x must be equal to 1
   D. x must be a real number less than or equal to 0
   E. No value for x satisfies the equation above.

A) Let x=0 → |0|+0=0
   0 is not negative

B) Let x=-1 → |-1|+(-1)=0
   -1 is not 0

C) Let x=1 → |1|+1=2
   2 is not 0

E) In proving A and B we showed that E is wrong.
   $\boxed{D}$ must be correct.

4. Which of the following represents a rational number?

F. $\sqrt{\dfrac{7}{49}}$

G. $\sqrt{\dfrac{5}{25}}$

H. $\sqrt{\dfrac{1}{49}}$

J. $\sqrt{\dfrac{1}{5}}$

K. $\sqrt{\dfrac{1}{7}}$

5. For real numbers x and y such that $y - x < 0$, which of the following *must* be true?

A. $x = y$

B. $x > y$

C. $x < y - x$

D. $x < -y$

E. $x < y$

6. Consider the expression $\dfrac{4x^2}{3}$. Which of the following represents the solution set of x that *must* yield a rational result?

F. Any rational number

G. Any irrational number

H. $x = 1$

J. $x = \dfrac{4}{3}$

K. $x = \dfrac{2\sqrt{3}}{3}$

7. If x is a negative odd integer, what must be true about y so that the expression $x^3 y^3$ results in a positive even integer?

A. y is even and positive

B. y is even and negative

C. y is odd and positive

D. y is odd and negative

E. y is any integer

8. If $-7 \leq x \leq -3$ and $2 \leq y \leq 7$, what is the smallest possible value of the expression $x - y$?

F. -21

G. -14

H. -10

J. -9

K. -4

9. If $3 \leq x \leq 8$ and $-5 \leq y \leq -1$, what is the greatest possible value of the expression $\dfrac{6}{x - y}$?

A. $\dfrac{6}{1}$

B. $\dfrac{3}{2}$

C. $\dfrac{2}{3}$

D. $\dfrac{6}{13}$

E. $-\dfrac{3}{1}$

10. If x is a positive even integer and y is a positive odd integer, then $[(-5)(+5)]^{xy}$ is:

    F. positive and even.
    G. positive and odd.
    H. zero.
    J. negative and even.
    K. negative and odd.

11. Which of the following inequalities is the solution for the equation below?

    $$|x| = -x$$

    A. $x \leq 0$
    B. $x \geq 0$
    C. $x = 0$
    D. x is irrational
    E. x is not a real number

12. The equation below demonstrates which property of numbers?

    $$(a + b) + cd = cd + (a + b)$$

    F. Associative: $(x + y) + z = x + (y + z)$
    G. Commutative: $x + y = y + x$
    H. Distributive: $x(y + z) = xy + xz$
    J. Identity: $x + 0 = x$
    K. Inverse: $x + (-x) = 0$

13. Which of the following operations will produce the largest result when substituted for the blank in the expression $5 \underline{\quad} \left(-\dfrac{2}{99}\right)$?

    A. Multiplied by
    B. Plus
    C. Minus
    D. Divided by
    E. Averaged with

$$i = \sqrt{-1}$$

$$i^0 = 1$$
$$i^1 = i$$
$$i^2 = -1$$
$$i^3 = -i$$
- - - - - - -
$$i^4 = 1$$
$$i^5 = i$$
$$i^6 = -1$$

Didn't think you could take square roots of negative numbers?

THINK AGAIN

$$i^{2000} \rightarrow \frac{2000}{4} = 500\tfrac{0}{4} \rightarrow \text{remainder of } 0 \rightarrow i^{2000} = i^4 = 1$$

$$i^{3502} \rightarrow \frac{3502}{4} = 875\tfrac{2}{4} \rightarrow \text{remainder of } 2 \rightarrow i^{3502} = i^2 = -1$$

Graphing

imaginary

$$A + Bi \text{ is a "complex number."}$$

real imaginary

$$A + Bi$$

$$A - Bi \text{ is its "conjugate."}$$

The product of a complex number and its conjugate is a real number.

$$\rightarrow (A + Bi)(A - Bi) = A^2 + B^2$$

When a complex number is on the bottom of a fraction, you MUST multiply Top & Bottom by the conjugate

This makes the bottom Rational, making it a legal (proper) fraction.

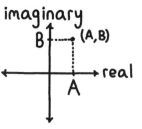

1. Which of the following complex numbers is a sum of $\sqrt{-54}$ and $\sqrt{-24}$?

   A. $5\sqrt{6}$
   B. $6\sqrt{6}$
   C. $5i\sqrt{6}$
   D. $6i\sqrt{6}$
   E. $36i\sqrt{6}$

$$\sqrt{-54} + \sqrt{-24}$$
$$\sqrt{-1}\sqrt{54} + \sqrt{-1}\sqrt{24}$$
$$i\sqrt{9}\sqrt{6} + i\sqrt{4}\sqrt{6}$$
$$3i\sqrt{6} + 2i\sqrt{6}$$
$$\boxed{5i\sqrt{6}}$$

2. Which of the following expressions is equivalent to the expression $\dfrac{4 + 2i}{3 - 6i}$?

   F. $40i$

   G. $12 + 12i$

   H. $\dfrac{4 - 2i}{3 + 6i}$

   J. $\dfrac{24 + 30i}{3 + 6i}$

   K. $\dfrac{30i}{45}$

$$\frac{(4+2i)}{(3-6i)} \cdot \frac{(3+6i)}{(3+6i)}$$
$$\downarrow$$
$$\frac{12 + 30i + 12i^2}{9 - 36i^2}$$
$$\downarrow$$
$$\frac{12 + 30i - 12}{9 + 36} = \boxed{\frac{30i}{45}}$$

3. Which of the following is NOT a solution to i^x if x is a positive integer?

   A. 0
   B. i
   C. -1
   D. $-i$
   E. 1

→ Recall that the only possible values of i^x for any x as a positive integer are $i, -1, -i,$ and 1.

→ The correct answer must be $\boxed{0}$.

4. Which of the following is the conjugate of $a + bi$?

 F. $a - bi$

 G. $b + ai$

 H. $b - ai$

 J. $a + bi$

 K. $ai + b$

7. The solution of the equation $3^{x^2+1} = 1$ contains:

 A.   2 imaginary numbers.

 B.   2 positive real numbers.

 C.   1 imaginary and 1 positive real number.

 D.   1 negative real number only.

 E.   an empty set.

5. The product of 2 numbers if 61. If 1 of the numbers is the complex number $5 + 6i$, what is the other number?

 A. $36 + 25i$

 B. $5 - 6i$

 C. $305 + 366i$

 D. $\dfrac{5}{61} + \dfrac{6}{61}i$

 E. $\dfrac{36}{11} + \dfrac{25}{11}i$

8. What is the distance, in coordinate units, between $-3 + 4i$ and $2 - 8i$?

 F.   5

 G.   12

 H.   13

 J.   17

 K.   25

6. For all pairs of nonzero real numbers m and n, the product of the complex number $m + ni$ and which of the following complex numbers is a real number?

 F. mni

 G. $m + ni$

 H. $m - ni$

 J. $n + mi$

 K. $n - mi$

9. Which of the following expressions would result in a real number when multiplied by $3 + 5i$?

 A. $6 - 10i$

 B. $3 - 5i$

 C. $9 - 25i$

 D. $8i^2$

 E. $-5i$

10. Which of the following expressions is equivalent to $\frac{\sqrt{x}}{i + \sqrt{x}}$?

   F. i
   G. x
   H. $\frac{i-1}{x+1}$
   J. $\frac{i\sqrt{x}+1}{1-x}$
   K. $\frac{x - i\sqrt{x}}{1+x}$

11. Which of the following complex numbers equals $(5 - 6i)(\pi + 5i)$?
   A. $5\pi - 30i$
   B. $(5 + \pi) - i$
   C. $(5 + \pi) + i$
   D. $(5\pi + 30) + (25 - 6\pi)i$
   E. $(5\pi - 30) + (25 - 6\pi)i$

12. What is the distance, in coordinate units, between $1 - 2i$ and $2 + 2i$?
   F. $\sqrt{2}$
   G. $\sqrt{3}$
   H. $\sqrt{4}$
   J. $\sqrt{5}$
   K. $\sqrt{17}$

13. Which of the following expressions is equivalent to $\frac{1}{2+i}\left(\frac{2-i}{2-i}\right)$?
   A. $\frac{2+i}{5}$
   B. $\frac{2+i}{3}$
   C. $2 - i$
   D. $\frac{2-i}{5}$
   E. $\frac{2-i}{3}$

14. Which of the following is equivalent to the expression $25x^2 + 64$?
   F. $(5x + 8)^2$
   G. $(5x + 8i)^2$
   H. $(5x - 8i)^2$
   J. $(5x + 8)(5x - 8)$
   K. $(5x + 8i)(5x - 8i)$

15. The solution of the equation $3^{x^2+1} = 0$ contains:
   A. 2 imaginary numbers.
   B. 2 positive real numbers.
   C. 1 imaginary and 1 positive real number.
   D. 1 negative real number only.
   E. an empty set.

① Finding the nth term of a periodic list:

→ What is the 196th term in the following repeating decimal?

0.719682719682...

note that we have 6 terms that repeat.

7 1 9 6 8 2

Divide 196 by 6 → $\frac{196}{6} = 32\frac{4}{6}$ → remainder: 4

7 1 9 6 8 2

↘ 4th term = 196th term

② Some formulas to know:

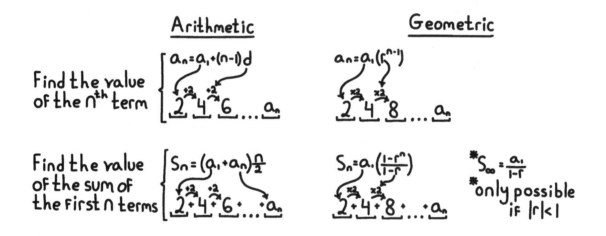

Arithmetic | Geometric

Find the value of the nth term

$a_n = a_1 + (n-1)d$

$2 \quad 4 \quad 6 \ldots a_n$

$a_n = a_1(r^{n-1})$

$2 \quad 4 \quad 8 \ldots a_n$

Find the value of the sum of the first n terms

$S_n = (a_1 + a_n)\frac{n}{2}$

$2 + 4 + 6 + \ldots + a_n$

$S_n = a_1 \cdot \left(\frac{1-r^n}{1-r}\right)$

$2 + 4 + 8 + \ldots + a_n$

$*S_\infty = \frac{a_1}{1-r}$

$*$ only possible if $|r| < 1$

Note that for Method 1, if you get "0" for your remainder, that means the answer is the LAST number in the core repeating sequence.

1. The sum of the first 50 positive integers is $1,275$. Which of the following is the sum of the first 100 positive integers?

A. $1,275^2$
B. $1,825$
C. $2,550$
D. $5,050$
E. $12,175$

$\underline{1},\ \underline{2},\ \underline{3}\ \ldots\ \underline{100}$

$S_n = (a_n + a_1)\frac{n}{2}$

$S_n = (100 + 1)\frac{100}{2} = \boxed{5050}$

2. What is the 47th digit to the right of the decimal point in the repeating number $0.\overline{26817}$

F. 2
G. 6
H. 8
J. 1
K. 7

$0.2\ 6\ 1\ 8\ 7$

1st 2nd 3rd 4th 5th

$\frac{47}{5} = 9\frac{2}{5} \rightarrow$ remainder: 2

$0.2\ \boxed{6}\ 1\ 8\ 7$

3. For any integer $n > 0$, the pyramid number P_n is the number of dots in a pyramid shape with n levels, where each level has three more dots than the previous one. The figure below shows the first 3 pyramid numbers. What is the value of P_{31}?

$P_1 = 1 \qquad P_2 = 5 \qquad P_3 = 12$

A. 900
B. 930
C. 961
D. 1,426
E. 1,524

①

n	# of dots on level n (ℓ_n)	# of dots in a pyramid with n levels (P_n)
1	1	$1 \rightarrow P_1 = \ell_1 = 1$
2	4	$5 \rightarrow P_2 = \ell_1 + \ell_2 = 1 + 4 = 5$
3	7	$12 \rightarrow P_3 = \ell_1 + \ell_2 + \ell_3 = 1 + 4 + 7 = 12$
$\vdots$	$\vdots$	$\vdots$
n	$\ell_n = \ell_1 + (n-1)d$	$P_n = \frac{(\ell_1 + \ell_n)n}{2}$

(with $+3$ between level 1 and 2, $+3$ between level 2 and 3)

② $P_{31} = \frac{(\ell_1 + \ell_{31})31}{2}$

$\ell_1 = 1$

$\ell_{31} = 1 + (31-1)3 = 91$

$P_{31} = \frac{(1+91)31}{2} = \boxed{1426}$

4. The fraction $\dfrac{2176}{9999}$ is equivalent to the repeating decimal $0.\overline{2176}$. What is the 80th digit to the right of the decimal point?

  F. 1
  G. 2
  H. 6
  J. 7
  K. 9

5. During the month of July, Gilesh resolves to do one more push-up each day than he did the previous day. If Gilesh does 3 push-ups on July 1st and sticks to his resolution exactly, how many total pushups will Gilesh complete during the month of July?
(Note: July has 31 days)

  A. 33
  B. 93
  C. 540
  D. 556
  E. 558

6. Jack opens a new savings account and deposits \$5 the first month. Every month for the next two years, Jack plans to deposit 5 more dollars than he did the previous month. If he meets but does not exceed his goal, how much much money will Jack have in his account after two years?

  F. \$120
  G. \$245
  H. \$390
  J. \$1,500
  K. \$2,880

7. The sum of a geometric sequence S can be found by the equation $S = \dfrac{a_1}{1 - r}$ where a_1 is the first term of the series and r is the common ratio where $0 < r < 1$.

What is the sum of the sequence whose first term is 100 and whose common ratio is 0.2?

  A. 20
  B. 80
  C. 120
  D. 125
  E. 180

8. Jill opens a savings account and deposits $200 the first month. Jill will deposit $15 *more* each month into her account every month for the a total of 12 months in order to save enough money for her dream vacation. If the amount of money in her account will be exactly enough to pay for her vacation, how much will her vacation cost?

   F. $2,000
   G. $3,000
   H. $3,390
   J. $3,570
   K. $45,000

9. A finite arithmetic sequence has 5 terms and the first term is 2. What is the difference between the mean and the median of the 5 terms?

   A. 0
   B. 2
   C. 5
   D. $5/2$
   E. 7

10. Which of the following represents the sum of all even integers from 1-100?

    F. 50!
    G. 100!
    H. 2,550
    J. 5,050
    K. 10,000

11. For any integer $n > 0$, the triangle number T_n is the number of dots in a triangle shape with n levels, where each level has one more dot than the previous one. The figure below shows the first four triangle numbers. What is the value of T_{66}?

$$T_1 = 1 \qquad T_2 = 3 \qquad T_3 = 6 \qquad T_4 = 10$$

    A. 264
    B. 524
    C. 666
    D. 2,211
    E. 66!

<u>Given</u>: A number of objects placed evenly apart.

<u>Goal</u>: The space between each object.

6 objects, when placed in a row,

●———●———●———●———●———●

have 5 gaps between them.

$$\text{gap distance} = \frac{\text{total distance}}{(\#\ \text{objects}) - 1}$$

1. Suzanne wants to plant a row of evenly spaced sunflowers along the outside of the northern wall of her house. If she only has 15 sunflower seeds and the northern wall of her house is 42 feet long, how far apart, to the nearest tenth of an inch, should she plant each sunflower?

  A. 2.8
  B. 3.0
  C. 4.3
  D. 33.6
  E. 36.0

objects = 15 flowers

total distance = 42 feet

$$\frac{42}{15-1} = 3 \leftarrow \text{careful this is in feet we need it in inches.}$$

$$3(12) = \boxed{36}$$

Some problems can be represented by the equation :
(# of gaps) = (# of objects) - 1

2. In the town of Bel-Air the clock tower rings three times for the 3 o'clock hour and four times for the 4 o'clock hour. For every hour, 3 seconds elapses between consecutive strikes of the bell. If 24 seconds elapses between the first and last strike of the bell, what hour is it?

F. 6
G. 7
H. 8
J. 9
K. 10

gap distance = 3
total distance = 24

$$3 = \frac{24}{rings - 1} \rightarrow rings = \boxed{9}$$

3. The Chesterville City Council decides to install a flag pole every 15 meters on Main Street, with one flag pole at the beginning of the street and one flag pole at the end of the street. If Main Street is 240 meters long, how many total flag poles will be installed?

A. 14
B. 15
C. 16
D. 17
E. 18

4. Amari is decorating his teacher's classroom for her birthday. He has 14 total posters he can hang along one wall of the classroom, which has a length of 44 feet. Amari plans to place one poster at each end of the wall, and evenly space the remaining posters between them. Approximately how far apart, to the nearest hundredth of a foot, should Amari hang each poster?

F. 2.93
G. 3.14
H. 3.38
J. 3.67
K. 4.00

5. A volcanic geyser in Yellowstone National Park erupts at regular intervals. On a certain day a scientist records one eruption at 12:00 P.M., one eruption at 6:00 P.M., and 17 eruptions between the hours of 12:00 P.M. and 6:00 P.M. Approximately how many minutes elapsed between each eruption of the geyser?

A. 0.32
B. 18.95
C. 20.00
D. 21.18
E. 46.12

6. Monique decides to build a border fence between her backyard and her neighbor's backyard. The fence must be 80 feet long to stretch the length of her yard. Monique decides to plant one rose bush every 8 feet, with a rose bush at either end of the fence. How many rose bushes should Monique plant in total?

F. 8
G. 9
H. 10
J. 11
K. 12

7. At the lumber mill in Smithtown, a bell rings at the beginning and end of each work day, with an additional bell every 20 minutes. Angel begins his work day at 8:00 A.M. and hears a total of 31 bells during the work day. At what time does Angel finish his work day?

A. 5:00 P.M.
B. 5:20 P.M.
C. 5:40 P.M.
D. 6:00 P.M.
E. 6:20 P.M.

8. The Westlake City Pool decides to purchase fold-out chairs for its guests. The pool is in the shape of a rectangle with sides equal to 45 feet by 30 feet. The manager of the pool would like one chair to be at each corner of the pool, with one chair spaced every 5 feet along all four sides of the pool's border. How many total chairs should the manager purchase?

F. 20
G. 24
H. 28
J. 30
K. 31

$$\log_a b = c \leftrightarrow a^c = b$$

$$\log b = c \leftrightarrow 10^c = b$$

$$\ln b = c \leftrightarrow e^c = b$$

"e" is just
a number

Logarithmic properties:

$$\log_a x + \log_a y = \log_a(xy)$$

$$\log_a x - \log_a y = \log_a\left(\frac{x}{y}\right)$$

$$\log_a x^y = y\log_a x$$

$$\log_a x = \frac{\log x}{\log a}$$

If you have a log expression that contains no variables, it is a NUMBER. Plug it into your calculator!

If you have a variable in your log, you have it unpack it with these properties.

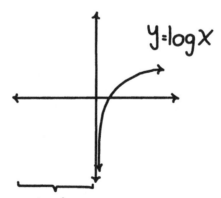

$y = \log x$

you cannot plug in negative values or zero for x.

↓

ex. $y = \log(-2)$ would never work.

1. If $\log_a x = m$ and $\log_a y = n$, then $\log_a (xy)^3 =$?

   A. $3(m+n)$
   B. $m+n$
   C. $3mn$
   D. mn
   E. $\dfrac{3m}{n}$

   $\log_a(xy)^3$ $\log_a x = m$

   $3\log_a(xy)$ $\log_a y = n$

   $3(\log_a x + \log_a y)$

   $3(\ m\ +\ n\ )$

   $\boxed{3(m+n)}$

2. If n is a real number such that $\log_2 (16) = 2n + 7$, then $n=$?

   F. -2
   G. $-\dfrac{3}{2}$
   H. $-\dfrac{5}{7}$
   J. 4
   K. 8

   $\log_2 16 = 2n+7 \rightarrow 2^{2n+7} = 16$

   $2^{2n+7} = 2^4$

   $2n+7 = 4$
   $\quad -7\ -7$

   $\dfrac{2n}{2} = \dfrac{-3}{2}$

   $n = \boxed{\dfrac{-3}{2}}$

3. What is the value of x in $\log_5 x = 3$?
    A. 3
    B. 5
    C. 25
    D. 125
    E. 243

4. What is the value of $\log_2(64)$?
    F. 3
    G. 4
    H. 6
    J. 8
    K. 32

5. If w is a positive number such that $\log_w (32) = 5$, then w=?
    A. $5/32$
    B. 1
    C. 2
    D. $32/5$
    E. 27

6. If a is a positive number such that $\log_a \left(\frac{1}{27}\right) = -3$, then a=?
    F. $1/27$
    G. 2
    H. 3
    J. 9
    K. 27

7. Which of the following is a possible value of x that satisfies $\log_x 81 = 2$?
    A. 3
    B. 6
    C. 9
    D. 18
    E. 36

8. The value of $\log_3(3^{\frac{7}{2}})$ is between which of the following pairs of consecutive integers?
    F. 0 and 1
    G. 1 and 2
    H. 2 and 3
    J. 3 and 4
    K. 4 and 5

9. For all $x > 5$, $\log(x - 5) + \log(x^2) = ?$
   A. $\log(-5)$
   B. $\log(x^2 + x - 5)$
   C. $\log(x^3 - 5x^2)$
   D. $\log\left(\dfrac{x^2}{x - 5}\right)$
   E. $\log\left(\dfrac{x - 5}{x^2}\right)$

10. If $\log_b 3 = x$ and $\log_b 5 = y$ what is $\log_b 45$?
    F. $2x - y$
    G. $2x + y$
    H. $x^2 + y$
    J. $2xy$
    K. $\dfrac{x^2}{y}$

11. Which value of x would satisfy the following equation?
$$4^{(2x+2)} = 8^{(3x-2)}$$

    A. -6
    B. 0
    C. $3/2$
    D. 2
    E. 4

12. If $\log_a(x) = q$ and $\log_a(y) = r$, which expression is equivalent to $\log_a(x/y)^2$?
    F. $2q + r$
    G. $2(q - r)$
    H. $2(r - q)$
    J. $2q/r$
    K. $2qr$

Vocabulary:

y varies <u>directly</u> with $x \rightarrow y = kx$

y varies <u>inversely</u> with $x \rightarrow y = \frac{k}{x}$

note: "k" is the proportionality constant... it's just a number that doesn't change.

If $D = \sqrt{\frac{72}{r^4}}$, what happens to D when r triples?

→ Remove all unchanging terms.

$$D = \sqrt{\frac{\cancel{72}}{r^4}} \rightarrow D = \sqrt{\frac{1}{r^4}}$$

→ Plug in a number for the changing term.

$r = 3$ $D = \sqrt{\frac{1}{3^2}} \rightarrow D = \boxed{\frac{1}{3}}$

we chose 3 because r tripled.

The LAV method is when a shape's dimension is changed and the effect on another dimension is the goal. Make a chart and plug in!

ex. When side length doubles, what happens to area?

① Length Area Volume

L	A	V
x	x^2	x^3
2		

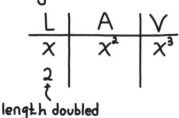

length doubled

② Length Area Volume

L	A	V
x	x^2	x^3
2	$\boxed{4}$	8

1. The recommended dosage of a certain medicine is directly proportional to the square root of the patient's weight, in kilograms. If the recommended dosage for a person weighing 64 kilograms is 80 milligrams, what is the recommended dosage for a patient weighing 36 kilograms?
   A. 36 milligrams
   B. 40 milligrams
   C. 45 milligrams
   D. 60 milligrams
   E. 140 milligrams

① d = dosage w = weight
$d = k\sqrt{w}$ $K = 10$
$\dfrac{80 = k\sqrt{64}}{\sqrt{64}} \quad \dfrac{}{\sqrt{64}}$

② $d = 10\sqrt{36}$
$d = \boxed{60}$

2. For a certain copper spring, the length in time, t seconds, for a complete period of a simple spring can be modeled by the equation $t = 2\pi\sqrt{\dfrac{m}{12}}$, where m is the mass, in kilograms, of the object. If the time required for a complete period of Spring 1 is triple the time required for a complete period of Spring 2, the mass of the object attached to Spring 1 is how many times the mass of the object attached to Spring 2?
   F. $1/3$
   G. 3
   H. 6
   J. 9
   K. 27

$t = 2\pi\sqrt{\dfrac{m}{12}}$

① Remove all constants
$t = \cancel{2\pi}\sqrt{\dfrac{m}{\cancel{12}}}$
$t = \sqrt{m} \quad t^2 = m$

② $t_1 = 3 \quad t_2 = 1 \quad \dfrac{m_1}{m_2} = \dfrac{9}{1} = \boxed{9}$
$m_1 = 9 \quad m_2 = 1$

3. Cylinder A and Cylinder B are similar. Cylinder B has four times the surface area of Cylinder A. What is the ratio of the height of Cylinder B to the height of Cylinder A?
   A. $1/4$
   B. $1/2$
   C. 1
   D. 2
   E. 4

①
L	A	V
x	x^2	x^3
	4	
area increased by a factor of 4.

② Fill in the necessary values
L	A	V
x	x^2	x^3
②	4	8
└ height is a length

4. Let k be a constant of proportionality and let variables w, x, y and z be positive real numbers. Which of the following equations does x vary directly with y, directly with the cube of z, and inversely with w?

F. $x = \dfrac{ky}{wz^3}$

G. $x = \dfrac{kz^3}{wy}$

H. $x = \dfrac{kyz^3}{w}$

J. $x = \dfrac{kw}{yz^3}$

K. $x = kyz^3w$

5. Two cubes have surface areas in a ratio of 4:9. What is the ratio of their volumes?

A. 1:2

B. 2:3

C. 4:9

D. 6:13.5

E. 8:27

6. If F varies directly with m and d but inversely with the square of t, which of the following is an expression of F in terms of m, d, and t?

F. $\dfrac{t^2}{md}$

G. $\dfrac{md}{t^2}$

H. $\dfrac{m}{dt^2}$

J. $\dfrac{d}{mt^2}$

K. mdt^2

7. In a roller coaster loop, the force exerted on the car by the rails is directly proportional to the square of the car's velocity in meters per second and inversely proportional to the loop's radius in meters. Which of the following expressions could represent the amount of force exerted on a car, traveling at a speed of v meters per second, by the rails in a loop of radius r meters?

A. $\dfrac{r}{4v^2}$

B. $\dfrac{4v^2}{r}$

C. $\dfrac{4}{v^2r}$

D. $4\left(\dfrac{v}{r}\right)^2$

E. $4(vr)^2$

8. For children ages 3-17, the recommended dosage, in milligrams, of a medicinal supplement varies directly with the cube root of three less than their age. If the recommended dosage for a 4 year old is 5 mg, what would the recommend dosage be for an 11 year old?

F. 10 mg

G. 12 mg

H. 15 mg

J. 21 mg

K. 35 mg

9. The volume of a right circular cylinder with radius r and height h is $\pi r^2 h$, where r and h have the same unit of measure. Cylinders A and B are both right circular cylinders. The radius of Cylinder B is 4 times the radius of Cylinder A. Cylinder B's height is $\frac{1}{4}$ Cylinder A's height. Compared to the volume of Cylinder A, the volume of Cylinder B is:

A. the same.

B. $^1/_2$ as great.

C. $^1/_4$ as great.

D. 2 times as great.

E. 4 times as great.

10. The distance a ball travels when thrown at a $45°$ angle of elevation is directly proportional to the square of the initial velocity in meters per second and inversely proportional to the acceleration due to gravity in meters per second per second. If k represents the constant of variation, which of the following expressions represents the distance such a ball travels when thrown with initial velocity v meters per second when the acceleration due to gravity is g meters per second per second?

F. kvg

G. $\dfrac{kv}{g}$

H. $\dfrac{kv^2}{g^2}$

J. $\dfrac{kv^2}{g}$

K. $\dfrac{k}{vg}$

11. The ratio of the areas of two similar triangles is 16:49. What is the ratio of their perimeters?

A. 4:7

B. 7:4

C. 16:49

D. 49:16

E. 64:343

12. The force of an object, F, can be modeled by the equation $F = \dfrac{md}{t^2}$, where m is the mass of the object, d is the distance the object is from a target, and t is the time in seconds it takes the object to reach the target. If Object A and Object B have the same mass and are the same distance away from their target, how many times more force will Object A exert compared to Object B, if Object A reaches its target twice as fast as Object B?

F. 1.5 times more force

G. 2 times more force

H. 2.25 times more force

J. 4 times more force

K. 6 times more force

Vector Addition:

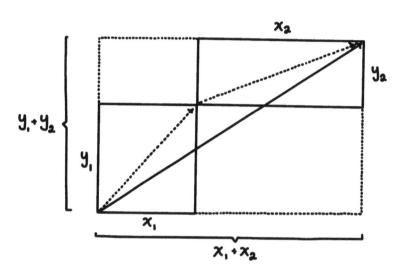

vectors are like diagonals of a rectangles.

$$\vec{v_1} + \vec{v_2} = \vec{v_3}$$

$$\langle a,b \rangle + \langle c,d \rangle = \langle a+c, b+d \rangle$$

Unit Vector:

$i \rightarrow$ unit vector in the x direction
$j \rightarrow$ unit vector in the y direction

ex: $\langle 6,9 \rangle = 6i + 9j$
$\quad\quad\;\; \Delta x \;\; \Delta y$

> Notice how the components of the vector are the sides of the rectangle, and the magnitude is the diagonal. Sides add but diagonals become something else, not a linear sum!

$$\|v_1\| = \sqrt{a^2 + b^2} \leftarrow \text{diagonal of rectangle}$$

$$\frac{v_1}{\|v_1\|} = \left\langle \frac{a}{\sqrt{a^2+b^2}}, \frac{b}{\sqrt{a^2+b^2}} \right\rangle$$

1. For vector $\overline{A} = <4,6>$ and $\overline{B} = <3,-1>$, which of the following is equal to $\overline{A} + \overline{B}$?

    A. $<10,-2>$
    B. $<7,-5>$
    C. $<2,-2>$
    D. $<7,5>$
    E. $<24,-3>$

$$\vec{A} \cdot \vec{B}$$
$$<x_A \cdot x_B, y_A \cdot y_B>$$
$$<4+3, 6\cdot 1>$$
$$\boxed{<7,5>}$$

2. Vectors AB and CD are shown in the coordinate plane below. Which of the following is the unit vector notation of $AB + CD$?

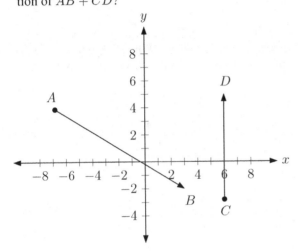

① Draw rectangles, visualize slope

② $\overrightarrow{AB} \cdot \overrightarrow{CD}$
$<x_A \cdot x_B, y_A \cdot y_B>$
$<10 \cdot 0, -6 \cdot 8>$
$<10, 2>$

③ write as $xi \cdot yj$
$$\boxed{10i \cdot 2j}$$

    F. $10i + 14j$
    G. $10i + 2j$
    H. $10i - 14j$
    J. $-10i + 14j$
    K. $-10i - 2j$

3. The component forms of vectors **j** and **k** are given by $u = <2,-7>$ and $v = <5,-3>$. Given that $4u + -3v + w = 0$, what is the component form of w?

    A. $<7,19>$
    B. $<-7,4>$
    C. $<-10,21>$
    D. $<-4,3>$
    E. $<-14,9>$

$4u - 3v \cdot w = 0$
$<4\cdot x_u - 3\cdot x_v \cdot x_w , 4\cdot y_u - 3\cdot y_v \cdot y_w> = <0,0>$

$4(2) - 3(5) \cdot x_w = 0$ $4(-7) - 3(-3) \cdot y_w = 0$
$8 - 15 \cdot x_w = 0$ $-28 \cdot 9 \cdot y_w = 0$
$x_w = 7$ $y_w = 19$

$$\boxed{\vec{w} = <7,19>}$$

4. What is the sum of the vectors $< 2, 3 >, < -4, 5 >$ and $< 3, -7 >$?

   F. $< 9, 15 >$

   G. $< -9, -15 >$

   H. $< -5, -1 >$

   J. $< 1, 1 >$

   K. $< 1, -1 >$

7. The component forms of two vectors are $a = < -3, 2 >$ and $b = < 1, 5 >$. Given that $-2a - c = b$, what is the component form of c?

   A. $< 5, -9 >$

   B. $< 5, 9 >$

   C. $< 7, -9 >$

   D. $< -5, -9 >$

   E. $< -5, 9 >$

5. What is the sum of the vectors $< -2, 6 >, < -4, 1 >$ and $< 5, -2 >$?

   A. $< 9, 1 >$

   B. $< -7, -2 >$

   C. $< -1, 5 >$

   D. $< -1, -1 >$

   E. $< -2, -1 >$

8. Vectors $\overline{AM}$ and $\overline{NT}$ are shown in the standard (x, y) coordinate plane below. Which of the following is the unit vector notation of the vector $\overline{AM} + \overline{NT}$?

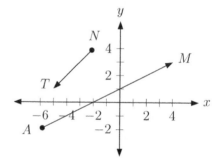

6. For vector $\overline{m} = < 5, 5 >$ and $\overline{b} = < 12, 12 >$, which of the following is equal to $\overline{m} - \overline{b}$?

   F. $< -12, -12 >$

   G. $< -7, -7 >$

   H. $< 7, 7 >$

   J. $< 12, 12 >$

   K. $< 14, 14 >$

   F. $-7\mathbf{i} + \mathbf{j}$

   G. $-2\mathbf{i} + 3\mathbf{j}$

   H. $2\mathbf{i} - 3\mathbf{j}$

   J. $7\mathbf{i} + \mathbf{j}$

   K. $7\mathbf{i} + 2\mathbf{j}$

9. The component forms of three vectors are $a = < 1, 1 >$, $b = < -1, -2 >$, and $c = < 2, 2 >$. Given that $-3a - 4b + 5c = 10d$, what is the component form of d?

A. $\left\langle \dfrac{11}{10}, \dfrac{3}{2} \right\rangle$

B. $\left\langle \dfrac{11}{10}, -\dfrac{3}{2} \right\rangle$

C. $\left\langle -\dfrac{11}{10}, \dfrac{3}{2} \right\rangle$

D. $\left\langle -\dfrac{11}{10}, -\dfrac{3}{2} \right\rangle$

E. $\left\langle -\dfrac{3}{2}, -\dfrac{11}{10} \right\rangle$

11. For vector $\overline{w} = < -10, -2 >$ and $\overline{z} = < -4, -5 >$, which of the following is equal to $\overline{w} - \overline{z}$?

A. $< -14, -7 >$

B. $< -14, -3 >$

C. $< -6, \ 3 >$

D. $< -6, -3 >$

E. $< \ 14, \ 3 >$

10. Vectors A and B are shown in the standard (x, y) coordinate plane below. Which of the following is the unit vector notation of $A + B$?

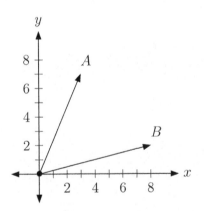

F. $< 5, 5 >$

G. $< 7, 6 >$

H. $< 10, 10 >$

J. $< 11, 9 >$

K. $< 24, 14 >$

12. Vectors $\overline{AB}$ and $\overline{CD}$ are shown in the standard (x, y) coordinate plane below. Which of the following is the unit vector notation of the vector $\overline{AB} + \overline{CD}$?

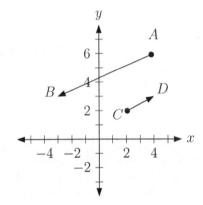

F. $-5\mathbf{i} - 2\mathbf{j}$

G. $-5\mathbf{i} + 2\mathbf{j}$

H. $5\mathbf{i} - 5\mathbf{j}$

J. $9\mathbf{i} + 4\mathbf{j}$

K. $9\mathbf{i} + 6\mathbf{j}$

Law of sines and law of cosines are for NON-RIGHT TRIANGLES only. Use SOHCAHTOA and pythagorean theorem for right triangles.

3 given pieces of info about a triangle	proper law
AAA	none
SAA/ASA	law of sines
SSA	law of sines
SAS	law of cosines
SSS	law of cosines

Law of cosines

$$c^2 = a^2 + b^2 - 2ab\cos C$$

Law of sines

$$\frac{\sin A}{a} = \frac{\sin B}{b} = \frac{\sin C}{c}$$

Law of Sines works for non-right triangles where a side and the angle OPPOSITE it are given.

Law of Cosines is for all other situations when three pieces of information are given.

1. While on a hiking expedition, Dominique can head in one of two directions. Dominique is $54°$ east of north and $10,250$ feet away from Basecamp A, and $45°$ west of north and x feet away from Basecamp B, as shown in the figure below. Which of the following expressions gives the value of Dominique's distance in feet, x, from Basecamp B?

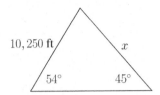

A. $\dfrac{10,250 \ \sin 45°}{\sin 54°}$

B. $\dfrac{10,250 \ \sin 54°}{\sin 45°}$

C. $\dfrac{\sin 54°}{10,250 \ \sin 45°}$

D. $\dfrac{\sin 45°}{10,250 \ \sin 54°}$

E. $\dfrac{10,250 \cdot 54}{45}$

2. Which of the following expressions could be used to calculate the measure of $\angle \theta$ in triangle ABC shown below?

(Note for any triangle ABC, the law of cosines states that $c^2 = a^2 + b^2 - 2(a)(b)cos(C)$ and the law of sines states that $\dfrac{sin(A)}{a} = \dfrac{sin(B)}{b} = \dfrac{sin(C)}{c}$.)

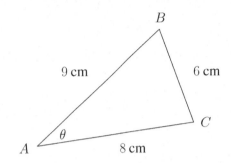

F. $6^2 = 9^2 + 8^2 - 2(9)(8)cos(\theta)$

G. $8^2 = 9^2 + 6^2 - 2(9)(6)cos(\theta)$

H. $9^2 = 6^2 + 8^2 - 2(6)(8)cos(\theta)$

J. $\dfrac{sin(\theta)}{6} = \dfrac{1}{8}$

K. $\dfrac{sin(\theta)}{6} = \dfrac{1}{9}$

Given: SAA
Use: law of sines

$\dfrac{\sin A}{a} = \dfrac{\sin B}{b}$
↓
$\dfrac{\sin 45}{10,250} = \dfrac{\sin 54}{x}$ → $x = \boxed{\dfrac{10,250 \cdot \sin 54}{\sin 45}}$

a = 10,250
b = x
sin A = sin 45
sin B = sin 54

Given: SSS
Use: law of cosines

$c^2 = a^2 + b^2 - 2abcosC$
↓
$\boxed{6^2 = 9^2 + 8^2 - 2(9)(8)cos\theta}$

a = 9
b = 8
c = 6
C = θ

3. In $\triangle MNP$ below, what is the approximate length of side $\overline{MP}$?

(Note: For an triangle, if a, b, and c are the lengths of the sides opposite $\angle A$, $\angle B$, and $\angle C$, respectively, then $a^2 = b^2 + c^2 - 2bc \cos \angle A$. The value of $\cos 104°$ is approximately -0.24.)

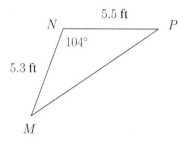

A. 6.7 feet
B. 7.2 feet
C. 7.7 feet
D. 8.1 feet
E. 8.5 feet

4. In triangle GHJ, $m\angle G = 65°$, $m\angle H = 40°$, and $\overline{HJ} = 50$ inches. What is the approximate measure of $\overline{GH}$?

(Note: For a triangle with sides of length a, b and c, which are opposite $\angle A$, $\angle B$ and $\angle C$, respectively, $\dfrac{\sin \angle A}{a} = \dfrac{\sin \angle B}{b} = \dfrac{\sin \angle C}{c}$.)

F. 35.5 inches
G. 46.9 inches
H. 53.3 inches
J. 70.5 inches
K. 75.1 inches

5. The isosceles triangle shown below has two equal sides of length z and one side of length 3. Which of the expressions below correctly relates z and $\angle W$, the angle opposite the side of length 3?

(Note: For an triangle, if a, b, and c are the lengths of the sides opposite $\angle A$, $\angle B$, and $\angle C$, respectively, then $a^2 = b^2 + c^2 - 2bc \cos \angle A$.)

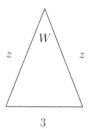

A. $\cos \angle W = 1 - \dfrac{9}{2z^2}$

B. $\cos \angle W = \dfrac{9}{2z^2} - 1$

C. $\cos \angle W = \dfrac{2z^2 - 9}{2z}$

D. $\cos \angle W = \dfrac{9}{2z^2} + 1$

E. $\cos \angle W = \dfrac{9}{2z^2} + 2$

6. An artist wants to create a uniquely shaped pennant for his son's baseball team. He has determined the side lengths and the angle shown below for the pennant. When the pennant is completed, what will be the approximate value of its perimeter?

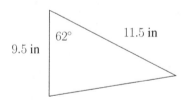

F. 10.4 inches
G. 11.0 inches
H. 32.0 inches
J. 35.3 inches
K. 56.3 inches

Questions 7-9 pertain to the following information.

Law of cosines: $c^2 = a^2 + b^2 - 2ab \cos C$

Law of sines: $\dfrac{\sin A}{a} = \dfrac{\sin B}{b} = \dfrac{\sin C}{c}$

Area of a triangle: $k = \dfrac{ab \sin C}{2}$

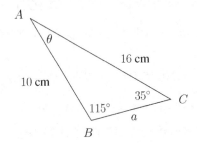

7. Which of the following is NOT true for angle θ shown above?

A. $\theta = 180° - (115° + 35°)$

B. $\dfrac{\sin(\theta)}{a} = \dfrac{\sin(115°)}{16}$

C. $a^2 = 16^2 + 10^2 - 2(16)(10) \cos(\theta)$

D. $\dfrac{\sin(\theta)}{a} = \dfrac{\sin(35°)}{10}$

E. $\sin \theta = \sqrt{\sin^2(115°) + \sin^2(35°)}$

8. To the nearest tenth of a centimeter, what is the length of side a?

F. 5.9 cm

G. 9 cm

H. 12.5 cm

J. 18.9 cm

K. 26.1 cm

9. To the nearest whole number, what is the area, in square centimeters, of triangle ABC?

A. 30 cm^2

B. 40 cm^2

C. 46 cm^2

D. 73 cm^2

E. 80 cm^2

10. An isosceles triangle has two 50° angles and two sides of length d. Which of the following is a correct expression for the length of the third side?

(Note: The law of sines states that, given

$\triangle XYZ, \dfrac{\sin \angle X}{x} = \dfrac{\sin \angle Y}{y} = \dfrac{\sin \angle Z}{z}.$

The law of cosines states that given $\triangle XYZ$,

$z^2 = x^2 + y^2 - 2xy \cos \angle Z.$)

F. $\dfrac{d \sin 50°}{\sin 80°}$

G. $\dfrac{d \sin 80°}{\sin 50°}$

H. $\sqrt{2d^2 - 2d \cos 80°}$

J. $\sqrt{2d^2(1 - \cos 50°)}$

K. $\sqrt{\dfrac{2d^2}{2d \cos 80°}}$

<u>Given</u>: one trig value and a specific domain (ex: $\frac{\pi}{2} < \theta < \pi$).

<u>Goal</u>: another trig value.

① Find the other trig value by following the steps in section 4.7. IGNORE any negative values (make all sides positive).

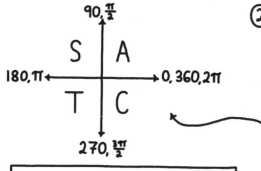

② Use the given angle domain to determine whether the angle should be positive or negative.

the letter in each quadrant indicates which trig function is positive.

"All Students Take Calc" is a popular mnemonic

(A="All", S="Sine", C="Cosine", T="Tangent")

You actually need to memorize this ASTC quadrant concept, as a calculator cannot properly indicate when the trig functions are positive and negative as needed.

Splitting these problems into finding side length (part 1) and finding the proper sign (part 2) is best for accuracy.

1. If $\tan\theta = 1$ and $\frac{\pi}{2} \le \theta \le \frac{3\pi}{2}$, what is the value of $\cos\theta$?

    A. -1

    B. $-\dfrac{2}{2}$

    C. $-\dfrac{1}{2}$

    D. $-\dfrac{\sqrt{2}}{2}$

    E. $\dfrac{\sqrt{2}}{2}$

① $\tan\theta = 1 \to$

$\cos\theta = \dfrac{1}{\sqrt{2}} = \dfrac{\sqrt{2}}{2}$

② cosine is negative in the II and III quadrants.

$$\boxed{-\dfrac{2}{2}}$$

2. If $\sec\theta = -2$ and $0 \le \theta \le \pi$, what is the value of $\sin\theta$?

    F. -1

    G. $-\dfrac{2}{2}$

    H. $-\dfrac{1}{2}$

    J. $\dfrac{\sqrt{2}}{2}$

    K. $\dfrac{\sqrt{3}}{2}$

① $\sec\theta = \dfrac{1}{\cos\theta} = \dfrac{H}{A}$

$\sin\theta = \dfrac{\sqrt{3}}{2}$

② sine is positive in the I and II quadrants.

$$\boxed{\dfrac{\sqrt{3}}{2}}$$

3. If $\sin\theta \leq 0$ and $\tan\theta \leq 0$, which constraints are true for θ?

   A. $0 \leq \theta \leq \dfrac{\pi}{2}$

   B. $\dfrac{\pi}{2} \leq \theta \leq \pi$

   C. $\pi \leq \theta \leq \dfrac{3\pi}{2}$

   D. $\dfrac{3\pi}{2} \leq \theta \leq 2\pi$

   E. $0 \leq \theta \leq 2\pi$

4. If $\cos\theta < 0$ and $\sin\theta > 0$, which constraints are true for θ?

   F. $0 \leq \theta \leq \dfrac{\pi}{2}$

   G. $\dfrac{\pi}{2} \leq \theta \leq \pi$

   H. $\pi \leq \theta \leq \dfrac{3\pi}{2}$

   J. $\dfrac{3\pi}{2} \leq \theta \leq 2\pi$

   K. $0 \leq \theta \leq 2\pi$

5. If $\cos\theta = \dfrac{\sqrt{3}}{2}$ and $0 \leq \theta \leq \pi$, what is the value of $\sin\theta$?

   A. 0

   B. $\dfrac{1}{2}$

   C. $\dfrac{\sqrt{2}}{2}$

   D. $\dfrac{\sqrt{3}}{2}$

   E. 2

6. If $\sin\theta = -\dfrac{\sqrt{3}}{2}$ and $\pi \leq \theta \leq \dfrac{3\pi}{2}$, what is the value of $\cos\theta$?

   F. -1

   G. $-\dfrac{2}{2}$

   H. $-\dfrac{1}{2}$

   J. $\dfrac{\sqrt{2}}{2}$

   K. 1

7. If $\tan\theta = 1$ and $0 \leq \theta \leq \pi$, what is the value of $\sin\theta$?

   A. 0

   B. $\dfrac{1}{2}$

   C. $\dfrac{\sqrt{2}}{2}$

   D. $\dfrac{\sqrt{3}}{2}$

   E. 2

8. If $\sin\theta = \dfrac{4}{5}$ and $0 \leq \theta \leq 2\pi$, what is the value of $\cos\theta$?

   F. $-\dfrac{3}{5}$ only

   G. $\dfrac{3}{5}$ only

   H. $\dfrac{4}{5}$ only

   J. $-\dfrac{3}{5}$ and $\dfrac{3}{5}$

   K. $-\dfrac{4}{5}$ and $\dfrac{4}{5}$

9. If $\tan\theta = \dfrac{12}{5}$ and $\pi \leq \theta \leq 2\pi$, what is the value of $\sin\theta$?

   A. $-\dfrac{12}{13}$ only

   B. $\dfrac{12}{13}$ only

   C. $\dfrac{5}{13}$ only

   D. $-\dfrac{5}{13}$ and $\dfrac{5}{13}$

   E. $-\dfrac{12}{13}$ and $\dfrac{12}{13}$

5.11 CHAPTER 5 QUIZ

As the test approaches the end, the writers create difficulty with more obscure topics rather than multi-step problems. These topics are not covered as well in school, so if you hit speedbumps while taking the quiz, be sure to *log* some extra hours of review on those concepts.

Speaking of Logs, don't forget that a logarithm with no variables inside of it is just a number. Use your calculator to find the value.

And speaking of remembering stuff, don't forget that the quiz is going to use the techniques explained in this Chapter. If a question seems overly confusing, figure out which system applies to it.

CHAPTER FIVE QUIZ
25 Minutes — 20 Questions

DIRECTIONS: Solve each problem, choose the correct answer, and then fill in the corresponding oval on your answer document.

Do not linger over problems that take too much time. Solve as many as you can; then return to the others in the time you have left for this test.

You are permitted to use a calculator on this test. You may use your calculator for any problems you choose,

but some of the problems may be best done without using a calculator.

Note: Unless otherwise stated, all of the following should be assumed.
1. Illustrative figures are NOT necessarily drawn to scale.
2. Geometric figures lie in a plane.
3. The word *line* indicates a straight line.
4. The word *average* indicates arithmetic mean.

---

1. In the standard (x, y) coordinate plane, when $a \neq 0$ and $b \neq 0$, the graph of $f(x) = \dfrac{3x - a}{2x + b}$ has a horizontal asymptote at:
   A. $y = -b/2$
   B. $y = -b$
   C. $y = -b/a$
   D. $y = 3/2$
   E. $y = a$

2. Which of the following expressions is equivalent to the expression $(6 - 3i)(2 + 4i)$?
   F. $20i$
   G. $12 + 12i$
   H. 24
   J. $30 + 6i$
   K. $24 + 18i$

3. What is the 66th digit to the right of the decimal point in the repeating number $0.\overline{15478}$?
   A. 1
   B. 5
   C. 4
   D. 7
   E. 8

4. If $\log_a x = Q$ and $\log_a y = P$, then $\log_a \left(\dfrac{x}{y}\right)^5 =?$
   F. $5Q - P$
   G. $5QP$
   H. $5(Q + P)$
   J. $5(Q - P)$
   K. $5Q^P$

Use the following information to answer questions 5-7.

Consider the function $f(x) = \dfrac{3x^2 + 27}{x^2 - 16}$

5. For which value(s) of x is the function undefined?
   A. $\{0\}$
   B. $\{-4\}$
   C. $\{0, 4\}$
   D. $\{-4, 4\}$
   E. $\{-4, 0, 4\}$

6. At which point(s) will the asymptotes of the function intersect?
   F. $(3, 4)$ only
   G. $(3, 4)$ and $(3, -4)$
   H. $(4, 3)$ only
   J. $(4, 3)$ and $(-4, 3)$
   K. The asymptotes will not intersect

7. If $(x + 3i)$ is a factor of the numerator, which of the following correctly lists additional factor(s)?
   A. $(x + 4)(x - 4)$
   B. $(x + 4i)(x - 4i)(x - 3i)$
   C. $(3x - 3i)$
   D. $(3x + 9i)$
   E. $(3x - 9i)$

---

8. For vectors $\vec{M} = <2,4>$, $\vec{N} = <3,-3>$, and $\vec{P} = <-1,0>$, which of the following is equal to $\vec{M} + \vec{N} + \vec{P}$?

    F. $<4,-1>$
    G. $<4,0>$
    H. $<4,1>$
    J. $<-1,-1>$
    K. $<-12,-5>$

9. The first four terms of a certain arithmetic sequence are shown below: 9, 16, 23, 30, ... What is the mean of the first 10 terms of this sequence?

    A. 38
    B. 40.5
    C. 43.25
    D. 45
    E. 47.75

10. The value of $\log_2 18$ is between of the following pairs of consecutive integers?

    F. 0 and 1
    G. 1 and 2
    H. 2 and 3
    J. 3 and 4
    K. 4 and 5

11. The volume of a right circular cylinder with radius r and height h is $\pi r^2 h$, where r and h have the same unit of measure. Cylinders X and Y are both right circular cylinders. The radius of Cylinder Y is 10 times the radius of Cylinder X. Cylinder Y's height is $\frac{1}{2}$ Cylinder X's height. Compared to the volume of Cylinder X, the volume of Cylinder Y is:

    A. the same
    B. $1/50$ as great
    C. $1/25$ as great
    D. 25 times as great
    E. 50 times as great

Use the following information to answer questions 12-14.

Consider the equation $\log_a \dfrac{b}{c^2} = d$

12. If $\log_a b = x$ and $\log_a c = y$, which of the following expressions is also equal to d?

    F. $2(x-y)$
    G. $2x - y$
    H. $x - 2y$
    J. $2(y-x)$
    K. $2y - x$

13. If the value of b is increased by a factor of 10, d:

    A. increases by $\log_a 10$.
    B. decreases by $\log_a 10$.
    C. increases by $\log_a 1$.
    D. decreases by $\log_a 1$.
    E. increases by a^{10}.

14. What is the value of c in terms of a, b, and d?

    F. $\sqrt{\dfrac{b}{a^d}}$
    G. $\sqrt[d]{\dfrac{b}{a}}$
    H. $\dfrac{\sqrt{a^d}}{b}$
    J. $\dfrac{\sqrt{b}}{a^d}$
    K. $\sqrt[d]{\dfrac{a}{b^2}}$

15. What are the vertical asymptotes of the function

$f(x) = \dfrac{3x^2 - 2x - 5}{2x^2 - 2}$ when graphed in the standard

(x, y) coordinate plane?

  A. $x = 1$ only
  B. $x = -1$ only
  C. $x = -1$ and $x = 1$
  D. $x = {}^3/_2$
  E.   This function has no vertical asymptotes

16. The product of two numbers is 145. If one of the numbers is the complex number $8 + 9i$, what is the other number?

  F. $9 + 8i$
  G. $8 - 9i$
  H. $\frac{8}{9} + \frac{9}{8}i$
  J. $72i$
  K. 17

17. If $-2 \le x \le 1$ and $2 \le y \le 4$, what is the greatest

possible value of the expression $\dfrac{10}{y - x}$?

  A. 10
  B. $3.\overline{3}$
  C. 2.5
  D. 1.25
  E. 0.10

> Use the following information to answer questions 18-20.

Consider triangle SOR below, where α is formed by the x-axis and $\overline{SO}$, and β is formed by $\angle SOR$.

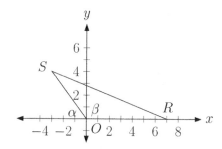

18. What is the correct unit vector notation of the vector $\overrightarrow{OR} + \overrightarrow{OS}$?

  F. $10\mathbf{i} + 4\mathbf{j}$
  G. $-10\mathbf{i} + 4\mathbf{j}$
  H. $4\mathbf{i} - 4\mathbf{j}$
  J. $-4\mathbf{i} - 10\mathbf{j}$
  K. $4\mathbf{i} + 4\mathbf{j}$

19. Which of the following expressions does NOT represent the length of $\overline{SR}$?

  A. $\sqrt{5^2 + 7^2 - 2(5)(7)\cos(\beta)}$
  B. $\sqrt{(-3 - 7)^2 + (4 - 0)^2}$
  C. $\sqrt{[5\sin(\alpha)]^2 + [5\cos(\alpha) + 7]^2}$
  D. $\dfrac{7\sin(\beta)}{\sin(\alpha)}$
  E. $|10 + 4i|$

20. Which of the following correctly states the sine and the cosine of $\angle \beta$?

  F. $\sin \beta = 0.6, \cos \beta = 0.8$
  G. $\sin \beta = 0.6, \cos \beta = -0.8$
  H. $\sin \beta = 0.8, \cos \beta = 0.6$
  J. $\sin \beta = 0.8, \cos \beta = -0.6$
  K. $\sin \beta = -0.8, \cos \beta = -0.6$

Congratulations are in order!

But first, this Chapter deals with many of the intense Mathematical concepts that consistently appear in the last portion of the exam.

Given the potential depth of study possible for each of these topics, we will frequently dive into additional guess & check procedures.

☐ Understand the topic at hand.

☐ Learn an analysis trick.

☐ Plug in a guess and check the answers.

The ACT will not delve too deep into these fringe topics, so hopefully that should make these problems rather consistent in their apperance and solutions.

So it will be a strong mix of "tough concepts" and workarounds, tricks, and substitution methods.

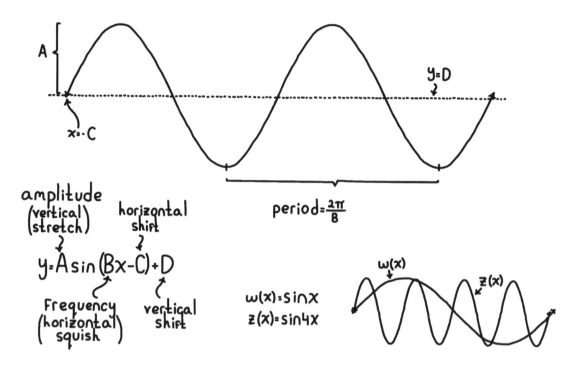

amplitude
(vertical)
(stretch)

horizontal
shift

$$y = A \sin (Bx - C) + D$$

Frequency
(horizontal
squish)

vertical
shift

$x = -C$

$y = D$

period $= \frac{2\pi}{B}$

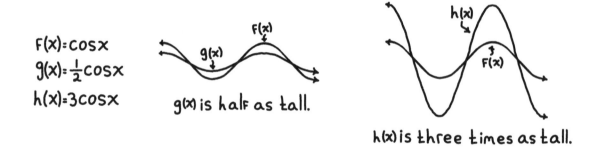

$w(x) = \sin x$
$z(x) = \sin 4x$

in one cycle of $w(x)$, $z(x)$ happens 4 times.

$F(x) = \cos x$
$g(x) = \frac{1}{2} \cos x$
$h(x) = 3 \cos x$

$g(x)$ is half as tall.

$h(x)$ is three times as tall.

Try to get a good feel for what A, B, C, and D do to the function.

Important : A & D are "direct" ..

.. and B & C are "inverse".

While B affects the Period, note that Tangent always has HALF the period of Sine or Cosine

1. What is the range of the function $f(x) = 3\sin(x) - 2$

   A. All real numbers

   B. $-1 < x < 1$

   C. $-3 < x < 3$

   D. $-3 < x < 1$

   E. $-5 < x < 1$

→ First, try graphing on your calculator and observe the low and high values.

→ If you're feeling formulas,

   A=3, B=1, C=0, D=-2

   Range = [D-A, D+A]

        [-2-3, -2+3]

         [-5, 1]

2. Which of the following MUST be true about the graph of $f(x) = A\cos(Bx - C) + D$?

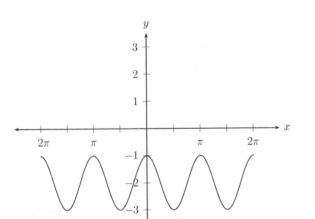

   F. $|A| = -3, B = 2$

   G. $|A| = 3, D = 0$

   H. $B = 2, D = 0$

   J. $B = 2, C = \pi$

   K. $C = 2\pi, D = 3$

① Amplitude is half the vertical coverage.

   -3 → -1 covers 2 thus |A|=1

② The function is clearly shifted down, so D is negative. D=-2

③ cos starts at the top, so C=0 or some multiple of the period.

④ $\frac{2\pi}{B} = \pi$, B=2.

You don't have to do every step listed here. Step 1 eliminated F & G, while step 2 eliminated H & K. Down to 1 means we're done!

Functions that are referred to as "odd" and "even" are curves with a certain symmetry.

"Odd" functions are symmetric around the origin. Examples include sine, tangent, and odd powers of x.

"Even" functions are symmetric around the y-axis. Examples include cosine, absolute value of x, and quadratic functions (as well as other even powers).

3. The graph of the function $y = 2\sin(2x)$ is shown below in the standard (x, y) coordinate plane. What are the amplitude and period of the function?

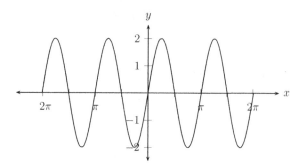

A. Amplitude: 2, Period: 2
B. Amplitude: π, Period: 2
C. Amplitude: 2, Period: 4π
D. Amplitude: 2, Period: π
E. Amplitude: $\frac{1}{2}$, Period: π

4. The graph of the function $y = a\sin bx$ is shown below for certain positive values of a and b. Which of the following values is equal to a?

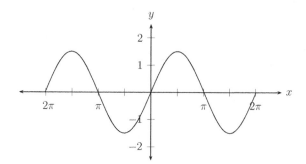

F. $1/2$
G. $2/3$
H. 1
J. $3/2$
K. 2

5. Which of the following statements is true about the graph of $f(x) = 3\sin(x)$?
A. It is an odd function
B. It is symmetrical to the y-axis
C. It is symmetrical to the x-axis
D. It has a period of 3
E. It has an amplitude of 2π

6. What is the value of A in the graph of $f(x) = -A\sin(2x - \pi)$ shown below?

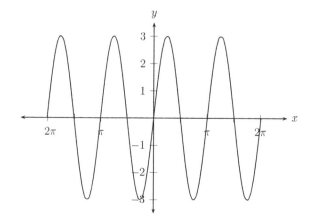

F. -3
G. 1
H. 2
J. 3
K. π

7. What is the range of the function shown below:

$$f(x) = -2\cos(x) + 2$$

A. All real numbers
B. $-1 \le x \le 1$
C. $-2 \le x \le 2$
D. $0 \le x \le 2$
E. $0 \le x \le 4$

8. The graph of the function $y = \cos x$ is shown in the standard (x, y) coordinate plane below. What is the period of $\cos x$?

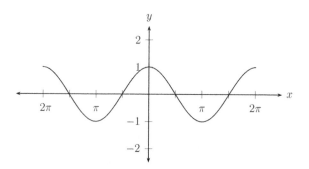

F. $\frac{\pi}{4}$
G. $\frac{\pi}{2}$
H. π
J. 2π
K. 4π

9. Which of the following is NOT true about the cosine graph below?

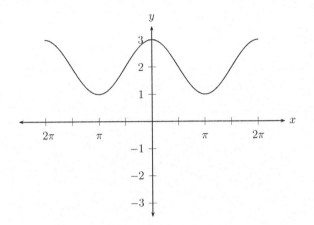

A. It has a vertical shift two units up
B. It has a period of 2π
C. It has an amplitude of 1
D. It is an even function ($f(x) = f(-x)$)
E. It is an odd function ($f(-x) = -f(x)$)

10. The graph of the function $y = a\sin(bx + c)$ is shown below for certain positive values of a, b and c. Which of the following values is equal to b?

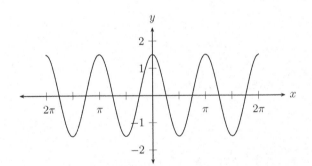

F. $\dfrac{\pi}{2}$

G. 2

H. $\dfrac{3\pi}{2}$

J. 2π

K. $\dfrac{5\pi}{2}$

11. The graph of the function $y = \cot x$ is shown in the standard (x, y) coordinate plane below. What is the period of $\cot x$?

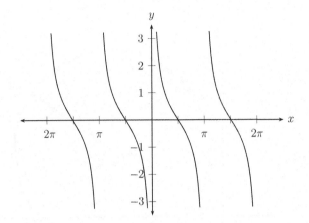

A. $\dfrac{\pi}{4}$

B. $\dfrac{\pi}{2}$

C. π

D. 2π

E. 4π

12. Below is the graph of $f(x) = \sec x$. What is the period of this function?
(Note: $\sec x = \dfrac{1}{\cos x}$)

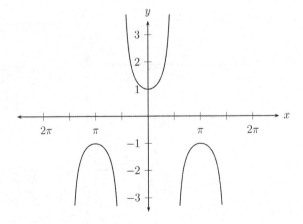

F. $\dfrac{\pi}{2}$

G. 1

H. π

J. 2

K. 2π

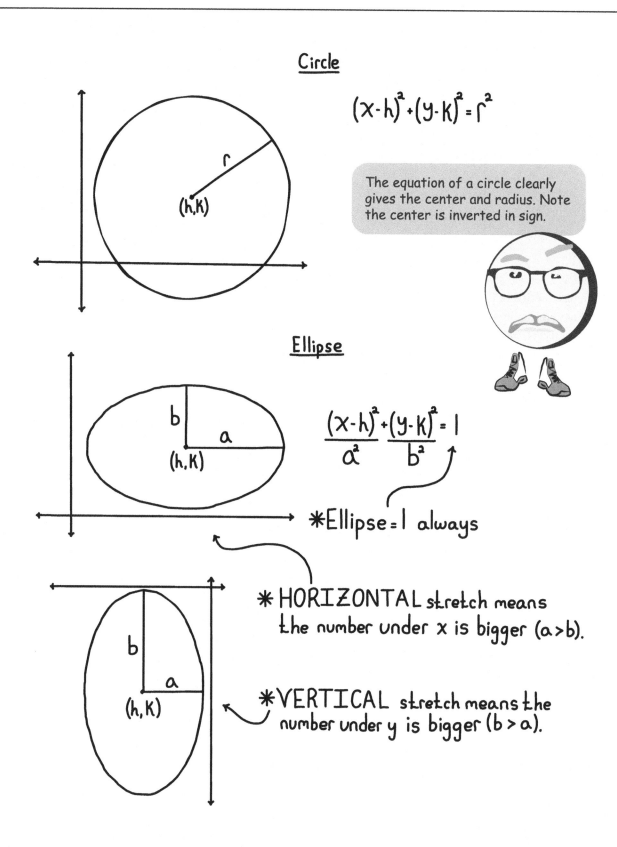

Circle

$$(x-h)^2+(y-k)^2=r^2$$

The equation of a circle clearly gives the center and radius. Note the center is inverted in sign.

Ellipse

$$\frac{(x-h)^2}{a^2}+\frac{(y-k)^2}{b^2}=1$$

✳Ellipse = 1 always

✳ HORIZONTAL stretch means the number under x is bigger (a>b).

✳ VERTICAL stretch means the number under y is bigger (b>a).

1. Which of the following is an equation of the circle shown in the standard (x, y) coordinate plane below?

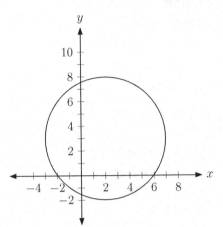

center = (2,3)   radius = 5

$(x-h)^2 + (y-k)^2 = r^2$

$\boxed{(x-2)^2 + (y-3)^2 = 25}$

A. $(x - 2)^2 + (y - 3)^2 = 25$

B. $(x - 2)^2 + (y - 3)^2 = 5$

C. $(x + 2)^2 + (y + 3)^2 = 25$

D. $(x - 2)^2 + (y - 3)^2 = 5$

E. $(x + 2)^2 + (y - 3)^2 = 25$

2. Which of the following lines would be *tangent* to the graph of $\dfrac{x^2}{36} + \dfrac{y^2}{9} = 1$

F. $y = 6$

G. $x = 3$

H. $y = -3$

J. $y = 6x$

K. $y = x - 3$

→ Tangent means "touches at one point."

→ If you plug in the answer choices and solve for x, a tangent line should have ONE solution.

$\frac{x^2}{36} + \frac{y^2}{9} = 1 \rightarrow x^2 + 4y^2 = 36$

F) $x^2 + 4(6)^2 = 36$
$x^2 = -108 \rightarrow$ no solutions ✗

G) $3^2 + 4y^2 = 36$
$4y^2 = 27$
$y = \pm\sqrt{\frac{27}{4}} \rightarrow$ two solutions. ✗

H) $x^2 + 4(-3)^2 = 36$
$x^2 + 36 = 36$
$x^2 = 0 \rightarrow$ one solution. ✓

3. Which of the following is an equation of the ellipse shown in the standard (x, y) coordinate plane below?

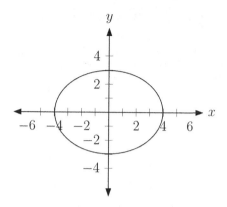

A. $x^2 - y^2 = 1$

B. $y^2 = x^2 + 1$

C. $\left(\dfrac{y}{4}\right)^2 + \left(\dfrac{x}{4}\right)^2 = 1$

D. $\left(\dfrac{y}{4}\right)^2 + \left(\dfrac{x}{3}\right)^2 = 1$

E. $\left(\dfrac{y}{3}\right)^2 + \left(\dfrac{x}{4}\right)^2 = 1$

From the picture, we know
1. ellipse
2. center is (0,0)
3. horizontal stretch,

so the answer must be

$$\frac{x^2}{a^2} + \frac{y}{b^2} = 1,$$

where $a > b$ ... $a \neq b$
$\qquad\qquad a \not< b.$

only Ⓔ has this.

---

4. What is the equation of a circle in the standard (x, y) coordinate plane with center at $(2, 3)$ and radius of 5?

F. $(x + 2)^2 + (y + 3)^2 = 25$

G. $(x + 2)^2 - (y + 3)^2 = 25$

H. $(x - 2)^2 + (y + 3)^2 = 25$

J. $(x - 2)^2 + (y - 3)^2 = 5$

K. $(x - 2)^2 + (y - 3)^2 = 25$

5. What are the coordinates of the center of the circle whose equation is $(x - 3)^2 + (y + 4)^2 = 25$

A. $(5, -5)$

B. $(3, 4)$

C. $(3, -4)$

D. $(-3, 4)$

E. $(-3, -4)$

6. Which of these represents the equation of a circle that has a diameter whose endpoints are at $(0, 2)$ and $(0, 6)$?

F. $x^2 + (y - 4)^2 = 4$

G. $x^2 + (y - 4)^2 = 2$

H. $(x + 4)^2 + y^2 = 6$

J. $x^2 + (y + 4)^2 = 9$

K. $(x - 4)^2 + y^2 = 9$

7. Which of the following circles has the largest area?

A. $(x - 15)^2 + (y + 6)^2 = 1$

B. $(x + 2)^2 + (y - 4)^2 = 5^2$

C. $(x - 11)^2 + (y - 3)^2 = \sqrt{71}$

D. $(x + 5)^2 + (y - 2)^2 = 3\pi$

E. $(x - 4)^2 + y^2 = 33$

8. Which of the following is the equation of the ellipse shown below?

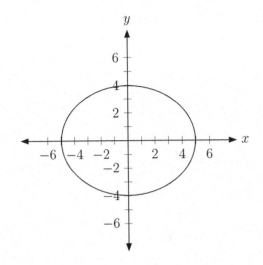

10. Which of the following is the equation of the ellipse on the coordinate plane below?

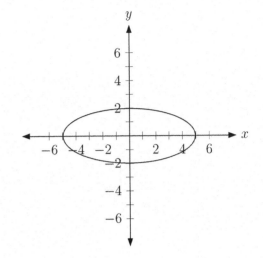

F. $\dfrac{x^2}{25} + \dfrac{y^2}{16} = 1$

G. $\dfrac{x^2}{16} + \dfrac{y^2}{25} = 1$

H. $\dfrac{(x-5)^2}{25} + \dfrac{(y-4)^2}{16} = 1$

J. $\dfrac{(x-5)^2}{16} + \dfrac{(y-4)^2}{25} = 1$

K. $\dfrac{(x+5)^2}{25} + \dfrac{(y+4)^2}{16} = 1$

F. $\dfrac{x^2}{4} + \dfrac{y^2}{25} = 1$

G. $\dfrac{x^2}{4} - \dfrac{y^2}{25} = 1$

H. $\dfrac{x^2}{5} + \dfrac{y^2}{2} = 1$

J. $\dfrac{x^2}{25} - \dfrac{y^2}{4} = 1$

K. $\dfrac{x^2}{25} + \dfrac{y^2}{4} = 1$

9. When graphed in the standard (x, y) coordinate plane, the ellipse $\dfrac{(x-2)^2}{9} + \dfrac{(y+1)^2}{16} = 1$ and the line $y = 6x + 10$ intersect at how many points?

A. 0

B. 1

C. 2

D. 3

E. 4

11. What is the equation of the ellipse shown on the coordinate plane below?

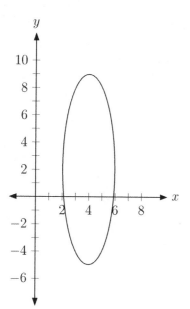

12. Which of the following is an equation of the ellipse shown in the standard (x, y) coordinate plane below?

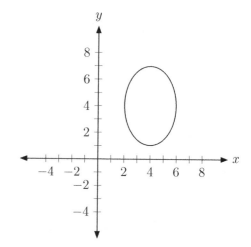

A. $\dfrac{x^2}{4} + \dfrac{y^2}{49} = 1$

B. $\dfrac{(x-4)^2}{4} + \dfrac{(y-2)^2}{49} = 1$

C. $\dfrac{(x+4)^2}{4} + \dfrac{(y+2)^2}{49} = 1$

D. $\dfrac{(x-4)^2}{49} + \dfrac{(y-2)^2}{4} = 1$

E. $\dfrac{(x+4)^2}{49} + \dfrac{(y-2)^2}{4} = 1$

F. $(x+4)^2 + (y+4)^2 = 1$

G. $(x+4)^2 - (y+4)^2 = 1$

H. $(x-4)^2 + (y-4)^2 = 1$

J. $\dfrac{(x-4)^2}{4} + \dfrac{(y-4)^2}{9} = 1$

K. $\dfrac{(x-4)^2}{4} - \dfrac{(y-4)^2}{9} = 1$

Negatives and Ellipses don't mix. In number 12, options G & K are HYPERBOLAS, a whole different shape.

13. Which of the following is the correct graph of the equation $\dfrac{(x+1)^2}{9} + \dfrac{(y-4)^2}{25} = 1$?

A.

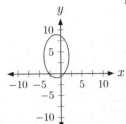

D.

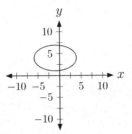

B.

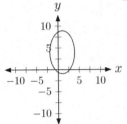

E.

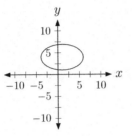

C.

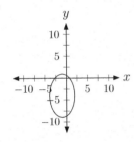

14. The figure below shows the graph of an ellipse. To the nearest tenth, what is the value of $|a| + |b|$?

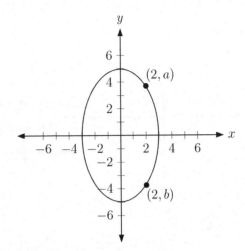

F. 5

G. 6.7

H. 7.5

J. 8.4

K. 9.8

①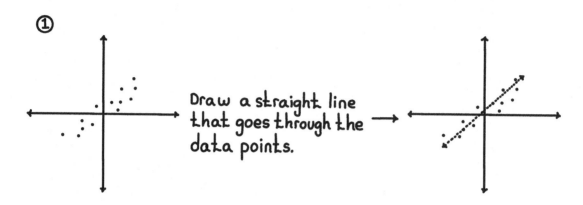

Draw a straight line that goes through the data points.

②
→ Calculate the slope of the line you created.

→ Determine the y-intercept.

---

x	y
5.5	6.6
4.1	4.5
3.9	4.7
2.3	2.8
1.4	1.7

① Determine the slope of the line that connects these points.

→ Calculate $\frac{y}{x}$ for each point.

$\frac{6.6}{5.5} = 1.2$ $\frac{4.5}{4.1} = 1.1$ $\frac{4.7}{3.9} = 1.2$ $\frac{2.8}{2.3} = 1.2$ $\frac{1.7}{1.4} = 1.2$

→ All of the quotients are 1.2 or close to it, so the answer is $\boxed{1.2}$.

Many statistics questions are more Vocabulary than Math.

For example, if you see the term "Residual", it is essentially the distance of a scatter plot point to the Line of Best Fit. The largest Residual will come from the farthest away point.

1. Which of the following values is the slope of a line of best fit for the points shown below in the standard (x, y) coordinate plane?

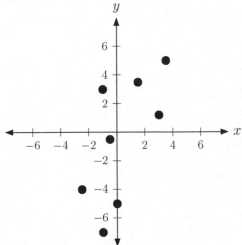

A. -2
B. -1
C. 0
D. 2
E. 4

① Draw the line of best fit.

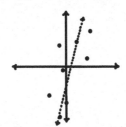

② Find the slope between two points that lie on the line.

→ (1.5, 3.5) & (-1, -7.5)

$$\frac{-7.5-3.5}{-1-1.5} = \frac{-11}{-2.5} = 4.4$$

the best answer is ④.

2. For an experiment in physics class, students collected data values for variables x and y shown in the table below. Theory predicts that y varies directly with x. Based on the experimental data, which of the following values is closest to the constant of variation?

x	y
4.62	0.601
7.11	0.924
8.65	1.125
12.40	1.612
14.75	1.917

(Note: The variable y varies directly with the variable x provided that $y = kx$ for some nonzero constant k, the constant of variation.)

F. -1.42
G. 0.13
H. 2.45
J. 10.12
K. 16.00

① $k=\frac{y}{x}$; solve for k for every point.

$$\frac{0.601}{4.62} = 0.13 \qquad \frac{0.924}{7.11} = 0.13$$

$$\frac{1.125}{8.65} = 0.13 \qquad \frac{1.612}{12.40} = 0.13$$

$$\frac{1.917}{14.75} = 0.13 \quad \text{the answer is } \boxed{0.13}.$$

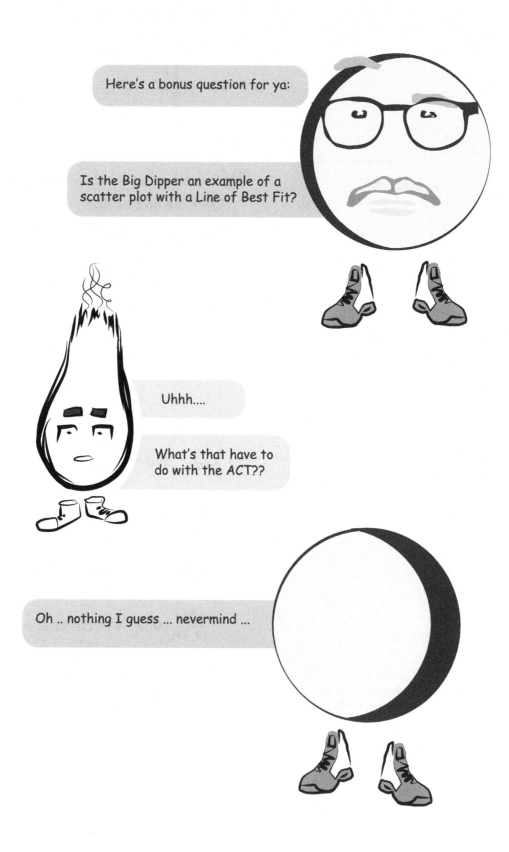

3. For an experiment in chemistry class, students collected data values for variables x and y shown in the table below. Chemistry theory predicts that y varies directly with x. Based on the experimental data, which of the following values is closest to the constant of variation?

x	y
0.211	1.10
0.410	2.18
0.808	4.41
1.221	6.63

(Note: The variable y varies directly with the variable x provided that $y = kx$ for some nonzero constant k, the constant of variation.)

A. 0.19
B. 1.10
C. 2.08
D. 4.12
E. 5.35

4. The figure below shows a scatterplot of data points graphed in the standard (x, y) coordinate plane. Which of the following is closest to the y-intercept of the line of best fit of these data points?

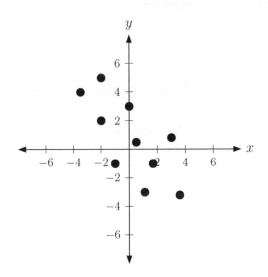

F. -3
G. -1
H. 1
J. 5
K. 5.5

5. The points $(1, 2), (2, 4.1), (3, 6.3), (4, 7.9), (5, 9.6)$ are plotted in the standard (x, y) coordinate plane. Which of the following equations best models these points for positive values of a, b and c?

A. $y = a\sin(bx) + c$
B. $y = ax^{-2}$
C. $y = a \cdot \log_b(x)$
D. $y = ax^2 + bx + c$
E. $y = ax + b$

6. In an experiment in Physics class, Martin is recording the velocity of a steel ball in meters per second, v, versus the time elapsed since the start of the experiment in seconds, t. He records the following (t, v) data points: $(0, 0), (1, 1.4), (2, 3.9), (3, 4.4), (4, 6.0), (5, 7.6)$. Martin then calculates the line of best fit for these data points using the function $y = ax + b$. Which of the following values is closest to the value of a for this line?

F. -3.0
G. -1.5
H. 0.5
J. 1.5
K. 3.0

7. The Willis family drove 2,800 miles in 6 days from Baltimore, Maryland to Los Angeles, California. The points on the graph below show the family's cumulative distance traveled at the end of each day. After the Willis family began their trip, they traveled the least number of miles on which of these 6 days?

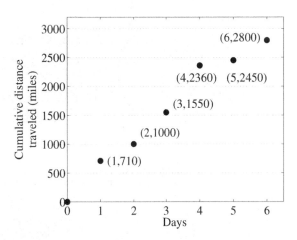

A. Day 1
B. Day 2
C. Day 4
D. Day 5
E. Day 6

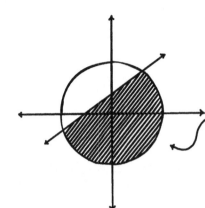

Method 1: Check points!
Find a point that works in the given, and try out in every answer choice.

(0,0) is in the shaded region; plug it into every equation.

<u>Method 2:</u>

① Check shading

y > line   y < line

y > circle   y < circle

y > parabola   y < parabola

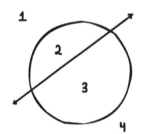

1: ABOVE line   >   2: ABOVE line   >
   OUTSIDE circle   >   INSIDE circle   <

3: BELOW line   <   4: BELOW line   <
   INSIDE circle   <   OUTSIDE circle   >

② If that doesn't solve, check the y-intercept & slope.

That's pretty clean!

Kinda cool that < is inside and > is outside for circles

1. The shaded region in the standard (x, y) coordinate plane below is bounded by a parabola and a line. The shaded region and its boundary is the solution set of which of the following systems of inequalities?

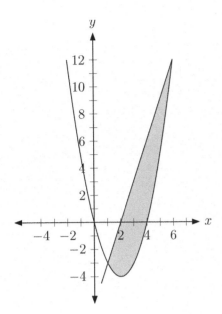

A. $y \geq x^2 - 4x$
$y \leq 3x - 6$

B. $y \geq x^2 - 4x$
$y \geq 3x - 6$

C. $y \leq x^2 - 4x$
$y \leq 3x + 6$

D. $y \geq x^2 + 4x$
$y \leq 3x + 6$

E. $y \leq x^2 - 4x$
$y \geq 3x + 6$

2. Which of the following is the correct graph of the inequality $|x - y| < 1$?

F.

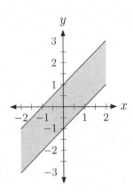

J.

G.

K.

H.

Method 2: ①

3 → ABOVE parabola
BELOW line

$y > x^2$ A
$y < x$ ~~B~~
~~C~~
D
~~E~~

② y-intercept of the line is
NEGATIVE. → A

Method 1: try (0,0)

|0-0|=0 → 0<1 ✓
only J & K have (0,0)
(2,0) is in K not J
|2-0|=|2| → 2<1 ✗
J

3. Which of the following inequalities is graphed in the standard (x, y) coordinate plane below?

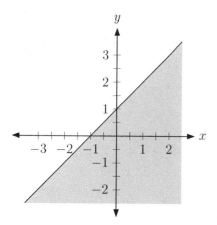

  A. $y \leq -x - 1$

  B. $y \geq -x - 1$

  C. $y \leq -x + 1$

  D. $y \leq x - 1$

  E. $y \leq x + 1$

4. What is the area of the region bounded by the inequalities below?

$$y > 0$$
$$x > 0$$
$$x + y < 4$$

  F. 2

  G. 4

  H. 6

  J. 8

  K. 16

5. For some positive integers a and b, which of the following could be the inequality of the figure listed below?

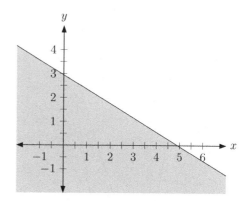

  A. $y < -ax + b$

  B. $y < -ax - b$

  C. $y < ax + b$

  D. $y > -ax - b$

  E. $y > -ax + b$

6. What is the area of the region bounded by the inequalities:

$$y + 3 > 0$$
$$x + 2 < 0$$
$$2y - 3x < 12$$

  F. 9

  G. 12

  H. 27

  J. 44

  K. 48

7. Which of the following sets of inequalities defines the inequality shown below?

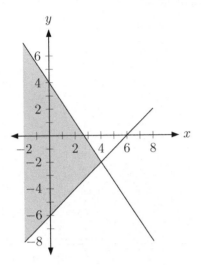

A. $-3x + 2y \geq 8$
$x - y \leq 6$

B. $-3x + 2y \leq 8$
$x - y \geq 6$

C. $-3x + 2y \geq 8$
$-x - y \leq 6$

D. $3x + 2y \geq 8$
$x - y \geq 6$

E. $3x + 2y \leq 8$
$x - y \leq 6$

8. The shaded region in the standard (x, y) coordinate plane below is bounded by a parabola and a line. The shaded region and its boundary is the solution set of which of the following systems of equations?

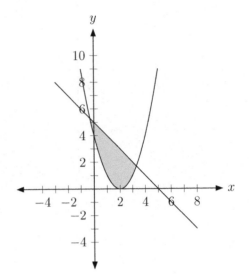

F. $y \geq x^2 + 4x + 4$
$y \leq -x + 5$

G. $y \geq x^2 + 4x - 4$
$y \leq -x + 5$

H. $y \geq x^2 - 4x + 4$
$y \leq x - 5$

J. $y \geq x^2 - 4x + 4$
$y \leq -x + 5$

K. $y \geq x^2 - 4x + 4$
$y \geq -x - 5$

9. For $f(x) = (x + 2)^4$ and $g(x) = x + 2$, over which x values is the inequality $g(x) > f(x)$ true?

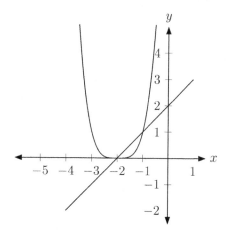

A. $x < -2$
B. $x > 0$
C. $-1 < x < 0$
D. $-2 < x < -1$
E. $x < -2$ or $x > 0$

10. Two functions, $(x+3)^2 + (y-1)^2 = 5^2$ and $y = 3x+5$, are graphed in the standard (x, y) coordinate plane below. Which of the following sets of inequalities defines the shaded region?

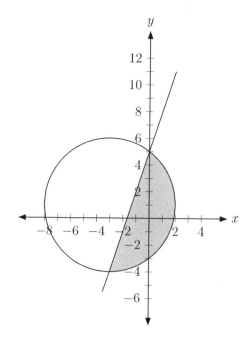

F. $(x + 3)^2 + (y - 1)^2 \leq 25$
   $y \leq 3x + 5$

G. $(x + 3)^2 + (y - 1)^2 \leq 25$
   $y \geq 3x + 5$

H. $(x + 3)^2 + (y - 1)^2 \geq 25$
   $y \leq 3x + 5$

J. $(x + 3)^2 + (y - 1)^2 \geq 25$
   $y \geq 3x + 5$

K. $(x + 3)^2 + (y - 1)^2 = 25$
   $y = 3x + 5$

11. One of the following graphs in the standard (x, y) coordinate plane is the graph of $y \leq ax + b$ for some negative a and negative b. Which graph?

A.

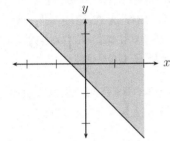

D.

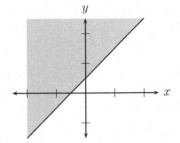

B.

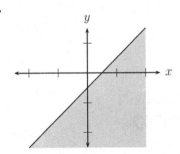

E.

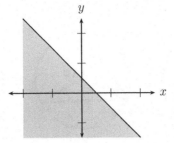

C.

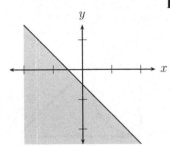

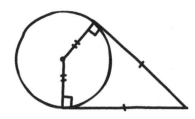

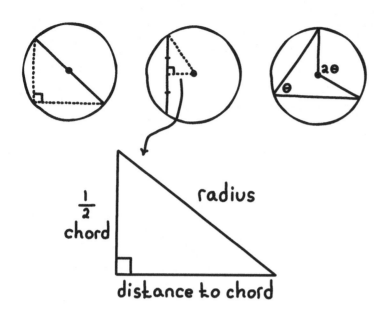

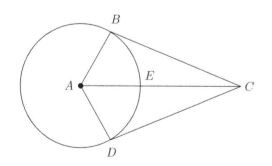

radius

$\frac{1}{2}$ chord

distance to chord

① Two tangents from a circle that meet at a point are congruent.

② Tangents are ⊥ to the radius.

1. As shown in the figure below, line $\overline{BC}$ is tangent to a circle A at point B and line DC is tangent to circle A at point D. If the circle has a diameter of 18 meters and line $\overline{BC} = \overline{DC} = 12$ meters, what is the length, in meters, of $\overline{EC}$?

(Note: Figure not drawn to scale.)

diameter = 18 → radius = 9
AB = AD = AE = 9, BC = 12

BC is a tangent ⎫
& AB is a radius ⎬ AB ⊥ BC
 ⎭

A
9 ⌐ 15 → 3:4:5 triangle
B ⌐ C
  12

AC = 15, AE = 9, so EC = ⎡6⎤

A. 5
B. 6
C. 8
D. 9
E. 11

The radius/chord right triangle is MAGIC for any questions addressing chords & distance from the center. It establishes a Pythagorean relationship between the values.

2. In the figure shown below, circle F has an area of 400π square feet and chord $\overline{GH} = 32$ feet. What is the distance, in feet, from the center of circle F to point I, the midpoint of chord $\overline{GH}$?

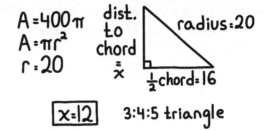

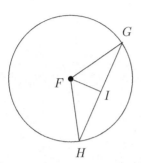

F. 12
G. 15
H. 16
J. 17
K. 18

3. Circle O is shown below with diameter $\overline{AB}$. If chords $\overline{AC}$ and $\overline{CB}$ are drawn, what would be the measure of $\angle ACB$?

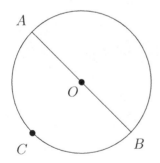

A. 45°
B. 60°
C. 75°
D. 90°
E. 105°

4. Circle O is shown below with points M, N, and P on the circle. If the measure of arc $\overset{\frown}{MN} = 106°$, what is the measure of $\angle MPN$?

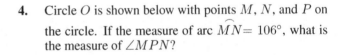

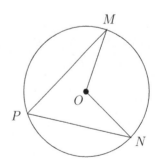

F. 21.5°
G. 53°
H. 106°
J. 169°
K. 180°

5. Circle O is shown below with points M, N, and P on the circle. If the measure of arc $\overset{\frown}{MN} = 106°$, what is the measure of central $\angle MON$?

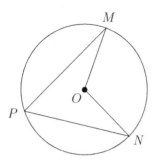

    A. 21.5°
    B. 53°
    C. 106°
    D. 169°
    E. 180°

6. In the diagram below, chord $\overline{TV}$ is parallel to diameter $\overline{WX}$. The length of $\overline{TV}$ is 12 inches and the length of $\overline{WX}$ is 20 inches. What is the distance, in inches, from Y, the center of the circle, to U, the midpoint of $\overline{TV}$?

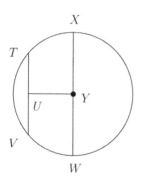

    F. 7
    G. 8
    H. $8\sqrt{2}$
    J. 9
    K. $9\sqrt{3}$

7. In the circle shown below, radius $\overline{AE}$ is 25 inches long, chord $\overline{DC}$ is 18 inches long, and $\overline{AE}$ is perpendicular to $\overline{DC}$ at point B. To the nearest tenth of an inch, how long is $\overline{AB}$?

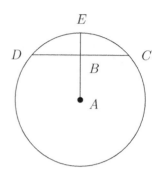

    A. 7
    B. 14.4
    C. 17.3
    D. 23.3
    E. 30.8

8. In the figure below, $\overline{DE}$ is tangent to circle B at point C, and $\overline{DB}$ is twice the length of radius $\overline{BC}$. Which of the following angles or minor arcs has the *greatest* degree measure?

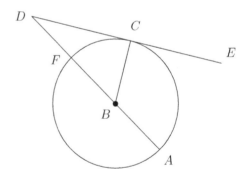

    F. $m\angle D$
    G. $\overset{\frown}{AC}$
    H. $m\angle BCD$
    J. $\overset{\frown}{FC}$
    K. $m\angle BCE$

9. In the figure shown below, circle with center J have radii tangent to lines $\overline{KL}$ and $\overline{LM}$ at points K and M, respectively. If $\overline{KL} = \overline{LM} = 16$ feet and $\overline{NL} = 12$ feet, what is the approximate length, in feet, of chord $\overline{KM}$?

(Note: Figure not drawn to scale.)

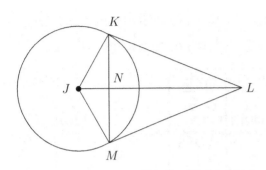

A. 5
B. 7
C. 11
D. 16
E. 21

10. Consider circle O below with central angle $AOB = 90°$. What is the *sum* of angles CAO and CBO?

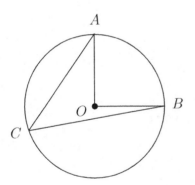

F. 45°
G. 58°
H. 60°
J. 80°
K. 90°

11. Circles Q, R, and S, have radii q, r and s, respectively, and are situated such that all three circles are tangent to one another. If the perimeter of triangle QRS is 42, what is the value of $q + r + s$?

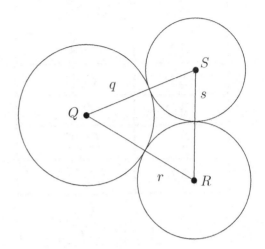

A. 21
B. 42
C. 63
D. 82
E. 105

value	probability
-$2	0.2
-$1	0.1
$0	0.5
+$1	0.15
+$2	0.05

should add up to 1

① EXPECTED VALUE

Value × probability for each case, then add them all up.

value	prob.		
-2 MULTIPLY	0.5	= -1	THEN ADD DOWN
0	ACROSS 0.2	= 0 +	
+1	0.3	= 0.3	

$$\boxed{-0.7}$$

② "At least" or "At most"

Probability is quite easy, as usual.

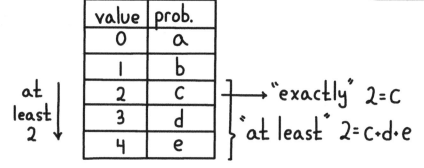

value	prob.
0	a
1	b
2	c
3	d
4	e

at least 2 ↓

→ "exactly" 2 = c
"at least" 2 = c+d+e

NOTE: "at least" 2 = 1 - "exactly 0" - "exactly 1"

= 1 - a - b

use if some of the probabilities are unknown ("prob" column doesn't sum to 1).

1. In a carnival game, players get a random score from 0-6 in each round of play. Chuck thinks the game might be rigged, so he spent an afternoon evaluating the outcomes. The results are shown in the table below. Based on the results, what is the *expected* value of any one round of play?

Score	Probability
0	$1/6$
1	$1/8$
2	$1/4$
3	$1/24$
4	$1/12$
5	0
6	$1/3$

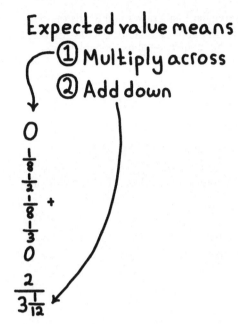

Expected value means
① Multiply across
② Add down

0
$\frac{1}{8}$
$\frac{1}{2}$
$\frac{3}{8}$ +
$\frac{0}{3}$
0
2
$\overline{3\frac{1}{12}}$

A. $1/7$
B. 1
C. $1^5/8$
D. $2^7/8$
E. $3^1/12$

2. A librarian tracked the chances that an overdue book would be returned on any given day. The results for up to four books are shown in the table below. Based on her data, what is the probability that at least 1 overdue book is returned today?

→ Probabilities don't add to 1.
1 - "exactly 0"
1 - 0.136 = 0.864

Books Returned	Probability
0	0.136
1	0.215
2	0.262
3	0.148
4	0.127

F. 0.738
G. 0.752
H. 0.822
J. 0.864
K. 0.888

3. Tina is calculating her final grade for U.S. History. Her grade averages, along with their respective weights, are tabulated in her course syllabus shown below:

Type	Average	Weight
Exams	92	70%
Homeworks	100	20%
Participation	88	10%

To the nearest whole number, what is Tina's final grade in U.S. History?

A. 88
B. 91
C. 93
D. 95
E. 96

4. Beth has tracked her 10-question quiz results all year and has determined the probability of missing x number of questions, as documented in the table below. Based on these results, what is her *expected* number of questions missed on her next quiz?

Questions Missed (x)	Probability
0	0.50
1	0.30
2	0.15
3	0.05

F. 0
G. 0.5
H. 0.75
J. 1
K. 3

5. The Peekskill Hotel has 120 rooms. Based on many previous years' occupancy rates, the owners of the Peekskill Hotel constructed the table below showing the daily occupancy rates and their probabilities for the coming summer season. Based on the probability distribution in the table, to the nearest whole number, what is the expected number of rooms that will be occupied on any day during the coming summer season?

Occupancy Rate	Probability
0.6	0.40
0.7	0.25
0.8	0.20
0.9	0.15

A. 54
B. 66
C. 71
D. 75
E. 85

6. In a game of chance, Mary selects one token at random from a pot of 100 tokens. Each token has a number amount on it. The denominations and frequency of each token is shown in the table below. What is the expected value of Mary's random token?

Value	Frequency
1	50
2	25
5	10
10	10
25	5

F. 1
G. 2
H. 3.75
J. 8.6
K. 43

7. Mr. Belvedere noticed his class never had full attendance, so he tracked his classes attendance over the course of a semester. The probability of attendance on any given day is shown in the table below. He teaches a total of 144 students. Approximately how many students, on average, can he expect to see on any given day?

Attendence	Probability
0.9	0.20
0.8	0.30
0.7	0.40
0.6	0.10

A. 76
B. 89
C. 101
D. 109
E. 125

8. At a certain factory, the Cog Construtor produces 1000 metal gears a day. The number of cracked gears produced by this machine each day is recorded for 80 days. Based on the distribution given below, what is the expected value of the number of cracked gears produced by the Cog Constructor in any single day?

Cracked Gears	Probability
6	0.715
8	0.010
10	0.105
12	0.100
14	0.070

F. 0.76
G. 7.60
H. 80
J. 760
K. 1,000

A basic note about Probability: sequential events in Probability always multiply. If we have multiple possible outcomes (such as "Draw a 2 or a 3"), we add to find the total Probability of that event. Expected Value is another combination of Multiplication and Addition - don't mix them up!.

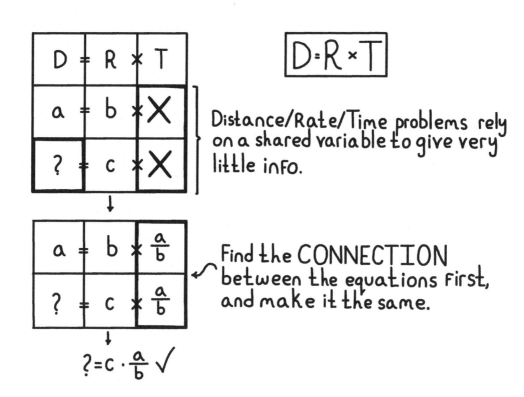

$$\boxed{D = R \times T}$$

Distance/Rate/Time problems rely on a shared variable to give very little info.

Find the CONNECTION between the equations first, and make it the same.

$$? = c \cdot \frac{a}{b} \checkmark$$

1. Two runners run 20 laps around a 400 meter track. The faster runner runs at an average rate of 600 meters per minute. The slower runs at a rate of 510 meters per minute. When the faster runner finishes her race, how many laps did the slower runner have remaining?

A. 1 lap
B. 2 laps
C. 3 laps
D. 4 laps
E. 5 laps

This DRT table is simply a visualization of Distance equals Rate times Time. The visual helps us to "line up" the hidden link that makes these problems tick.

① The last sentence tells us TIME is the shared quantity.

② Write rate in terms of laps.

$R_1 = 1.5 \quad R_2 = 1.275$

$T = \frac{20}{1.5} = 13.3$

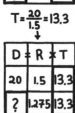

$? = R \times T$
$? = (1.275)(13.3) = 17$ laps

③ laps left

2. At the start of his cross country season, Stephen completes a run of 5 miles in a time of 38 minutes. At what average speed must Stephen run if he wants to run the race 6 minutes faster by the end of the season?

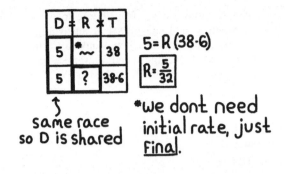

F. $\dfrac{32}{5}$ miles/minute

G. $\dfrac{38}{5}$ miles/minute

H. $\dfrac{6}{5}$ miles/minute

J. $\dfrac{5}{6}$ miles/minute

K. $\dfrac{5}{32}$ miles/minute

3. Nasir went on a road trip that began and ended at his house. He used all the time on the trip driving, sleeping, or sightseeing. Nasir began his trip on Monday at 10:00 A.M. when he left his house. During his driving time, he drove 880 miles at an average speed of 40 miles per hour. His driving time was twice as long as his sightseeing time, and his resting time was 26 hours. When did Nasir end his road trip?

A. Wednesday at 1:00 P.M.

B. Wednesday at 9:00 P.M.

C. Thursday at 1:00 P.M.

D. Thursday at 9 P.M.

E. Friday at 4:00 A.M.

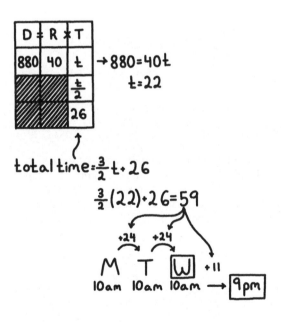

4. On a typical day, Jenny's drive from home to work takes her 20 minutes, and she drives at an average speed of 40 miles/hour. If Jenny gets stuck in traffic and can only drive at an average speed of 30 miles per hour, approximately how long will it take her to get to work?

   F. 24 minutes

   G. 27 minutes

   H. 29 minutes

   J. 31 minutes

   K. 34 minutes

5. A new highway just opened up near where Eamon lives. His commute to work used to take him 40 minutes at an average speed of 25 miles per hour. On the new highway, his total distance is the same but he can now average 60 miles per hour on his commute. How much time will he save on each trip to work by taking the new highway?

   A. 15 minutes

   B. 16 $2/3$ minutes

   C. 20 minutes

   D. 23 $1/3$ minutes

   E. 25 minutes

6. Jack and Jill are running around the track of their high school. It takes Jack 60 seconds to complete 1 lap and it takes Jill 45 seconds to complete 1 lap. If Jack and Jill start at the same point on the track, how many seconds will have elapsed until Jill is exactly one lap ahead of Jack?

   F. 45

   G. 60

   H. 90

   J. 120

   K. 180

7. Dante was riding a bicycle with wheels 15 inches in radius. During 1 minute of Dante's ride, the wheels made exactly 160 revolutions. Approximately what was the average speed, in feet per second, for Dante's ride?

   A. 21

   B. 44

   C. 72

   D. 88

   E. 400

8. In her physical education class, Lucia runs 1 lap around a circular track with a diameter of 120 meters. On her first week, she runs at a speed of 1.5 meters per second. On the last week of the class, she runs at a speed of 2.8 meters per second. Approximately how much faster did Lucia complete the lap on the last week of class than on the first week of class?

   F. 37 seconds

   G. 52 seconds

   H. 58 seconds

   J. 1 minute 16 seconds

   K. 1 minutes 56 seconds

9. Maria drives to and from work five days a week. On the morning of a workday, Maria averages 60 miles per hour driving to work. On the evening of a workday, Maria averages 40 miles per hour driving from work. What is Maria's average speed, in miles per hour, for the round-trip commute to and from work?

   A. 40

   B. 48

   C. 50

   D. 60

   E. 100

Questions 10-13 pertain to the following
information.

The graph below shows the height of a surveillance drone
during a 60-second vertical flight.

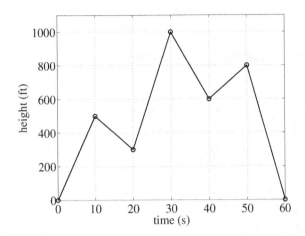

12. The graph below compares the time the drone was in
the air to which of the following variables?

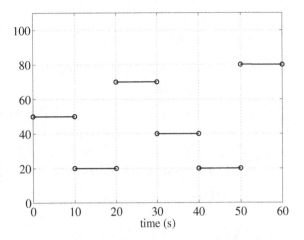

F. Height

G. Speed

H. Acceleration

J. Distance

K. Time

10. What was the speed of the drone, in feet per second,
over the first 10 seconds of the flight?

F. 5 ft/s

G. 20 ft/s

H. 25 ft/s

J. 50 ft/s

K. 500 ft/s

13. What was the average speed of the drone over the last
30 seconds of the flight?

A. 25 ft/s

B. 33 1/3 ft/s

C. 46 2/3 ft/s

D. 50 ft/s

E. 200 ft/s

11. What was the total distance that the drone traveled over
the course of the flight?

A. 1,000 ft

B. 2,000 ft

C. 2,800 ft

D. 3,600 ft

E. 6,000 ft

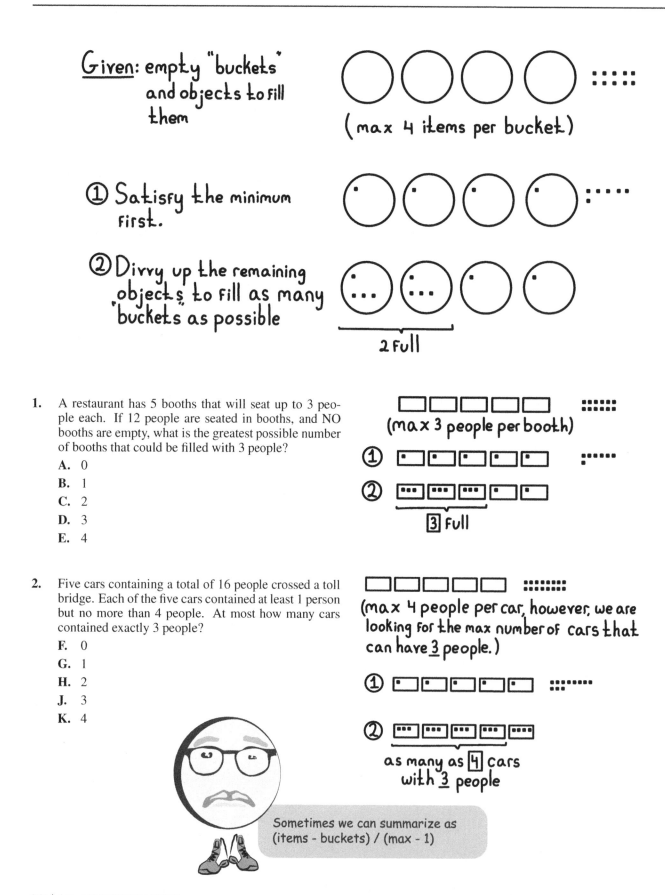

Given: empty "buckets" and objects to fill them

(max 4 items per bucket)

① Satisfy the minimum first.

② Divvy up the remaining objects to fill as many "buckets" as possible

2 Full

1. A restaurant has 5 booths that will seat up to 3 people each. If 12 people are seated in booths, and NO booths are empty, what is the greatest possible number of booths that could be filled with 3 people?

A. 0
B. 1
C. 2
D. 3
E. 4

(max 3 people per booth)

①

②

[3] Full

2. Five cars containing a total of 16 people crossed a toll bridge. Each of the five cars contained at least 1 person but no more than 4 people. At most how many cars contained exactly 3 people?

F. 0
G. 1
H. 2
J. 3
K. 4

(max 4 people per car, however, we are looking for the max number of cars that can have 3 people.)

①

②

as many as [4] cars with 3 people

Sometimes we can summarize as (items - buckets) / (max - 1)

3. Link is brewing a powerful potion to help improve his combat awareness. He needs 3 Blue Mountain flowers and 4 Giant's toes for each potion. In his inventory Link has 10 Blue Mountain flowers and 11 Giant's toes. How many potions can Link brew?

A. 0
B. 1
C. 2
D. 3
E. 4

4. Amanda invited 30 people to her birthday party at a local restaurant, which has 7 booths that will seat up to 6 people each. If NO booths are empty, what is the greatest possible number of booths that could be filled with 6 people?

F. 0
G. 1
H. 2
J. 3
K. 4

5. Carrie is baking brownies for a fund raiser. A recipe for 500 brownies calls for 6 cups of sugar, 9 cups of flour, and 4 cups of butter. If Carrie has 20 cups of sugar, 20 cups of flour, and 20 cups of butter in her kitchen, what is the maximum number of brownies she can bake for her fund raiser?

A. 500
B. 1,000
C. 1,500
D. 2,000
E. 2,500

6. Brett builds houses for a living. The house requires 150 bricks and 200 lbs of cement. If Brett has an inventory of 2,217 bricks and 1,629 lbs of cement, how many houses can Brett build with his current supplies?

F. 8
G. 9
H. 10
J. 11
K. 14

7. Elizabeth is painting the walls of her local mall as part of a charity fund raiser. Each wall requires 3 quarts of red paint and 2 quarts of white paint. If Elizabeth is supplied with 10 quarts of red paint and 9 quarts of white paint, how many walls can Elizabeth paint in full?

A. 0
B. 1
C. 2
D. 3
E. 4

8. Dave is playing a video game and needs to escort 40 survivors of a zombie apocalypse across a bridge. He has 10 cars available, each of which contain at least 1 person but no more than 5 people. To beat the game, Dave must escort all 40 survivors across the bridge with as many cars containing 5 survivors as possible and no cars empty. At most how many cars must Dave fill with 5 survivors to beat the game?

F. 5
G. 6
H. 7
J. 8
K. 9

9. Three butterfly wings and two dragon's tongues form a Dartwing. Two butterfly wings and five fish eggs form a Spynyte. One Dartwing and a one Spynyte form a Zen. If there are 15 butterfly wings, 12 dragon's tongues, and 11 fish eggs available, what is greatest number of Zens that can be formed?

A. 0
B. 1
C. 2
D. 3
E. 4

Step 1: SIZE

① Matricies are measured as HEIGHT × WIDTH

$$\begin{bmatrix} 1 & 0 \\ 2 & 3 \\ 1 & 4 \end{bmatrix} \begin{bmatrix} a & b & c \\ 0 & 0 & 1 \end{bmatrix}$$
3×2   2×3

$$\begin{bmatrix} 1 & 3 & 4 \end{bmatrix}$$
1×3

② To be ABLE to multiply MIDDLE dimensions must be the SAME.

3×<u>2</u>·<u>2</u>×1 ✓   ⟶ 3×1

3×<u>3</u>·<u>2</u>×1 ✗   ⟶ ∅

A×<u>B</u>·<u>B</u>×C ✓   ⟶ A×C

③ The resulting matrix will have the dimensions of the two outside terms.

Step 2: ALIGNMENT

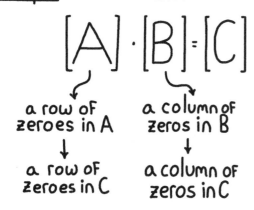

$$[A] \cdot [B] = [C]$$

a row of zeroes in A
↓
a row of zeroes in C

a column of zeros in B
↓
a column of zeros in C

Determinants:

The determinant of

$$\begin{bmatrix} A & B \\ C & D \end{bmatrix} = \begin{vmatrix} A & B \\ C & D \end{vmatrix} = AD - BC$$

Here, we are focusing on Tricks to help solve quickly, as opposed to teaching actual Matrix Multiplication.

Real multiplication is long and annoying, and often at the end of the test you do not have the luxury of time.

However, these tricks may not last forever, and you may need to learn the real deal.

1. What is this matrix product? $\begin{bmatrix} 1 \\ 0 \\ -1 \end{bmatrix} \begin{bmatrix} x & 2y & 3z \end{bmatrix}$

A. $\begin{bmatrix} 0 \end{bmatrix}$

B. $\begin{bmatrix} -2 \end{bmatrix}$

C. $\begin{bmatrix} -6xy^2z^3 \end{bmatrix}$

D. $\begin{bmatrix} x & 2y & 3z \\ 0 & 0 & 0 \\ -x & -2y & -3z \end{bmatrix}$

E. $\begin{bmatrix} x & 0 & -x \\ 2y & 0 & -2y \\ 3z & 0 & -3z \end{bmatrix}$

① $3 \times \underline{1} \cdot \underline{1} \times 3 \checkmark \rightarrow 3 \times 3$

~~A~~ ~~B~~ ~~C~~ D E

② First matrix has a row of zeros $\rightarrow \begin{bmatrix} 1 \\ 0 \\ -1 \end{bmatrix}$

↓

answer needs a row of zeros $\boxed{D}$

2. If the determinant of the matrix below is equal to 0, what is one possible value for x?

$$\begin{vmatrix} x & 10 \\ 2 & x \end{vmatrix}$$

F. $\sqrt{2}$
G. 1
H. 2
J. $\sqrt{5}$
K. $2\sqrt{5}$

$\begin{vmatrix} x & 10 \\ 2 & x \end{vmatrix} = x^2 - 20 = 0$

$+20 \ +20$

$x^2 = 20$

$x = \sqrt{20} = \boxed{2\sqrt{5}}$

3. What is the determinant of the matrix shown below?

$$\begin{vmatrix} 1 & -5 \\ 3 & 0 \end{vmatrix}$$

A. -16
B. -15
C. 0
D. 15
E. 16

4. What is the matrix product of:

$$\begin{bmatrix} 1 & -1 \end{bmatrix} \begin{bmatrix} 2 & 2 \\ -4 & 4 \end{bmatrix}$$

F. $\begin{bmatrix} -6 & -6 \end{bmatrix}$

G. $\begin{bmatrix} -6 & 6 \end{bmatrix}$

H. $\begin{bmatrix} 6 & -2 \end{bmatrix}$

J. $\begin{bmatrix} 6 \\ -2 \end{bmatrix}$

K. $\begin{bmatrix} -6 \\ -6 \end{bmatrix}$

5. What is the determinant of the matrix shown below?

$$\begin{vmatrix} x & y \\ y & x \end{vmatrix}$$

A. $(x+y)(x-y)$
B. $(y+x)(y-x)$
C. $x^2 + y^2$
D. $y^2 + x^2$
E. 0

6. Four matrices are given below.

$$A = \begin{bmatrix} 4 & 2 & 4 \end{bmatrix} \quad B = \begin{bmatrix} -2 & 5 & 3 \\ -5 & 3 & -2 \\ -1 & -2 & -3 \end{bmatrix}$$

$$C = \begin{bmatrix} 1 & -5 \\ 3 & -3 \\ 1 & -1 \end{bmatrix} \quad D = \begin{bmatrix} 5 & -5 & 5 \\ -1 & 1 & -1 \end{bmatrix}$$

Which of the following matrix products is undefined?
F. AB
G. AC
H. CD
J. BA
K. DB

Consider the following matrices:

$$V = \begin{bmatrix} 4 & 2 \\ 6 & 3 \end{bmatrix} \quad W = \begin{bmatrix} 2 & 4 & 6 \\ 1 & 3 & 5 \end{bmatrix} \quad X = \begin{bmatrix} 5 & 10 \\ 15 & 20 \end{bmatrix}$$

$$Y = \begin{bmatrix} 3 & -3 \\ 2 & -2 \\ 1 & -1 \end{bmatrix} \quad Z = \begin{bmatrix} 8 & -3 \\ -6 & 4 \end{bmatrix}$$

7. Which of the following matrix products is undefined?
   A. VW
   B. WY
   C. YZ
   D. ZV
   E. WX

8. Which matrix product would result in a 3 by 3 matrix?
   F. WY
   G. YW
   H. YZ
   J. XW
   K. VY

9. Which matrix product would yield the following result?
$$\begin{bmatrix} 13 & 23 & 33 \\ -8 & -12 & -16 \end{bmatrix}$$
   A. VW
   B. XW
   C. ZW
   D. YV
   E. YZ

10. Which of the following matrices has a determinant equal to 0?
   F. $\begin{bmatrix} 4 & 6 \\ 6 & 9 \end{bmatrix}$

   G. $\begin{bmatrix} 4 & 9 \\ 6 & 6 \end{bmatrix}$

   H. $\begin{bmatrix} 9 & 6 \\ 4 & 6 \end{bmatrix}$

   J. $\begin{bmatrix} 6 & 6 \\ 4 & 9 \end{bmatrix}$

   K. $\begin{bmatrix} 6 & 4 \\ 6 & 9 \end{bmatrix}$

11. If it can be determined, what is the matrix product of:
$$\begin{bmatrix} 3 & 5 & 7 \end{bmatrix} \begin{bmatrix} 2 \\ 4 \\ 6 \end{bmatrix}$$
   A. $\begin{bmatrix} 27 \end{bmatrix}$

   B. $\begin{bmatrix} 68 \end{bmatrix}$

   C. $\begin{bmatrix} 6 & 10 & 14 \\ 12 & 20 & 28 \\ 18 & 30 & 42 \end{bmatrix}$

   D. $\begin{bmatrix} 6 & 12 & 18 \\ 10 & 20 & 30 \\ 14 & 28 & 32 \end{bmatrix}$

   E. Cannot be determined because the matrix product is undefined

1. If $\sin\theta = \dfrac{5}{8}$, what is the value of $\cos\theta\tan\theta$?

A. $\dfrac{5}{8}$

B. $\dfrac{\sqrt{89}}{5}$

C. $\dfrac{\sqrt{39}}{5}$

D. $\dfrac{\sqrt{89}}{5}$

E. $\dfrac{\sqrt{39}}{8}$

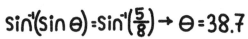

$$\sin^{-1}(\sin\theta)=\sin^{-1}\left(\tfrac{5}{8}\right)\rightarrow\theta=38.7$$

$$\cos(38.7)\tan(38.7)=\boxed{\tfrac{5}{8}}$$

The little negative 1 means "inverse trig function". An Inverse Trig Function is equal to the ANGLE that we would use to find the targeted ratio of sides.

2. Consider right triangle ABC with legs a and b opposite angles A and B, respectively, and hypotenuse $\sqrt{a^2 + b^2}$ opposite angle C. In terms of a and b, what is $\cot\left[\sin^{-1}\left(\dfrac{b}{\sqrt{a^2+b^2}}\right)\right]$?

F. $\dfrac{a}{b}$

G. $\dfrac{b}{a}$

H. $\dfrac{a}{\sqrt{a^2+b^2}}$

J. $\dfrac{\sqrt{a^2+b^2}}{b}$

K. $\dfrac{\sqrt{a^2+b^2}}{a}$

Let $a=3$ & $b=4$, therefore $\sqrt{a^2+b^2}=5$

$$\frac{1}{\tan\left[\sin^{-1}\left(\tfrac{4}{5}\right)\right]}=\frac{3}{4}=\boxed{\frac{a}{b}}$$

When given hypothetical values of angles and sides, pick easy ones and plug in for equations and answer choices!

3. Which of the following expressions is equivalent to $\dfrac{\sin\theta\csc\theta}{\cot\theta}$?

Note: $\csc\theta = \dfrac{1}{\sin\theta}$ and $\cot\theta = \dfrac{\cos\theta}{\sin\theta}$

A. $\csc^2\theta$
B. $\sin\theta$
C. $\cos\theta$
D. $\sin^2\theta$
E. $\tan\theta$

Let $\theta=50$

$$\frac{\sin 50\left(\frac{1}{\sin 50}\right)}{\left(\frac{\cos 50}{\sin 50}\right)}=0.84$$

A) $\csc^2 50 = 1.70$ ✗
B) $\sin 50 = 0.77$ ✗
C) $\cos 50 = 0.64$ ✗
D) $\sin^2 50 = 0.59$ ✗
E) $\tan 50 = 0.84$ ✓

I prefer 3 - 4 - 5 for sides and 50 degrees for any angles. Makes for clear differences between sine and cosine.

4. If $\cos x = -1$ then what is the value of $\tan x + \sin x$?

   F. -2

   G. -1

   H. 0

   J. 1

   K. 2

5. If $3\cos x = 3$ and $2\sin(90° - y) = 2$, what is the value of $x + y$?

   A. 0

   B. 1

   C. 2

   D. 3

   E. 5

6. For all x such that $\sin x \neq 0$, the expression $\dfrac{\cos x \tan x}{\sin x}$ is equivalent to which of the following?

   F. $\cos x$

   G. $\sin x$

   H. $\dfrac{\cos^2 x}{\sin x}$

   J. $\dfrac{\sin x}{\cos^2 x}$

   K. 1

7. If $\sin^2 \theta = 0.64$, what is the value of $\cos \theta$?

   A. 0.36

   B. 0.60

   C. 0.75

   D. 0.80

   E. 1.33

8. If $\tan x = -1$, what is the value of $\cos x \sec x$?

   F. $-2\sqrt{2}$

   G. -2

   H. $2 + \sqrt{2}$

   J. 1

   K. $2\sqrt{2}$

9. Consider right triangle ABC with legs a and b opposite angles A and B, respectively, and hypotenuse c opposite angle C. What is the value of $\sin^2 A + \cos^2 B$?

   A. a^2

   B. b^2

   C. c^2

   D. $\left(\dfrac{a}{b}\right)^2$

   E. $2\left(\dfrac{a}{c}\right)^2$

10. Which of the following is equal to $\tan \theta \sin \theta$ if $\cos \theta = \frac{\sqrt{3}}{2}$ and $0 < \theta < \frac{\pi}{2}$?

   F. $\dfrac{\sqrt{3}}{6}$

   G. $\dfrac{\sqrt{3}}{2}$

   H. $\dfrac{2\sqrt{3}}{3}$

   J. $\sqrt{3}$

   K. 1

11. For all x such that $\cos x \neq 0$, the expression $\dfrac{\csc x \sin x}{\cos x}$ is equivalent to which of the following?

   A. $\csc x$

   B. $\sec x$

   C. $\sin x$

   D. $\cos x$

   E. $\tan x$

12. Consider right triangle ABC with hypotenuse $\overline{AB}$. If the lengths of $\overline{AC}$ and $\overline{CB}$ are $12\sin \theta$ and $12\cos \theta$, respectively, what is the length of $\overline{AB}$?

   F. 1

   G. 5

   H. $5\sin \theta$

   J. $12\tan \theta$

   K. 12

The final level of difficulty in the ACT is know-it-or-don't questions. They don't often take a long time, but the time is spent trying to remember exactly how to do a random specific topic. For other quizzes and tests we have encouraged an open-book approach to emphasize proper form, but for this quiz the extra time exists mostly to meditate and remember concepts.

On the real test, 48-60 is the "difficult" section. But the internal difficulty of the section varies wildly. Often two or three problems at the beginning (such as 49, 50, 51) will be fantastically difficult, and then the test will cool down and be reasonable in the mid-50's. 60 is almost always pretty simple, but 58 or 59 will be super tough.

Accordingly, don't get attached to going in order. Find problems you can solve easily and crush them. Each question is worth the same amount of points, so missing an easy one while working on a hard one is inefficient.

CHAPTER SIX QUIZ
30 Minutes — 20 Questions

DIRECTIONS: Solve each problem, choose the correct answer, and then fill in the corresponding oval on your answer document.

Do not linger over problems that take too much time. Solve as many as you can; then return to the others in the time you have left for this test.

You are permitted to use a calculator on this test. You may use your calculator for any problems you choose,

but some of the problems may be best done without using a calculator.

Note: Unless otherwise stated, all of the following should be assumed.
1. Illustrative figures are NOT necessarily drawn to scale.
2. Geometric figures lie in a plane.
3. The word *line* indicates a straight line.
4. The word *average* indicates arithmetic mean.

---

1. Tyrese and Rachel are side by side when they begin a race around a circular track. Tyrese runs at a constant rate of 40 seconds per lap and Rachel runs at a constant rate of 56 seconds per lap. How many seconds after the race begins will Tyrese have run exactly 1 more lap than Rachel?

   A. 96
   B. 122
   C. 140
   D. 155
   E. 160

2. The graph of the function $y = \sin(4x)$ is shown below in the standard (x, y) coordinate plane. What are the amplitude and period of the function?

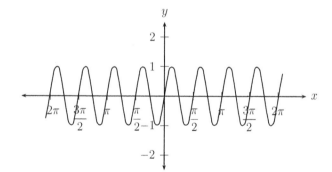

   F. Amplitude: 1; Period: 4
   G. Amplitude: π; Period: 4
   H. Amplitude: 1; Period: $\frac{\pi}{2}$
   J. Amplitude: 4; Period: π
   K. Amplitude: $\frac{1}{2}$; Period: $\frac{1}{2}$

3. Which of the following equations represents an ellipse graphed in the standard (x, y) coordinate plane with center $(4, 4)$, major axis of length 6 and minor axis of length 4?

   A. $(x + 4)^2 + (y + 4)^2 = 1$
   B. $(x + 4)^2 - (y + 4)^2 = 1$
   C. $(x - 4)^2 + (y - 4)^2 = 1$
   D. $\dfrac{(x - 4)^2}{4} + \dfrac{(y - 4)^2}{9} = 1$
   E. $\dfrac{(x - 4)^2}{4} - \dfrac{(y - 4)^2}{9} = 1$

4. Which of the following matrices is equal to the matrix product:

$$\begin{bmatrix} 5 & -1 \\ 6 & 2 \end{bmatrix} \begin{bmatrix} -2 \\ 3 \end{bmatrix}$$

   F. $\begin{bmatrix} -13 \\ -6 \end{bmatrix}$

   G. $\begin{bmatrix} -13 \\ 6 \end{bmatrix}$

   H. $\begin{bmatrix} -10 & 2 \\ -12 & 6 \end{bmatrix}$

   J. $\begin{bmatrix} 10 & 16 \\ 12 & 6 \end{bmatrix}$

   K. $\begin{bmatrix} -5 & 1 \\ -12 & 6 \end{bmatrix}$

Carly and Willie are playing a dart game. A dart hitting the outer ring is worth 1 point, with each additional inner ring creasing in value by 1 point. The board they are using is shown in the figure below.

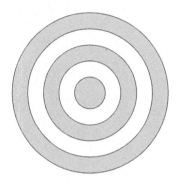

Carly and Willie have been charting their scores in an attempt to find the empirical probability of getting any one score on a throw of a dart. The results of 1,000 throws each are shown in the table below. All throws count, but only throws that hit the dartboard score points.

Score	Willie	Carly
1	0.042	0.113
2	0.121	0.159
3	0.214	0.192
4	0.281	0.221
5	0.342	0.255

5. What is the expected value of the number of points Willie will get on any given throw?

   A. 0.342

   B. 1

   C. 3.17

   D. 3.76

   E. 5

6. If a game consists of 25 throws, what is Carly's average score per game to the nearest whole number?

   F. 3

   G. 31

   H. 79

   J. 94

   K. 125

7. If Carly throws 50 darts, how many darts can she expect to completely miss the dartboard?

   A. 0

   B. 1

   C. 3

   D. 6

   E. 7

8. Zarya is making particle beam cannons. She needs 2 liters of hydrogen gas, 3 neodymium magnets, and 2 glass photon emitter to create a single particle beam cannon. In her laboratory, Zarya has 11 liters of hydrogen gas, 20 neodymium magnets, and 10 glass photon emitters. How many particle beam cannons can Zarya make?

   F. 1

   G. 2

   H. 3

   J. 4

   K. 5

9. If $\sin x = \dfrac{\sqrt{3}}{2}$ and $\cos x < 0$, what is the value of $\cos x \tan x$?

   A. $-\dfrac{\sqrt{3}}{2}$

   B. $-\dfrac{1}{2}$

   C. $\dfrac{1}{2}$

   D. $\dfrac{\sqrt{3}}{2}$

   E. $2\sqrt{2}$

Use the following information to answer questions 10-12.

The figure below depicts a dirt bike tire. The diameter of the outer rim of the tire is 20 inches and the diameter of the inner rim is 15 inches. Point V represents the air valve and is located on the inner rim of the tire.

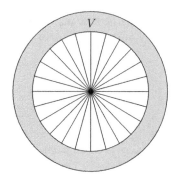

10. If the dirt bike runs over a nail, the tire will begin to deflate after traveling approximately 1,000 feet. In that span, approximately how many times will the nail hit the ground?

     F.   100
     G.   170
     H.   190
     J.   200
     K.   240

11. If the tire made 840 rotations in 1 minute, what was the approximate speed of the dirt bike in miles per hour?

(Note: 1 mile = 5,280 feet)

     A.   40 mph
     B.   45 mph
     C.   50 mph
     D.   55 mph
     E.   60 mph

12. If the 24 spokes of the wheel are equally spaced and form an angle with the center of the wheel, what is the distance along the inner rim of the tire between any two spokes?

     F. $\dfrac{15\pi}{2}$

     G. $\dfrac{30\pi}{4}$

     H. 15π

     J. $\dfrac{5\pi}{4}$

     K. $\dfrac{5\pi}{8}$

13. If the valve starts at the highest point on the tire at the beginning of a race, which of the following equations represents the position of the valve relative to the ground as the wheel spins $\theta°$ forward, so long as the tire remains grounded?

     A. $V(\theta) = 7.5\cos(\theta) + 10$
     B. $V(\theta) = 7.5\cos(\theta)$
     C. $V(\theta) = 15\cos(\theta) + 20$
     D. $V(\theta) = 7.5\sin(\theta) + 10$
     E. $V(\theta) = 10\sin(\theta) + 7.5$

14. As shown below, irregular quadrilateral $QRST$ is inscribed in circle P with a radius of 5 inches. Lines $\overline{QP}$ and $\overline{TP}$ (not shown) are perpendicular. What is the length, in inches of chord $\overline{QT}$?

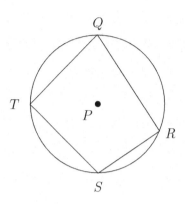

F. 5
G. $5\sqrt{2}$
H. $5\sqrt{3}$
J. $8\sqrt{2}$
K. 10

15. The graph of the function $y = A\cos(Bx)$ is shown below for certain positive values of A and B. Which of the following values is equal to A?

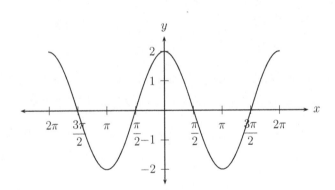

A. 0.5
B. 1
C. 2
D. π
E. 2π

16. Which of the following values is closest to the slope of the line of best fit for the scatterplot shown below?

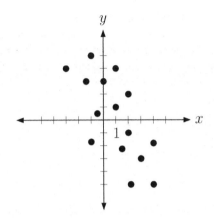

F. -10
G. -2
H. -1
J. 1
K. 3

17. If the determinant of the matrix below is equal to 0, what is one possible value for x?

$$\begin{vmatrix} 6 & x \\ x & 3 \end{vmatrix}$$

A. 2
B. 3
C. $2\sqrt{3}$
D. $3\sqrt{2}$
E. 18

Use the following information to answer questions 18-20.

The figure below depicts an ellipse, $f(x, y)$, on the standard (x, y) coordinate plane. All coordinates that lie on the ellipse are contained in the set Ω. The angle θ is defined by the positive ray of the x-axis and line l, which passes through point (a, b) on the ellipse.

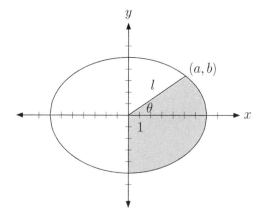

18. What is the equation of the ellipse?

F. $\dfrac{x^2}{7} + \dfrac{y^2}{5} = 1$

G. $\dfrac{x^2}{14} + \dfrac{y^2}{10} = 1$

H. $\dfrac{x^2}{10} + \dfrac{y^2}{14} = 1$

J. $\dfrac{x^2}{49} + \dfrac{y^2}{25} = 1$

K. $\dfrac{x^2}{25} + \dfrac{y^2}{49} = 1$

19. Which of the following represents the values of a and b for any given value of θ?

A. $a = 5\sin\theta$
$b = 7\cos\theta$

B. $a = 7\tan\theta$
$b = 5\tan\theta$

C. $a = 5\sin\theta$
$b = 7\sin\theta$

D. $a = 7\cos\theta$
$b = 5\cos\theta$

E. $a = 7\cos\theta$
$b = 5\sin\theta$

20. The shaded region is bounded by line l, the y-axis, and the ellipse. Which of the following systems of inequalities bounds the shaded region?

F. $y \leq \dfrac{b}{a}x$

$x \geq 0$

$f(\Omega) \leq 1$

G. $y \leq \dfrac{b}{a}x$

$x \leq 0$

$f(\Omega) \leq 1$

H. $y \geq \dfrac{b}{a}x$

$x \geq 0$

$f(\Omega) \geq 1$

J. $y \leq \dfrac{b}{a}x$

$x \leq 0$

$f(\Omega) \geq 1$

K. $y \geq \dfrac{a}{b}x$

$x \geq 0$

$f(\Omega) \geq 1$

CHAPTER 7

CLASSIFIED

CHAPTER CLASSIFIED QUIZ
~~30~~ Minutes — 21 Questions
99

DIRECTIONS: Solve each problem, choose the correct answer, and then fill in the corresponding oval on your answer document.

Do not linger over problems that take too much time. Solve as many as you can; then return to the others in the time you have left for this test.

You are permitted to use a calculator on this test. You may use your calculator for any problems you choose,

but some of the problems may be best done without using a calculator.

Note: Unless otherwise stated, all of the following should be assumed.
1. Illustrative figures are NOT necessarily drawn to scale.
2. Geometric figures lie in a plane.
3. The word *line* indicates a straight line.
4. The word *average* indicates arithmetic mean.

---

1. A parabola and circle are graphed on the standard (x, y) coordinate plane. The parabola has a vertex at $(0, -3)$ and crosses the x-axis at ± 4. The circle has a center at $(0, 5)$ with a radius of 4. How many points of intersection are there between the parabola and circle?

  A. 0
  B. 1
  C. 2
  D. 3
  E. 4

2. Which of the following number properties is illustrated in the statement below?

$$7 + (2 + 3) = (2 + 3) + 7$$

  F. Associative: $x + (y + z) = (x + y) + z$
  G. Commutative: $x + y = y + x$
  H. Distributive: $x(y + z) = xy + xz$
  J. Identity: $x + 0 = x$
  K. Inverse: $x + (-x) = 0$

3. What is the distance in coordinate units between $3 + 5i$ and $-5 + 2i$ in the complex plane?

  A. 1
  B. 3
  C. 11
  D. $\sqrt{73}$
  E. $\sqrt{80}$

4. Which of the following lists of numbers could be the sides lengths, in inches, of a triangle?

  F. 1, 2, 4
  G. 4, 6, 9
  H. 5, 7, 13
  J. 8, 9, 18
  K. 10, 10, 20

5. Which of the following data sets has the greatest standard deviation?

  A. 2, 2, 2, 12, 12, 12
  B. 2, 2, 7, 7, 11, 12
  C. 2, 3, 4, 5, 6, 7
  D. 6, 6, 6, 6, 6, 6
  E. 6, 7, 8, 10, 11, 12

6. A plane contains 17 horizontal lines and 13 vertical lines. These lines divide the plane into disjoint regions. How many of these disjoint regions have a finite nonzero area?

  F. 221
  G. 192
  H. 169
  J. 57
  K. 30

7. What is the minimum degree possible for the polynomial function whose graph is shown in the standard (x, y) coordinate plane below?

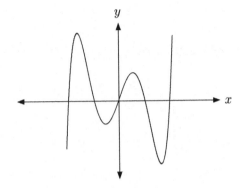

- **A.** 1
- **B.** 2
- **C.** 3
- **D.** 4
- **E.** 5

8. What is the tangent of the angle formed by $\overline{AB}$ and $\overline{AC}$ in the graph shown below?

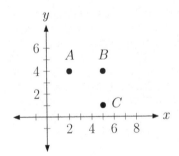

- **F.** $\dfrac{1}{\sqrt{2}}$
- **G.** $\dfrac{3}{\sqrt{3}}$
- **H.** 1
- **J.** $\sqrt{2}$
- **K.** $3\sqrt{3}$

9. A circle with center $(0, 3)$ is graphed in the standard (x, y) coordinate plane below. Suppose the circle rolls along the positive x-axis for 2 rotations and then stops. Which of the following is an equation of the circle in its new position?

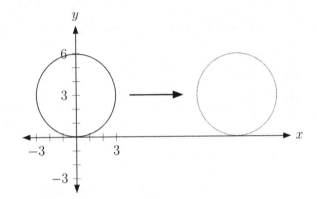

- **A.** $(x + 3)^2 + (y - 3)^2 = 9$
- **B.** $(x - 6\pi)^2 + (y - 3)^2 = 3$
- **C.** $(x - 6\pi)^2 + (y - 3)^2 = 9$
- **D.** $(x - 12\pi)^2 + (y - 3)^2 = 3$
- **E.** $(x - 12\pi)^2 + (y - 3)^2 = 9$

10. A polynomial in x has r nonzero terms. Another polynomial in x has s nonzero terms, where $r < s$. These polynomials are multiplied and all like terms are combined. The resulting polynomial in x has a maximum of how many nonzero terms?

- **F.** r
- **G.** rs
- **H.** $\frac{1}{2}(r + s)$
- **J.** $r + s$
- **K.** $\frac{1}{2}rs$

11. Which one of the following expressions could be a factor of the expression below. $x^3 + 8y^{12}$?

- **A.** $x^2 - 2xy^4 + 4y^8$
- **B.** $x^2 + 2xy^4 + 4y^8$
- **C.** $x^2 - 2x^2y^4 + 4y^8$
- **D.** $x^2 + 2x^2y^4 - 4y^8$
- **E.** $x^2 - 2xy^4 - 4y^8$

12. Points $O(0,0)$ and $A(2,0)$ lie on the standard (x,y) coordinate plane. The collection of all points such that each is twice as far from A as from O forms a circle. The point $\left(0, \frac{2\sqrt{3}}{3}\right)$ is one point on the circle. What are the coordinates of the center of the circle?

F. $\left(-\frac{2}{3}, 0\right)$
G. $(-2, 0)$
H. $\left(\frac{2}{3}, \frac{\sqrt{3}}{2}\right)$
J. $(2, 0)$
K. $\left(\frac{3}{2}, 0\right)$

13. A right circular cylinder is intersected by a plane that is not parallel to the base and does not intersect the base, as shown in the figure below.

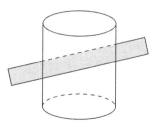

Which one of the following figures shows the shape of the intersection?

A.

D.

B.

E.

C.

14. Right $\triangle ABC$ shown below will be rotated about the x-axis to form a right circular cone. If $\overline{BC} = 6$ and $\angle BCA = 60°$, how long, in coordinate units, is the diameter of the base of the cone?

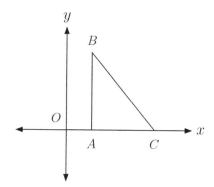

F. 2
G. 3
H. $3\sqrt{3}$
J. 6
K. $6\sqrt{3}$

15. Suppose that equally spaced dots are marked one each side of a regular polygon, with a dot at each vertex, and the distance between consecutive dots is the same of all sides. The figure below shows 4 equally spaced dots per side, including a dot at each vertex, for a regular pentagon. Which of the following expressions represents the number of dots for a regular polygon with n equally spaced dots, including one at each vertex, marked on each of its s sides?

A. ns
B. $ns - s$
C. $ns - 1$
D. $ns + s$
E. $ns - n$

16. In the standard (x, y) coordinate plane below, D is on the positive x-axis, the measure of $\angle COD$ is $120°$, and the length of $\overline{CO}$ is 1 coordinate unit. What are the coordinates of C?

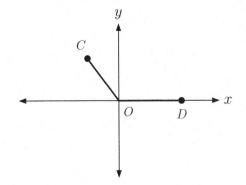

F. $\left(-\dfrac{\sqrt{3}}{2}, \dfrac{1}{2}\right)$

G. $\left(-\dfrac{1}{2}, \dfrac{\sqrt{3}}{2}\right)$

H. $\left(-\dfrac{\sqrt{2}}{2}, \dfrac{\sqrt{2}}{2}\right)$

J. $\left(\dfrac{1}{2}, \dfrac{\sqrt{3}}{2}\right)$

K. $\left(\dfrac{\sqrt{2}}{2}, \dfrac{\sqrt{2}}{2}\right)$

17. As shown in the (x, y, z) coordinate space below, cube P with vertices A through H has edges that are 0.5 coordinate units long. The coordinates of F are $(0, 0, 0)$ and H is on the positive y-axis. P', not shown below, is P reflected over the z-axis and multiplied by a factor of 2. What are the coordinates of D'?

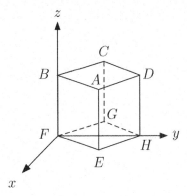

A. $(1, -1, 1)$
B. $(1, \sqrt{2}, 1)$
C. $(1, \sqrt{2}, 0)$
D. $(0, 0, 1)$
E. $(0, -\sqrt{2}, 1)$

18. Which of the following polar coordinates represents the same location as $\left(5, -\dfrac{\pi}{4}\right)$?

F. $\left(5, \dfrac{15\pi}{4}\right)$

G. $\left(5, \dfrac{3\pi}{4}\right)$

H. $\left(5, \dfrac{\pi}{4}\right)$

J. $\left(5, -\dfrac{3\pi}{4}\right)$

K. $\left(5, -\dfrac{15\pi}{4}\right)$

19. The force due to gravity, F, between two masses, m_1 and m_2, varies directly with the product of the two masses and the gravitational constant, and varies indirectly with the square of the distance between them, r. On a certain celestial body the gravitational constant is 13 m/s^2. Which of the following graphs shows the force due to gravity, F, on this celestial body between two objects with masses m_1 and m_2 for all values of r in the (r, F) coordinate plane?

A.

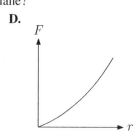

D.

B.

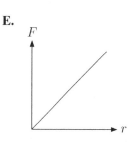

E.

C.

21. In the figure below, a band is wrapped tightly around two pulleys. The center of the pulleys are 16 inches apart. The band wraps two-thirds around the larger pulley, which has a radius of 10 inches, and one-third of the way around the smaller pulley, which has a radius of 2 inches. What is the length of the band, in inches?

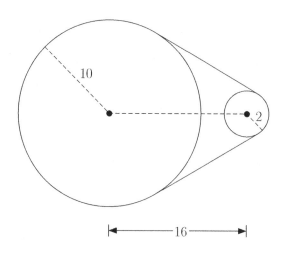

A. $34\pi + 16$

B. $34\pi + 16\sqrt{3}$

C. $\dfrac{44\pi}{3} + 16$

D. $\dfrac{44\pi}{3} + 16\sqrt{2}$

E. $\dfrac{44\pi}{3} + 16\sqrt{3}$

20. A teacher assigns each of her 14 students a different integer from 1 through 14. The teacher forms pairs of study partners by using rule that the sum of the pair of numbers is a perfect square. Assuming the 7 pairs of students follow this rule, the student assigned which number must be paired with the student assigned the number 4?

F. 12

G. 9

H. 5

J. 2

K. 1

CHAPTER 8

CALCULATOR GUIDE

Hold on - I thought we were done with all of this!

Almost! We've got one last thing to discuss. Because you can bring a calculator, you're not alone on the Math section.

A calculator is like a perfect soldier... it simply follows orders so you need to know how to use it. I'm going to walk you through some of the most useful features of the TI-84 Plus Graphing Calculator.

I know how to use a calculator *yawn*

Really? Did you know that a calculator can solve any equation almost instantly?

Wait, say what?

Haha. Now that I've got your attention, let's explore some of the lesser-known tools your TI-84 gives you!

Is there a "Right Answer" button? That, you know, gives me the right answer every time?

Not quite - BUT !! You can access a menu of math expressions by hitting "Alpha" then "Window"

1. What is $|(6)(-7) - (5)(-3)|$?
   A. -57
   B. -27
   C. 9
   D. 27
   E. 57

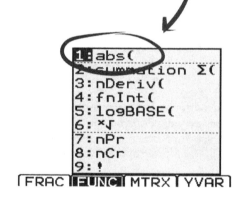

Oh sweet! So there *is* an absolute value button on the calculator. That's useful.

What else we got?

Well, option 9 gives us the "!" needed for factorials. Option 5 allows for alternate base logarithms. And Options 7 & 8 are useful when you need to solve the ACT's new favourite topic : nPr or nCr!

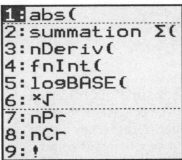

```
1:abs(
2:summation Σ(
3:nDeriv(
4:fnInt(
5:logBASE(
6:×√
7:nPr
8:nCr
9:!
[FRAC [FUNC] MTRX [YVAR]
```

2. If $f(x) = 5x^2 - 3x + 7$, what is $f(-3)$?
   - **F.** -47
   - **G.** -29
   - **H.** 1
   - **J.** 43
   - **K.** 61

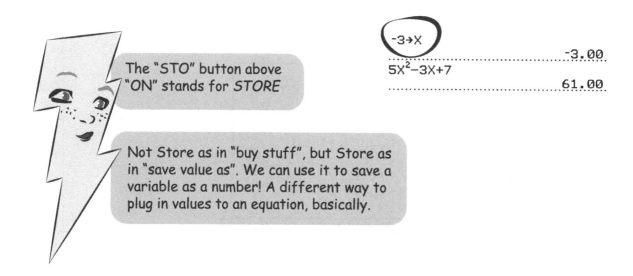

The "STO" button above "ON" stands for *STORE*

Not Store as in "buy stuff", but Store as in "save value as". We can use it to save a variable as a number! A different way to plug in values to an equation, basically.

3. Which of the following is the factored form of $x^2 + 15x - 34$?

A. $(x - 17)(x - 2)$

B. $(x + 17)(x - 2)$

C. $(x - 1)(x + 34)$

D. $(x + 1)(x + 34)$

E. $(x - 6)(x - 6)$

```
-3→X
................................... -3.00
```

```
X²+15X-34
................................... -70.00
(X+17)(X-2)
................................... -70.00
```

Interesting! So, I can type in equations so they look just like the problem...that's kind of nice.

Yup! And once stored, you can type in as many equations as you want, and it will use the same value.

This is quite useful for checking answer choices against the original equation.

Ok ok! What else you got for me?

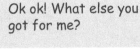

4. If $\log_b 3 = x$ and $\log_b 5 = y$ what is $\log_b 45$?

F. $2x - y$

G. $2x + y$

H. $x^2 + y$

J. $2xy$

K. $\dfrac{x^2}{y}$

Let's combine our lessons: use Alpha & Window to pull up a Logarithm base 4.

Then, use STO to save X and Y as versions of that Logarithm.

Lastly, check each answer choice quickly using X & Y. Boom.

```
1:abs(
2:summation Σ(
3:nDeriv(
4:fnInt(
5:logBASE(
6:ˣ√
7:nPr
8:nCr
9:!
FRAC  FUNC  MTRX  YVAR
```

```
log₄(3)→X
                          .79
log₄(5)→Y
                         1.16
log₄(45)
                         2.75
2X-Y
                          .42
2X+Y
                         2.75
2XY
                         1.84
X²+Y
                         1.79
```

5. For all x such that $\cos x \neq 0$, the expression $\dfrac{\csc x \sin x}{\cos x}$ is equivalent to which of the following?

A. $\csc x$

B. $\sec x$

C. $\sin x$

D. $\cos x$

E. $\tan x$

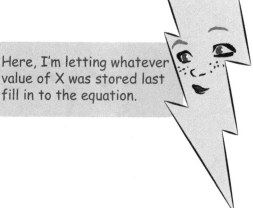

Here, I'm letting whatever value of X was stored last fill in to the equation.

```
  1
─────sin(X)
sin(X)
─────────────
   cos(X)
                        -1.41
    1
  ──────
  sin(X)
                         1.41
    1
  ──────
  cos(X)
                        -1.41
```

```
tan(X)
                        -1.00
sin(X)
                          .71
cos(X)
                         -.71
```

6. Consider right triangle ABC with hypotenuse $\overline{AB}$. If $\cos A = \dfrac{4}{5}$, what is $\sin B \tan B$?

F. $\dfrac{3}{4}$

G. $\dfrac{3}{5}$

H. $\dfrac{4}{3}$

J. $\dfrac{5}{4}$

K. $\dfrac{16}{15}$

```
cos⁻¹(4/5)→A
                         36.87
90-A→B
                         53.13
sin(B)tan(B)
                          1.07
Ans▶Frac
                           16
                           15
```

I get it. It's useful.

Yup. And feel free to get creative with it! You can define one variable using another, etc.

I feel like I need to redo the whole book using these techniques.

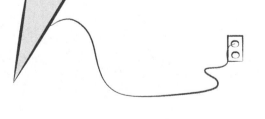

Well, the tricks and tips we taught are super important for speed. Remember the calculator is just a tool - if you don't know what you want it to do, you won't be able to use it well.

Any equation equality can be solved with the graphing ability of the Calculator.

Access the "Y=" menu and type in your equation as (LEFT SIDE) - (RIGHT SIDE)

Ok, I've used the Y= graphing before. I think it's the main reason we are supposed to use "graphing calculators" in the first place...

7. Which value of x satisfies the equation:

$$\frac{5}{2x + 7} = -\frac{10}{4x + 2}$$

A. -10
B. -2
C. 2
D. 10
E. 40

Definitely. Let's tack on a few tricks to that ability :)

First, I'm using Alpha & Y= to access Fraction mode. Makes everything pretty!

```
Plot1   Plot2   Plot3
■\Y₁=
■\Y₂=
■\Y₃=
■\Y₄=
 1:n/d
 2:Un/d
 3:▶n/d◀▶Un/d
 4:▶F◀▶D
FRAC  FUNC  MTRX  YVAR
```

```
Plot1   Plot2   Plot3
■\Y₁⊟( 5/2X+7 )−( −10/4X+2 )
```

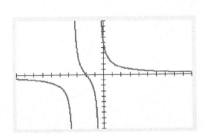

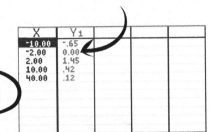

TABLE SETUP
 TblStart=1■
 △Tbl=1
 Indpnt: Auto **Ask**
 Depend: **Auto** Ask

X	Y1			
-10.00	-.65			
-2.00	0.00			
2.00	1.45			
10.00	.42			
40.00	.12			

> Second, you can use the table to plug in whatever numbers you want by hitting 2nd Table Setup (Window) and switching the independent variable from *auto* to *ask*. Switching this setting will let you plug in any numbers you want: fractions decimals, mixed numbers, radicals, trig items etc....

> Usually I set the X values equal to the five answer choices in the problem. When the Y value is zero, the sides are equal, which was the goal!

8. Which value of x would satisfy the following equation?

$$4^{(2x+2)} = 8^{(3x-2)}$$

F. -6
G. 0
H. $3/2$
J. 2
K. 4

Plot1　Plot2　Plot3

■\Y1 ⊟ $(4^{(2x+2)}) - (8^{(3x-2)})$

■\Y2=
■\Y3=
■\Y4=
■\Y5=
■\Y6=
■\Y7=

X	Y1			
-6.00	9.5E-7			
0.00	15.98			
1.50	842.98			
2.00	0.00			
4.00	-1.1E9			

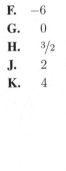

> Alright. So Y=, enter LEFT minus RIGHT side. Then graph it, go to the table, make Indpnt "Ask" and enter the five answer choices, then look for the value that equals zero?

> Baller. I'm into it.

9. Which of the following correctly lists all asymptotes

   of the equation $f(x) = \dfrac{3}{x+1}$?

   A. $x = -1$
   B. $y = 0$
   C. $x = 0, y = -1$
   D. $x = -1, y = 0$
   E. $x = 1, y = 3$

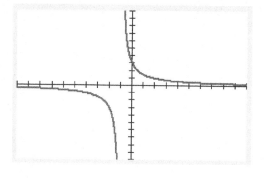

What else can we use graphing for?

How about quickly visualizing vertical asymptotes...

10. What is the range of the function shown below:

$$f(x) = -2\cos(x) + 2$$

   F. All real numbers
   G. $-1 \leq x \leq 1$
   H. $-2 \leq x \leq 2$
   J. $0 \leq x \leq 2$
   K. $0 \leq x \leq 4$

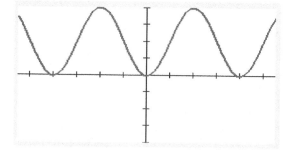

... or quickly visualizing the range of a function?

11. Which of the following is the graph of the inequality $|2x - 5| < 11$?

A.

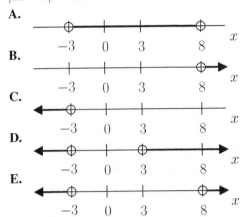

B.

C.

D.

E.

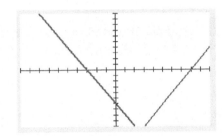

```
Plot1  Plot2  Plot3
■\Y₁=|2X-5|-11
```

```
ZOOM MEMORY
1:ZBox
2:Zoom In
3:Zoom Out
4:ZDecimal
5:ZSquare
6:ZStandard
7:ZTrig
8:ZInteger
9↓ZoomStat
```

```
WINDOW
 Xmin=-495
 Xmax=495
 Xscl=90
 Ymin=-4
 Ymax=4
 Yscl=1
 Xres=1
 △X=3.75
 TraceStep=7.5
```

12. If $3x + 5y = 7$ and $6x + 8y = 10$, what is the value of $9x + 11y$?

  F. 3

  G. 9

  H. 13

  J. 14

  K. 20

Ok, what about when I have two equations that I can't just do LEFT - RIGHT?

Plot1   Plot2   Plot3

$\blacksquare \diagdown Y_1 \blacksquare\triangleright \dfrac{7-3X}{5}$

$\blacksquare \diagdown Y_2 \blacksquare \dfrac{10-6X}{8}$

$\blacksquare \diagdown Y_3 =$

The Y= menu has a lot of room to enter equations. However, first you'll need to solve for Y to plug them in properly.

Alright. I see where the lines are intersecting, but how do I get the correct value quickly?

The CALC button brings up some analytical options. Let's examine the intersect option!

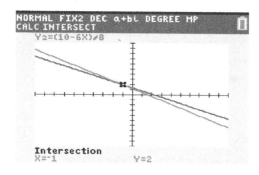

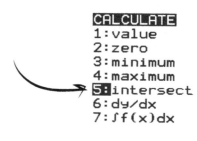

```
CALCULATE
1:value
2:zero
3:minimum
4:maximum
5:intersect
6:dy/dx
7:∫f(x)dx
```

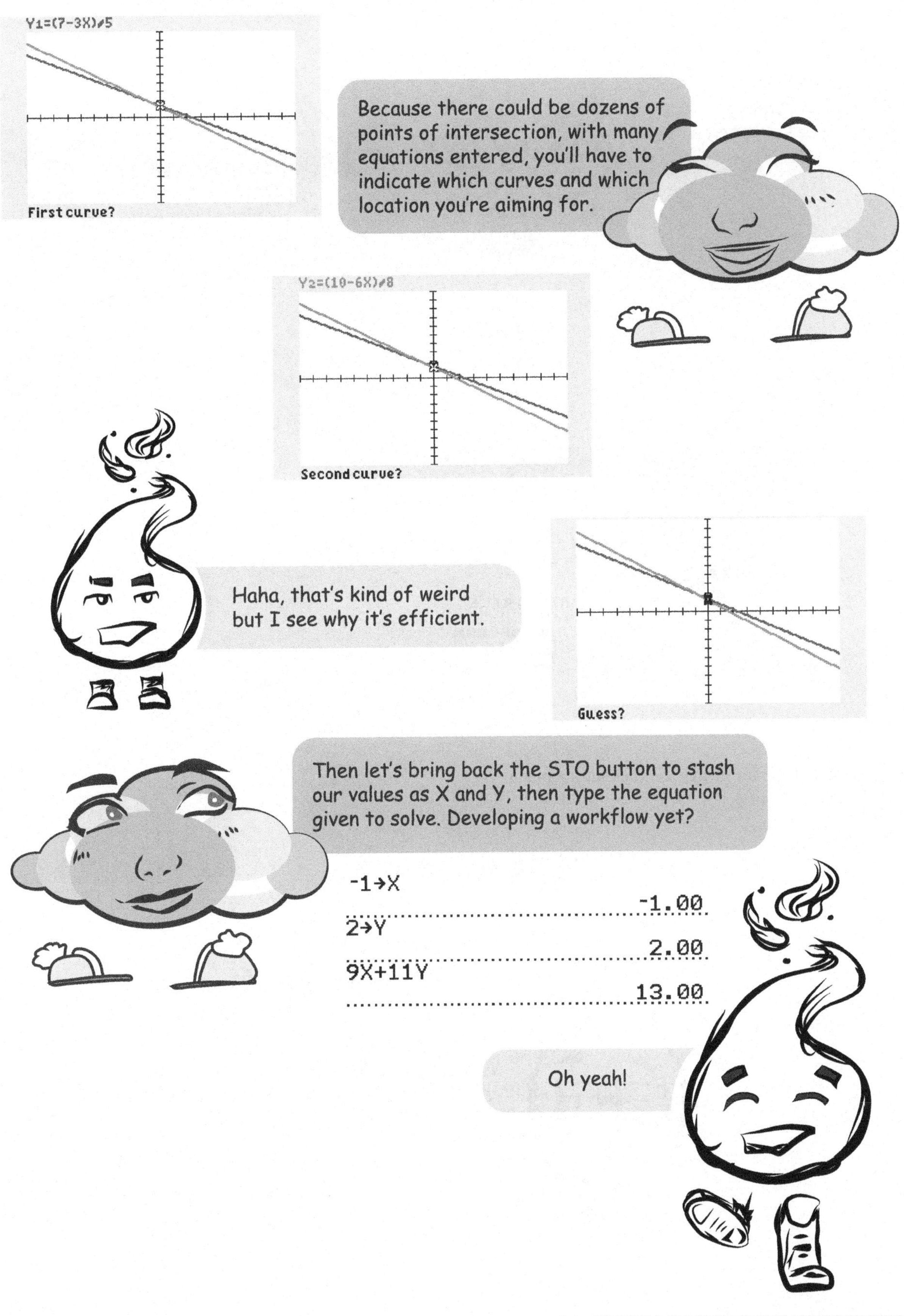

Y1=(7-3X)/5

First curve?

Because there could be dozens of points of intersection, with many equations entered, you'll have to indicate which curves and which location you're aiming for.

Y2=(10-6X)/8

Second curve?

Haha, that's kind of weird but I see why it's efficient.

Guess?

Then let's bring back the STO button to stash our values as X and Y, then type the equation given to solve. Developing a workflow yet?

-1→X
⠀⠀⠀⠀⠀⠀⠀⠀⠀-1.00
2→Y
⠀⠀⠀⠀⠀⠀⠀⠀⠀2.00
9X+11Y
⠀⠀⠀⠀⠀⠀⠀⠀⠀13.00

Oh yeah!

Let's take a pit stop and make sure you've got your MODES set properly.

Did you know with a quick change, you can use "i", the imaginary number, on your TI-84?

```
NORMAL FIX2 DEC a+bi DEGREE MP
MATHPRINT  CLASSIC
NORMAL   SCI   ENG
FLOAT   0 1 2 3 4 5 6 7 8 9
RADIAN   DEGREE
FUNCTION  PARAMETRIC  POLAR   SEQ
THICK  DOT-THICK  THIN  DOT-THIN
SEQUENTIAL   SIMUL
REAL   a+bi   re^(θi)
FULL   HORIZONTAL   GRAPH-TABLE
FRACTIONTYPE: n/d   Un/d
ANSWERS: AUTO   DEC   FRAC-APPROX
GO TO 2ND FORMAT GRAPH: NO   YES
STAT DIAGNOSTICS: OFF   ON
STAT WIZARDS: ON   OFF
```

13. Which of the following complex numbers equals
$(5 - 6i)(\pi + 5i)$?

A. $5\pi - 30i$

B. $(5 + \pi) - i$

C. $(5 + \pi) + i$

D. $(5\pi + 30) + (25 - 6\pi)i$

E. $(5\pi - 30) + (25 - 6\pi)i$

```
(5-6i)(π+5i)
                    45.71+6.15i
(5π+30)+(25-6π)i
                    45.71+6.15i
(5π-30)+(25-6π)i
                   -14.29+6.15i
```

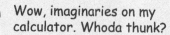

Wow, imaginaries on my calculator. Whoda thunk?

```
NORMAL FIX2 DEC a+bi DEGREE MP                    ▯

MATHPRINT  CLASSIC
NORMAL  SCI   ENG
FLOAT  0 1 2 3 4 5 6 7 8 9
RADIAN  DEGREE
FUNCTION  PARAMETRIC  POLAR  SEQ
THICK DOT-THICK THIN DOT-THIN
SEQUENTIAL  SIMUL
REAL  a+bi  re^(θi)
FULL  HORIZONTAL  GRAPH-TABLE
FRACTION TYPE: n/d  Un/d
ANSWERS: AUTO  DEC  FRAC-APPROX
GO TO 2ND FORMAT GRAPH: NO  YES
STAT DIAGNOSTICS: OFF  ON
STAT WIZARDS: ON  OFF
```

I always set my calculator to only display 2 or 3 decimal places so that my numbers fit nicely on the screen, and I always store any long decimals using the store function so I never have to worry about rounding errors! Notice that I also have my calculator set to a+bi mode, have all stat items turned on, and can choose here whether it defaults to fractions or decimals, improper fractions or mixed numbers, and degrees or radians.

Wow, that's a lot. Won't that change the way I'm used to working on my calculator?

Not really! If anything, it should help make the calculator work more like you expect it to.

14. What is the median of the following data set:

$$3, -4, 7, 5, -2, 5, 0$$

Now, let's explore the STAT menu!

F. 0
G. 2
H. 3
J. 5
K. 14

On the stat menu, you can type in and evaluate lists of data in a snap. In this first example here, I've just typed the numbers in by editing list L1, and then went to the calculate menu in the stat screen (not the one for graphs!) and selected 1-Variable Statistics.

```
EDIT CALC TESTS
1:Edit…
2:SortA(
3:SortD(
4:ClrList
5:SetUpEditor
```

L₁	L₂	L₃	L₄	L₅
3.00	0.00	5.00	4.62	.60
-4.00	1.00	12.00	7.11	.92
7.00	2.00	9.00	8.65	1.13
5.00	3.00	5.00	12.40	1.61
-2.00	4.00	2.00	14.75	1.97
5.00	5.00	2.00	------	------
0.00	------	------		

You didn't need to put the numbers in order?

```
   1-Var Stats
List:L₁
FreqList:
Calculate
```

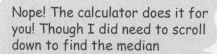

```
   1-Var Stats
x̄=2.00
Σx=14.00
Σx²=128.00
Sx=4.08
σx=3.78
n=7.00
minX=-4.00
↓Q₁=-2.00
Med=3.00
Q₃=5.00
maxX=7.00
```

Nope! The calculator does it for you! Though I did need to scroll down to find the median

1-Variable stats give you mean, sum, variance, sample deviation, standard deviation, count, minimum, lower quartile, median, upper quartile, and maximum respectively for your set of data.

15. Evan completed a survey at his local mall. He recorded the number of siblings for 35 random people and tabulated his data in the data shown below.

Siblings	Frequency
0	5
1	12
2	9
3	5
4	2
5	2

To the nearest tenth, what is the average number of siblings per person surveyed?

A. 1

B. 1.8

C. 2

D. 2.5

E. 5.8

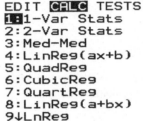
So if I have a frequency table, do I want to do 2-Variable Statistics?

```
EDIT CALC TESTS
1:1-Var Stats
2:2-Var Stats
3:Med-Med
4:LinReg(ax+b)
5:QuadReg
6:CubicReg
7:QuartReg
8:LinReg(a+bx)
9↓LnReg
```

NOOOOO!!!!!!! You NEVER want 2-Variable stats. To evaluate a frequency table like in the above example, you need to make sure that the numbers in the lists are on the same row (like they are coordinates) and pick the 2nd list as the frequency list. The list buttons are above the numbers 1-6 using the 2nd function. Notice that n=35 and the question mentions 35 people - it's a good way to check that you've typed everything in properly.

```
1-Var Stats
List:L₂
FreqList:L₃■
Calculate
```

```
1-Var Stats
x̄=1.80
Σx=63.00
Σx²=175.00
Sx=1.35
σx=1.33
n=35.00
minX=0.00
↓Q₁=1.00
 Med=2.00
 Q₃=3.00
 maxX=5.00
```

16. For an experiment in physics class, students collected data values for variables x and y shown in the table below. Theory predicts that y varies directly with x. Based on the experimental data, which of the following values is closest to the constant of variation?

x	y
4.62	0.601
7.11	0.924
8.65	1.125
12.40	1.612
14.75	1.917

(Note: The variable y varies directly with the variable x provided that $y = kx$ for some nonzero constant k, the constant of variation.)

F. -1.42
G. 0.13
H. 2.45
J. 10.12
K. 16.00

LinReg(ax+b)
Xlist:L4
Ylist:L5
FreqList:
Store RegEQ:
Calculate

1:Y1 6:Y6
2:Y2 7:Y7
3:Y3 8:Y8
4:Y4 9:Y9
5:Y5 0:Y0

FRAC FUNC

YVAR

LinReg
y=ax+b
a=.13
b=-.03
r²=1.00
r=1.00

If you need to find a line of best fit or determine which equation mirrors a table, the Linear Regression function will do just that. You can even use the Alpha F4 (Trace) to get the calculator to plug the equation directly into the y= menu for further evaluation! The correlation value (r) will tell you how strongly your equation matches the data!

Plot1 Plot2 Plot3
\Y1=
\Y2=
\Y3=.13X+-.03

17. In a game of chance, Mary selects one token at random from a pot of 100 tokens. Each token has a number amount on it. The denominations and frequency of each token is shown in the table below. What is the expected value of Mary's random token?

Value	Frequency
1	50
2	25
5	10
10	10
25	5

A. 1
B. 2
C. 3.75
D. 8.6
E. 43

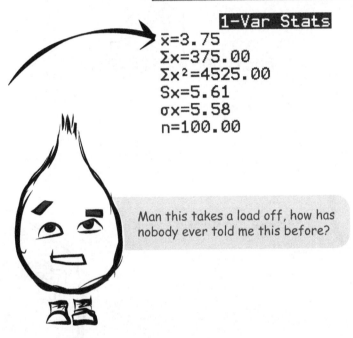

Man this takes a load off, how has nobody ever told me this before?

Well, you never asked!

18. What is the value of y in the matrix equation shown below?

$$-2 \begin{bmatrix} -3 & 4 \\ -1 & 1 \end{bmatrix} + \begin{bmatrix} 4 & -2 \\ 0 & 6 \end{bmatrix} = \begin{bmatrix} 10 & x \\ 2 & y \end{bmatrix}$$

F. -10
G. 0
H. 2
J. 4
K. 8

I feel like I've learned so much.

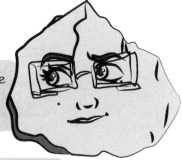

One last thing! Let's examine how Alpha & Zoom can help us out a ton with Matrices.

The Alpha F3 (Zoom) shortcut will bring up the Matrix menu. Here, you can pick the appropriate dimensions for the matrix and, as usual, match the calculator screen to what you see in your question. It's also useful in reminding yourself that rows come first when you name a matrix!

Consider the following matrices:

$$V = \begin{bmatrix} 4 & 2 \\ 6 & 3 \end{bmatrix} W = \begin{bmatrix} 2 & 4 & 6 \\ 1 & 3 & 5 \end{bmatrix} X = \begin{bmatrix} 5 & 10 \\ 15 & 20 \end{bmatrix}$$

$$Y = \begin{bmatrix} 3 & -3 \\ 2 & -2 \\ 1 & -1 \end{bmatrix} Z = \begin{bmatrix} 8 & -3 \\ -6 & 4 \end{bmatrix}$$

```
[4 2][2 4 6]
[6 3][1 3 5]
         [10.00 22.00 34.00]
         [15.00 33.00 51.00]
[2 4 6][5  10]
[1 3 5][15 20]
                       Error
```

19. Which of the following matrix products is undefined?
- **A.** VW
- **B.** WY
- **C.** YZ
- **D.** ZV
- **E.** WX

```
ERROR: DIMENSION MISMATCH
1:Quit
2:Goto
```

Remember the rules for multiplying matrices. If the dimensions don't match properly, you'll get an error.

Ok, so an error is a useful thing here!

20. Which of the following matrices has a determinant equal to 0?

F. $\begin{bmatrix} 4 & 6 \\ 6 & 9 \end{bmatrix}$

G. $\begin{bmatrix} 4 & 9 \\ 6 & 6 \end{bmatrix}$

H. $\begin{bmatrix} 9 & 6 \\ 4 & 6 \end{bmatrix}$

J. $\begin{bmatrix} 6 & 6 \\ 4 & 9 \end{bmatrix}$

K. $\begin{bmatrix} 6 & 4 \\ 6 & 9 \end{bmatrix}$

```
NAMES MATH EDIT
1:det(
2:ᵀ
3:dim(
4:Fill(
5:identity(
6:randM(
7:augment(
8:Matr▶list(
9↓List▶matr(
```

$\det\left(\begin{bmatrix} 4 & 6 \\ 6 & 9 \end{bmatrix}\right)$

....0.00

$\det\left(\begin{bmatrix} 4 & 9 \\ 6 & 6 \end{bmatrix}\right)$

....-30.00

If they ask you to find the determinant of a matrix, as in the example here, the determinant function is the first item on the Math page IN the matrix menu (not the Math button on the calculator)

I'm just gonna go lie down and take a little nap ....

CHAPTER 9

PRACTICE TEST 1

MATHEMATICS TEST
60 Minutes — 60 Questions

DIRECTIONS: Solve each problem, choose the correct answer, and then fill in the corresponding oval on your answer document.

Do not linger over problems that take too much time. Solve as many as you can; then return to the others in the time you have left for this test.

You are permitted to use a calculator on this test. You may use your calculator for any problems you choose,

but some of the problems may be best done without using a calculator.

Note: Unless otherwise stated, all of the following should be assumed.
1. Illustrative figures are NOT necessarily drawn to scale.
2. Geometric figures lie in a plane.
3. The word *line* indicates a straight line.
4. The word *average* indicates arithmetic mean.

---

1. If $\dfrac{5}{x} = 0.2$, then $x =$?

　　A. 0.05
　　B. 0.5
　　C. 5
　　D. 10
　　E. 25

2. The statement $\triangle RST \cong \triangle XYZ$ is true. Which of the following statements must be true?

　　F. $\overline{RS} \cong \overline{XZ}$
　　G. $\overline{RT} \cong \overline{YZ}$
　　H. $\overline{ST} \cong \overline{XZ}$
　　J. $\angle R \cong \angle Z$
　　K. $\angle T \cong \angle Z$

3. $(7m - 3n) - (4m + 6n)$ is equivalent to:

　　A. $3m - 9n$
　　B. $3m - 3n$
　　C. $3m - 6n$
　　D. $11m - 9n$
　　E. $11m - 6n$

4. $4x^5 \cdot 6x^8$ is equivalent to:

　　F. $10x^{13}$
　　G. $10x^{40}$
　　H. $24x^8$
　　J. $24x^{13}$
　　K. $24x^{40}$

5. What is the value of $3\,|3 - 6| - 2(5 + 1)$?

　　A. -15
　　B. -3
　　C. 1
　　D. 3
　　E. 6

6. Eduardo recorded the noon temperature, in degrees Celsius, on 4 consecutive day as part of a school science project. On the 1st day, the noon temperature was $-5°$. On the 4th day, the noon temperature was $14°$. What was the change in the noon temperature from the 1st day to the 4th day?

　　F. $-19°$
　　G. $-5°$
　　H. $5°$
　　J. $9°$
　　K. $19°$

7. What is the least common multiple of 35, 28, and 8?

　　A. 40
　　B. 280
　　C. 980
　　D. 1,120
　　E. 7,840

8. If $g(x) = 3x^2 - 6x - 5$, then $g(-2)$?

　　F. -29
　　G. -5
　　H. 4
　　J. 19
　　K. 29

9. The cost of a long-distance call to City X is $1.15 for the first minute and $0.20 for each additional minute or part thereof. What is the cost of a 15-minute call to City X?

A. $1.25
B. $1.85
C. $3.00
D. $3.95
E. $4.15

10. Lynn programs her calculator to evaluate a certain linear function, but she does not identify what the function is. When she enters the number 12, the calculator displays the number 20. When she enters the number 16, the calculator displays the number 28. Which of the following expressions represents what the calculator will display when any number, n, is entered?

F. $\frac{5}{3}n$
G. $\frac{7}{4}n$
H. $n - 8$
J. $n - 12$
K. $2n - 4$

11. Tianna is saving money to buy a stereo that costs $515, including tax. Tianna opens a savings account with a deposit of $65 and deposits $40 at the end of each month. If Tianna makes no other deposits or withdrawals, what is the minimum number of months she will need to make deposits until she has enough money in her account to buy the stereo?

A. 9
B. 10
C. 11
D. 12
E. 13

12. The dimensions of the rectangle shown below are given in inches. Which of the following expressions gives the area, in square inches, of the rectangle?

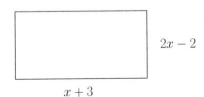

$2x - 2$

$x + 3$

F. $2x - 6$
G. $x^2 + 4x - 6$
H. $2x^2 - 6$
J. $2x^2 + 4x - 6$
K. $2x^2 + 8x - 6$

13. Which of the following expressions is equal to $(4x^2 - 6x - 4) - (-x^2 + 5x + 8)$ for all real values of x?

A. $3x^2 - 11x - 12$
B. $3x^2 - x - 4$
C. $5x^2 - 11x - 4$
D. $5x^2 - 11x - 12$
E. $5x^2 - x + 4$

14. Given that $\cos^2 x = \dfrac{5}{12}$, what is $\sin^2 x$?

F. $\dfrac{5}{13}$
G. $\dfrac{7}{12}$
H. $\dfrac{5}{7}$
J. $\dfrac{12}{5}$
K. $\dfrac{13}{12}$

15. The figure below shows line $\overline{AC}$, line segments $\overline{AB}$ and $\overline{BC}$, and 2 angle measures. What is the measure of $\angle ABC$?

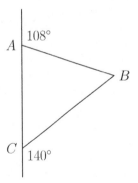

A. $28°$
B. $34°$
C. $68°$
D. $112°$
E. $142°$

16. In the standard (x, y) coordinate plane, what is the slope of the line $13x + 5y = 4$?

F. $-\dfrac{13}{5}$

G. $-\dfrac{4}{5}$

H. $\dfrac{5}{13}$

J. $\dfrac{4}{5}$

K. 13

17. Ashley earned scores of 76, 82, 94, 90 and 78 on her first 5 chemistry tests, and she has 1 more chemistry test before the end of the semester. What is the minimum score Ashley needs to earn on the 6th chemistry test so that the mean of her scores on all 6 tests is at least 2 points more than the mean of the scores she earned on the first 5 tests?

A. 86

B. 88

C. 92

D. 96

E. 98

18. What is the median of the list of numbers below?

$$4, 7, 11, 4, 8, 12, 16, 9, 19, 1$$

F. 7

G. 8.5

H. 9

J. 10

K. 11

19. Given that $a \leq 3$ and $a + b \geq 7$, what is the LEAST value that b can have?

A. -10

B. -4

C. 0

D. 4

E. 10

20. Manuela decides to make a budget for the month of April, allowing herself a total of \$3,200 for all expenses. She records her budget for 5 different categories in the table shown below.

Expense category	Budget amount
Rent	\$1,200
Food	\$900
Entertainment	\$250
Savings	\$450
Other	\$400

In a circle graph illustrating the 5 budget amounts in the table, what should be the approximate measure of the central angle of the Savings sector?

F. $28°$

G. $45°$

H. $51°$

J. $101°$

K. $135°$

21. Right triangle $\triangle ABC$ is shown below. Two side lengths are given in centimeters. What is $\sin A$?

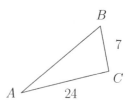

A. $\dfrac{7}{24}$

B. $\dfrac{7}{25}$

C. $\dfrac{24}{25}$

D. $\dfrac{25}{24}$

E. $\dfrac{25}{7}$

22. What is the area, in square coordinate units, of the parallelogram $ABCD$ shown in the standard (x, y) coordinate plane below?

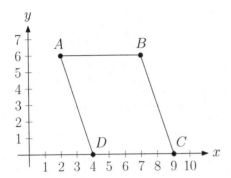

F. 20

G. 24

H. 30

J. 45

K. 54

23. In the standard (x, y) coordinate plane, a translation maps a point (x, y) to its image $(x+6, y-4)$. To what image does the translation map the point $(-5, -3)$?

A. $(-11, -7)$

B. $(-1, 1)$

C. $(1, -7)$

D. $(1, -1)$

E. $(1, 1)$

24. The system of equations below has one solution (c, d). What is the value of d?

$$5c - 3d = 15$$
$$c + 2d = 16$$

F. -6

G. -4

H. 5

J. 6

K. 12

Use the following information to answer questions 25-27.

In the figure shown below, trapezoid $WXYZ$ is formed by $\triangle WXY$ and $\triangle WYZ$. The lengths are given in inches.

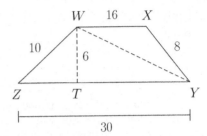

25. What is the area of $\triangle WYZ$, in square inches?

A. 90

B. 138

C. 180

D. 274

E. 300

26. Which of the following ratios is equal to $\csc Z$?

(Note: $\csc A = \dfrac{1}{\sin A}$)

F. $\dfrac{3}{4}$

G. $\dfrac{4}{5}$

H. $\dfrac{3}{5}$

J. $\dfrac{5}{4}$

K. $\dfrac{5}{3}$

27. Suppose $WXYZ$ is placed in the standard (x, y) coordinate plane such that Z is at $(0, 0)$, Y is at $(30, 0)$, and W and X have positive x and y coordinates. What is the x-coordinate of point X?

A. 16

B. 18

C. 20

D. 22

E. 24

28. Which of the expressions below is a factor of the polynomial $2x^3 - 5x^2 - 3x$?
    I. x
    II. $x + 3$
    III. $2x + 1$

    F. I only
    G. I and II only
    H. I and III only
    J. II and III only
    K. I, II and III

29. In Johnstown on Thursday, the high temperature was 28° Celsius and the low temperature was 16° Celsius. What was the difference between the high and low temperatures, in degrees Fahrenheit?

    (Note: The relationship between the temperature, f, in degrees Fahrenheit, and the temperature, c, in degrees Celsius, is given by $f = \frac{9}{5}c + 32$.)

    A. $-20\frac{9}{10}$
    B. $-8\frac{8}{9}$
    C. $21\frac{3}{5}$
    D. 42
    E. $53\frac{3}{5}$

30. To determine the height of a tree in a local park, a surveyor sets his equipment 44 meters from the base of the tree. He measures the angle of elevation between his equipment and the top of the tree to be 29°. Which of the following correctly gives the height of the tree, in meters?

    F. $44\sin 29°$
    G. $44\cos 29°$
    H. $44\tan 29°$
    J. $\dfrac{44}{\sin 29°}$
    K. $\dfrac{44}{\tan 29°}$

31. The product of the complex number $2 + 7i$ and which of the following numbers is equal to 53?

    A. 7
    B. 14
    C. $2 - 7i$
    D. $7 + 2i$
    E. $9i$

32. The function $f(x) = 0.5\cos(5x) + 0.5$ is graphed below for $-2\pi \le x \le 2\pi$. What is the period of the function?

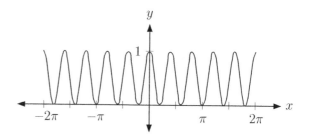

    F. 0.5
    G. $\dfrac{2\pi}{5}$
    H. $\dfrac{5}{2\pi}$
    J. 5
    K. 2π

33. The sum of the measures of $\angle X$ and $\angle Y$ is 90°. The sum of the measures $\angle X$ and $\angle Z$ is 180°. The sum of the measures of $\angle Y$ and $\angle Z$ is 180°. What is the measure of $\angle Z$?

    A. $45°$
    B. $90°$
    C. $135°$
    D. $180°$
    E. $360°$

34. Point T lies at $(3, 7)$ and point R lies at $(-4, 12)$ in the standard (x, y) coordinate plane below. What is the length, in coordinate units, of $\overline{RT}$?

    F. 5
    G. 7
    H. $\sqrt{26}$
    J. $\sqrt{74}$
    K. $\sqrt{362}$

Use the following information to answer questions 35-37.

At Bay Village High School, the 30 cast members of the drama club sold 2 types of tickets - youth and adult - for the Saturday night and Sunday afternoon performances of the new musical. The price of each youth ticket was $3 and the price of each adult ticket was $5. The table below gives the number of tickets sold, by type and by performance.

Ticket Sales per Performance		
Ticket Type	Day of Performance	
	Saturday	Sunday
Youth	168	122
Adult	121	136

The stem-and-leaf plot below shows the number of tickets, regardless of type, sold by each of the 30 cast members.

Stem	Leaf
0	7, 8, 9
1	0, 0, 1, 2, 4, 9
2	1, 2, 2, 3, 5, 6, 6, 7, 8
3	0, 1, 1, 2, 3, 3, 5, 7, 9
4	1, 2, 3

The auditorium where the musical will be performed has 12 seats in the 1st (front) row. Each row behind the 1st row has 6 more seats than does the row in front of it.

35. Suppose 1 cast member will be picked at random from the 30 cast members who sold tickets to receive a prize. What is the probability of picking a cast member who sold more than 30 tickets?

A. $\dfrac{2}{5}$

B. $\dfrac{1}{4}$

C. $\dfrac{11}{30}$

D. $\dfrac{1}{2}$

E. $\dfrac{2}{3}$

36. For which performance was the total amount collected for the tickets greater, and by how many dollars was it greater?

F. Saturday by $42
G. Saturday by $63
H. Saturday by $108
J. Saturday by $108
K. Sunday by $42

37. How many seats are in the 10th row of the auditorium?

A. 48
B. 60
C. 66
D. 72
E. 102

_____

38. In $\triangle XYZ$, $\overline{XY} = 8$ cm, $\overline{XZ} = 14$ cm, and $m\angle X = 110°$. Which of the following statements about the measures of the angles in $\triangle XYZ$ must be true?

(Note: $m\angle A$ denotes the measure of angle A.)

F. $m\angle X = m\angle Y = m\angle Z$
G. $m\angle Z > m\angle X > m\angle Y$
H. $m\angle X = m\angle Y > m\angle Z$
J. $m\angle Y > m\angle Z > m\angle X$
K. $m\angle X > m\angle Y > m\angle Z$

39. The circumference of a circle is 80 cm. What is the length, in centimeters, of the diameter of the circle?

A. $\dfrac{40}{\pi}$

B. $\dfrac{80}{\pi}$

C. 80

D. 40π

E. 80π

40. Twelve years ago, Shaneke invested $3,200$ at 5% interest compounded monthly. Which of the following expressions represents today's value of the investment?

F. $3,200e^{0.5}$

G. $3,200(1+0.05)^{12}$

H. $3,200(1+\frac{0.05}{4})^{48}$

J. $3,200(1+\frac{0.05}{12})^{144}$

K. $3,200 + 3,200(0.05)(12)$

41. Consider the equation $\sqrt{3x+4}+6=10$. What is the value of $3x$?

A.   4

B.   12

C.   36

D.   64

E. 512

42. Two concentric circles are shown below. The radius of the larger circle is 12 centimeters and the radius of the smaller circle is 6 centimeters. What is the area, in square centimeters, of the shaded region bounded by the circles?

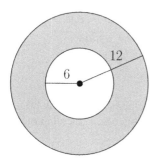

F. 36π

G. 72π

H. 108π

J. 180π

K. 324π

43. The value of a social media photo is modeled by the following equation $P = \dfrac{25L}{D}$, where P is the value of the photo, L is the number of likes per hour, and D is the number of dislikes per hour. Which of the following gives the number of likes per hour of the photo if the value of the photo is 150 units with 2 dislikes per hour?

A. $\dfrac{(2)(150)}{25}$

B. $\dfrac{(2)(25)}{150}$

C. $\dfrac{(25)(150)}{2}$

D. $\dfrac{2}{(150)(25)}$

E. $\dfrac{25}{(150)(2)}$

44. A box contains a combination of four solid-colored beads: $\dfrac{1}{12}$ of the beads are blue, $\dfrac{1}{2}$ are green, $\dfrac{1}{3}$ are yellow, and the remaining 40 beads are red. How many green beads are in the box?

F.   40

G. 160

H. 200

J. 240

K. 480

45. During a rainstorm, the relationship between the height of water in a bucket, y, initially at 2 centimeters, and the elapsed time in hours, x, was modeled by the equation $3x - 6y = -12$. Which of the following graphs in the standard (x, y) coordinate plane models the equation for positive values of x and y?

A.
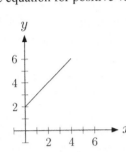

D.
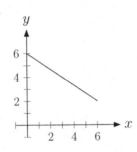

B.
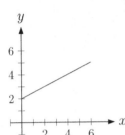

E.
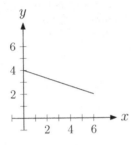

C.
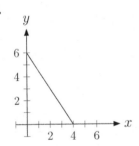

46. Arturo is designing a 9-foot-by-13-foot rectangular piece of poster board for a science project. He will cover both diagonals of the front of the poster board with straight lengths of clear tape. Which of the following values is closest to the total length, in feet, of the 2 pieces of tape Arturo will need for the poster board?

F. 11
G. 16
H. 22
J. 28
K. 32

47. A circle with a radius of 20 cm is divided into 6 congruent arcs. What is the length, in centimeters, of each of the 6 arcs?

A. $\dfrac{20\pi}{3}$

B. $\dfrac{20\pi}{6}$

C. 20π

D. $\dfrac{40\pi}{3}$

E. 40π

48. Paco writes a check for $40. When he records the check in his check register, he accidentally adds $40 to his balance instead of subtracting $40, which causes a discrepancy between what Paco's check register shows and what it should show. Because of his mistake, Paco's check register shows:

F. $80 less than it should
G. $40 less than it should
H. $10 more than it should
J. $40 more than it should
K. $80 more than it should

49. The graph of $y = \dfrac{5x - 1}{2x + 6}$ in the standard (x, y) coordinate plane has a vertical asymptote with equation

$x =$?
A. -3

B. $-\dfrac{1}{5}$

C. $-\dfrac{1}{6}$

D. $\dfrac{5}{2}$

E. 3

50. The fraction $\frac{4}{7}$ is equivalent to $0.\overline{428571}$. What is the digit in the 999th decimal place of $0.\overline{428571}$?

(Note: the digit in the 3rd decimal place of $0.\overline{428571}$ is 8.)

F. 2
G. 4
H. 5
J. 7
K. 8

51. The volume, V, of a right circular cone with radius r and height h is $V = \frac{1}{3}\pi r^2 h$, where r and h have the same unit of measure. Cones W and X are both right circular cones. The radius of Cone W is 8 times the radius of Cone X. Cone W's height is one-eighth Cone X's height. Compared to the volume of Cone X, the volume of Cone W is:

- **A.** the same
- **B.** $\frac{1}{2}$ as great
- **C.** $\frac{1}{8}$ as great
- **D.** 4 times as great
- **E.** 8 times as great

52. Let x be a negative odd integer. The expression $3xy^5$ is a positive even integer whenever y is any member of which of the following sets?

- **F.** All integers
- **G.** Positive odd integers
- **H.** Positive even integers
- **J.** Negative odd integers
- **K.** Negative even integers

53. Consider the cylinder shown below with a radius of 14 centimeters. The distance from a point on the circumference of the bottom base to the center of the top base is $2\sqrt{193}$. Which of the following is closest to the volume, in cubic centimeters, of the cylinder?

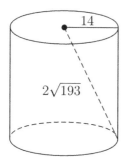

- **A.** 196
- **B.** 772
- **C.** 1,444
- **D.** 4,704
- **E.** 14,778

54. The employees at an electric company are assigned a unique 9-digit personal identification number (PIN). The first and last digit in each PIN are always 7. The other 7 digits can be any digit 0 through 9, and digits may be repeated. How many possible 9-digit PINs are there?

- **F.** 7^7
- **G.** 7^9
- **H.** 9^7
- **J.** 9^9
- **K.** 10^7

55. Yellow Camp and Orange Camp lie on the opposite sides of Lake Stevens. A waterslide is located 1,400 yards from Yellow Camp. The campers estimated the angles between these 3 locations to be as shown on the map below. Using these estimates, which of the following expressions gives the distance, in yards, between Yellow Camp and Orange Camp?

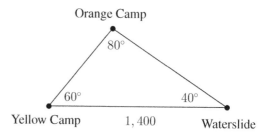

- **A.** $\dfrac{1,400}{40}$
- **B.** $\dfrac{1,400}{\cos 40°}$
- **C.** $\dfrac{1,400 \sin 40°}{\sin 80°}$
- **D.** $\dfrac{1,400 \sin 80°}{\sin 40°}$
- **E.** $\dfrac{\sin 80°}{1,400 \sin 40°}$

56. Given that $3\cos r = 3$ and $3\sin(\pi + t) = 3$, which of the following could be a value, in radians, of $r + t$?

- **F.** $-\frac{1}{2}\pi$
- **G.** 0
- **H.** $\frac{1}{2}\pi$
- **J.** π
- **K.** 2π

57. Which of the following matrices is equal to the matrix product shown below?

$$\begin{bmatrix} 6 & -1 \\ 4 & -2 \end{bmatrix} \begin{bmatrix} 3 \\ -4 \end{bmatrix}$$

A. $\begin{bmatrix} 18 & -3 \\ -16 & 8 \end{bmatrix}$

B. $\begin{bmatrix} -24 & -3 \\ 12 & 8 \end{bmatrix}$

C. $\begin{bmatrix} 22 & -18 \\ 20 & -16 \end{bmatrix}$

D. $\begin{bmatrix} 15 \\ -8 \end{bmatrix}$

E. $\begin{bmatrix} 22 \\ 20 \end{bmatrix}$

58. The graph of $y = \cos x$ in the standard (x, y) coordinate plane is first reflected over the x-axis, then shifted down b units, and then finally shifted right 1.5π units. Which of the following equations represents the graph after the 3 transformations?

F. $y = -\cos(x - 1.5\pi) + b$

G. $y = -\cos(x + 1.5\pi) + b$

H. $y = -\cos(x - 1.5\pi) - b$

J. $y = \cos(x - 1.5\pi) - b$

K. $y = \cos(x + 1.5\pi) - b$

59. Which of the following is an equation of the ellipse shown in the standard (x, y) coordinate plane below?

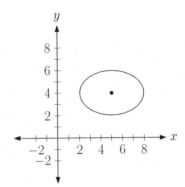

A. $(x + 4)^2 + (y + 5)^2 = 1$

B. $(x - 4)^2 - (y - 5)^2 = 1$

C. $\dfrac{(x - 5)^2}{9} + \dfrac{(y - 4)^2}{4} = 1$

D. $\dfrac{(x - 5)^2}{4} + \dfrac{(y - 4)^2}{9} = 1$

E. $\dfrac{(x + 5)^2}{9} + \dfrac{(y + 4)^2}{4} = 1$

60. For what real value of x, if any, is $\log_{(x+2)}(x^2 + 6) = 2$ true?

F. -2

G. -1

H. 0.5

J. 2

K. There is no such value of x

CHAPTER 10

PRACTICE TEST 2

MATHEMATICS TEST
60 Minutes — 60 Questions

DIRECTIONS: Solve each problem, choose the correct answer, and then fill in the corresponding oval on your answer document.

Do not linger over problems that take too much time. Solve as many as you can; then return to the others in the time you have left for this test.

You are permitted to use a calculator on this test. You may use your calculator for any problems you choose,

but some of the problems may be best done without using a calculator.

Note: Unless otherwise stated, all of the following should be assumed.
1. Illustrative figures are NOT necessarily drawn to scale.
2. Geometric figures lie in a plane.
3. The word *line* indicates a straight line.
4. The word *average* indicates arithmetic mean.

---

1. A muffin recipe requires $2\frac{1}{2}$ cups of flour and yields a dozen muffins. Marcy has a small oven that can only fit an 8 muffin tin. If she adjusts her recipe proportionally, how much flower will she need for 8 muffins?
   A. $\frac{5}{16}$ cup
   B. $1\frac{1}{4}$ cup
   C. $1\frac{1}{2}$ cup
   D. $1\frac{2}{3}$ cup
   E. $3\frac{3}{4}$ cup

2. Rita, a junior, is running for president of the key club. There are 9 other juniors running for the same position. If, historically, a junior only has a 1 in 3 chance of being elected president of the club, what are Rita's chances of becoming president of the key club?
   F. $1/3$
   G. $1/9$
   H. $1/10$
   J. $1/27$
   K. $1/30$

3. Which value of x would make equation $(81)(3^x) = 3^{10}$ true?
   A. 3
   B. 4
   C. 5
   D. 6
   E. 9

4. For the function defined by $f(x) = 3x^2 - 5(2x + 11)$, what is the value of $f(5)$?
   F. -180
   G. -30
   H. 30
   J. 80
   K. 120

5. One streaming movie service offers unlimited movies for $10.99 per month. Another streaming service offers a package where the user pays $3.50 per month and then $0.75 per movie watched. How many movies must Kara watch in a month in order for the unlimited movie subscription to be the cheaper service?
   A. 7
   B. 8
   C. 9
   D. 10
   E. 11

6. In planning her outdoor wedding, Kathleen looked up data for the last 20 years and found that, on the day that she picked, it was sunny 12 times, cloudy 5 times, and rainy 3 times. What is the the empirical probability that her wedding day will turn out to be a sunny day?
   F. $2/5$
   G. $3/5$
   H. $1/4$
   J. $3/20$
   K. $9/25$

7. In the figure below, ABCD is an isosceles trapezoid, $\overline{AD}$ is twice the length of $\overline{AB}$, $\angle A$ is twice the measure of $\angle ADB$, and $\overline{AB} \perp \overline{BD}$. What is the measure of $\angle C$?

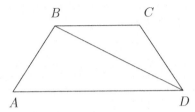

A. 30°

B. 60°

C. 90°

D. 120°

E. 150°

8. Which of the following augmented matrices represents the system of linear equations below?

$$x + 3y = 12$$
$$7x - y = 1$$

F. $\begin{bmatrix} 1 & 3 & | & 12 \\ 7 & 1 & | & 1 \end{bmatrix}$

G. $\begin{bmatrix} 1 & 3 & | & 12 \\ 7 & -1 & | & 1 \end{bmatrix}$

H. $\begin{bmatrix} 1 & 3 & | & 12 \\ 7 & -1 & | & -1 \end{bmatrix}$

J. $\begin{bmatrix} 1 & 3 & | & 12 \\ -7 & -1 & | & 1 \end{bmatrix}$

K. $\begin{bmatrix} 1 & 3 & | & 12 \\ -7 & -1 & | & 1 \end{bmatrix}$

9. Point A is at $(5, -8)$, Point B is at $(-10, 12)$, and $\overline{AB}$ is the diameter of a circle in the standard (x, y) coordinate plane. What are the coordinates of the center of the circle?

A. $(-5, 4)$

B. $(-2.5, 2)$

C. $(-15, 20)$

D. $(-7.5, 10)$

E. $(-2, 2.5)$

10. At a carnival, admission costs \$15. Each basic ride costs \$2 to ride and each premium ride costs \$5 to ride. If Evan went to the carnival, spent \$12 on food, rode 13 rides, and paid a total of \$68, how many premium rides did Evan ride?

F. 4

G. 5

H. 6.5

J. 8

K. 9

11. This semester in Math class, Sven scored a 98 on each of his first and second tests and then a 90 on each of his remaining tests, finishing with a test average of 92. If all tests are weighted equally, how many tests must Sven have taken this semester?

A. 2

B. 4

C. 6

D. 7

E. 8

12. What is the length of the diagonal of a rectangle whose perimeter is 34 and whose area is 60?

F. 69

G. 49

H. 26

J. 17

K. 13

13. For winning a chess tournament, the captain, Ayleen, will receive one-third of what is left of a \$500 prize after the team's coach gets \$20. What remains after Ayleen gets her share will be split evenly among the other team members. If the team has a total of 5 players, how much will Ayleen's teammate Brenda receive?

A. \$40

B. \$80

C. \$96

D. \$100

E. \$160

14. If $(a,b)\Delta(c,d) = \dfrac{ac-bd}{ad-bc}$, what is the value of $(1,2)\Delta(3,4)$?

   F. -2
   G. $2/3$
   H. $3/2$
   J. $5/2$
   K. 2

15. In how many different ways can the letters of the word TIGERS be rearranged?

   A. 30
   B. 36
   C. 240
   D. 512
   E. 720

16. Which of the following expressions is equivalent to $x^{\frac{3}{2}}y^{\frac{5}{2}}$?

   F. $\sqrt[3]{x}\sqrt[5]{y}$
   G. $\left(\sqrt[4]{xy}\right)^{15}$
   H. $(xy)^4$
   J. $\sqrt[4]{xy}$
   K. $\sqrt{x^3y^5}$

17. Which of the following equations represents the line perpendicular to the line $3x + 5y = 10$ at the y-axis?

   A. $y = \dfrac{5}{3}x + 2$

   B. $y = \dfrac{3}{5}x + 3\frac{1}{3}$

   C. $y = -\dfrac{5}{3}x + 2$

   D. $y = -\dfrac{3}{5}x + 2$

   E. $y = \dfrac{5}{3}x + 3\frac{1}{3}$

18. Which of the following operations will produce the largest result when substituted for $\oint$ in the expression $(42)\oint\left(-\frac{7}{5}\right)$?

   F. Averaged with
   G. Divided by
   H. Multiplied by
   J. Plus
   K. Minus

19. In the figure below, the midpoint, M, of hypotenuse $\overline{BC}$ is equidistant from the vertices of $\triangle ABC$. How far is midpoint M from $\angle A$?

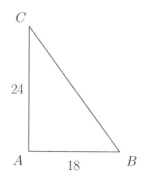

   A. 9
   B. 12
   C. 15
   D. 27
   E. 30

20. A map is scaled such that $\frac{1}{4}$ of an inch represents 20 actual miles. Two towns that are $6\frac{3}{4}$ inches apart on this map are how far apart in reality?

   F. 22
   G. 27
   H. 68
   J. 130
   K. 540

21. What is the first value of x for which the sum of the consecutive numbers $1 + 2 + 3 + ... + x$ will yield a 3 digit number?

   A. 5
   B. 10
   C. 14
   D. 20
   E. 45

22. If x is a positive odd integer and y is a negative odd integer such that $|x| \neq |y|$, which of the following *must* produce a positive even integer?

   F. y^x
   G. x^y
   H. xy
   J. $x - y$
   K. $\dfrac{y^2}{x}$

Questions 23-26 pertain to the following information.

In the figure below, Point A is located at $(9, 0)$, Point B is located at $(0, 12)$, and Point C is located at $(-5, 0)$.

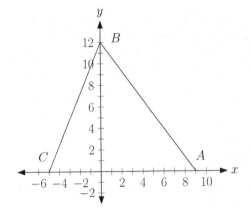

23. What is the area of $\triangle ABC$?

    A. 13

    B. 42

    C. 78

    D. 84

    E. 130

24. What is the perimeter of $\triangle ABC$?

    F. 16

    G. 28

    H. 40

    J. 42

    K. 84

25. Which of the following is equal to $\tan(A)\tan(C)$?

    A. $16/5$

    B. $3/13$

    C. $4/3$

    D. $12/5$

    E. $48/65$

26. Which of the following inequalities correctly lists the *absolute value* of the slopes of the sides of $\triangle ABC$?

    F. $\overline{AC} < \overline{AB} < \overline{BC}$

    G. $\overline{AC} < \overline{BC} < \overline{AB}$

    H. $\overline{AB} < \overline{AC} < \overline{BC}$

    J. $\overline{AB} < \overline{BC} < \overline{AC}$

    K. $\overline{BC} < \overline{AB} < \overline{AC}$

27. Which of the following could be the equation of a circle that passes through the origin?

    A. $(x-3)^2 + (y-4)^2 = 5$

    B. $(x-3)^2 + (y-4)^2 = 7$

    C. $(x-3)^2 + (y-4)^2 = 10$

    D. $(x-3)^2 + (y-4)^2 = 25$

    E. $(x-3)^2 + (y-4)^2 = 49$

28. At a point in time, the Earth was 9.2×10^6 miles from the sun, while Pluto was 4.6×10^9 miles from the sun. At that point in time, how many more times farther from the sun was Pluto than Earth?

    F. 2.0×10^{-3}

    G. 5.0×10^2

    H. 4.2×10^3

    J. 5.0×10^3

    K. 4.2×10^{16}

29. In terms of π, what is the volume of a cylinder whose diameter is 8 and whose height h is three times its radius?

    A. 192π

    B. 384π

    C. 576π

    D. 768π

    E. 1536π

30. If $\tan A = \dfrac{a}{b}$, what is the value of $\cos A$ in terms of a and b?

    F. $\dfrac{a}{\sqrt{a^2 + b^2}}$

    G. $\dfrac{b}{\sqrt{a^2 + b^2}}$

    H. $\dfrac{\sqrt{a^2 + b^2}}{a}$

    J. $\dfrac{\sqrt{a^2 + b^2}}{b}$

    K. $\dfrac{b}{a}$

31. Which of the following expressions is a factor of the expression $x^2 + 64$?

    A. $x + 8i$

    B. $x - 4i$

    C. $x + 8$

    D. $x - 8$

    E. $x - 4$

Questions 32-34 pertain to the following information.

The figure below depicts a 9-ball pool rack. The spherical pool balls are $2\frac{1}{4}$ inches in diameter and tangent to one another. The rack has an outer perimeter of 34 inches and each of the outer sides of the rack is approximately 17% longer than each of the inner sides. The distance between the closest vertices of the rack is $1/2$ inch more than 6 times the radius of a ball in the rack.

(Note: The surface area of a sphere, S_A, is $S_A = 4\pi r^2$. The volume of a sphere, V, is $V = \frac{4}{3}\pi r^3$.)

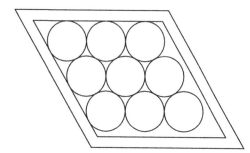

32. What is the perimeter of the *inside* of the rack?
    F.   27 inches
    G.   28 inches
    H.   29 inches
    J.   30 inches
    K.   31 inches

33. To the nearest tenth of a cubic inch, what is the combined volume of the 9 balls in the rack?
    A.   6.0
    B.   17.1
    C.   47.7
    D.   53.7
    E.   143.1

34. The surface area of a pool ball is $5\frac{1}{16}\pi$ in². If the surface area of a cue ball is 11% larger than the surface area of a pool ball, what is the approximate diameter of a cue ball?
    F.   2.49 inches
    G.   2.37 inches
    H.   2.30 inches
    J.   2.03 inches
    K.   1.18 inches

Questions 35-37 pertain to the following information.

A local boys club has 11 members while the local girls club has 14 members. They frequently participate in a number of different activities together.

35. If one member from each club will elected president of their club, how many different combinations of one president from the boys club and one president from the girls club are possible?
    A.   3
    B.   25
    C.   154
    D.   625
    E.   3,850

36. At a fair, each boy is paired with a different girl, with the remaining girls serving as judges for the event. Pairs are randomly selected and change following each event. What is the probability that Annie, the president of the girls club, will judge two consecutive events?

    F. $\dfrac{3}{14}$

    G. $\dfrac{6}{121}$

    H. $\dfrac{3}{196}$

    J. $\dfrac{9}{28}$

    K. $\dfrac{9}{196}$

37. If 5 total members of the clubs will be chosen at random for a cruise trip, which of the following expressions represents the probability that exactly 2 boys and 3 girls are chosen for the cruise trip?

    A. $\dfrac{(_{11}C_2)(_{14}C_3)}{_{25}C_5}$

    B. $\dfrac{(_{25}C_2)(_{25}C_3)}{_{25}C_5}$

    C. $\dfrac{(_{11}C_3)(_{14}C_2)}{_{25}C_5}$

    D. $\dfrac{(_{25}C_{11})(_{25}C_{14})}{_{25}C_5}$

    E. $\dfrac{_{25}C_5}{_{25}P_5}$

38. Which expression is equivalent to $\dfrac{2}{(\sqrt{3}+7)}$?

F. $\dfrac{14-2\sqrt{3}}{-46}$

G. $\dfrac{14-2\sqrt{3}}{-4}$

H. $\dfrac{-14+\sqrt{3}}{-46}$

J. $\dfrac{-14+2\sqrt{3}}{-46}$

K. $\dfrac{-14+2\sqrt{3}}{-4}$

39. In the system of equations shown below, what value of d will create a system of equations that has no solutions?

$$10x+7y=12$$
$$15x+dy=14$$

A. 5
B. $4\,{}^{2}/_{3}$
C. 10.5
D. 12
E. 21

40. Two functions, $f(x)$ and $g(x)$, are defined by $f(x) = \dfrac{x+5}{2-x}$ and $g(x) = x^2 + 5x + 4$. What is the value of $f(g(-3))$?

F. $\dfrac{3}{4}$

G. $\dfrac{154}{25}$

H. $-\dfrac{51}{44}$

J. -2

K. Undefined

41. The distance a ball travels when thrown at a $45°$ angle of elevation is directly proportional to the square of the initial velocity in meters per second and inversely proportional to the acceleration due to gravity in meters per second squared. If k represents the constant of variation, which of the following expressions represents the distance such a ball travels when thrown with with initial velocity v meters per second when the acceleration due to gravity is a meters per second squared?

A. kva

B. $\dfrac{kv}{a}$

C. $\dfrac{kv^2}{a^2}$

D. $\dfrac{kv^2}{a}$

E. $\dfrac{k}{va}$

42. The stem and leaf plot below depicts the daily average temperature (rounded to the nearest degree) for Treesville over a two week period, with weekend leafs—W, X, Y, and Z—absent:

stem	leaf
5	$8, W, 9$
6	$X, 2, 4, 4, Y, 6, 6, 9$
7	$7, 7$
8	Z

If the *median* daily temperature was $65°$, what could be the *mode* of the data set?

F. $59°$
G. $64°$
H. $66°$
J. $77°$
K. Cannot Be Determined

43. In a tennis league, players earn 3 points for winning a Singles match, 2 points for winning a Doubles Match, and 1 point for winning a Mixed Doubles match. The statistics for Jenathy's season are shown in the table below. Based on the data, how many points did Jenathy score for her team?

Type of Match	Matches Played	Winning %
Singles	40	75%
Doubles	30	60%
Mixed Doubles	30	50%

A. 185

B. 141

C. 126

D. 100

E. 63

44. $\triangle KLM$ is an obtuse triangle whose side lengths are all whole numbers. If $\overline{KL}$ is 10 inches long and $\overline{LM}$ is 4 inches long, which of the following sets of numbers represents all possible lengths of $\overline{KM}$ in inches?

F. $\{6, 7, 8, 9\}$

G. $\{11, 12, 13, 14\}$

H. $\{7, 8, 9, 11, 12, 13\}$

J. $\{7, 8, 9, 10, 11, 12, 13\}$

K. $\{6, 7, 8, 9, 10, 11, 12, 13, 14\}$

45. Each of the figures below consist of four cubes of equal volume. On the left, the cubes are stacked one on top of the other. On the right, the two cubes from the top have been moved such that the cubes are arranged in a row. By moving the cubes from the top and placing them on the side, by what percent did the surface area of the figure increase?

A. 2.0%

B. 10.0%

C. 11.1%

D. 12.5%

E. 16.7%

46. A bowling ball has a volume of approximately 320 cubic inches. A lidless rectangular shipping crate measuring 3 feet in length, 2.5 feet in width, and 2.5 feet in height, contains 24 un-drilled bowling balls. A leak above the crate causes the crate to begin filling with water. To the nearest tenth of a cubic foot, how much water would need to leak into the crate before it begins to overflow?

F. 2.8

G. 7.2

H. 11.1

J. 13.4

K. 14.3

47. Suppose $\log_7 4 = f$ and $\log_7 5 = t$, which of the following is equal to 20?

A. 7^{f+t}

B. 7^{ft}

C. $7^f + 7^t$

D. $(7^f)^t$

E. $7(f + t)$

48. The table below shows the earnings each player in a golf tournament took home based on their order of finish:

Position	Name	Earnings
1	Justin Dohnson	$1,000,000
2	Dayson Jay	$800,000
3	Ron Jahm	$640,000
4	Fickie Rowler	?
5	Rich McMillian	?

If the earnings of the five positions form a geometric sequence, how much money would 5th place finisher Rich McMillian have earned?

F. $200,000

G. $320,000

H. $327,640

J. $409,600

K. $512,000

Questions 49-51 pertain to the following information.

In a certain set of vectors, vector $\overrightarrow{AB} = \mathbf{u}$, vector $\overrightarrow{CD} = \mathbf{v}$, and vector $\overrightarrow{EF} = \mathbf{w}$. Two of these vectors, $\overrightarrow{AB}$ and $\overrightarrow{CD}$, are shown in the figure below:

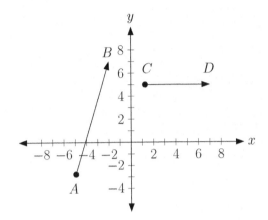

49. What is the unit vector notation of $\overrightarrow{AB} + \overrightarrow{CD}$?

   A. $-3\mathbf{i} + 6\mathbf{j}$

   B. $3\mathbf{i} + 9\mathbf{j}$

   C. $3\mathbf{i} + 10\mathbf{j}$

   D. $9\mathbf{i} + 10\mathbf{j}$

   E. $10\mathbf{i} + 9\mathbf{j}$

50. If $\overrightarrow{CD}$ is translated so that Point C lies on Point B, what would be the distance between points A and D?

   F. $\sqrt{164}$

   G. $\sqrt{181}$

   H. $\sqrt{208}$

   J. $\sqrt{244}$

   K. $\sqrt{109} + 6$

51. Given that $3\mathbf{u} + (-2\mathbf{v}) + \mathbf{w} = 0$, what is the component form of $\mathbf{w}$?

   A. $\langle 3, -30 \rangle$

   B. $\langle 16, -20 \rangle$

   C. $\langle 3, -10 \rangle$

   D. $\langle 21, -30 \rangle$

   E. $\langle -3, 30 \rangle$

---

52. If the function $f(x) = 3x^2 + bx + 7$ has two imaginary roots, which of the following gives the possible values for b?

   F. $|b| < \sqrt{84}$

   G. $|b| < \sqrt{21}$

   H. $|b| < \sqrt{10}$

   J. $|b| > \sqrt{21}$

   K. $|b| > \sqrt{84}$

53. As shown in the figure below, a square brick patio has been inscribed in a circular pavilion 10 decimeters in diameter. The remaining area around the patio will be filled with potting soil. Each barrel of potting soil will cover 1 square decimeter of space. How many barrels of potting soil will be needed to fill in the area surrounding the patio?

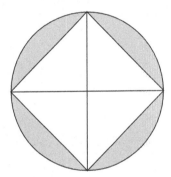

   A. 22

   B. 29

   C. 79

   D. 115

   E. 215

54. If $f(x) = 3x - 7$ and $g(x) = 5x + b$, what value of b would make $g(f(x)) = f(g(x))$?

   F. -21

   G. -17.5

   H. -14

   J. -10.5

   K. -7

55. The graph of the function $f(x) = \sec(2x) + 1$ is shown in the figure below. What is the period of the function?

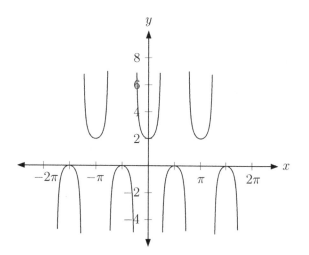

A. $\dfrac{\pi}{4}$

B. $\dfrac{\pi}{2}$

C. π

D. 2π

E. 4π

56. As a reward for getting an A in Math class, Justine gets to reach into a bag of money that contains twelve \$1 bills, seven \$5 bills, five \$10 bills, and three \$20 bills and randomly pull out a single bill. What is the expected amount of money that Justine will earn for pulling a bill?

F. \$0.75

G. \$1.00

H. \$1.33

J. \$5.00

K. \$5.81

57. What is the distance, in the imaginary plane, between the complex numbers $-2 + 7i$ and $6 + i$?

A. 6

B. $\sqrt{80}$

C. 10

D. $\sqrt{130}$

E. 14

58. What value(s) of x would make the determinant of the matrix below equal to 10?

$$\begin{vmatrix} (x+2) & 10 \\ 2 & (x-5) \end{vmatrix}$$

F. $\{-2, 5\}$

G. $\dfrac{3 \pm \sqrt{89}}{2}$

H. $\{-5, 8\}$

J. $\dfrac{3 \pm \sqrt{129}}{2}$

K. $\{-8, 5\}$

59. For which of the following values of θ for $-\dfrac{\pi}{2} \le \theta \le \dfrac{\pi}{2}$ is the value of $\tan^2 \theta = 1$?

A. 0 only

B. $\dfrac{\pi}{4}$ only

C. $\left\{ -\dfrac{\pi}{4}, \dfrac{\pi}{4} \right\}$

D. $\left\{ -\dfrac{\pi}{2}, 0, \dfrac{\pi}{2} \right\}$

E. $\left\{ -\dfrac{\pi}{4}, 0, \dfrac{\pi}{4} \right\}$

60. For the first 5 possible values of x, the table below gives the probability, $P(x)$, that a certain baseball team will make x errors in a given baseball game. Which of the following values is closest to the probability that this baseball team will make at least 1 error in any given baseball game?

x errors	$P(x)$
0	0.0724
1	0.2526
2	0.2639
3	0.1842
4	0.1363

F. 0.2526

G. 0.3756

H. 0.8352

J. 0.9076

K. 0.9276

CHAPTER 11

ANSWER KEYS

You can find handwritten explanations to the chapter quizzes at the following address:
https://privateprep.com/blog/love-of-act-math-answers/

Handwritten explanations to our full-length practice tests are located at the back of this book.

0.1	
1	E
2	G
3	A
4	H
5	B
6	H
7	A
8	G

0.2	
1	E
2	H
3	B
4	F
5	A
6	F
7	C
8	F

0.3	
1	D
2	G
3	D
4	G
5	E
6	J
7	A
8	H

0.4	
1	A
2	J
3	A
4	H
5	D
6	F
7	C
8	H

0.5	
1	C
2	K
3	B
4	F
5	B
6	K

0.6	
1	A
2	J
3	B
4	H
5	A
6	G
7	E
8	G

0.7	
1	D
2	H
3	C
4	J
5	D
6	H
7	D
8	J

0.8	
1	E
2	F
3	E
4	G

0.9	
1	A
2	H
3	D
4	G
5	D
6	G

0.10	
1	D
2	J
3	B
4	K
5	E
6	H

Explanations here: https://privateprep.com/blog/love-of-act-math-answers/

4096
8192
16384

1.1	
1	D
2	H
3	A
4	F
5	B
6	G
7	E
8	F
9	A
10	H
11	C
12	G
13	B
14	H
15	D

1.1 cont'd	
16	G
17	A
18	J
19	D
20	K
21	C
22	K
23	A
24	F

1.2	
1	C
2	G
3	E
4	G
5	B
6	J
7	C
8	G
9	E
10	K
11	C

1.3	
1	A
2	K
3	A
4	K
5	E
6	F
7	B
8	F

1.4	
1	A
2	F
3	B
4	G
5	D
6	H
7	D
8	J
9	A
10	K
11	B
12	K
13	C
14	K
15	D

1.4 cont'd	
16	G
17	E
18	J
19	A
20	F
21	A
22	J
23	D
24	F

1.5	
1	C
2	F
3	E
4	G
5	D
6	H
7	C
8	J
9	B
10	J
11	C

1.6	
1	C
2	G
3	B
4	K
5	C
6	H
7	E
8	K
9	E
10	F

1.7	
1	E
2	J
3	D
4	G
5	E
6	K
7	A
8	H
9	D
10	H

1.8	
1	A
2	J
3	C
4	J
5	D
6	J
7	B
8	K
9	A
10	H

1.9	
1	D
2	J
3	D
4	J
5	B
6	K
7	C
8	G
9	C
10	G
11	D
12	K

1.10	
1	D
2	H
3	C
4	F
5	D
6	G
7	A
8	J
9	C
10	G

Ch.1 quiz			
1	C	11	C
2	G	12	F
3	D	13	D
4	K	14	K
5	B	15	C
6	H	16	G
7	B	17	B
8	K	18	F
9	E	19	E
10	H	20	J

Explanations here: https://privateprep.com/blog/love-of-act-math-answers/

2.1

1	E
2	K
3	D
4	J
5	B
6	H
7	D
8	H
9	A
10	F

2.2

1	C
2	G
3	D
4	J
5	C
6	J
7	B
8	H
9	C
10	G
11	A

2.3

1	D
2	H
3	E
4	H
5	A
6	H
7	C
8	J
9	A
10	F
11	D

2.4

1	C
2	J
3	C
4	G
5	B
6	G
7	B
8	K
9	C
10	K
11	D
12	G

2.5

1	B
2	H
3	C
4	G
5	A
6	K
7	D
8	F
9	A
10	G
11	D
12	F
13	A
14	H
15	B

2.6

1	C
2	G
3	B
4	H
5	A
6	G
7	D
8	J
9	D
10	G
11	B
12	G
13	B
14	K
15	A
16	H
17	B
18	H
19	A

2.7

1	B
2	J
3	D
4	F
5	C
6	G
7	D
8	G
9	B
10	G

2.8

1	D
2	G
3	A
4	F
5	C
6	H

Ch.2 quiz

1	D	11	D
2	J	12	F
3	B	13	C
4	H	14	G
5	E	15	D
6	J	16	J
7	D	17	A
8	F	18	H
9	A	19	C
10	H	20	G

Explanations here: https://privateprep.com/blog/love-of-act-math-answers/

11.4 CHAPTER 3

3.1	
1	A
2	H
3	A
4	G
5	B
6	J
7	B
8	H
9	C
10	F

3.2	
1	B
2	J
3	C
4	F
5	A
6	F
7	B
8	G
9	D
10	J

3.3	
1	D
2	H
3	B
4	F
5	A
6	H
7	C
8	G
9	A
10	H

3.4	
1	E
2	H
3	E
4	F
5	C
6	J
7	A
8	J
9	D

3.5	
1	B
2	G
3	C
4	K
5	E
6	F
7	B
8	J
9	C
10	F
11	E

3.6	
1	A
2	F
3	C
4	J
5	B
6	G
7	E
8	G
9	B
10	H

3.7	
1	D
2	J
3	C
4	F
5	A
6	H
7	D
8	K

3.8	
1	C
2	K
3	B
4	G
5	D
6	K
7	D
8	H
9	B
10	F
11	D
12	K

3.9	
1	E
2	G
3	A
4	F
5	B
6	H
7	A
8	F
9	D
10	K
11	C
12	J

Ch.3 quiz			
1	B	11	E
2	K	12	H
3	E	13	D
4	G	14	F
5	B	15	A
6	H	16	K
7	C	17	C
8	J	18	G
9	E	19	D
10	F	20	F

Explanations here: https://privateprep.com/blog/love-of-act-math-answers/

1	D	11	D	21	C
2	J	12	H	22	J
3	A	13	A	23	C
4	G	14	J	24	F
5	C	15	C	25	B
6	K	16	F	26	J
7	C	17	C	27	A
8	F	18	J	28	F
9	D	19	C	29	A
10	J	20	F	30	G

31	B	41	C	51	B
32	F	42	G	52	F
33	B	43	C	53	B
34	G	44	H	54	K
35	A	45	D	55	D
36	J	46	K	56	J
37	D	47	D	57	A
38	J	48	G	58	F
39	D	49	C	59	B
40	J	50	J	60	K

Explanations here: https://privateprep.com/blog/love-of-act-math-answers/

4.1	
1	C
2	H
3	E
4	J
5	D
6	F
7	A
8	F
9	B
10	J
11	D
12	H

4.2	
1	C
2	H
3	D
4	J
5	C
6	G
7	D
8	J
9	B
10	H
11	C
12	J
13	A
14	H
15	D

4.3	
1	A
2	K
3	D
4	F
5	C
6	K
7	C
8	K
9	B

4.4	
1	D
2	J
3	B
4	F
5	B
6	J
7	B
8	H
9	C
10	J

4.5	
1	A
2	K
3	E
4	J
5	B
6	G
7	B
8	J
9	A
10	G
11	D

4.6	
1	D
2	F
3	D
4	H
5	B
6	K
7	C
8	H
9	B
10	H

4.7	
1	B
2	H
3	C
4	G
5	B
6	K
7	C
8	F
9	C
10	K
11	E
12	G
13	D
14	J

4.8	
1	A
2	J
3	D
4	G
5	E
6	K
7	B
8	H
9	B

4.9	
1	E
2	F
3	A
4	J
5	A
6	G
7	C
8	H
9	D
10	K
11	A
12	J
13	A
14	K
15	E
16	F

Ch.4 quiz			
1	B	11	D
2	J	12	K
3	C	13	B
4	F	14	H
5	C	15	D
6	F	16	F
7	B	17	C
8	K	18	G
9	C	19	B
10	F	20	J

Explanations here: https://privateprep.com/blog/love-of-act-math-answers/

5.1	
1	C
2	J
3	A
4	J
5	B
6	H
7	B
8	F
9	D
10	G

5.2	
1	B
2	J
3	D
4	H
5	B
6	F
7	B
8	G
9	B
10	G
11	A
12	G
13	C

5.3	
1	C
2	K
3	A
4	F
5	B
6	H
7	A
8	H
9	B
10	K
11	D
12	K
13	D
14	K
15	E

5.4	
1	D
2	G
3	D
4	H
5	E
6	J
7	D
8	H
9	A
10	H
11	D

5.5	
1	E
2	J
3	D
4	H
5	C
6	J
7	D
8	J

5.6	
1	A
2	G
3	D
4	H
5	C
6	H
7	C
8	J
9	C
10	G
11	D
12	G

5.7	
1	D
2	J
3	D
4	H
5	E
6	G
7	B
8	F
9	E
10	J
11	A
12	J

5.8	
1	D
2	G
3	A
4	J
5	C
6	G
7	A
8	K
9	A
10	J
11	C
12	F

5.9	
1	B
2	F
3	E
4	H
5	A
6	H
7	E
8	G
9	B
10	G

5.10	
1	D
2	K
3	D
4	G
5	B
6	H
7	C
8	J
9	A

Ch.5 quiz			
1	D	11	E
2	K	12	H
3	A	13	A
4	J	14	F
5	D	15	A
6	J	16	G
7	E	17	A
8	H	18	K
9	B	19	D
10	K	20	J

Explanations here: https://privateprep.com/blog/love-of-act-math-answers/

6.1

1	E
2	J
3	D
4	J
5	A
6	F
7	E
8	J
9	E
10	G
11	C
12	K

6.2

1	A
2	H
3	E
4	K
5	C
6	F
7	E
8	F
9	A
10	K
11	B
12	J
13	A
14	H

6.3

1	E
2	G
3	E
4	H
5	E
6	J
7	D

6.4

1	A
2	J
3	E
4	J
5	A
6	G
7	E
8	J
9	D
10	F
11	A

6.5

1	B
2	F
3	D
4	G
5	C
6	G
7	D
8	G
9	E
10	F
11	A

6.6

1	E
2	J
3	C
4	H
5	E
6	H
7	D
8	G

6.7

1	C
2	K
3	B
4	G
5	D
6	K
7	A
8	K
9	B
10	J
11	C
12	G
13	B

6.8

1	D
2	K
3	C
4	K
5	B
6	F
7	D
8	H
9	C

6.9

1	D
2	K
3	D
4	H
5	A
6	J
7	E
8	G
9	C
10	F
11	B

6.10

1	A
2	F
3	E
4	H
5	A
6	K
7	B
8	J
9	E
10	F
11	B
12	K

Ch.6 quiz

1	C	11	C
2	H	12	K
3	D	13	A
4	F	14	G
5	D	15	C
6	H	16	G
7	C	17	D
8	K	18	J
9	D	19	E
10	H	20	F

Explanations here: https://privateprep.com/blog/love-of-act-math-answers/

1	A	11	A
2	G	12	F
3	D	13	B
4	G	14	K
5	A	15	B
6	G	16	G
7	E	17	E
8	H	18	F
9	E	19	B
10	G	20	F
		21	E

Explanations here: https://privateprep.com/blog/love-of-act-math-answers/

1	E
2	K
3	A
4	J
5	B
6	K
7	B
8	J
9	D
10	K

11	D
12	J
13	D
14	G
15	C
16	F
17	D
18	G
19	D
20	H

21	B
22	H
23	C
24	H
25	A
26	K
27	E
28	H
29	C
30	H

31	C
32	G
33	C
34	J
35	C
36	G
37	C
38	K
39	B
40	J

41	B
42	H
43	A
44	J
45	B
46	K
47	A
48	K
49	A
50	K

51	E
52	K
53	E
54	K
55	C
56	F
57	E
58	H
59	C
60	H

Explanations here: https://privateprep.com/blog/love-of-act-math-answers/

1	D	11	E	21	C
2	K	12	K	22	J
3	D	13	B	23	D
4	G	14	J	24	J
5	D	15	E	25	A
6	G	16	K	26	F
7	D	17	A	27	D
8	G	18	K	28	G
9	B	19	C	29	A
10	G	20	K	30	G

31	A	41	D	51	A
32	H	42	H	52	F
33	D	43	B	53	B
34	G	44	H	54	H
35	C	45	D	55	C
36	K	46	K	56	K
37	A	47	A	57	C
38	J	48	J	58	H
39	C	49	D	59	C
40	F	50	G	60	K

Explanations here: https://privateprep.com/blog/love-of-act-math-answers/

CHAPTER 12

PRACTICE TEST EXPLANATIONS

Question 1: E

Cross Multiply

$$\frac{5}{x} = \frac{0.2}{1}$$

$$\frac{0.2}{0.2} = \frac{5}{0.2}$$

$$x = 25$$

or plug in answer choices for x

Question 2: K

Corresponding sides and angles are in the same position

$$\angle R \cong \angle X \quad \overline{RS} \cong \overline{XY}$$
$$\angle S \cong \angle Y \quad \overline{ST} \cong \overline{YZ}$$
$$\angle T \cong \angle Z \quad \overline{RT} \cong \overline{XZ}$$

Question 3: A

Distribute the negative and drop the parentheses

$$7m - 3n - 4m - 6n$$

Combine Like Terms

$$7m - 4m - 3n - 6n$$

$$3m - 9n$$

Can check or solve by plugging in the concrete numbers for m and n

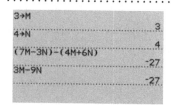

Question 4: J

Multiply coefficients and Add Exponents

$$4 \cdot 6x^{5+8} = 24x^{13}$$

Also can use concrete number for x

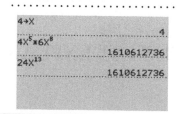

Question 5: B

Plug as is into the calculator, or follow order of operations like so

$$3|-3|-2(6)$$
$$3 \cdot 3 - 12$$
$$9 - 12$$
$$-3$$

Question 6: K

Find the range using subtraction, but be careful of the negatives

Last - First

$$14 - (-5)$$
$$14 + 5$$
$$19°$$

Question 7: B

Find unique factors

$$35 \quad 28 \quad 8$$
$$5 \cdot 7 \quad 2^2 \cdot 7 \quad 2^3$$

$$2^3 \cdot 5 \cdot 7 = 280$$

You can also see which is the smallest answer choice evenly divisble by all 3.

Question 8: J

$$3(-2)^2 - 6(-2) + 5$$
$$3 \cdot 4 + 12 - 5 = 12 + 7 = 19$$

```
-2→X
                          -2
3X²-6X-5
                          19
```

Question 9: D

Mind the Gap!
First min = $1.15
14 additional min (not 15)
$1.15 + 14 ($0.20) = $3.95

Question 10: K

$$an + b = F(n)$$

Use elimination to solve the system of equations

$$-16a + b = 28$$
$$\underline{12a + b = 20}$$
$$4a = 8$$
$$a = 2$$

Now that we have "a" we can plug back in to either equation to solve for "b"

$$12(2) + b = 20$$
$$16(2) + b = 28 \quad b = -4$$

$$2n - 4 = F(n)$$

....

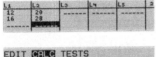

```
EDIT CALC TESTS
1:1-Var Stats
2:2-Var Stats
3:Med-Med
4:LinReg(ax+b)
```

```
        LinReg
y=ax+b
a=2
b=-4
r²=1
r=1
```

Question 11: D

$$65 + 40m = 515$$
$$40m = 450$$
$$m = 11.25$$

Since she will be short after the 11 month, she must save for 12 months

Question 12: J

Area = length × width

$$(x+3)(2x-2)$$

FOIL

$$2x^2 - 2x + 6x - 6$$

$$\searrow \text{combine}$$

$$2x^2 + 4x - 6$$

....

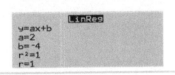

```
12→X
                    12
(X+3)(2X-2)
                   330
2X²+4X-6
                   330
```

Question 13: D

Same procedure as #4

$$4x^2 - 6x - 4 + x^2 - 5x - 8$$

$$4x^2 + x^2 - 6x - 5x - 4 - 8$$

$$5x^2 - 11x - 12$$

....

Or, substitute a number in for x, we picked 13:

```
13→X
                    13
(4X²-6X-4)-(-X²+5X+8)
                   690
5X²-11X-12
                   690
```

Question 14: G

$$\sin^2 x + \cos^2 x = 1$$
$$\sin^2 x + \frac{5}{12} = 1$$
$$\sin^2 x = 1 - \frac{5}{12}$$
$$\sin^2 x = \frac{7}{12}$$

....

```
cos⁻¹(√(5/12))→X
              49.79703411
sin(X)²▶Frac
                    7/12
```

Question 15: C

$$180° - 108° = 72° = \angle BAC$$
$$180° - 140° = 40° = \angle BCA$$
$$\angle ABC + \angle BCA + \angle BAC = 180°$$
$$\angle ABC + 72° + 40° = 180°$$
$$\angle ABC = 68°$$

Also, trust your eyes!

Question 16: F

In the standard form of a line $Ax + By = C$ the slope "m" $= -\frac{A}{B}$

$$13x + 5y = 4$$

$$m = -\frac{13}{5}$$

Question 17: D

Get to the sum total and work backwards

$$76 + 82 + 94 + 90 + 78 = 420$$

average

$$\frac{420}{5} = 84$$

# of tests

new average

$$84 + 2 = 86$$

$$86 \cdot 6 = 516$$

$$516 - 420 = 96$$

Question 18: G

Can put the numbers in order by hand

$$1, 4, 4, 7, \boxed{8, 9,} 11, 12, 16, 19$$

$$\frac{8+9}{2} = 8.5$$

....

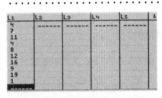

```
EDIT CALC TESTS
1:1-Var Stats
        1-Var Stats
↑Sx=5.586690533
σx=5.3
n=10
minX=1
Q₁=4
Med=8.5
Q₃=12
maxX=19
```

Question 19: D

If $a = 3$ (maximum)

$$3 + b \geq 7$$
$$b \geq 4$$
$$b = 4$$

Question 20: H

The savings to total expenses is equal to the angle out of $360°$

$$\frac{450}{3200} = \frac{\theta}{360°}$$

$3200\theta = 162000$

$\theta = 50.625$

$\theta \approx 51°$

Question 21: B

You CAN use Pythagorean theorem to find the hypotenuse $\overline{AB}$, but the answer choices will dictate that $\overline{AB} = 25$

$$\sin A = \frac{opp}{hyp} = \frac{\overline{BC}}{\overline{AB}} = \frac{7}{25}$$

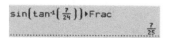

$\sin(\tan^{-1}(\frac{7}{24})) \blacktriangleright \text{Frac}$

$\frac{7}{25}$

Question 22: H

Area = base × height

base = $9 - 4 = 5$

height = $6 - 0 = 6$

$5 \cdot 6 = 30$

Question 23: C

Plug in -5 for "x" and -3 for "y"

$(-5 + 6, -3 - 4) = (1, -7)$

Question 24: H

Use Elimination...

$5(c + 2d = 16)$

$5c + 10d = 80$

$-(5c - 3d) = 15$

$$\frac{13d}{13} = \frac{65}{13}$$

$d = 5$

Question 25: A

Area = $\frac{1}{2}$ base · height

base = $\overline{ZY} = 30$

height = $\overline{WT} = 6$

Area $\triangle WYZ = \frac{1}{2}(30)(6)$

Area $\triangle WYZ = 90 \text{ in}^2$

Question 26: K

$$\text{sine} = \frac{\text{Opposite}}{\text{Hypotenuse}}$$

$$\text{cosecant} = \frac{\text{Hypotenuse}}{\text{Opposite}}$$

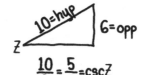

$$\frac{10}{6} = \frac{5}{3} = \csc Z$$

Must be J or K from the outset, as the larger number must be in the numerator

$\sin^{-1}(6/10) \rightarrow Z$

$.64$

$\frac{1}{\sin(Z)} \blacktriangleright \text{Frac}$

$\frac{5}{3}$

Question 27: E

$\triangle WZT$ is the 2nd multiple of the 3:4:5 Pythagorean triple, the 6:8:10, so $\overline{ZT} = 8$ horizontally the x value of point X will be

$\overline{ZT} + \overline{WX} = 8 + 16 = 24$

Question 28: H

By factoring (Grouping)

First factor out an x

$x(2x^2 - 5x - 3)$

split

$x(2x^2 - 6x + x - 3)$

$x(2x(x-3) + 1(x-3))$

factor groups

$x(2x + 1)(x - 3)$

$2(-3) = -6$ ⎱ can be split
$-6 + 1 = 5$ ⎰ in either order

Also, what makes the factor 0 will also make the polynomial 0

$I = F(0) = 0 \checkmark$

$II = F(3) = 90 \times$

$III = F(-\frac{1}{2}) = 0 \checkmark$

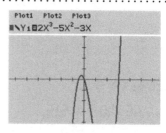

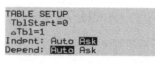

Question 29: C

You can plug in each to get the temperatures and then subtract the results

$F(28) - F(16) = 21\frac{3}{5}$

but since it's a CHANGE, you can plug in the difference If you ignore the constant

$F = \frac{9}{5}(28 - 16) \cancel{+32} = 21\frac{3}{5}$

342

Question 30: H

$$Tan = \frac{opposite}{adjacent}$$

$$Tan(29°) = \frac{h}{44m}$$

$$h = 44 \cdot Tan(29°)m$$

Question 31: C

$$(2+7i)x = 53$$

$$x = \frac{53}{2+7i} = 2-7i$$

If 2 complex numbers multiply to a real number, they MUST be conjugates or multiples of conjugates

$$x^2 + y^2 = (x+yi)(x-yi)$$

$$2^2 + 7^2 = 53 = (2+7i)(2-7i)$$

....

53/(2+7i)

2.00-7.00i

Question 32: G

$$A sin(Bx) \quad |A| = Amplitude$$

$$\frac{2\pi}{B} = Period \qquad B = 5$$

$$\frac{2\pi}{5} = G$$

From the graph, there are 2.5 cycles from 0 to π

so $B = \frac{\pi}{2.5} = \frac{2\pi}{5}$

Question 33: C

$$\angle X + \angle Z = 180$$

$$\angle Y + \angle Z = 180$$

$$\angle X + \angle Z + \angle Y + \angle Z = 360$$

$$\underbrace{\angle X + \angle Y} + 2\angle Z = 360$$

$$90 + 2\angle Z = 360$$

$$2\angle Z = 270$$

$$\angle Z = 135$$

Can also be done by showing that $\angle X = \angle Y$

Question 34: J

Distance IS Pythagorean Theorem

$$\underbrace{\Delta y^2 + \Delta x^2} = d^2$$

$$|3-(-4)| = 7 \qquad |7-12| = 5$$

$$\sqrt{7^2 + 5^2} = \sqrt{74}$$

....

$\sqrt{(3--4)^2 + (7-12)^2}$

8.60

$\sqrt{74}$

8.60

Question 35: C

From the plot, there are 11 students who sold more than 30 tickets

$$3 \mid 0\ 1\ 1\ 2\ 3\ 3\ 5\ 7\ 9$$
$$\quad \underset{1\ 2\ 3\ 4\ 5\ 6\ 7\ 8}{}$$

$$4 \mid 1\ 2\ 3 \qquad \frac{11}{30}$$
$$\quad \underset{9\ 10\ 11}{}$$

Question 36: G

$$Sat = 168(3) + 121(5)$$
$$= \$1109$$

$$Sun = 122(3) + 136(5)$$
$$= \$1046$$

$$1109 - 1046 = \$63$$

$$Sat > Sun\ by\ \$63$$

Question 37: C

Seats form an arithmetic sequence

$$a_n = a_1 + d(n-1)$$

$$s_n = 12 + 6(n-1)$$

$$s_n = 12 + 6(n-10)$$

$$s_n = 66\ seats$$

Question 38: K

The largest angle is across from the largest side. If $\angle X$ is equal to $110°$, then $\overline{YZ}$ is the longest side. If the sides are in the relationship $\overline{YZ} > \overline{XZ} > \overline{ZY}$, the angles across will be the same.

$$\angle X > \angle Y > \angle Z$$

$$\angle X + \angle Y + \angle Z = 180$$

$$\angle Y + \angle Z = 70$$

$$\angle Y < 70°\ and$$

$$\angle Z < 70°$$

Question 39: B

The definition of π is the ratio of the circumference of a circle to its diameter

$$\pi = \frac{Circumference}{Diameter}$$

$$\frac{\pi}{1} = \frac{80}{D} \qquad D = \frac{80}{\pi}$$

Can always swap diagonal terms when 2 fractions are set equal to each other, and can always put contants over 1.

Question 40: J

Annual Interest Formula

$$A_t = A_o(1+r)^t$$

Monthly Interest Formula

$$A_t = A_o\left(1+\frac{r}{12}\right)^{12t}$$

$$A_{12} = 3200\left(1+\frac{.05}{12}\right)^{12(12)}$$

$$= 3200\left(1+\frac{.05}{12}\right)^{144}$$

Question 41: B

$$\left(\sqrt{3x+4}\right)^2 = 4^2$$
$$3x+4 = 16$$
$$3x = 12$$

or
let $3x = y$
and solve for y
$$\sqrt{y+4} + 6 = 10$$

You can also plug in answer choices for $3x$, but don't confuse with 'x'

Question 42: H

Area of shaded region is
Area of whole − Area of inner circle

$$\pi R^2 - \pi r^2 = \text{Area}$$
$$\pi 12^2 - \pi 6^2 = \text{Area}$$
$$\pi 144 - \pi 36 = \text{Area}$$
$$108\pi = \text{Area}$$

Question 43: A

Substitute 150 for 'P' and 2 for 'D', then solve for 'L'

$$150 = \frac{25L}{2}$$

Multiply by 2
$$2(150) = 25L$$

Divide by 25
$$\frac{2(150)}{25} = L$$

Question 44: J

$$\frac{1}{12} + \frac{1}{2} + \frac{1}{3} = \frac{1}{12} + \frac{6}{12} + \frac{4}{12} = \frac{11}{12}$$

The remaining $\frac{1}{12}$ are red

$$\frac{1}{12} = \text{red total} = \frac{40}{x} \quad x = 480$$

There are 480 beads in the box. If half are green, then there are 240 greens.

Question 45: B

Can plug in concrete numbers and math with the right graph.

When x is 0, y is 2
When x is 4, y is 4

Or solve for y and match.

$$3x - 6y = -12$$
subtract $-6y = -3x - 12$
divide $y = \tfrac{1}{2}x + 2$

Question 46: K

The length and width of the poster board will be the legs of a right triangle, with the diagonals being the hypotenuse. Since there are two diagonals

$$\text{total length} = 2\sqrt{9^2 + 13^2}$$
$$= 2\sqrt{81 + 169}$$
$$= 2\sqrt{250}$$
$$\approx 32 \text{ ft.}$$

....

$2\sqrt{9^2+13^2}$ 31.62

Question 47: A

Circumference $= 2\pi r$

$$2(20)\pi = 40\pi$$
$$\frac{40\pi}{6} = \frac{20\pi}{3}$$

Question 48: K

What Paco did...
$$B_o + \$40 = B_n$$
What Paco should've done...
$$B_o - \$40 = B_n$$

Say he started with $100,
it now reads $140,
but it should read $60,
So it now reads $80 (140−60) more than it should.

Question 49: A

Vertical asymptote is where the denominator is equal to 0

$$2x + 6 = 0$$
$$2x = -6$$
$$x = -3$$

Question 50: K

We have 6 repeating digits, so $\frac{999}{6} = 166\frac{3}{6}$ cycles. Since the remainder is 3, the 999th digit must be the 3rd digit in the repeating sequence, which is '8'.

Question 51: E

You can use concrete numbers here, but $r_w = 8r_x$
and $h_w = \frac{h_x}{8}$

$$V_x = \tfrac{1}{3}\pi r_x^2 h_x$$

$$V_w = \tfrac{1}{3}\pi (8r)^2 \left(\frac{h_x}{8}\right)$$

$$\frac{V_w}{} = \frac{\tfrac{1}{3}\pi \frac{8 \cdot 8 r_x^2 h_x}{8}}{\tfrac{1}{3}\pi r_x^2 h_x} = 8$$

V_w is 8 times as great as V_x

Question 52: K

If x is odd and negative, then 3x is also odd and negative, so for $3xy^5$ to be even and positive, y^5 must be even, since an odd must be multiplied by and even to get an even result, and y^5 must be negative, as a negative times a negative is a positive. Since odd exponents keep their sign, 'y' must be negative and even.

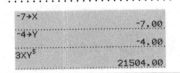

```
-7→X
                    -7.00
-4→Y
                    -4.00
3XY⁵
               21504.00
```

Question 53: E

Use Pythagorean theorem to find the height of the cylinder $h^2 + 14^2 = (2\sqrt{193})^2$
$$h^2 + 196 = 772$$
$$h^2 = 576$$
$$h = 24$$

$$\text{Volume} = \pi r^2 h$$
$$= \pi(14)^2(24)$$
$$= 4704\pi$$
$$\approx 14{,}778$$

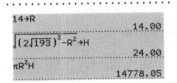

```
14→R
                    14.00
√((2√193)²-R²)→H
                    24.00
πR²H
               14778.05
```

Question 54: K

Since the first and last digit are always 7, we only have 1 option for each of those digits. For The other 7, there are 10 options, so the total number of possible pins
$$= 1 \cdot 10 \cdot 10 \cdot 10 \cdot 10 \cdot 10 \cdot 10 \cdot 10 \cdot 1$$
$$= 10^7$$

Question 55: C

In Law of Sines, the proportion of the side length to the sine of the angle across is the same for all 3 side,

so $\dfrac{\sin 40}{d_{y-o}} = \dfrac{\sin 80}{1400}$

$$d_{y-o} = \frac{1400 \sin 40}{\sin 80}$$

Question 56: F

$$3\cos r = 3 \qquad 3\sin(\pi + t) = 3$$
$$\cos r = 1 \qquad \sin(\pi + t) = 1$$
$$\cos^{-1}(1) = r \qquad \sin^{-1}(1) = \pi + t$$
$$0 = r \qquad \frac{\pi}{2} = \pi + t$$
$$r + t = -\frac{\pi}{2} \qquad -\frac{\pi}{2} = t$$

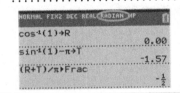

```
NORMAL FIX2 DEC REAL RADIAN MP
cos⁻¹(1)→R
                         0.00
sin⁻¹(1)-π→T
                        -1.57
(R+T)/π▸Frac
                          -½
```

Question 57: E

$$\begin{bmatrix} a & b \\ c & d \end{bmatrix} = \begin{bmatrix} x \\ y \end{bmatrix} = \begin{bmatrix} ax + by \\ cx + dy \end{bmatrix}$$

$$\begin{bmatrix} 6 & -1 \\ 4 & -2 \end{bmatrix} \begin{bmatrix} 3 \\ -4 \end{bmatrix} = \begin{bmatrix} 6(3) + -1(-4) \\ 4(3) + -2(-4) \end{bmatrix}$$
$$= \begin{bmatrix} 22 \\ 20 \end{bmatrix}$$

A×B · B×C
(2×2)(2×1)=(2×1)
A×C

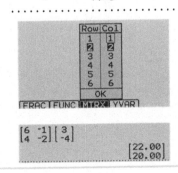

```
              Row Col
               1   1
               2   2
               3   3
               4   4
               5   5
               6   6
                OK
FRAC FUNC MTRX YVAR
```

```
[6  -1][3 ]
[4  -2][-4]
                  [22.00]
                  [20.00]
```

Question 58: H

x-axis reflection
① $F(x) = -F(x)$

Vertical shift
② $F(x) = F(x) + Y$

Horizontal shift
③ $F(x) = F(x-h)$

$y = \cos x$

$y = -\cos(x - 1.5\pi) - b$

Question 59: C

$$\frac{(x-h)^2}{a^2} + \frac{(y-k)^2}{b^2} = 1$$

center $(h, k) = (5, 4)$
Major Axis $a = 3$
minor axis $b = 2$

$$\frac{(x-5)^2}{3^2} + \frac{(y-4)^2}{2^2} = 1$$

$$\frac{(x-5)^2}{9} + \frac{(y-4)^2}{4} = 1$$

Question 60: H

$$\log_{(x+2)}(x^2 + 6) = 2$$
$$(x+2)^2 = x^2 + 6$$
$$x^2 + 4x + 4 = x^2 + 6$$
$$4x = 2$$
$$x = \tfrac{1}{2}$$

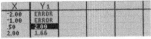

```
Plot1
Y₁=   1:abs(
       2:summation Σ(
       3:nDeriv(
Y₂=   4:fnInt(
Y₃=   5:logBASE(
Y₄=   6:×√
Y₅=   7:nPr
Y₆=   8:nCr
Y₇=   9:♦
FRAC FUNC MTRX YVAR
Plot1  Plot2  Plot3
Y₁■log_{x+2}(x²+6)
```

```
X      Y₁
-2.00  ERROR
-1.00  ERROR
.50    2.00
2.00   1.66
```

Question 1: D

CROSS MULTIPLY

$$\frac{2.5}{12} = \frac{X}{8}$$

$$12X = 20$$

$$X = \frac{20}{12} = \frac{5}{3} = 1\frac{2}{3}$$

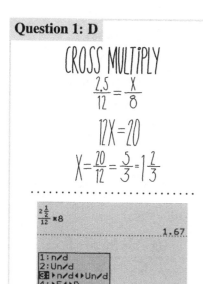

Question 2: K

TOTAL JUNIORS = 10

9 OTHER JUNIORS

TOP JUNIOR PROBABILITY = $\frac{1}{10}$

$$\frac{1}{10} \times \frac{1}{3} = \frac{1}{30}$$

CHANCE OF
ANY JUNIOR

Question 3: D

$$81 = 3^4$$

$$3^4 \cdot 3^X = 3^{10}$$

$$4 + X = 10 \rightarrow X = 6$$

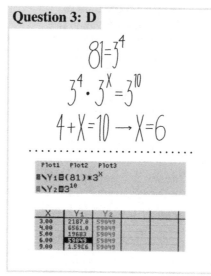

Question 4: G

$$3(5^2) - 5(2(5) + 11)$$

$$3 \cdot 25 - 5(10 + 11)$$

$$75 - 5(21)$$

$$75 - 105 = \ominus 31$$

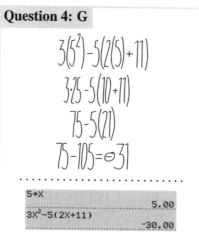

Question 5: D

$$3.50 + 0.75m > 10.99$$

$$0.75m > 7.49$$

$$m > 9.99 \approx 10$$

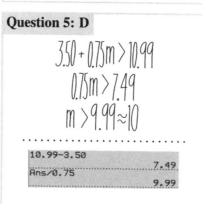

Question 6: G

$$\frac{\text{FAVORABLE}}{\text{ALL POSSIBLE}} = \frac{12}{20} = \frac{3}{5}$$

Question 7: D

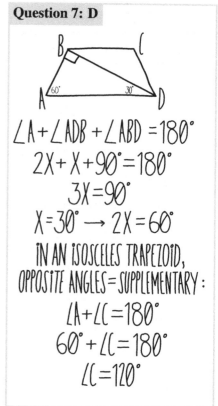

$$\angle A + \angle ADB + \angle ABD = 180°$$

$$2X + X + 90° = 180°$$

$$3X = 90°$$

$$X = 30° \rightarrow 2X = 60°$$

IN AN ISOSCELES TRAPEZOID,
OPPOSITE ANGLES = SUPPLEMENTARY:

$$\angle A + \angle C = 180°$$

$$60° + \angle C = 180°$$

$$\angle C = 120°$$

Question 8: G

MATCH COEFFICIENTS (INCLUDING SIGNS):

$$\begin{array}{l} 1X + 3Y = 12 \\ 7X + (-1Y) = 1 \end{array} \rightarrow \begin{bmatrix} 1 & 3 & | & 12 \\ 7 & -1 & | & 1 \end{bmatrix}$$

Question 9: B

MIDPOINT OF A DIAMETER IS THE CIRCLE
CENTER → USE AVERAGE OF COORDINATES

$$\left(\frac{5 + (-10)}{2}, \frac{-8 + 12}{2}\right) = (-2.5, 2)$$

Question 10: G

SYSTEM OF EQUATION

$\$15 + \$12 + \$2b + \$5p = \$68$

$\$2b + \$5p = 41$

$b + p = 13$

3-STEP HACK

1 ASSUME ALL 13 WERE BASIC
$\$2 \cdot 13 = \$26$

2 ALL RIDES ACTUALLY COST $\$41$
$\$41 - \$26 = \$15$

3 DIFFERENCE MUST BE PREMIUM RIDES
$5 - 2 = \$3$ A RIDE $\rightarrow \frac{\$15}{3} = 5$ PREMIUM RIDES

Question 11: E

LET X = NUMBER OF TESTS $\frac{1}{3}$

$X - 2 \longrightarrow$ TESTS SCORING 90

$\frac{98 + 98 + 90(X-2)}{X} = 92$

$196 + 90X - 180 = 92X$

$16 = 2X$

$8 = X$

Question 12: K

$2\ell + 2\omega = 34$

$\ell + \omega = 17$

$\ell + \omega > d$

$d < 17 \rightarrow$ ONE ANSWER

OR SET-UP A SYSTEM OF EQUATIONS

$\ell \cdot \omega = 60$

$\omega = 17 - \ell$

$\ell(17 - \ell) = 60$

$17\ell - \ell^2 = 60$

$\ell^2 - 17\ell + 60 = 0$

$(\ell - 12)(\ell - 5)$

$\ell = 12 \rightarrow \omega = 5$

OR $\ell = 5 \rightarrow \omega = 12$

Question 13: B

$500 - 20 = \$480$ LEFT FOR THE TEAM

FOR THE OTHER MEMBERS: $\frac{\$320}{4} = \$80$

Question 14: J

$\frac{1(3) - 2(4)}{1(4) - 2(3)} = \frac{3 - 8}{4 - 6} = \frac{-5}{-2} = \frac{5}{2}$

2→B	2.00
3→C	3.00
4→D	4.00
$\frac{AC-BD}{AD-BC}$ ▶Frac	$\frac{5}{2}$

Question 15: E

NO REPITION MEANS PERMUTATIONS/FACTORIALS

$6!$ OR $_6P_6 = 720$

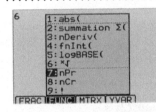

6	1:abs(
	2:summation Σ(
	3:nDeriv(
	4:fnInt(
	5:logBASE(
	6:×√
	7:nPr
	8:nCr
	9:!

| FRAC | FUNC | MTRX | YVAR |

$_6P_6$	720.00
$6!$	720.00

Question 16: K

$$C^{a/b} = \sqrt[b]{C^a}$$

$X^{3/2} = \sqrt{X^3}$ $\frac{1}{3}$ $Y^{5/2} = \sqrt{Y^5}$
  $\frac{1}{1}$

$\sqrt{X^3} \cdot \sqrt{Y^5} = \sqrt{X^3 Y^5}$

16→X	16.00
25→Y	25.00
$X^{\frac{3}{2}} Y^{\frac{5}{2}}$	200000.00
$\sqrt{X^3 Y^5}$	200000.00
16→X	16.00
25→Y	25.00
$X^{\frac{3}{2}} Y^{\frac{5}{2}}$	200000.00
$\sqrt{X^3 Y^5}$	200000.00

Question 17: A

$3X + 5Y = 10$

$5Y = -3X + 10$

$Y = \frac{-3}{5}X + 2$

$m = \frac{-3}{5}, b = 2$

$m_\perp = \frac{5}{3} \rightarrow Y = \frac{5}{3}X + 2$

Question 18: K

AVERAGED WITH → DIVIDED SUM = SMALLER VALUE

DIVIDED BY → YIELD NEGATIVE VALUE

MULTIPLIED BY → YIELD NEGATIVE VALUE

PLUS → YIELD SMALLER VALUE

MINUS → SUBTRACTING A NEGATIVE = ADDITION

$$42 - \left(\frac{-7}{5}\right) = 42 + \left(\frac{7}{5}\right) = 43\frac{2}{5}$$

$\frac{42 + \frac{-7}{5}}{2}$	20.30
$42 / \frac{-7}{5}$	-30.00
$42 \ast \frac{-7}{5}$	-58.80
$42 + \frac{-7}{5}$	40.60
$42 - \frac{-7}{5}$	43.40

Question 19: C

$$\overline{AB}^2 + \overline{AC}^2 = \overline{BC}^2$$
$$18^2 + 24^2 = \overline{BC}^2$$
$$\sqrt{900} = \overline{BC}$$
$$30 = \overline{BC}$$

SIXTH MULTIPLE OF THE 3-4-5 TRIPLE
$$6 \cdot (3:4:5) = 18:24:30$$
IF $\overline{BC} = 30$ AND ITS MIDPOINT IS
EQUIDISTANT FROM $\angle A, \angle B, \frac{1}{3} \angle C$

$$\frac{30}{2} = 15 \text{ UNITS}$$

Question 20: K

$$\frac{\frac{1}{4}}{20} = \frac{6\frac{3}{4}}{X}$$

CROSS MULTIPLY

$$\frac{X}{4} = 135$$
$$X = 540$$

Question 21: C

THREE DIGIT NUMBER = 100

$$S_n = \frac{n(a_1 + a_n)}{2} \qquad a_1 = 1$$

HERE $a_n = n$
BECAUSE $d = 1$

$$100 = \frac{n(1 + a_n)}{2}$$
$$200 = n + n^2$$
$$n^2 + n - 200 = 0$$
$$= \frac{-1 \pm \sqrt{1^2 - 4(1)(200)}}{2} = \frac{-1 \pm \sqrt{1 + 800}}{2}$$

↳ ANSWER MUST BE POSITIVE

$$= \frac{-1 \pm \sqrt{801}}{2} = \frac{-1 + 28.302}{2}$$

$$n = 13.65 \rightarrow 14 \text{ IS CLOSEST}$$

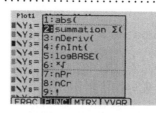

Question 22: J

$X = +$ ODD INTEGER → LIKE $+5$
$Y = -$ ODD INTEGER → LIKE -3

F. $y^x = (-3)^5 = -243 \ominus$ ODD INTEGER

G. $x^y = 5^{-3} = \frac{1}{125}$ NOT AN INTEGER

H. $XY = (5)(-3) = -15 \ominus$ ODD INTEGER

J. $5 - (-3) = 8 \oplus$ EVEN INTEGER

K. $\frac{y^2}{X} = \frac{(-3)^2}{5} = \frac{9}{5} = 1.8$ NOT AN INTEGER

11→X	11.00
-17→Y	-17.00
Y^X	-3.43E13
X^Y	1.98E-18
XY	-187.00
X-Y	28.00
Y²/X	26.27

Question 23: D

AREA = ½ (BASE)(HEIGHT)
$$= ½ (9 - (-5))(12 - 0)$$
$$= ½ (14)(12) = 84$$

Question 24: J

$$\overline{AC} = 9 - (-5) = 14$$
$$\overline{BC} = \sqrt{(-5)^2 + 12^2} = 13$$
$$\overline{AB} = \sqrt{9^2 + 12^2} = 15$$
$$14 + 13 + 15 = 42$$

Question 25: A

$$\tan(A) = \frac{12}{9} \quad \tan(C) = \frac{12}{5}$$
$$\tan(A)\tan(C) = \frac{12}{9} \cdot \frac{12}{5} = \frac{144}{45} = \frac{16}{5}$$

Question 26: F

$$|m\overline{AC}| = 0 \quad |m\overline{BC}| = \frac{12}{5} \quad |m\overline{AB}| = \frac{12}{9}$$
$$\overline{AC} < \overline{AB} < \overline{BC}$$

Question 27: D

$$X = 0, Y = 0$$
$$(0 - 3)^2 + (0 - 4)^2$$
$$(-3)^2 + (-4)^2 = 9 + 16 = 25$$

Question 28: G

$$\frac{4.6 \times 10^9}{9.2 \times 10^6} \rightarrow \frac{4.6}{9.2} \times \frac{10^9}{10^6} = 0.5 \times 10^3$$

$$0.5 \times 10^3 \rightarrow 5.0 \times 10^2$$

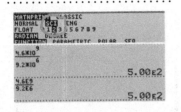

Question 29: A

$$V = \pi r^2 h$$
$$d = 8 \rightarrow r = 4$$
$$h = 3r \rightarrow 3 \cdot 4 = 12$$
$$V = \pi \, 4^2 \cdot 12 = 192\pi$$

Question 30: G

$$h = \sqrt{a^2 + b^2}$$

$$\tan A = \frac{a}{\sqrt{a^2 + b^2}} \quad \begin{array}{l} \text{OPPOSITE} \\ \text{HYPOTENUSE} \end{array}$$

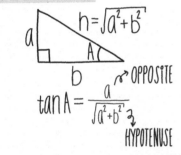

Question 31: A

USE QUADRATIC EQUATION

$$X = \frac{-0 \pm \sqrt{0^2 - 4(1)(64)}}{2(1)}$$

$$X = \pm \frac{\sqrt{-256}}{2} = \pm \frac{16i}{2}$$

$$X = \pm 8i \rightarrow X + 8i \quad X - 8i$$

$-8i \rightarrow X$	$-8.00i$
$X^2 + 64$	0.00
$4i \rightarrow X$	$4.00i$
$X^2 + 64$	48.00

Question 32: H

$$P_{OUTSIDE} = 1.17 \times P_{INSIDE}$$

$$34 \, iN = 1.17 \times P_{INSIDE}$$

$$P_{INSIDE} = \frac{34}{1.17} = 29 \, iN$$

Question 33: D

$$V_{1-BALL} = \frac{4}{3}\pi r^3$$
$$d = 2\tfrac{1}{4} \, iN = 2r$$
$$r = 1\tfrac{1}{8} \, iN$$
$$V_{1-BALL} = \frac{4}{3}\pi \left(1\tfrac{1}{8}\right)^3 = 5.96 \, iN^3$$
$$\text{TOTAL VOLUME} = 9 \cdot 5.96 \, iN^3 = 53.7 iN^3$$

Question 34: G

$$5\tfrac{1}{16} \cdot 1.11 = 17.65 \, iN$$

$$A = 4\pi r^2 = 17.65 \, iN^2$$

$$r = \sqrt{\frac{17.65}{4\pi}} \approx 1.185$$

$$d = 2r = 2 \cdot 1.185 = 2.37 \, iN$$

Question 35: C

COUNTING PRINCIPLE

11 BOYS × 14 GIRLS = 154 COMBINATIONS

Question 36: K

INDEPENDENT EVENTS

$$P(JUDGE) = \tfrac{3}{14}$$

$$P(TWICE) = \tfrac{3}{14} \cdot \tfrac{3}{14} = \tfrac{9}{196}$$

Question 37: A

$$P(2 BOYS) = 2 \text{ BOYS OUT OF } 11 = {}_{11}C_2$$
$$P(3 GIRLS) = 3 \text{ GIRLS OUT OF } 14 = {}_{14}C_3$$
$$\text{ALL POSSIBLE OUTCOMES} = 5 \text{ STUDENTS OUT OF } 25 = {}_{25}C_5$$

$$\frac{P(2 BOYS) \cdot P(3 GIRLS)}{\text{ALL POSSIBLE OUTCOMES}} = \frac{({}_{11}C_2) \cdot ({}_{14}C_3)}{{}_{25}C_5}$$

Question 38: J

MULTIPLY BY CONJUGATE

$$\frac{2}{(\sqrt{3} + 7)} \cdot \frac{(\sqrt{3} - 7)}{(\sqrt{3} - 7)} = \frac{-14 + 2\sqrt{3}}{3 - 49} = \frac{-14 + 2\sqrt{3}}{-46}$$

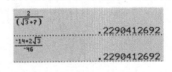

Question 39: C

IF $AX + BY = C$ AND
$DX + EY = F$ HAS NO SOLUTION, THEN

$$\frac{A}{D} = \frac{B}{E} \neq \frac{C}{F}$$

$$\frac{10}{15} \times \frac{7}{D} \quad \text{CROSS MULTIPLY}$$

$$10D = 105 \rightarrow D = 10.5$$

Question 40: F

$$f(g(-3)) = \frac{g(-3) + 5}{2 - g(-3)}$$

$$g(-3) = (-3^2) + 5(-3) + 4 = -2$$

$$f(g(-3)) = \frac{-2 + 5}{2 - (-2)} = \frac{3}{4}$$

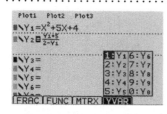

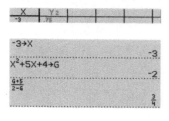

Question 41: D

DIRECT = NUMERATOR

INVERSE = DENOMINATOR

K = CONSTANT

$$\frac{KV^2}{a}$$

Question 42: H

↳ NUMBER DATA POINTS

$$n = 14$$

MEDIAN = AVERAGE OF 7TH AND 8TH POSITIONS

7TH POSITION = 64 8TH POSITION = Y

$$\frac{64 + Y}{2} = 65$$

$$Y = (65 \cdot 2) - 64$$

$$Y = 130 - 64$$

$$Y = 66$$

Question 43: B

$$40 \cdot 0.75 \cdot 3 = 90$$

$$30 \cdot 0.6 \cdot 2 = 36$$

$$30 \cdot 0.5 \cdot 1 = 15$$

$$90 + 36 + 15 = 141$$

Question 44: H

TRIANGLE INEQUALITY THEOREM

$$A + B > C$$

$$10 - 4 < KL < 10 + 4$$

$$6 < KL < 14$$

FOR AN OBTUSE TRIANGLE

$$A^2 + B^2 < C^2$$

$4^2 + (KL)^2 < 10^2$ OR $4^2 + 10^2 < (KL)^2$

$KL < \sqrt{84}$ $KL > \sqrt{116}$

7, 8, 9   11, 12, 13

$$\{7, 8, 9, 11, 12, 13\}$$

Question 45: D

$$SA_{LEFT} = 16 \left(\begin{smallmatrix} 8 \text{ VISIBLE} \\ 8 \text{ HIDDEN} \end{smallmatrix}\right)$$

$$SA_{RIGHT} = 18 \left(\begin{smallmatrix} 9 \text{ VISIBLE} \\ 9 \text{ HIDDEN} \end{smallmatrix}\right)$$

$$\Delta SA = 18 - 16 = 2$$

$$\frac{\Delta SA}{ORIGINAL\ SA} = \frac{2}{16} \times 100\% = 12.5\%$$

Question 46: K

$$1 FT^3 = (12\ IN)^3 = (12^3) IN^3 = 1728\ IN^3$$

$$BOWLING\ BALL = 320\ IN^3 \times \frac{1 FT^3}{1728\ IN^3} = 0.185\ FT^3$$

24 BOWLING BALLS = $24 \times 0.185\ FT^3 = 4.44\ FT^3$

CRATE = $3 FT \times 2.5 FT \times 2.5 FT = 18.75\ FT^3$

$18.75\ FT^3 - 4.44\ FT^3 \approx 14.3\ FT^3$ OF WATER
COULD FIT BEFORE OVERFLOWING

Question 47: A

LOG ROLL

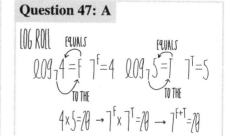

$$4 \times 5 = 20 \rightarrow 7^F \times 7^T = 20 \rightarrow 7^{F+T} = 20$$

Question 48: J

$$a_n = a_1 \times r^{(n-1)}$$

$n=5$
$a_1 = 1\,000\,000$ $r = \dfrac{800\,000}{1\,000\,000} = 0.8$

$$a_5 = 1\,000\,000 \times (0.8)^{5-1}$$
$$a_5 = 1\,000\,000 \times (0.8)^4$$
$$a_5 = \$409\,600$$

- - - - - - - - - - - - - - - - - - - -

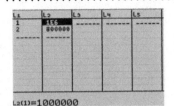

```
L1    L2      L3    L4    L5
1     1E6     ----- ----- -----
2     800000  ----- ----- -----
----- ------- ----- ----- -----


L2(1)=1000000
```

```
EDIT CALC TESTS
2↑2-Var Stats
3:Med-Med
4:LinReg(ax+b)
5:QuadReg
6:CubicReg
7:QuartReg
8:LinReg(a+bx)
9:LnReg
0↓ExpReg
```

```
          ExpReg
Xlist:L1
Ylist:L2
FreqList:
Store RegEQ:Y1░
Calculate
```

```
          ExpReg
y=a*b^x
a=1250000
b=.8
r²=1
r=-1
```

```
Plot1  Plot2  Plot3
■\Y1■1250000*.8^X
```

```
X     Y1
1     1E6
2     800000
3     640000
4     512000
5     409600
```

	1000000
Ans*.8	
	800000
Ans*.8	
	640000
Ans*.8	
	512000
Ans*.8	
	409600

Question 49: D

$$\overrightarrow{AB} = 3i + 10j$$
$$\overrightarrow{CD} = \dfrac{6i + 0j}{9i + 10j}$$

Question 50: G

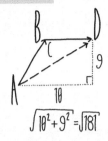

$$\sqrt{10^2 + 9^2} = \sqrt{181}$$

Question 51: A

$$3\langle 3+10\rangle + \small{-}2\langle 6,0\rangle + W = 0$$
$$\langle 9+30\rangle + \langle \small{-}12,0\rangle + W = 0$$
$$\langle \small{-}3, 30\rangle + W = 0$$
$$W = \langle 3, -30\rangle$$

Question 52: F

DISCRIMINANT $= \overset{\frown \; b^2-4ac}{\ominus}$ FOR IMAGINARY ROOTS

$$F(X) = 3X^2 + bX + 7$$
$$b^2 - 4(3)(7) < 0$$
$$b^2 - 84 < 0$$
$$b^2 < 84 \longrightarrow |b| < \sqrt{84}$$

↳ SQUARE ROOT OF AN INEQUALITY YIELDS AN ABSOLUTE VALUE

Question 53: B

RADIUS $= \dfrac{\text{DIAMETER}}{2} = \dfrac{10}{2} = 5$

PAVILION AREA $= \pi(5)^2 = 25\,dm^2$

SIDE LENGTH OF SQUARE BRICK PATIO → $\sqrt{50}$

(triangle with height 5, base segments 5 and 5)

PATIO AREA $= (\sqrt{50}) \cdot (\sqrt{50}) = 50\,dm^2$
POTTING AREA $= 25\pi - 50 = 29.5 \rightarrow 29$ BARRELS

Question 54: H

$$F(g(X)) = 3(5X+b) - 7$$
$$g(F(X)) = 5(3X-7) + b$$
$$F(g(X)) = g(F(X))$$
$$3(5X+b) - 7 = 5(3X-7) + b$$
$$\cancel{15X} + 3b - 7 = \cancel{15X} - 35 + b$$
$$3b - 7 = -35 + b$$
$$2b = -28 \longrightarrow b = -14$$

Question 55: C

PERIOD $= \dfrac{2\pi}{B}$ TRUE FOR sin, cos, sec AND csc

$F(X) = A\sec(BX-C) + D$
↳ HERE B=2

PERIOD $= \dfrac{2\pi}{2} = \pi$

Question 56: K

EXPECTED VALUE $= \dfrac{\text{TOTAL AMOUNT OF MONEY}}{\text{NUMBER OF BILLS}}$

TOTAL AMOUNT OF MONEY $= 1(12) + 5(7) + 10(5) + 20(3) = \$157$
NUMBER OF BILLS $= 12 + 7 + 5 + 3 = 27$ BILLS

EXPECTED VALUE $= \dfrac{\text{TOTAL AMOUNT OF MONEY}}{\text{NUMBER OF BILLS}} = \dfrac{\$157}{27\;\text{BILLS}}$

- - - - - - - - - - - - - - - - - - - -

```
L1    L2    L3    L4    L5    3
1     12    ----- ----- ----- 
5     7     ----- ----- -----
10    5     ----- ----- -----
20    3     ----- ----- -----
----- ----- ----- ----- -----
```

```
     1-Var Stats
List:L1
FreqList:L2
Calculate
```

```
     1-Var Stats
x̄=5.81
Σx=157.00
Σx²=1887.00
Sx=6.12
σx=6.01
n=27.00
```

Question 57: C

USE THE MODULUS

$(-2+7i)-(6+i) = (-2-6) + (7i-i)$

$d = |(-2-6) + (7i-i)| = \sqrt{(-8)^2 + (6)^2}$

$= \sqrt{64 + 36} = \sqrt{100} = 10$

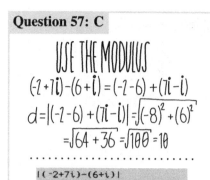

```
|(-2+7i)-(6+i)|
                        10
```

Question 58: H

$\det \begin{vmatrix} (X+2) & 10 \\ 2 & (X-5) \end{vmatrix} = (X+2)(X-5) - (2)(10) = 10$

$(X^2 + 2X - 5X - 10) - 20 = 10$

$X^2 - 3X - 40 = 0$

$(X-8)(X+5) = 0 \longrightarrow X = -5 \text{ OR } 8$

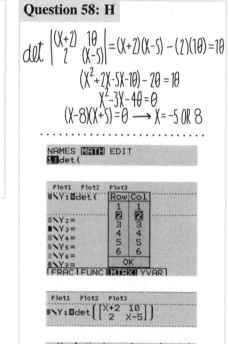

Question 59: C

$\tan^2\theta = 1 \longrightarrow \tan\theta = \pm\sqrt{1}$

$\tan^{-1}(+1) = \frac{\pi}{4} \qquad \tan^{-1}(-1) = -\frac{\pi}{4}$

CALCULATOR MAY READ 45° AND -45°

$\frac{\pi}{4} = \frac{180°}{4} = 45°$

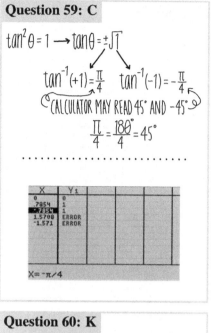

Question 60: K

ATLEAST 1 ERROR IS NOT 0 ERRORS

$P(\text{NOT } 0) = 1 - P(0) = 1 - 0.0724 = 0.9276$

EQUATION SHEETS

COMMON EQUATIONS and FORMULAS: algebra 1

GIVEN TWO POINTS

(X_1, Y_1) (X_2, Y_2)

MIDPOINT FORMULA

$\left(\dfrac{X_1 + X_2}{2}, \dfrac{Y_1 + Y_2}{2} \right)$

DISTANCE FORMULA

$d = \sqrt{(X_2 - X_1)^2 + (Y_2 - Y_1)^2}$

EQUATION OF A LINE

slope-intercept

$Y = mX + b$

point-slope

$(Y - Y_1) = m(X - X_1)$

SLOPE

$m = \dfrac{RISE}{RUN} = \dfrac{\Delta Y}{\Delta X} = \dfrac{Y_2 - Y_1}{X_2 - X_1}$

Y-intercept $(0, b)$ X-intercept $\left(-\dfrac{b}{m}, 0 \right)$

FACTORING PATTERNS

FACTORS OF

$1X^2 + bX + c$ $aX^2 + bX + c$

THAT ADD UP TO   FACTORS OF $(A \times C)$ THAT ADD UP TO

$X^2 - Y^2 = (X + Y)(X - Y)$

$(X - Y)^2 = X^2 - 2XY + Y^2$

$(X + Y)^2 = X^2 + 2XY + Y^2$

QUADRATICS

$aX^2 + bX + c$

$X = \dfrac{-b \pm \sqrt{b^2 - 4ac}}{2a}$ IF NEGATIVE, THEN IMAGINARY

NUMBER TERMINOLOGY

ALL INTEGERS & RATIONAL NUMBERS

$0, -759, 2$

$\frac{1}{3}, 0.25, \frac{-7}{4}$

$\pi, \sqrt{2}, \sqrt{16.6}, -0.25798\ldots$

$1 - 2i$

$3i, -i$

$2, 3, 5, 7$

__REAL__ - ANY NUMBER THAT CAN EXIST ON A NUMBER-LINE

__INTEGER__ - COUNTING WHOLE NUMBERS INCLUDING ZERO AND NEGATIVES

__RATIONAL__ - TERMINATING AND REPEATING DECIMALS

__IRRATIONAL__ - PATTERNLESS NON-TERMINATING DECIMALS

__COMPLEX__ - COMBINATION OF A REAL AND COMPLEX NUMBER

__IMAGINARY__ - MULTIPLES OF i

__PRIME__ - NUMBER WITHOUT DIVISORS. CANNOT BE ONE

PATTERNS OF i

$i = \sqrt{-1}$ $i^m = -1$ MULTIPLE OF TWO

MULTIPLE OF FOUR

$i^n = 1$

ODD NUMBER

$i^p = +\text{ OR }- i$

ALTERNATES SIGNS

COMMON EQUATIONS AND FORMULAS: *algebra 2*

LOGARITHMS

$$\log_a b = c \Rightarrow a^c = b$$

EQUALS

TO THE

$$\log a = \log_{10} a$$

NO BASE? NO WORRIES!

$$\log_a b = \frac{\log b}{\log a}$$

$$\log \frac{a}{b} = \log a - \log b$$

$$\log ab = \log a + \log b$$

$$\log 1 = 0 \qquad \log_b b = 1 \qquad \log_b b^n = n$$

SAME   SAME

ARITHMETIC SEQUENCES

COMMON DIFFERENCE BETWEEN TERMS

TERM NUMBER

$$a_n = a_1 + (n-1)d$$

NEW TERM   FIRST TERM

TERM NUMBER   FIRST TERM

$$S_n = \frac{n(a_1 + a_n)}{2}$$

LAST TERM IN SEQUENCE

SUM OF "n" TERMS

GEOMETRIC SEQUENCES

TERM NUMBER

$$a_n = a_1 \times r^{n-1}$$

NEW TERM   FIRST TERM   COMMON RATIO BETWEEN TERMS

TERM NUMBER

FIRST TERM

$$S_n = \frac{a_1(1 - r^n)}{1 - r}$$

COMMON RATIO BETWEEN TERMS

SUM OF "n" TERMS

EXPONENT RULES

MULTIPLICATION IS ADDITION

$$a^m \times a^n = a^{(m+n)}$$

DIVISION IS SUBTRACTION

$$\frac{a^m}{a^n} = a^{(m-n)}$$

DISTRIBUTE TO BOTH DENO. AND NUMER.

$$\left(\frac{a}{b}\right)^m = \frac{a^m}{b^m}$$

DISTRIBUTE TO BOTH

$$(ab)^m = a^m b^n$$

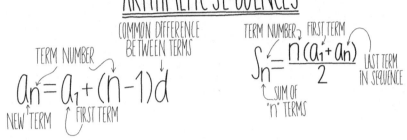

ANY NUMBER TO THE POWER OF ZERO IS ONE

$$a^0 = 1$$

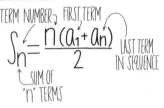

$$a^{-m} = \frac{1}{a^m}$$

NEGATIVE EXPONENTS FLIP FRACTION SIDES

FRACTION EXPONENTS ARE ROOTS

$$a^{\frac{m}{n}} = \sqrt[n]{a^m}$$

COMMON EQUATIONS AND FORMULAS: *geometry*

2D SHAPES

CIRCLES

$A = \pi r^2 \quad C = \pi d = 2\pi r$

RECTANGLE

$P = 2L + 2W$
$A = L \times W$

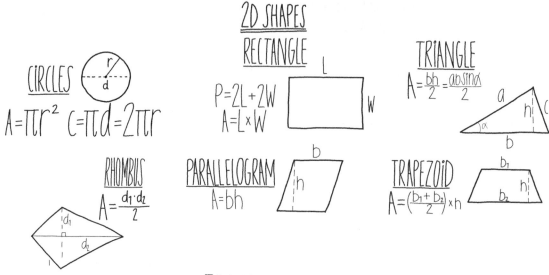

TRIANGLE

$A = \frac{bh}{2} = \frac{ab\sin\alpha}{2}$

RHOMBUS

$A = \frac{d_1 \cdot d_2}{2}$

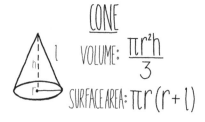

PARALLELOGRAM

$A = bh$

TRAPEZOID

$A = \left(\frac{b_1 + b_2}{2}\right) \times h$

3D SHAPES

GENERALLY: $V = A \times h$
(AREA) (HEIGHT) (VOLUME)

CYLINDER

VOLUME: $\pi r^2 h$
SURFACE AREA: $2\pi r(r+h)$

RECTANGULAR PRISM

VOLUME: $l \times w \times h$
SURFACE AREA: $2(lh + lw + hw)$

CONE

VOLUME: $\frac{\pi r^2 h}{3}$
SURFACE AREA: $\pi r(r+l)$

SPHERE

VOLUME: $\frac{4\pi r^3}{3}$
SURFACE AREA: $4\pi r^2$

COMMON EQUATIONS AND FORMULAS: *geometry*

ARC LENGTH AND SECTOR AREA

PART OR FRACTION OF A FULL CIRCLE

LENGTH OF $\overarc{AB}$ IS A PARTIAL CIRCUMFERENCE $= 2\pi r \times \dfrac{\theta°}{360°}$

$(C = 2\pi r)$

AREA OF SECTOR $\overarc{AB}$ IS A PARTIAL AREA $= \pi r^2 \times \dfrac{\theta°}{360°}$

$A = \pi r^2$

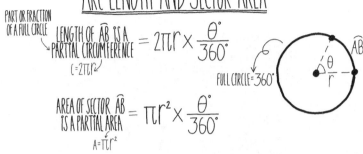

FULL CIRCLE = 360°

$\overarc{AB}$

PYTHAGOREAN THEOREM

RIGHT TRIANGLE NEEDED

$A^2 + B^2 = C^2$

LEGS   HYPOTENUSE

PYTHAGOREAN INEQUALITIES

OBTUSE → $A^2 + B^2 < C^2$

ACUTE → $A^2 + B^2 > C^2$

COMMON RIGHT TRIANGLE TRIPLES

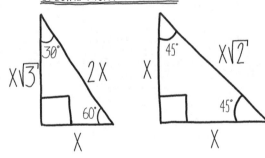

LEG "A"   HYPOTENUSE

LEG "B"

LEG "A" - LEG "B" - HYPOTENUSE

3 - 4 - 5

6 - 8 - 10

5 - 12 - 13

7 - 24 - 25

8 - 15 - 17

DECIDING IF 3 LENGTHS MAKE A TRIANGLE

THE LARGEST LENGTH IS BETWEEN THE DIFFERENCE AND SUM OF THE SMALLER SIDES

LARGEST LENGTH

$|a - b| < c < a + b$

DIFFERENCE OF SMALLER LENGTHS   SUM OF SMALLER LENGTHS

SPECIAL RIGHT TRIANGLES

30° $X\sqrt{3}$ $2X$ 60° X

45° X $X\sqrt{2}$ 45° X

COMMON EQUATIONS AND FORMULAS: *precalculus*

CONICS

PARABOLA
VERTEX: (h,k)

$$y = a(x-h)^2 + k$$

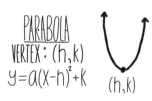
(h,k)

CIRCLE
CENTER: (h,k)

$$(x-h)^2 + (y-k)^2 = r^2 \text{ RADIUS}$$

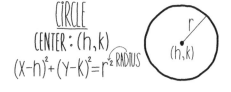
r
(h,k)

ELLIPSE
CENTER: (h,k)

$$\frac{(x-h)^2}{a^2} + \frac{(y-k)^2}{b^2} = 1$$

DISTANCE FROM CENTER ALONG X
DISTANCE FROM CENTER ALONG Y

b a
(h,k)

HYPERBOLA
CENTER: (h,k) MIDPOINT BETWEEN VERTICES

$$\frac{(x-h)^2}{a^2} - \frac{(y-k)^2}{b^2} = 1$$

(h,k)

MATRICES

MULTIPLICATION
✳ MULTIPLY ROWS BY COLUMNS ✳

RESULT MATRIX DIMENSIONS   NUMBER OF ROWS

$$(m \times n) \cdot (n \times q) = (m \times q)$$

MUST MATCH   NUMBER OF COLUMNS

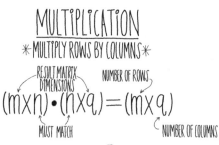

$$\begin{bmatrix} a & b & c \\ d & e & f \end{bmatrix} \times \begin{bmatrix} g & j \\ h & k \\ i & \ell \end{bmatrix} = \begin{bmatrix} (ag+bh+ci) & (aj+bk+c\ell) \\ (dg+eh+fi) & (dj+ek+f\ell) \end{bmatrix}$$

2×3 SAME 3×2 2×2
RESULT

ADDITION
DIMENSIONS MUST MATCH

SAME POSITIONS ADD

$$\begin{bmatrix} a & b \\ c & d \end{bmatrix} + \begin{bmatrix} e & f \\ g & h \end{bmatrix} = \begin{bmatrix} (a+e) & (b+f) \\ (c+g) & (d+h) \end{bmatrix}$$

SUM WILL HAVE SAME DIMENSIONS

DETERMINANT

SUBTRACT THE CROSS PRODUCTS

$$\det \begin{bmatrix} a & b \\ c & d \end{bmatrix} = ad - cb$$

COMMON EQUATIONS AND FORMULAS: *statistics*

MEAN = AVERAGE

SUM = MEAN × n ← NUMBER OF DATA POINTS

$$MEAN = \frac{SUM}{n}$$

MODE = MOST OCCURRING NUMBER

MEDIAN = MIDDLE NUMBER

RANGE = MAX – MIN

... IS REFLECTED IN THE

STANDARD DEVIATION = DIFFERENCE FROM MEAN

PROBABILITY

COMBINATION – FOR GROUPS, ORDER DOES NOT MATTER

$$_nC_r = \frac{n!}{(n-r)!\,r!}$$

PERMUTATION – FOR LISTS, ORDER MATTERS

KEYWORDS: "ALL POSSIBLE WAYS"

$$_nP_r = \frac{n!}{(n-r)!}$$

COMMON EQUATIONS AND FORMULAS: trigonometry

SOH-CAH-TOA

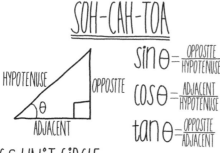

$$\sin\theta = \frac{\text{OPPOSITE}}{\text{HYPOTENUSE}}$$

$$\cos\theta = \frac{\text{ADJACENT}}{\text{HYPOTENUSE}}$$

$$\tan\theta = \frac{\text{OPPOSITE}}{\text{ADJACENT}}$$

TRIG. IDENTITIES

$$\sin^2\theta + \cos^2\theta = 1$$

$$\tan = \frac{\sin}{\cos} \quad \cot = \frac{1}{\tan}$$

$$\sec = \frac{1}{\cos} \quad \csc = \frac{1}{\sin}$$

ALL THINGS UNIT CIRCLE

TO CONVERT FROM RADIANS TO DEGREES, USE: $\pi = 180$

TO CONVERT $n°$ INTO RADIANS USE: $\frac{n\pi}{180}$

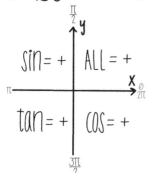

$\sin = +$ | $\text{ALL} = +$

$\tan = +$ | $\cos = +$

LAW OF SINES / COSINES
NO RIGHT TRIANGLE NECESSARY

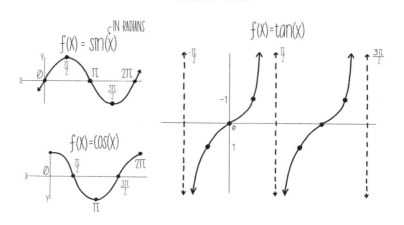

$$\frac{\sin A}{a} = \frac{\sin B}{b} = \frac{\sin C}{c}$$

$$a^2 = b^2 + c^2 - 2bc\cos A$$

$$c^2 = a^2 + b^2 - 2ab\cos C \quad b^2 = a^2 + c^2 - 2ac\cos B$$

TRIGONOMETRIC GRAPHS AND EQUATIONS

PERIOD FOR cos/sin → $\frac{2\pi}{B}$ AND TAN → $\frac{\pi}{B}$

AMPLITUDE = $|A|$

VERTICAL SHIFT

$$f(x) = A\sin([B]x - C) + D$$

ANY TRIG FUNCTION LIKE COS OR tan

HORIZONTAL SHIFT IN DEGREES OR RADIANS

COMMON VALUES

	$\cos\theta$	$\sin\theta$	$\tan\theta$
θ:	1	0	0
$30° = \frac{\pi}{6}$:	$\frac{\sqrt{3}}{2}$	$\frac{1}{2}$	$\frac{\sqrt{3}}{3}$
$45° = \frac{\pi}{4}$:	$\frac{\sqrt{2}}{2}$	$\frac{\sqrt{2}}{2}$	1
$60° = \frac{\pi}{3}$:	$\frac{1}{2}$	$\frac{\sqrt{3}}{2}$	$\sqrt{3}$
$90° = \frac{\pi}{2}$:	0	1	UNDEFINED
$180° = \pi$:	-1	0	0

IN RADIANS

$f(x) = \sin(x)$

$f(x) = \cos(x)$

$f(x) = \tan(x)$

ABOUT PRIVATE PREP

Private Prep is an education services company that offers individually customized lessons in all K-12 academic subjects, standardized test prep, and college admissions consulting. We believe personal attention is fundamental to academic achievement and lies at the forefront of every student-tutor relationship. Designing curriculum for each student's unique learning style, we focus not only on improving grades and increasing test scores but also on building confidence and developing valuable skills—like work ethic, growth mindset, and anxiety management—that will last a lifetime.

One of the most significant points of differentiation between us and other educational services companies is our team approach. Our directors work in tandem with tutors and support staff to provide comprehensive, collaborative support to families.

We also focus on giving back to the communities in which we work. Through the Private Prep Scholarship Program, we place high-achieving students from low-income or underserved backgrounds with individual tutors, who work with them to navigate the test prep and college application process and ultimately gain admission to best-fit colleges.

At Private Prep, we deliver a superior academic experience—in the U.S., abroad, and online—that is supported by diverse and excellent resources in recruitment, curriculum design, professional training, and custom software development.

Made in the USA
Las Vegas, NV
18 August 2021